White Captives

The University of North Carolina Press   Chapel Hill & London

Gender and Ethnicity on the American Frontier

White
CAPTIVES
JUNE NAMIAS

Library of Congress
Cataloging-in-Publication Data
Namias, June.

White captives : gender and
ethnicity on the American
frontier / by June Namias.

p. cm.

Includes bibliographical
references and index.

ISBN 0-8078-2079-2 (cloth:
alk. paper).

— ISBN 0-8078-4408-x (pbk.:
alk. paper)

1. Indians of North America—
Captivities. 2. Ethnicity—
United States—History.
3. Indians of North America—
Sexual behavior. 4. McCrea,
Jane, 1753–1777. 5. Jemison,
Mary, 1743–1833. 6. Wakefield,
Sarah F. I. Title.

E85.N34 1993

305.8'00973—dc20 92-31235

CIP

99 98 97 96 95
6 5 4 3 2

To My Parents,

Foster and Helen,

and for Barbara

Contents

Illustrations and Maps

Preface

Waterdrinker, priest of the Sioux, dreamed that outlandish creatures were weaving a huge spider web around his people. He awoke knowing that was how it was going to be and said to his people, When this happens, you shall live in square gray houses, in a barren land, and beside these square gray houses, you shall starve.
   —*Peter Nabokov,* Native American Testimony

Thus humanity is male and man defines woman not in herself but as relative to him; she is not regarded as an autonomous being.
   —*Simone de Beauvoir,* The Second Sex

As experience, the world belongs to the primary word I-It.
   The primary word I-Thou *establishes the world of relation.* . . .
   The primary word I-Thou *can be spoken only with the whole being.* . . . *I become through my relation to the* Thou. *As I become* I, *I say* Thou.
   All real living is meeting.
   —*Martin Buber,* I and Thou

The meeting of cultures is the greatest of the world's stories. These histories and the stories cultures produce of them contain amazement, recognition, pain, sorrow, hate, and, occasionally, love.

Two questions are often asked of me about this study. The first is, How did you ever get interested in this captivity business? and the second, What do you hope to accomplish? From the moment I read the first paragraph of the narrative of Mary Rowlandson, I felt a sense of amazement, recognition, pain, and sorrow. As a daughter of New England I should have been taught this story as a child, but nearly accidentally I fell across it in a Chicago archive, long after I had my own child. I continued through these English and American stories and histories of contact and meeting written in the first decades of English settlement by New Englanders. They brought me into a world I now see as deliberately forgotten but one which was central and well known to the first European settlers of North America. Those men and women were not my ancestors in any way; my grandparents did not set foot on American soil for some two hundred years and more after Rowlandson wrote her narrative. But I was something of an "other" in my native Massachusetts, and the power of these stories moved me to further inquiry as to their meaning. I noticed immediately that there was a playful aspect to this material (albeit at the expense of "others"), as well as a brutal side. As my mother put it when I showed her some of the illustrations I had uncovered, "Where did you ever find *this*?" and "It looks like you're going back to your childhood." As I moved from captivity literature through government documents, paintings, and beaded moccasins, I defined what I was doing as a personal quest to uncover a part of my own and America's history that had been denied me in my long trail of study through public school and university.

It is hard to say what I hope to accomplish even after ten years of traveling through this material and through Minnesota, western New York State, Colorado, and innumerable archives and museums. In the 1970s I worked on a collection of oral histories of twentieth-century immigrants. When I finished, I realized that I was interested in two questions involved in the migration process. First, what happens when people from one culture move and come in contact with those of a very different culture? Second, what part does the relationship of men and women play in this question of "what happens," especially when the men and women are from different cultures? I knew that this was a very old and enduring American problem. How enduring came to my attention in the mid-1970s in the living room of a Japanese-American woman who talked about having to ward off sexual advances while working in the home of a white family in California. Later, in talks with a Filipino farm worker in Delano, I became aware that the laws in California did not allow "Orientals" to marry whites until after World War II, with the result that this man and other Asian men with whom I spoke were fatherless and virtually without families.

Of course I knew about sexual taboos between blacks and whites, and cases like Scottsboro. But I was also interested in the Leo Frank case in which a Jew, who was accused in the early twentieth-century South of raping and murdering an Irish girl, was lynched. I perused graduate programs in history with the hope of finding a person or a place that could direct me toward understanding some of the root problems in these diverse cases and most troubling matters. I happily found both. In the summer of 1982 at the Newberry Library, the 1682 edition of *A True History of the Captivity & Restoration of Mrs. Mary Rowlandson* was placed on my desk. I gently opened the small book, looked at the brittle title page, and read the first paragraph.

North America is a land of encounters. It is my hope that this work will shed some light on the myths and realities of cross cultural encounters. We are a migrating people and always have been—both the indigenous peoples and the many immigrant groups who chose to come here, as well as the African Americans who did not so choose. The more we know about our early migrations and the meeting of people along the cultural boundaries that made up the earliest frontiers, the better chance we have to know the origins of our hopes and fears and perhaps deal with each other more humanely.

Like many another researcher, I never realized a major book would take a decade to write. The process was well worth it, because in that time and in the pursuit of information and clarity, I met many people who changed my life. Ten years is a long time, and I have incurred many debts. Virginia Woolf advised a woman who wanted to write that she needed financial support and a room of her own. Besides those basics, to do historical work one needs great libraries, museums, and historical societies to help you along, other scholars to read your work and offer needed criticism, and friends and family to urge you on.

John Demos became the first of these treasured friends. His advice and confidence, so important in the early years of this project, helped in the later years as well. Laurel Thatcher Ulrich and Neal Salisbury gave a close reading and clear directions for reshaping the final manuscript. I thank Joyce Antler, Pauline Maier, Elizabeth Pleck, Daniel Asher Cohen, Donald Worster, Jill K. Conway, Dorothy Gonson, Mary Moore, and Tona Hangen for reading all or large parts of the manuscript at earlier stages of its development.

Certain chapters were read and commented on by the History of American Civilization seminar and the Humanities Dissertation Group at Brandeis University, as well as by Theda Perdue, Carol Karlsen, Elise Marienstras, David Hackett Fischer, Estelle B. Freedman, Christine L. Heyrman, Allen R. Grossman, David D. Hall, Julie Roy Jeffrey, Daria Donnelly, Lissa Gifford, Carol Zemel, Rayna Green, Tom Cook, Arthur Kaledin, Wendy Gamber, Gary Clayton Anderson, William N. Fenton, Mimi Grosser, David Palmer, Adria Steinberg, Marisha Hydeman, and Anita Safran. Of course, any problems that still exist are my own responsibility.

I thank the Crown Fellowship and the History of American Civilization program at Brandeis University, which provided research assistance; the American Antiquarian Society for its support at the seminar of the History of the Book in American Culture; the National Museum of American History at the Smithsonian Institution for a short-term fellowship under the generous supervision of Rayna Green; the Newberry Library for a summer fellowship during which John Aubrey first handed me Mary Rowlandson's narrative and continued to provide good leads. The Massachusetts Institute of Technology and its History Faculty, Dianne Brooks and Mabel Chin, along with the Kelly Fund and the Undergraduate Research Opportunities Program and research assistant Tona Hangen deserve many thanks. Wheaton College also provided funds for copying, maps, and travel. The Millay Colony for the Arts and the

Blue Mountain Center provided me not only with rooms of my own for one and, in the case of Blue Mountain, two summers, but also gave me time in Iroquois country in the presence of great beauty and in the company of other writers and artists. Mimi and George Grosser helped assure the needed summer solace over the decade by allowing me to use their Little House in Vermont. Marisha and Lee Hydeman generously offered me the use of their home and garden in the Northeast Kingdom to work on the final draft.

At the Newberry Library, Tom Willcockson produced the maps of the New York and Minnesota frontiers. Ken Cain carefully reproduced most of the illustrations. Mary Porter Wyly helped arrange for their use. Of great assistance were Judith Humphreys and the staff of Brandeis's Goldfarb Library and Victor Berch, formerly of Special Collections; Kathleen Green of the Dewey Library at MIT; Peter Love at the Hilles Library at Harvard; James P. Roan at the National Museum of American History and Kathleen Baxter at the Anthropological Archives at the National Museum of Natural History at the Smithsonian; Barbara Taylor and Eric Grundset at the Genealogical Library, National Society, Daughters of the American Revolution, Washington, D.C.; Karl Kabelac of the Department of Rare Books and Special Collections at the University of Rochester Library; Peter J. Knapp, at the Library of Trinity College, Hartford; Jocquelyn Foy at Litchfield Historical Society in Litchfield, Connecticut; and Jerald Pepper at the Adirondack Museum in Blue Mountain Lake, New York. Papers from the American Board of Commissioners for Foreign Missions are used by permission of the Houghton Library, Harvard University, Cambridge, Massachusetts, and the United Church Board for World Ministries. Manuscripts from Yale University are used by permission of the Beinecke Library's Western Americana Collection and the Yale Medical School, Historical Library, in New Haven. Other libraries and institutions that provided assistance include, at the Harvard Libraries, the Tozzer, Schlesinger, Widener, and Houghton libraries; at Yale, the Western Americana Collection at the Beinecke Library; in Hartford, the library at the Wadsworth Atheneum; in New York, the New York Genealogical and Biographical Society and the New York Public Library; in Boston, the Boston Public Library and the New

England Historic Genealogical Society; in Buffalo, the Buffalo and Erie County Historical Society; in Geneseo, New York, the

staff at the College Libraries, State University of New York at Geneseo.

For work on Jane McCrea, Mary Jemison, and the Iroquois people, I thank the Fort Edward Historical Society, Fort Edward, New York; Tom Cook at the Pioneer and Indian Museum at Letchworth State Park in Castile, New York; Richard Rose, formerly of the Rochester Museum and Science Center; Ray and John Fadden at the Six Nations Indian Museum, Onchiota, New York; Kathy Skelly of the Collections Department of the Peabody Museum at Harvard University; and Susan Crawford at the National Museum of Natural History.

Research on Sarah Wakefield and the Dakota War was greatly assisted by the Minnesota Historical Society. Alan R. Woolworth was especially generous. I also thank Darla Schnurrer at Brown County Historical Society, New Ulm, Minnesota; the Blue Earth Historical Society, Mankato, Minnesota; the Faribault County Historical Society, Blue Earth, Minnesota; Marilyn Lass at the Mankato State University Library; and Carol Scott, court administrator at the Scott County Court House, Shakopee, Minnesota. At the National Archives, Robert Kvasnicka of the Scientific, Economic, and Natural Resources Bureau introduced me to the complexities and riches of those archives, and at the National Archives Records Office in Waltham, Helen Engle assisted me with census data.

It is a humbling experience to try to "do" Indian and white history. I thank Calvin Martin for urging me to take my own path and Pauline Turner Strong for handing me many key primary sources. I also owe a debt to Seneca and Mdewakanton people who spoke with me, especially G. Peter Jemison, Theresa Morrison, and Chris Cavender. Many scholars were generous with their thoughts on this project. They included Julie Roy Jeffrey, Susan Armitage, James T. Kloppenberg, Allan MacDougall, Janice L. Reiff, Herbert T. Hoover, R. H. Ives Goddard, Wilcomb E. Washburn, Frederick E. Hoxie, and John Lawrence. To Natasha Anisimov, Joan Brigham, Adria Steinberg, Carol Zemel, Ron Boucher, Will Stewart, Elizabeth MacMahon, Sonia Dettmann, and Dorothy Gonson, I can only say that without your friendship and encouragement there would hardly be a book at all.

Seeing a book through from an idea to a draft to a finished work takes tremendous faith and patience, especially when it isn't your own. The University of Alaska Anchorage generously provided funds for the last stages of the manuscript, and the College of Arts and Sciences and the Department of History and Geography assisted my move and warmly welcomed me to Alaska. Charlotte Cecil Raymond became the editor for my first book. She has since become a fine agent and great friend. She has helped me more than I can say. Trudie Calvert took great care with the copyediting. Lewis Bateman at the University of North Carolina Press saw the value in this work. I thank him, Sandra Eisdorfer, and others at the University of North Carolina Press for taking on this task.

Finally, my family has offered love and support. My mother, Helen (Needle) Namias, did not live to see this book completed, but she always had faith in my ability to do most anything. To the extent that she was right, it is because I inherited a small amount of her enthusiasm, energy, and warmth. My father, Foster Namias, has always been a model of excellence. He was most kind in donating funds for a new computer system. My son, Robert Victor Slavin, lived with the first years of this project; later he read and then proofread many pages, ran the printer often, dredged up last-minute citations, and gave me good advice. Finally, I thank my sister Barbara Meltzer for her great support and love, and Philip, Stephen, Beth, Jeffrey, and Faith Meltzer for their affection and good humor.

June Namias
Cambridge, Massachusetts
June 1992

White Captives

White Captives: An Introduction

From conventional literature and history we are used to a frontier of Indian fighters and war whoops—men clashing on horseback, surrounded by shooting arrows and firing rifles. This is the West as depicted in adventure novels, military accounts, movies, and television westerns. Reexamination finds this picture wanting—it is an exaggerated, one-dimensional, melodramatic view of America's frontier history. Recent studies of white migration and settlement in North America reveal a different picture, one less filled with critical battles, more involved with encounters across cultural lines, and including women and children as opposed to an all-male cast. Studying white captives verifies the coexistence of men, women, and children of a variety of cultures as the norm in American frontier life, a situation well recognized by earlier generations as at the heart of the American migratory experience. As Europeans and their descendants moved onto successive frontiers, they confronted their own gender and sexuality in new ways. Gender had to be viewed in the context of a competing culture. What can we tell about the way Euro-Americans think when confronted by danger from a group they consider "other"?

To earlier generations, the stories and depictions of white captives and the legends that grew up around them were well known. These stories had tremendous power and resonance. Why was this so? Why were the exploits and the hardships of a relatively few whites captured by a relatively few Indians so popular in political and local histories, literature, high and low art? This book explores the histories of European and American captives in the continental United States and the way these stories have been incorporated into American history. The experiences of early American white captives are not familiar in the culture at large. Among historians and students of literature, if known at all, they are read as "captivity narratives." An occasional name such as Hannah Dustan or Mary Jemison may be recognized, but a systematic analysis of these captives and some wider placement of their experiences in the context of American politics, society, and culture has been attempted by only a few scholars.[1]

What was the captivity experience about? What is the captivity literature? Why study it to learn more about gender and ethnicity on the frontier? Far from being an occasional act of a barbarous foe, the taking of captives was a centuries-old practice around the world. In the Americas before the arrival of Columbus it was a part of intertribal warfare; with the coming of Europeans it was used as a tactic of warfare between Indians and Euro-Americans for over 250 years. In the successive struggles for dominance on the North American continent, priests, soldiers, women, and children were held for ransom, adopted, or otherwise incorporated into the tribal life of an enemy. North American Indians were taken prisoner, enslaved, or forcibly taken on voyages to the other side of the Atlantic, where they were put on public display as showpieces of victory and novelty.[2]

Capture as seen by most whites in North America was an act of brutality and savagery against an innocent, civilized, and superior foe, one aspect of what was labeled "savage war." It employed elements not found in European warfare in the early modern or modern periods—a forced, prolonged imprisonment with the enemy, a fearful contamination, a separation from one's community, a loss of spouse and children, and a communion with or at least relentless exposure to representatives of the devil. But captivity was a complex enterprise. Its history pre-dated the European invasion of the Americas. Before investigating "white captives" these two earlier traditions of European capture of Indians and capture as a tactic, regardless of the race or culture of the enemy, need further explication.

Indian Ways of War

. . . . . .

Why did North American Indian groups employ capture? Capture was a widely used tactic of warfare in both the Northeast and the Southwest before European arrival in the Americas. In the Northeast in particular, adoption and ransom were the two major motives of Indian capture in the period from approximately 1500 through the American Revolution. The sex and age of the victim were important in determining the survival of the captive. Terror frequently accompanied the arrival of male captives (white or Indian) at the village of their captors. In many tribes east of the Mississippi to the southwest, males who got that far were greeted by grieving and angry Indians of all ages and both sexes mourning the loss of relatives. Male captives were usually forced to run the gauntlet, attempting to avoid attack. Lewis Henry Morgan wrote that among the Iroquois, "adoption or torture were the alternative chances of the captive." Only males were required to run the gauntlet. During the ordeal, they were pointed toward their future house, and if they made it through the "long avenue of whips" running naked to the waist they would be "treated with the utmost affection and kindness." Those who did not pass the test were "led away to torture, and to death." On the one hand, when a member of the Iroquois nations or a rival northeastern group went to war he knew such a fate was possible and that if captured he must prove "his courage was equal to any trial and above the power of death itself." On the other hand, adoption was so common that one scholar goes so far as to say that the Iroquois would have died out had they not taken captives. From colonial times we have accounts by survivors verifying that comrades were beaten, tortured, and sometimes burned to death and others that describe their lives as accepted members of tribal groups.[3]

Adoption was part of a wider social and cultural practice and, in the case of the many northeastern Indians, indicates the importance of women in the system of warfare. In the colonial Northeast, especially among the Iroquois, Hurons, and Delawares, for those who made it through the ordeal, a new family was often waiting. The choice of captives was left to the women of the village. To assuage their loss of a brother, husband, or son, they could choose among male or female captives to adopt. Either sex was considered a desirable substitute for a lost relative. In the late 1750s, Mary Jemison became a sister to women who had lost their brother. The elderly and those less able might be killed in a raid or on a forced march, but northeastern Indians knew enough about what we call acculturation to understand that a child could more readily learn and accept a new language and culture than could an adult, and they favored children for adoption. James Axtell's work demonstrates that young children took to Indian life better than did adults.[4]

In Daniel K. Richter's analysis, adoption is a cultural and political system. "Mourning war" was a complicated set of rituals for assuring that the family of deceased warriors were compensated for their loss both physically and psychologically. It was also a cultural system of bestowing power to avenge loss. Through their political power the women of the family, as leading older women in the clan, could call upon kin to make war on those who had killed a son, brother, or husband. After battle, the ceremonies of bringing the captives into the village and running the gauntlet enabled the family to express anger and loss as well as victory and dominance. The ritual mourning could then be transformed into new life with the adoption of a captive.[5] In the Northeast, especially among the Iroquois, adoption was common, but it was also common in other parts of the country, as in the Southeast among the Cherokees and Catawbas.[6]

Besides serving as a way to mourn and replenish population, in the early Indian wars in New England white captives were used to get ransom money from the French or English at the end of wars.[7] Mary Rowlandson was ransomed at the end of King Philip's War. Finally, the use of capture, or what we call the holding of prisoners of war (which sounds less "savage"), was a form of psychological warfare well known in the Americas. In an age in which the Carter administration fell because of its inability to get hostages back from Iran and the face of a downed U.S. pilot in the Persian Gulf War struck feelings of terror and vulnerability, one can appreciate the psychological dimension of capture, of holding an enemy warrior, never mind its women and children.

Indian Captives

. . . . . .

The Indian practice of taking captives dates back to the years before white settlement and appears to have had its origins in economic and social as well as diplomatic and psychological aspects of Indian life. But Indians were not the only perpetrators of this practice. All of the major European players in the conquest of the Americas captured American natives in war, for profit, for novelty, and for sexual misuse. There is substantial documentation of its widespread use among the Spanish, French, and British during the period of conquest and settlement.

In the Southeast and Southwest, capture of Indians by the Spanish and French predated English settlement. According to Peter Wood, kidnapping was a common tactic among sixteenth-century Spaniards and was practiced in the Southeast by three different explorers between 1521 and 1528, and in the sixteenth century Spaniards forcibly took "several thousand Southeast Indians to the West Indies." But in the Caribbean and the rest of the Americas, diseases and mistreatment were the main causes of Indian depopulation. By 1540 church resolutions against native slavery replaced a captive native labor force with a captive and enslaved African one. French attempts at abduction also began in the sixteenth century and were made by Giovanni da Verrazano (1524), Jacques Cartier (1534 and 1535), and Jean Ribault (1524). By the early eighteenth century apparently the French were looking for more than just a work force. Intertribal warfare in Canada was encouraged for the purpose of having Indians capture Indians and sell them to the French, who then shipped them downriver to Louisiana. Wood found that by 1708 "there were at least 80 Indian slaves in the province, most of them young women," and many "soon died after enslavement."[8]

Following Hernán Cortés's conquest of Mexico, what is today the American Southwest became the northern Spanish frontier. There the capture and enslavement of Indians was a common practice. Slaving expeditions were dispatched by Nuño de Guzman (1530s), the first governor of Mexico, who took twenty Acoma captives and sentenced them to servitude. Even though by 1526 slavery was illegal under Spanish law, raids were made against Plains Indian groups north of the Spanish borderlands and orphans were used as forced labor on Spanish building projects. Indians were bound by the *encomienda,* a system of forced labor and payment of tribute to Spanish landholders all over the empire and especially employed in mines and on plantations. Governor Juan de Eulate (1618–25) first sold Indians into slavery by shipping them to New Spain but was fined and had to release them and return them to Mexico. Another governor sponsored slave raids against Apaches, Utes, and Plains Indian groups and forced captives to work in Santa Fe. In 1716, when Comanches and Utes allied and attacked the Spanish in northern New Mexico, the Spanish responded by taking Indian captives; the governor and his brother divided them up and sold them.[9]

As had the Spanish, the British colonial enterprise in the Northeast required a means of enlisting Indians into the colonial labor force. One solution was to capture and enslave Indians. After the Pequot War (1637), forty-eight women and children were enslaved within the Massachusetts Bay Colony. And in a move that signaled the beginning of black slavery in New England, Pequot warriors were exchanged for black slaves in the West Indies. In King Philip's War (1675–76) Richard Waldron captured four hundred Abenakis and had them sold into slavery. Occasionally, colonists bought Indian captives from Indians. From 1500 to 1800, varieties of servitude were common. According to one scholar, Massachusetts Bay and Plymouth "sold Indian captives freely into slavery, both inside and outside their borders." Rhode Island was exceptional in making slavery illegal by 1676.[10] Although the numbers were minuscule compared with the contemporary black slave traffic and although Puritans saw their actions as part of activity initiated in a "just war," New England Puritans participated in both black and Indian slavery.

Colonial New Englanders were not the only British colonists to enslave Indians. In Virginia during Bacon's Rebellion (1675) Indians were also sold into slavery. In the Southeast during the early eighteenth century, British settlers arriving from the West Indies in Carolina made slaves of Indians captured in wars with the Coosas, Stonos, and Westos tribes. British colonists raided the Yamasees, Apalachees, and Timucuas of northern Florida. Wood finds that the fourteen hundred Indians captured "became about a quarter of the slave population" and that other captives were shipped off to other colonies, including New England and the West Indies. Thus in the Southeast, "numerous slave children were born of Black-Indian unions." During the Tuscarora Wars (1711 and 1713) more than four hundred Indian slaves were sold by the colonial government of North Carolina; in the Yamasee War that followed, South Carolina became a leader in Indian slaving.[11] And in central New York during the American Revolution General John Sullivan wrote to John Jay on September 30, 1779, concerning an order in regard to Indian women and children taken captive by American forces: one "of the women being very ancient & the Lad a cripple" were left but two others were "brought on . . . & joined the Army." [12]

As late as the era of the overland trail of the 1840s, Indians were sometimes captured to guide migrations west. Ironically, despite nineteenth-century fears of Indians sullying the honor of white women captives, it appears that Indian women were more often brutalized by white capture. According to Albert Hurtado, California Indian women experienced abductions, rape, and forced concubinage during the 1850s in the gold rush period on the California frontier.[13]

The White Captive Story
. . . . . .

But what of white captives? In New England alone, an estimated 1,641 white captives were taken between 1675 and 1763.[14] Capture was rarely an act of caprice. Rather, for many indigenous peoples of the Northeast it was a major strategy of warfare used against all enemies, regardless of race. Captives were taken to prevent expansion onto Indian lands. This was a direct threat to settler families and frontier fortresses. Prisoners were held in exchange for the purchase of weapons and goods and to replace lost relatives. Decimation by disease and intense warfare left woodland Indians of the seventeenth and eighteenth centuries fearing extinction, and, as mentioned, traditional practice encouraged the replacement of a dead brother, sister, or spouse by another person of either sex by ritual adoption.[15]

From the European perspective, the white captive was a centerpiece in history and literature from the earliest days of European and Native American contact. Although many natives, including Pocahontas, were kidnapped by the British, captivity by Indians made celebrities of John Smith, Mary Rowlandson, John and Eunice Williams, and Daniel Boone and his daughter Jemima.[16] The English and American authors who built their plots on actual or fictional themes of capture include James Fenimore Cooper, Nathaniel Hawthorne, Herman Melville, Henry David Thoreau, and Mark Twain.[17] In 1956, filmmaker John Ford cast John Wayne as Ethan Edwards in *The Searchers*. Edwards's goal was to recapture his two nieces from the Comanches. The young son of an American engineer was captured in Brazil by Amazonian Indians in John Boorman's *Emerald Forest* (1985). *Dances with Wolves* (1990), a recent box office hit, dramatized the fate of a white woman taken as a child and raised and renamed by Lakotas after her frontier family was killed by Pawnees. Both Stands with a Fist, as white captive, and John Dunbar (played by Kevin Costner), as white Indian, are contemporary recastings of the traditional themes of whites among the Indians.[18]

Captivity literature is the most extensive source of information concerning what happened to white captives. It includes personal narratives, depositions, biographies, oral testimonies, folk histories, and, later, novels and dime novels. Some of the best-selling captivity narratives were about known members of frontier communities, either recently returned or forever "lost" to Indian or French captors. Some are verifiable through travelers' accounts, colonial records, diaries, sermons, newspapers, and military and court records. For others, our ability to corroborate history is hopelessly clouded by folklore, exaggeration, and a lack of testimony from their Indian captors. The late eighteenth-century novels and later films copy their plots from earlier narratives. Though such responses were often influenced by literary styles of the period in which they were written, most accounts (at least until the late eighteenth century) were read as real responses to real situations.

Historic accounts were the best-sellers of their day in both Europe and America. Mary Rowlandson's *Soveraignty & Goodness of God* (1682) appeared in thirty editions. John Williams's *Redeemed Captive, Returning to Zion* (1707) sold over one hundred thousand copies and was reissued under various titles until its twentieth edition in 1918. Captivity stories were also popular abroad. Rowlandson's account was printed simultaneously with different titles in London and Cambridge, Massachusetts. James E. Seaver's narrative of Mary Jemison had four concurrent U.S. and British editions. Captivity themes appear in French and German popular literature into the eighteenth and nineteenth centuries.[19] Besides narratives, poetry, drama, and fiction for both adults and children appeared, along with widely published collected popular histories. In the public and private record are also newspaper accounts, trial records, legislative pronouncements and bills to compensate captives, local histories and records, and family papers. There is also a large body of visual records: paintings, woodblocks, etchings, murals, cartoons, statuary, playbills, and book cover designs.

But how will a study of white captives inform an understanding of gender and intergroup relations? The captive drama presents us with an intersection of cultures. In the Euro-American sources, we find a mine of firsthand experience of white and native contact, a diverse group of gendered sources. By focusing on these varied accounts and representations, *White Captives* provides an entrée into how Euro-Americans thought about gender and sexuality when confronted by a foreign enemy of another color and culture. The purpose of this book is to interpret the meaning behind these gendered and ethnic depictions of the American frontier.

How and why did capture and its perceived threat shape Anglo-American ideas of gender and culture from 1607 to 1862? In what ways did Anglo-American culture of particular periods shape responses, writings, and depictions of the frontier? What was the impact of age, sex, and tribal culture on the captive?

A TRUE

HISTORY

OF THE

Captivity & Restoration

OF

Mrs. *MARY ROWLANDSON*,

A Minifter's Wife in *New-England*.

Wherein is fet forth, The Cruel and Inhumane Ufage fhe underwent amongft the *Heathens*, for Eleven Weeks time: And her Deliverance from them.

Written by her own Hand, for her Private Ufe: And now made Publick at the earneft Defire of fome Friends, for the Benefit of the Afflicted.

Whereunto is annexed,

A Sermon of *the Poffibility of God's Forfaking a People that have been near and dear to him.*

Preached by Mr. *Jofeph Rowlandfon*, Husband to the faid Mrs. *Rowlandfon*: It being his Laft Sermon.

Printed firft at *New-England:* And Re-printed at *London*, and fold by *Jofeph Poole*, at the *Blue Bowl* in the *Long-Walk*, by *Chrifts-Church* Hofpital. 1682.

Title page from A True History of the Captivity & Restoration of Mrs. Mary Rowlandson *(1682). Courtesy of the Newberry Library*

What was the meaning of the continual showing and telling of these horror stories, tales of adventure and woe? Finally, how and why were particular stories of persistent interest? My findings suggest that captivity pictures, stories, and histories helped the Euro-American culture struggle through questions of cultural and gender identity during periods of extreme change and uncertainty.

Materials about white captives, especially those about white female captives, provide a window on North American society by showing us the anxieties of Euro-Americans of an earlier day under the threat or power of a "savage" and unknown enemy. An examination can provide insight into aspects of gender and intergroup conflict in American life. The popularity of the captive story came from a fascination with both the other and the self. One's own culture, one's own family, one's own gender, that whole complex of Anglo-American culture one inherited by being raised on the American continent, was brought into relief. All that was otherwise understood as given, true, and "natural" required reexamination of the ethnic—that is, cultural— origins of society. Although much in Indian-white relations involves race and racism, concepts of race were strongest in the nineteenth century. Despite the importance of race, I have preferred the term *ethnicity* because it indicates the full range of physical, social, and cultural differences, including those central to group identity. As elaborated upon by Harold R. Isaacs, these include body, name, language, history and origins, religion, and nationality.[20]

The experience of living with members of other societies heightened awareness and functioned as a foil for one's behavior, testing which values could endure. Surviving among others required some acceptance or at least understanding of their ways. Forced experience of another culture challenged Euro-Americans, demanded soul-searching, posed alternative solutions to race war, and might offer alternatives to the status quo between cultures and between the sexes.

My method is based on the presupposition that no one approach fully illuminates the complexity and richness of the sources, nor will only one perspective unlock their meaning and significance. I have therefore chosen to study these materials from a historical perspective over a long run (1607–1862) and to do that first at the macro level—surveying a wide range of documents, narratives, art, literature, local history, and newspapers—to get a sense of how these materials were produced and how they changed over time. Here, using gender as a variable for political and cultural study, the theoretical work of Joan Scott and Natalie Zemon Davis is a useful tool.[21] But a feminist interpretation is merged with the methods of historians who are interested in the nature of contact and conflict between Europeans and Euro-Americans with non-Europeans.[22]

In the second half of the book I proceed from the macro level to the micro level, adopting a case study approach of three women captives. I move chronologically from the American Revolution to the Dakota War of 1862. Although I have focused on women and Indians, two groups neglected by Frederick Jackson Turner, I have chosen his geographical perspective— moving from east to west, from the Hudson Valley frontier, to the Appalachians, and finally to the trans-Mississippi West. I have consciously adopted Turner's idea of a moving frontier although the definition of *frontier* has been called into question as an ethnocentric concept with no relevance or counterpart in Indian country. For studying the Euro-American mentalité I find the term *frontier* useful as redefined by Robert Utley as "not as a single frontier line, white on one side and lacking any discernible color at all on the other, but of groupings of frontier zones in which white and red met and mingled." My use of *frontier* here is also in keeping with recent studies of colonial and imperial contact between Europeans and aboriginal peoples in their first meetings on intercultural frontiers in Africa, Australia, and the Americas. Finally, with all its ethnocentric and imperial flaws, the term *frontier,* as William Cronon tells us, has useful narrative as well as explanatory power. It also illuminates the ways in which regional histories and mentalités contribute to the construction of the national culture.[23]

White Captives is divided into two parts. Part I is titled "White Actors on a Field of Red" and is an overview of the captivity materials. Its first two chapters are "White Women Held Captive" and "White Men Held Captive." Chapter 3, "Exploring Sexual Boundaries," examines forbidden intimacies: relationships between men and women across racial and cultural lines. The second half of *White Captives,* "Women in Times of Change," is devoted to a detailed analysis of three captive women at critical periods in American history and moves from the general to the specific. In so doing, the themes of gender and ethnic contrast are brought into focus in one case relating to the American

Revolution, another involving the life course of a woman who lived from the colonial period to the age of Andrew Jackson, and a third at the time of the Civil War.

Chapter 4, "Jane McCrea and the American Revolution," discusses the strange mythologizing of a New York woman who tried to run off with her Tory lover and her capture and death, which somehow became a symbol of revolutionary martyrdom. Chapter 5, "Mary Jemison: The Evolution of One Captive's Story," concerns a colonial captive from Pennsylvania during the Seven Years' War who lived with New York Senecas well into the age of early industrialization. In Chapter 6, "Sarah Wakefield and the Dakota War," the wife of a Yale-educated doctor defends a Dakota man who served as her protector after she was captured in a frontier conflagration in Minnesota.

The sources of this study are eclectic. First- and secondhand accounts include personal narratives, depositions, and experiences given to a second party and then reproduced in sermons, narratives, and collected biographies. A constant companion for this study's research has been the Newberry Library's reprint series of 111 volumes, *The Garland Library of Narratives of North American Indian Captivities.* Other rare editions have been examined in the collections of the Newberry Library; the American Antiquarian Society; the Library of Congress; the Boston Public and New York Public Library Special Collections; the Special Collections of the Rush Rhees Library at the University of Rochester; the Tozzer, Houghton, and Widener libraries at Harvard; the Western Collections of the Beinecke Library at Yale; and the Rare Book Collection of Goldfarb Library at Brandeis University. Some narratives of historical figures were verifiable through public records such as military and court records, government reports, sermons, newspapers, travelers' accounts, church records and correspondence, private letters and diaries, county histories, town histories, and local historical society records. National and state records were useful for some nineteenth-century cases. For the Dakota War (or Minnesota Sioux Uprising) of 1862, trial records in the National Archives were consulted, as was official correspondence between state, territorial, military, and federal officials. Claims and census records were also helpful. In Minnesota and New York local and state historical societies possess newspapers and personal papers and local and county histories. The county courts provided marriage and probate records and wills.

The visual history of whites among the Indians began with early settlement and contact literature. Drawings and illustrated maps accompanied texts that presented the European public with a strange New World.[24] From the earliest days of white-Indian contact in the Americas, the visual and written records—of fact and fiction—converge. By the nineteenth century stories appeared in national magazines and local newspapers, along with the continual output of narratives of individual experiences. These exist alongside a growing popular literature of plays, novels, and poems about "historic" and purely fictive captives. Paintings, etchings, lithographs, and sculpture also range from the historically based representation to the mythic and fantastical.

Any inventory of sources on white captives would show that the vast majority are from the Euro-American side, many by white males. To attempt to balance the overwhelmingly "white" nature of the sources is a necessary if daunting task. Museum collections and parks were invaluable. Talking with and writing to members of the Native American community has been helpful. Descendants of a few former captives who stayed with Indians were consulted. Ethnographic records for the Iroquois and Dakota have been studied. Because most of the ethnohistorical materials were written by European or American males, Native American religious writing, crafts, poetry, and art have been examined to provide a balance.[25] Combining these materials has helped to give a sense of the richness and power of the native world into which Euro-Americans were taken. A different perspective would emerge if we had Indian documents, paintings, films, and photographs. But rather than using the Euro-American materials to give us ethnographic certainty into the multiplicity of Indian cultures in North America, the masses of materials that do exist help document that most unusual white tribe of Anglo-Saxon Protestants along with some Irish, Germans, and Scandinavians.

To date, scholars have studied captivity from four perspectives: imperial, cultural, ethnohistorical, and gender-based. Twentieth-century historians and literary critics are the inheritors of a nineteenth-century tradition—writers from New England and New York entranced by the captivity experience.

The earliest perspective originates with students of the American empire. Captives were lionized in the nationalist historical writing of the nineteenth century. Books often placed frontier captives as bit-part players in the wider drama of America's rise to power. This nationalist or imperialist school includes the multivolume works of Francis Parkman, *France and England in North America*, and George Bancroft, *History of the United States*.[26] These historians assumed that whatever the sacrifice to the land or its peoples, expansion and conquest were a sign of "manifest destiny," "progress," and "civilization." In this tradition, an array of popular Victorian literature used captive male figures such as Captain John Smith and Daniel Boone to demonstrate Anglo-American superiority facing the "savages" of the Americas. Some of these histories showed their less-well-known, less-well-publicized female counterparts in chapters titled "heroic women" and "girl heroines." Such histories and adventure tales, complete with etchings, elaborate covers, and short, readable chapters, were popular family reading. The message was patriotic: the heroic triumph of white men, women, and children over red, good over evil.[27]

Much of twentieth-century western history is part of this adventurist, ethnocentric tradition. Indians and white women are usually absent or, if present, are stereotyped, while "patriotic" male heroism predominates. The imperialist side of the imperial tradition portrays Indian capture of whites as a mindless, brutal, and savage act. Western history in this tradition refers to Indians as "hostiles," has a strong sense of Anglo-Saxon superiority, and perceives the frontier as a heroic battlefield. This is Frederick Jackson Turner's frontier of "new opportunities" with a violent inevitability. A Turnerian imperial tradition of a more subtle sort exists in works that express a belief in the "democratic" nature of the move west and quest for "free" land.[28]

An anti-imperialist school has also made its mark on Western historiography and captivity analysis. This work argues that white America perpetrated violence on Native Americans in a series of colonialist assaults. Anti-imperialists present us with sympathetic portraits of Indian society as seen through the eyes of white captives who lived with Indians; they tend to cite positive experiences of capture and minimize, romanticize, or exclude negative ones. An example from film is Dustin Hoffman's portrayal of the white captive turned Cheyenne Indian in *Little Big Man*. Anti-imperialist analysis is helpful in heightening our awareness of the ways in which images perpetuate dominant ideologies.[29]

The cultural perspective has two traditions. The first evolved from two of the founding fathers of the American Studies movement, Roy Harvey Pearce and Henry Nash Smith, and two industrious offspring, Richard Slotkin and Leslie Fiedler. These scholars have seen the captivity narratives as an important American genre leaving clues to Euro-American character and society. They have examined frontier literature, including captivity narratives, as studies of American views of the "savage," as repositories of mythic themes, and as influences on other forms of American literature. Another tradition is derived from the work of Perry Miller, locating Puritan narratives as part of the religious and intellectual history of early New England.[30]

The third, or ethnohistorical, approach was prompted by William N. Fenton. His suggestions were based on both his own experience and the work of anthropologists A. Irving Hallowell and John Swanton. Addressing historians and anthropologists in the late 1950s, Fenton asked what each could learn from the other to get a clearer picture of Indian-white relations on this continent. Captivity literature was one area suggested as potentially bringing together the ethnologist and the historian. Following this lead, James Axtell pioneered the first essays studying white captives and adoptees. An earlier set of "ethnographers" spent a substantial amount of time "in the field" experiencing firsthand the effects of capture on white men. The *Jesuit Relations* is an inexhaustible supply of such data.[31]

Finally, there remains the perspective based on an analysis of gender. Here we want to know if a particular experience under study is affected by the sex of participant or observer. Similar questions have recently been applied to studies of women on various American frontiers.[32] The first work was done by Dawn Lander Gherman, Annette Kolodny, and Laurel Thatcher Ulrich. This study concurs with theirs that white women were a historic and dynamic presence on the frontier and in early American culture.[33] But unlike earlier interpretations it examines how women and men were depicted and in some cases behaved during the frontier experience to compare them and to observe gender and ethnic relations over the first 250 years of European settlement. Rather than assume that white women have been less racist and more open to the culture of others, as some feminists presume, or more racist and closed to the "wild," "more masculine" West, as some male critics have claimed, recent studies of gender and ethnicity have begun to look more closely at overall patterns and specific cases.[34] While doing the research I tried to suspend judgment on both white male and female relationships with Indians and instead look at the data and explore cases in depth. Gender and ethnic differences provide a core identity for white captives' lives with Indians and the basis for their stories when presented by themselves and others to their culture. It is the purpose of this book to provide answers to the questions of why and how gender and ethnicity were critical in integrating white captives into what became an American pantheon and what gains and losses that integration held for them and their society as well its implications for America's native people.

Earlier work has recognized the importance of white captives in American history, society, and culture, but the task of linking concerns of gender with those of ethnic or cultural identity is incomplete. In *White Captives* I hope to forge more of these linkages. As Frederick Jackson Turner indicated, the frontier *is* a key to understanding American society, not because of "free land" or democracy but because of what it tells us about Anglo-Americans in contact with others and with their own notions of gender, sexuality, and society.

Part One

White Actors on a Field of Red

White Women Held Captive

O, the wonderful power of God that I have seen, and the experiences that I have had! I have been in the midst of roaring Lions, and Salvage Bears, that feared neither God nor Man, nor the Devil, by night and by day, alone and in company, sleeping all sorts together, and yet not one of them ever offered the least abuse of unchastity to me in word or action.
　—*Mary Rowlandson*

They drank freely, and soon became stupid and senseless. With one of their tomahawks I might with ease have dispatched them all, but my only desire was to flee from them as quick as possible. I succeeded with difficulty in liberating myself by cutting the cord with which I was bound.
　—*Mrs. Jordan*

I was stripped of my gown, shawl, stockings and shoes; loaded with as many of the packs which the boat contained as could be piled upon me, and compelled in this manner to accompany the Indians through a pathless wilderness, for many a tedious mile—not privileged to embrace or nurse my infant babe, which

*was but eleven months old, and which was carried in a fur sack,
by one of their young squaws.*
—Eliza Swan

...
22
*White
Actors
on a
Field
of Red*

*To undertake to narrate their barbarous treatment would only
add to my present distress, for it is with feelings of the deepest
mortification that I think of it, much less to speak or write of it.*
—Rachel Plummer

"On the tenth of *February*, 1675 came the *Indians* with great numbers upon *Lancaster*." So begins the first narrative of North American captivity in the English language. In a single paragraph its writer, Mary Rowlandson, rivets her reader's attention on a catastrophic scene of a small community in mayhem—men's bodies split open, houses and barns in flames, members of her household "fighting for their Lives, others wallowing in their Blood! . . . Mothers and Children crying out for themselves, and one another, *Lord, what shall we do!*"[1]

Years after Mary Rowlandson wrote these lines, hundreds of captivity stories followed her lead. Men's and women's narratives almost always began with a frightful scene of capture, often accompanied by murder, dismemberment, or maiming of some family member, and perhaps fire to one's home or the violent interruption of migration. Progressing from a confrontation between whites and Indians, narratives continued en route with the Indians to the Indian camp, then followed, like Rowlandson's, with a discussion of life there and concluded with an escape, a rescue, or some other means of return (with the few exceptions of narratives of those who never returned).

For each sex and in different periods, there are many accounts of white captivity and many responses to it. For men and women, the once clear and penitent Puritan narrative later became more formulaic. The captivity stories of white men and women have many other similarities as well. But the details of the experience and the way the accounts—real and imagined— were described differ according to gender. By comparing accounts and representations by and about men with those about women but by both men and women, we notice some major differences not only in tone and style but in experience and response. We can also speculate on why such stories held an American readership for so long.

Joan Scott defines gender as "knowledge about sexual differ-ence" and "the understanding produced by cultures and soci-eties of human relationships, in this case of those between men and women." She finds that in historical presentation there has been a "remarkable absence or subordination of women," con-fining them to "the domestic and private" spheres, thus enforc-ing a set of "priorities" and "categories" which diminishes their importance.[2] But rather than being marginalized, subordinated, or totally missing, white women captives are the subject of a vast array of materials. In this literature white women participate fully in the so-called rise of civilization. In fact, what is signifi-cant about seventeenth-, eighteenth-, and nineteenth-century representations of this material is that women are not only there, but they are frequently at the center of stories, histories, and illustrations.

Looking at captivity materials from 1607 through the nine-teenth century one cannot miss the gendered nature of the de-pictions. Often European or American men and women were undergoing similar if not identical experiences, but these were represented in startlingly different ways. They also allegedly reacted to Indian attack and captivity or potential captivity dif-ferently and in very gendered ways. Here again, Scott is useful: "The story is no longer about the things that have happened to women and men and how they have reacted to them; instead it is about the subjective and collective meanings of women and men as categories of identity have been constructed." The use of gender as a lens is helpful here because women are so prominent. We need to ask how they are represented and why.[3]

Captivity materials, especially those from the late eighteenth century, are notorious for blending the real and the highly fic-tive. In this book, works about historical figures are examined, but it is the production, reproduction, and use to which these stories have been put rather than the veracity or lack of it in the accounts with which I am concerned. Besides folk heroes, folk heroines, and folk victims shaped to justify the ruling national political purpose, as Richard Slotkin and Roy Harvey Pearce have told us, there are gendered archetypes asserting a gender ideology as a piece of the national and domestic mission and, perhaps, as normative behavior.[4]

...

24

White
Actors
on a
Field
of Red

What constructions of gender do these materials show us? Despite the perils of overgeneralizing an enormous literature in surveying hundreds of captivity narratives, western history books, schoolbooks, newspaper accounts of capture, and the like, particular archetypes appear again and again. In the period between 1675 and 1870 these female types can be called the Survivor, the Amazon, and the Frail Flower.

This typology best describes female captives who appear in an analysis of over fifty North American captivity narratives.[5] All three types originate in the colonial era, but the preponderance of each varies over time and place. Survivors predominate in the colonial era, Amazons flourish in the period of the Revolution and the Early Republican era, and Frail Flowers are most evident in the period 1820–70. The archetypes themselves, although exhibiting continuities, change over time, territory, and with different Indian groups. Indian groups and practices change with the move west. After the Revolution the new republic pushed many native groups west, and nineteenth-century plains warfare grew increasingly ferocious. These political and ethnic dimensions had important implications for Anglo-American women.

But first, who were the white women captives? Except for young children, married women between the ages of twenty and forty-five predominated. Most were English or Anglo-American Protestants, usually from frontier regions. On the Pennsylvania frontier there were also German captives; on the Minnesota frontier, Germans and Scandinavians were among the white captives. Most were mothers of young children and, in the cases of the older women, were parents to both young and adolescent children. With the exception of ministers' wives and daughters, these women were usually homesteaders of yeoman, artisan, or middle-class backgrounds. Those who wrote their own narratives were better educated. What does the typology tell us about the way white women's captivity was written about and otherwise portrayed?

Survivors

. . . . ' .

Rowlandson most typifies the Survivor. She is not a passive victim, a racist, or a Puritan pawn. She is a woman supremely tried. She watches as her frontier Massachusetts fortress goes up in flames, her relatives and neighbors are murdered, her baby dies of exposure, and her other children disappear. Separated from her husband and children for thirteen weeks, not knowing, except for a brief meeting with her daughter, whether they are dead or alive, she renews and reconceives her faith in God. She also becomes a supreme negotiator with the Narragansetts and Wampanoags among whom she finds herself. She uses her considerable strength to learn to live among these Algonquians.[6] She sews and exchanges goods with them. After several weeks, she moves from disgust with native fare to relishing bear's foot. She makes fast friends with Metacomet (King Philip). Like Rowlandson, Survivors show a range of feelings from extreme powerlessness to aggressive hostility. Yet they all adapt, survive, and make sense of and, in a sense, bear witness without undue victimization, personal aggrandizement, or genocidal aggression.

Ten of the eleven Survivors were captured within the period 1675–1763; eight were New Englanders. The preponderance of the Survivor type in the early period neatly fits the quantitative findings of Alden Vaughan and Daniel K. Richter, which confirm the high survival rate of female captives. Of 392 known female captives of all ages they found that fewer than 10 percent died of various causes in captivity or were killed. Between 30 and 37 percent remained with French or Indians, and 44 percent returned to New England. The quantitative data fit the image portrayed in the Puritan narratives. But though the stories highlight inner fortitude, these women and girls survived forced winter marches like the Deerfield exodus through the New England wilderness into Canada often with the close cooperation of New England or Canadian Indians or the French. These early Anglo-American women and children were tough, both physically and emotionally. Over 20 percent (22.5) of their sex who were taken captive were prisoners for one or more years.[7] How did they manage?

...

26

White

Actors

on a

Field

of Red

First, their captors should be credited. Although many of the Survivors chose not to remain with Indians, and any number can be cited for venomous remarks about Indians, these women were willing to give credit when it was due. Others, as James Axtell has told us, did stay, were adopted by their captors, and refused several attempts to be "redeemed" or repatriated into white society.[8]

But for their own part, many English and Anglo-American women did well in marches through Indian country. Mary Rowlandson and Elizabeth Hanson expressed fear and depression. Rowlandson became despondent after losing her baby and being separated from her husband and children. At the site of their first encampment she was thrown into despair. "All was gone, my Husband gone (at least separated from me, he being in the Bay; and to add to my grief, the *Indians* told me they would kill him as he came homeward) my Children gone . . . all gone (except my life) and I knew not but the next moment that might be too." But almost immediately she assessed her choices: she remembered her earlier thoughts: "If the *Indians* should come, I should chuse rather to be killed by them, than taken alive, but when it came to the trial my mind changed: their glittering Weapons so daunted my Spirit, that I chose rather to go along with those (as I may say) ravenous Bears, than that moment to end my daies."[9]

Those days passed, and she felt lost in a "vast and desolate Wilderness, I know not whither." She lamented leaving behind "my own country, and traveling to the vast and howling Wilderness; and I understood something of *Lot's* Wife's Temptation, when she looked back." By their eighth site she was overwhelmed.

> When I was in the Cannoo, I could not but be amazed at the numerous Crew of Pagans, that were on the Banks of the other side. When I came ashore, they gathered all about me, I sitting alone in their midst. . . . Then my heart was began to faile: and I fell a weeping; which was the first time to my remembrance, that I wept before them. Although I had met with so much Affliction, and my heart was many times ready to break, yet I could not shed one tear in their sight; but rather

had been all this time in a maze, and like one astonished; but now I may say, as *Psal. 137.1 By the Rivers of Babylon, there we sate down and, yea, we wept when we remembered Zion.*

One Indian asked her why she was crying, and she said she was afraid they would kill her. "No, said he, none will hurt you." And one of the Indians came forward with "two spoonfuls of Meal (to comfort me)." [10] She went on to make the most of her stay and to befriend some of her captors.

Mary Rowlandson was clearly a remarkable woman. As a minister's wife she was not typical of New England women of her time. She was a member of the elite and a highly literate and powerful writer.[11] Her account shows a strength and self-awareness unusual in any period. But several accounts show that other daughters of New England employed accommodation and ingenuity for their own benefit. Elizabeth Hull Heard was the daughter of a minister, mother of five sons and five daughters, and a "widow of good estates." When Dover, New Hampshire, was attacked in 1689, the widow told her children to abandon her and "shift for themselves" because "through her despair and faintness"—according to Cotton Mather—she was "unable to stur any further." When they left she tried to move downriver surrounded by "blood and fire, and hideous outcries." She finally sat down by a bush and "poured out her ardent prayers to God for help in distress." Soon "an Indian came toward her, with a pistol in his hand." He came back twice but let her go.[12]

Cotton Mather presents this as a "Remarkable Escape," but Samuel G. Drake gives additional information. During an earlier attack on Dover in 1676, "this same Mrs. Heard secreted a young Indian in her house, by which means he escaped that calamitous day." Apparently, Heard's earlier generosity, not God's will, saved her.[13]

Mary Woodwell (Fowler) was sixteen years old in 1746 when she and her family and several others of the household were captured in Hopkinton, Massachusetts. She was taken to Canada and sold to an Indian woman. A French doctor urged her to feign a fatal illness. Her successful acting ability resulted in her return to New England.[14]

...

28

White

Actors

on a

Field

of Red

Isabella M'Coy was captured while she and her family were fleeing an attack on Epsom, New Hampshire, in August 1747. She owed her survival to the kindness of Indian captors, who, according to the account she gave a minister, fed her apples and carried her across rivers on their backs. To her they appeared "desirous of mitigating the distress of their prisoner." One suspects this young woman's behavior may have merited such kind treatment; something in her manner may have prompted a reciprocal kindness in theirs. The account does not say so directly, but we might assume that, as in the case of Heard, some sympathetic relationships were established.[15]

Jemima Howe, a Vernon, Vermont, captive of the mid-eighteenth century was a mother of seven who remained among the Indians and then the French for five years after her capture in July 1755. One infant child died, and two of her small boys were separated from her. Like Rowlandson, Hanson, Heard, and M'Coy, she seemed to be able to adapt to and deal with Indian captors. When she and her new Indian mistress and others settled in for the winter at St. Johns, her anxiety for her health and that of her nursing infant mounted. "I acquainted my new mother that I did not think it would be possible for me to endure it. . . . Listening to my repeated and earnest solicitations, that I might be disposed of among some of the French inhabitants of Canada, she, at length, set off with me and my infant, attended by some male Indians, upon a journey to Montreal, in hopes of finding a market for me there."[16] Howe later credited the Indians who took care of her two sons, both of whom she had given up for dead. She found her son Caleb, aged two or three, "under the protection of a fond Indian mother." Another Indian gave her directions to cross Lake Champlain in winter to see her son Squire.

> At my request he gave me the best directions he could to the place of his abode. . . . At length, having obtained my keepers' leave to be absent for one day, I set off early in the morning, and steering as well as I could, according to the directions which the friendly Indian had given me, I quickly found the place, which he had so accurately marked out. I beheld, as I drew nigh, my little son without the camp; but he looked, thought I, like a starved and mangy puppy, that had

been wallowing in the ashes. I took him in my arms, and he spoke to me these words in the Indian tongue: "Mother, are you come?" [17]

By Survivor, I mean the woman who experiences and feels a wide range of stress in, but ultimately adapts to, tries to make sense of, and comes to terms with her situation. When a captured Bible was given to Rowlandson by one of the Indians, Puritan faith became a means of spiritual support giving meaning to her suffering. Because Puritan narratives were carefully screened and served religious and political aims, we cannot guarantee that the behavior cited was accurate or exaggerated to serve these wider goals. Although their intent may have been to place the congregation of the new Zion in awe of God's Providence and infinite mercies, these narratives also told the Puritan community of the tremendous physical, emotional, and spiritual stamina of its women in times of trial.[18]

The Rise of the American Amazon

. . . . . .

During the mid-eighteenth to the early nineteenth centuries, two other images begin to emerge beside the Survivor. With the publication of Jemima Howe's narrative in 1788 and 1792 began romance, sentiment, and the elements of the Frail Flower. Earlier and more pronounced is the Amazonian response characterized by women of "singular prowess." Amazonian women of the period 1764–1820 are residents of the Appalachian frontier and the Ohio Valley. They serve as models for many a pistol-packin' momma in later western lore and appear on prominent western statues.[19] The colonial version arose, according to Laurel Thatcher Ulrich, out of necessity and English tradition and became an accepted role she calls "deputy husband." Husbands went away on long trips; husbands died. In such circumstances, society sanctioned women to serve in their stead for the sake of family survival. For protection from animals or Indian attack, women routinely learned to pick up a gun in defense of self or family. The first and most famous of these women was Hannah Dustan.[20]

...

30

White

Actors

on a

Field

of Red

Dustan's story comes to us from the pen of Cotton Mather, the renowned Puritan minister. On March 15, 1697, toward the end of King William's War, the frontier town of Haverhill, Massachusetts, was attacked and thirty-nine people were captured and several homes burned. Dustan, aged forty, was lying in after the delivery of her eighth child one week before. Her husband was away and a nurse was in attendance when the assault occurred. Mr. Dustan rushed back in time to rescue seven of the children and to retreat to the town garrison. Nurse Mary Neff, Mrs. Dustan, and the infant "fell into the hands of Formidable Salvages," who rifled and burned the house and led them away with approximately ten other "English *Captives*." En route, according to Mather, "those furious Tawnies" took and "dash'd out the Brains of the *Infant*, against a Tree," and when other captives began "to Tire in their sad *Journey*" they were "soon sent unto their *Long Home*." Dustan and Neff traveled nearly 150 miles in the next few days, later continuing north with an Indian family of twelve: two men, three women, and seven children. The family told them that on reaching the Indian town of Penacook (near present-day Concord, New Hampshire), they "must be Stript, and Scourg'd, and run the *Gantlet* through the whole Army of *Indians*." One evening, with Neff and a young boy to assist her, Dustan picked up a hatchet and murdered ten of the twelve Indians. The ten were then scalped, following which the colonial captives returned with their scalps to Massachusetts, where they received a bounty of fifty pounds from the General Assembly along with *"presents of Congratulation"* from friends and much press from Mather.[21]

Women in the Dustan tradition are found in profusion in captivity literature of the eighteenth and mid-nineteenth centuries. We also find women resisting capture using a variety of Amazonian tactics, exhibiting extraordinary ability with rifles, hoes, hatchets, and axes—masters of the arts of escape and hand-to-hand combat. The story of one such republican mother is found in Archibald Loudon's *Selection of Narratives of Outrages Committed by the Indians* (1808). Its author offers an account of a woman "in defense of her own life, and that of her husband and children." During March 1779 at Dunkard's Creek, Kentucky, several families, "who were afraid to stay at home, gathered to her house and there stayed; looking on themselves to be safer than when scattered about their own houses." One day the children "came running in from play in great haste, saying, there were ugly red men." When one of the men in the house stepped to the door, he was shot. Soon the men of the house were all killed or injured. "Now Mrs. Bozarth appears the only defense, who not finding a knife at hand, took up an axe that lay by, and with one blow cut out the brains of the Indian." She then turned to a second Indian wrestling with a man on the bed "and with her axe gave him several large cuts, some of which let his entrails appear." His cries of "murder" brought other Indians who had been "killing some children out of doors." On entering, one's head was "clove in two with her axe . . . which laid him flat upon the soil." In a final move, Experience Bozarth pushed another entering warrior from the door and, with the help of one of the recovering men, shut it "and made it fast."[22] Other nameless Amazons are discussed and graphically illustrated in any number of nineteenth-century histories. The overtly racist and bloodthirsty intent of many of these Amazon figures is obvious. Women not only defend their dwellings but often enjoy the gore and violence. One woodcut in a popular 1846 anthology shows Mrs. Merril with two dead Indians at her feet hovering over a third coming through the slats in her door. A smile is on her face; an ax is poised over the middle of his back.[23]

Other women of extraordinary prowess are athletic escape artists. One such woman was Frances Scott, a contemporary of Daniel Boone's from Washington County, Virginia. Scott escaped capture by following the Sandy River to its source, passing waterfalls, and climbing "impassable" mountains and "inaccessible Rocks." She jumped from rocks fifteen to twenty-five feet high and landed unhurt, was bitten by a "venomous snake, killed it and arrived with the help of two birds exhausted but alive at Clinch, her destination." Mrs. Davis, a James River, Virginia, captive of 1761, escaped by rafting down the Ohio on a log, surviving on shellfish, wild fruit, and roots. Massy Harbison also escaped capture. Carrying her nursing infant, she walked for four days along the headwaters of the Allegheny until she reached Pittsburgh.[24]

Less violent Amazons of this period were able to escape and elude capture, but unlike their colonial captive sisters they succeeded for reasons other than prayer and goodwill. Mrs. Arm-

Mrs. Bozarth defending her Dwelling, from John Frost,
Thrilling Adventures among the Indians *(1850). Courtesy of the*
Newberry Library

strong of Northumberland County, Pennsylvania, watched from under the bed as her husband, Andrew, was carried off. Mrs. Clendenin, of Greenbrier, Virginia, displayed "Surprising Conduct" when she and other neighboring settlers were cut off from help in 1763 by the warriors of Cornstalk after an attack on the Muddy Creek settlement. With no ax at hand, "Mrs. Clendenin did not fail to abuse the Indians with her tongue, with the most reproachful epithets she could command, although the tomahawk was brandishing at the same moment overhead." The Indians, rather than killing her, took to "lashing her in the face and eyes with the bleeding scalp of her dead husband!" When she and other prisoners were taken and marched off, she gave her baby to another female captive and escaped. The baby was brutally murdered. The unknowing mother returned that night to her house, "a distance of more than ten miles," where her dead husband was still lying with "one of his dead children in his arms." The narrator concludes: "Thus ends the remarkable, though short captivity of a woman, more to be admired for her courage than some other qualities not less desirable in the female character." [25]

Mrs. Daviess, wife of Samuel Daviess of Bedford County, Virginia, was captured in 1782 with her seven children but released with the help of her husband. Some time later, when her home was again threatened and the men were chasing after Indian robbers, Mrs. Daviess, "a woman of cool, deliberate courage and accustomed to handle the gun," picked one up and aimed it at an Indian who happened into her house and was about to take some whiskey. "She held him a prisoner, until the party of men returned and took him into their possession." [26] The determination of these women to escape and elude recapture does not bear out James Axtell's position that nearly all colonial captives wanted to stay within the Indian community "because they found Indian life to possess a strong sense of community, abundant love and uncommon integrity." [27]

Why were these women Amazons? Apparently, a personal threat to the survival of self and family required a woman to summon her physical power, her cunning, her stamina, and her anger. But these accounts and illustrations are part of a growing nationalistic necessity, which served the function of bringing women into active combat status in the national war against Indians.

Just as the prototype of the Amazonian figure came from the colonial story of Hannah Dustan, the evolution of the fighting frontier mother was first perpetuated in the colonial era in New England with another unlikely colonial captive—Mary Rowlandson. Nearly one hundred years after the 1682 original, a spate of five new Rowlandson editions appeared between 1770 and 1773. The first in 1770 followed a previous edition of 1720 by fifty years.[28] There were two major changes in these revolutionary era editions. First, the introductory and closing pieces that framed the early Puritan narrative were omitted.[29] Second, illustrations were provided. Although the first Boston editions came out with borders and the second with fleur-de-lis, it was not until the 1770 editions that woodcuts adorned Rowlandson's work. In Boyle's (1773) and Coverly's (1770 and 1771) editions, woodcuts employ the images of a patriotic mother and frontier fighter.[30] The illustrations recast Mrs. Rowlandson into what Linda Kerber has called an example of female patriotism, in this case a frontier mother in the American Amazon tradition.[31]

There are three woodcuts of the frontier fighter. The first shows up in the Coverly edition of 1770 as a frontispiece depicting Rowlandson with a three-cornered hat holding a musket at her side. According to bibliographer R. W. G. Vail, the woodcut used in the Coverly edition was "stock in trade" and had been used earlier in Fowle's edition of *A New Gift for Children* (1762).[32] A similar woodcut appeared on broadsides before the Revolution and on *A New Touch of the Times . . . by a Daughter of Liberty, living at Marblehead* (1778).[33] The woodcut of the woman with musket appears to have been an accepted and known symbol of patriotic women of the revolutionary era. A second fighter image (Coverly, 1771) is more a victim, with flames leaping around the Rowlandson garrison and a woman in distress.[34] A third, in Boyle's edition of 1773, shows a woman dressed in frontier dress aiming a musket at monstrous, hatchet-wielding, gun-toting Indians.

The image of the gun-wielding mother is accompanied by a domestic mother. The domestic woodcut on the final page of the 1771 Coverly edition is a small, very crowded triptych. The upper panel shows a woman rocking a baby in a cradle. The middle panel is so unclear that only a guess will do: there are birds over a river, animals on one side, a woman on the other. In the bottom panel, a woman is milking a cow. Such scenes of domesticity, nurturance, and peaceable wholeness—bees surround the outside of the entire woodcut—indicate a productive and reproductive importance. The pairing of the fighting woman with the domestic one was a good propaganda device for urging traditional women to take up arms, as if the use of violence would complement rather than compromise femininity and domesticity.

The publication history of the Rowlandson narrative in the 1770s was the work of four men, all of whom were prorevolutionary printers of political tracts.[35] Of the four, John Boyle (or Boyles), Nathaniel Coverly, and Zachariah Fowle printed in Boston. Timothy Green came from New London. Both Fowle and Boyle were publishers of revolutionary newspapers, Fowle working with Isaiah Thomas on the 1770 editions of the *Massachusetts Spy*, Boyle working with Richard Draper and then his widow, Margaret Draper, on the *Massachusetts Gazette*, a Tory paper he helped dissolve.[36] That Boyle saw an intimate connection between the events of the earlier Indian wars and the contemporary revolutionary crisis is clear from the preface to his 1775 edition of William Hubbard's *Narrative of the Indian Wars in New-England*, in which the "gracious hand of Divine Providence" preserved the early New England colonies from "Savages" who attacked "the first English adventurers, while they were few in number, yea very few, and strangers in the land." He concluded, "Our many frontier settlements are continually exposed to savage invasion."[37]

The Rowlandson imprints were all issued at a time of trouble for colonial Boston in particular and colonial America in general. Printers tried to establish a sense of identification for both male and female readers with a new and an old patriotic and religious tradition in America. That new tradition demanded active participation and self-defense by women on the frontier and in the seaports; it required women to identify the patriot cause as their own and as best for their families and their country. The choice of Rowlandson as a symbol in the new ideology and activism was not fortuitous but was part of a blending of two older frontier and literary American traditions with which

...

36

White
Actors
on a
Field
of Red

her revolutionary printers were familiar: the Survivor and the Amazon traditions of the Puritan narratives. The years of the Revolution were certainly different from those of the 1680s, but in New England the descendants of that earlier frontier were again about to be tried.[38] That their foremothers successfully came through afflictions in fighting their enemies and that this revolutionary generation was a link in that older chain could not have been lost on such a reader, nor was it lost on Rowlandson's newest publishers. They displayed women as national heroic figures in the war against Indians—fierce and defending mothers and needed warriors. As such, they sanctioned and even glorified white women's use of violence. As with the Dustan story, bold and bloody action was justified. One popular nineteenth-century anthology suggests that violent behavior was unnatural but necessary given the nature of the wilderness frontier.[39]

The Emergence of the Frail Flower

The Frail Flower is our third type. Like the others, her origins can be found in New England captivity narratives, especially Jemima Howe's in the late eighteenth century, and sentimental heroines of this type develop the "melodramatic possibilities of the narrative," as Richard VanDerBeets pointed out in writing of Mary Kinnan's 1795 narrative. But the most complete renditions of the Frail Flower do not appear until the 1830s and 1840s, and they correspond to the rise of True Womanhood and the mass marketing of sentimental fiction.[40] Roy Harvey Pearce characterized nineteenth-century captivities as "truly wild and woolly." In surveying the narratives of both men and women between 1813 and 1873, "all of which seem to stem from real enough experiences," he found the "language is most often that of the hack writer gone wild."[41] If this explains the violence in the writing, it does not account for the sentiment or for the shift from Amazon to Frail Flower. The rise of the sentimental heroine in the mid- to late eighteenth-century literature continued until a response almost unknown in the seventeenth and early eighteenth centuries becomes the dominant mode of the nineteenth. This heroine turns frailty, motherhood, cleanliness, and disgusting Indians into highly salable works. The Frail Flower appears frequently in such narratives. She is the poor, hapless woman who is taken unawares. She is shocked and distressed by her capture and by the deaths and dislocations that go with it. What makes her a candidate for Frail Flower status is that she rarely emerges from her shock, distress, and misery. Frail Flower narratives include brutality, sadomasochistic and titillating elements, strong racist language, pleas for sympathy and commiseration with the author's suffering, special appeals to her sad lot as a distressed mother, and occasional invectives against dirt and sex among Indians.[42]

Eliza Swan was captured near St. Louis and later saved by a Spanish trader. Under the burdens of captivity she wished she "possessed the courage of some of the heroines of my sex, whom history informs us, have distinguished themselves on similar occasions" so she might "revenge" her husband's death and escape. Instead, she complains that "an old bear skin" was thrown at her. Then, separated from her baby, she was marched over high mountains "in my weak and emaciated state." The mountain she climbed was "probably the highest in the western world." She was "tormented by painful bites of large black ants" and feared being attacked by giant rattlesnakes, one of which "coiled within two yards from my head! He was of an unusual size, seven or eight feet (as I judged) in length." Her sentiments of abandonment; her outrage and disgust; her dismay that anything might go wrong; her response to life as a tragic plight unfairly visited upon her, a poor suffering female; and the sexual imagery are typical of Frail Flower narratives. Although she was "saved," there is no Providence here.[43]

Caroline Harris, Clarissa Plummer, and their families were on their way to Texas when their party was captured by Comanche Indians. Both of their husbands were killed, and both were, in Harris's words, "compelled to co-habit with a barbarous and blood-thirsty savage." "Alas! however revolting the idea, such, indeed was my fate! for a poor, forlorn, and friendless captive, as I then was, there was no alternative." Plummer's "disgust" is followed by fainting and her recovery on "a filthy bed of leaves and moss." "Never, no never," she writes, "could a human being of my sex be reduced to a more wretched condition."[44]

Eliza Swan, Caroline Harris, and Clarissa Plummer all suf-

Frontispiece and title page from Mrs. Caroline Harris, History
of the Captivity and Providential Release Therefrom of
Mrs. Caroline Harris *(1838). Courtesy of the Newberry Library*

HISTORY

OF THE

CAPTIVITY AND PROVIDENTIAL RELEASE
THEREFROM OF

MRS. CAROLINE HARRIS,

Wife of the late Mr. *Richard Harris*, of Franklin County, State of New-York; who, with Mrs. *Clarissa Plummer*, wife of Mr. *James Plummer*, were, in the Spring of 1835, (with their unfortunate husbands,) taken prisoners by the Camanche tribe of Indians, while emigrating from said Franklin County (N. Y.) to Texas; and after having been made to witness the tragical deaths of their husbands, and held nearly two years in bondage, were providentially redeemed therefrom by two of their countrymen attached to a company of Santa Fe Fur Traders.

It was the misfortune of Mrs. *Harris*, and her unfortunate female companion (soon after the deaths of their husbands,) to be separated by, and compelled to become the companions of, and to cohabit with, two disgusting Indian Chiefs, and from whom they received the most cruel and beastly treatment.

NEW-YORK:

PERRY AND COOKE, PUBLISHERS.

1838.

. . .

40

White
Actors
on a
Field
of Red

Frontispiece from Clarissa Plummer, Narrative of the Captivity
and Extreme Sufferings of Mrs. Clarissa Plummer *(1838).*
Courtesy of the Newberry Library

fered from severe cases of "poor me," or Frail Flower syn-
drome. Why they did not refuse to go west or southwest to Texas
we never know; they preferred to mourn and fuss later. They
dreamed of being genteel wives but wedded men with cowboy
fantasies. Sarah Ann Horn's narrative discusses the trip west
as a disaster from start to finish. "From the first time the subject was talked of, and notwithstanding all the fortitude I could
command, my mind was a constant prey to the most distressing apprehensions. An undefinable sense of affliction seemed
constantly to haunt my imagination." But when her husband
offered to send her back to England until he found "a permanent home," she said no. She wanted to share the experience
with him: "He was my greatest earthly treasure." Later, as she
looked back, she concluded her narrative with this warning:
"Emigration has for two or three years past been the prevail-
ing principle which . . . in too many instances, has proved the
cause of the ruin of families once comfortably settled in a land
where the conveniences of life amply abound."[45] Perhaps such
writings functioned to warn women that following husbands
everywhere might prove dangerous.

Were the feelings which Swan, Harris, and Plummer expressed real or merely thought up by publishers to capture the dollars of readers? Massy Harbison was a frontier mother whose narrative acquired more Frail Flower elements in later editions. A look at her story's publication history might shed some light on the problems of reality versus sentiment, for in addition to several editions of the narrative, we have a court deposition of her case.[46] The deposition was given in Pittsburgh in 1792. The first publication of Harbison's "own" account appeared in Pittsburgh thirty-three years later (1825), one year after the commercial success of James E. Seaver's *Narrative of the Life of Mrs. Mary Jemison* and two years following James Fenimore Cooper's first Leatherstocking Tale, *The Pioneers: or the Sources of the Susquehanna.* The title page of *A Narrative of the Sufferings of Massy Harbison* assures the reader that the narrative is "COMMUNICATED BY HERSELF," but it is unclear to whom.[47] Did Harbison respond as her narrative claims, or was her tale published for pecuniary and nationalistic purposes? The 1825 edition is prefaced with a certificate of verification and a seal. The editors state their intent that "such deeds of valour, suffering, and privation, ought to be distinctly and minutely recorded, that our sons and daughters, and future generations, may know what was endured by those who first braved the dangers of the wilderness, exposing themselves to the scalp-knife and tomahawk, that they might turn the barren land into a fruitful field."[48] For the historical record they insert letters of Governor Arthur St. Clair to Secretary of War Henry Knox regarding the Miami, Ohio, campaigns of 1791. Harbison, a mother of two and seven months pregnant at the time of her captivity, describes the capture and murder of two children and appeals to mothers who now enjoy "sweet repose" to extend their sympathies to "a pioneer in the work of cultivation and civilization." The text with additions is sixty-six pages. The original deposition with basically the same information is five paragraphs. Feeling, sentiment, and suffering make up the difference along with "historic" pieces added by the editor to connect Harbison's plight after the loss of her husband to St. Clair's defeat in 1791.[49]

Such accounts contained historical elements but were also products of the market. They were created at a time when sentimental and yet adventurist writing was being produced for a

...

42

White
Actors
on a
Field
of Red

female readership as part of the wider emergence of mass news-paper, magazine, and book marketing. Frail Flower responses and the view of the brutal Indian described by these women were also shaped by the periods in which they lived.[50] The threat to woman as nurturing mother and protector of her children was frequently a central piece in these narratives and their accompanying illustrations, a piece which corresponds directly with the Cult of True Womanhood and the Victorian focus on motherhood as the center of female and domestic life.

Of course, not all of these women were exaggerating their plight. Rachel Plummer, daughter of Reverend James Parker, was a captive from the attack by Comanche bands on Fort Parker, Texas, in 1836. She saw her uncle killed before her eyes. She was beaten and tied up. She watched as her eighteen-month-old son, James Pratt, was taken from her. After she gave birth in captivity, her six- or seven-week-old infant was tortured to death. She watched as he was continually thrown into cactus plants. Although released in 1839, she died the next year.[51]

Carroll Smith-Rosenberg tells us that in the pre–Civil War period of the overland trail "true" women married men with Davy Crockett visions of moving west. Women found them-selves in new situations outside the home in an age of increasing domesticity. And the move west was a difficult one—a period of hard times for women and their families.[52] These narratives thus appear to have had another function, allowing women of the period whether on or off the trail to express their sense of loss and powerlessness in the face of decisions made by personal and impersonal forces. They gave women credit for, however imperfectly, carrying on in the face of adversity. In so doing, in a different way from the Puritan pieces from which they originated, they acknowledged the central role of women in the westering enterprise.

By the post–Civil War period, both the dime novel and the romance had become popular market products. With the stereo-type of the evil, brutal Indian long in place, a shockingly illus-trated dime novel appeared. It tells of how Massachusetts-born Mary Barber, with her own consent, married a Sioux chief by the name of Squatting Bear in the year 1867. She excuses her-self by saying, "I never stopped to think at all, for if I had I should never have taken the step I did." Her "zeal" in her effort to convert the heathen tribes was her sole motivation. She asks her reader: "Did I love him? perhaps some may ask. No, I did not." These thoughts gave her much "uneasiness." "'Twas a sin to marry a man whom I did *not* love. But, reader, pray your lenience. Remember I was young and blind with what I then considered a religious duty."[53] Even so, it was not long before Barber conceived of herself as a captive. The cover of her narrative reads, *Five Years of Terrible Suffering among the Indians.* Part of the "suffering" included her witnessing her husband's fourth marriage. She was outraged when he gave his new Indian bride the same gold chain and locket she "had worn before our marriage." And even worse, the woman was a widow with a nine-year-old boy. Me-em-ole became one of Barber's "greatest tormentors." Her husband "became a perfect tyrant," beating her often. She "resolved to escape." This was a step in the right direction, but she fainted instead, first from a rattlesnake bite, then in the process of recovery from "another severe shock," which left her "again prostrated." She attempted another escape but was recaptured. Eventually a white man "saved" her.[54]

The drawings in Barber's book unite the key elements of nineteenth-century captive women's responses. First we see a young "lady" being wed in front of a minister to a dark, painted Indian. This is followed by a page depicting a dainty and domestic Mary slightly lifting her skirt to put the kettle on the fire as a strange creature looks on. The caption reads: "My Domestic Duties Practiced Under Difficulty. Jealousy of Me-em-ole." Later we find a sadomasochistic picture of her husband pulling her hair and beating her, subtitled "My Suffering Knew No Bounds. The Fiend Was at No Loss to Devise Schemes of Torture." There is also a picture of the two wives battling it out with tomahawks, a scheme Barber claims was thought up by her husband to see the two women fight in an "Amazonian encounter."[55] This and other nineteenth-century narratives along with accompanying artistic renditions of captivity exaggerated two stereotypic images: the Indian as savage and the white woman as delicate vessel. Visually and in print, Indian men were depicted as a wild and "savage" race, antithetical to domestic purity.[56] By midcentury, these works contributed to an emerging

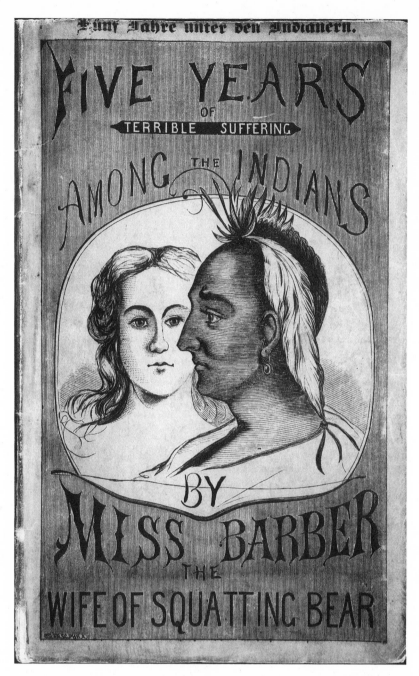

Cover from Miss Mary Barber, Five Years of Terrible Suffering among the Indians *(1872). Courtesy of the Newberry Library*

Attempt to Escape. My Capture, and Cruel Treatment, from Miss Mary Barber, Five Years of Terrible Suffering among the Indians *(1872). Courtesy of the Newberry Library*

gender ideology contrasting powerful white men with totally powerless white women overpowered by villainous and brutal Indians.

White
Actors
on a
Field
of Red

Among women captured between 1675 and the mid-nineteenth century, there were three common gender ideologies. Seventeenth-century women had God to lean on and in a real sense were never totally alone. They felt fear and abandonment in captivity but rarely so total an abandonment as to leave them helpless. Many exhibited physical strength and a willingness to negotiate. By the late eighteenth and early nineteenth centuries, a model of an undaunted frontier mother had developed, a carryover from the colonial era and a mixture of tall-tale folklore and down-home necessity. This Amazonian model, however, included strong racist overtones and encouraged murder rather than accommodation. It added to the conception of the Indian as savage other. It supported female strength but in the service of expansion; it defended family and virginity but only for Euro-American women and their families. Alternatively, by the 1830s, a culture of delicate femininity had so infiltrated much of the ideology of white middle-class womanhood and an ever-present God had become so modified and removed that for some captive women, most of whom were mothers of small children, the loss of a protective husband brought a sense of overwhelming defenselessness and powerlessness. By the postrevolutionary period it was acceptable to cry terror, suffering, and inability to cope.

The line between actual response and literary and artistic style makes it hard to say categorically that women of the three periods in question actually and consistently behaved in distinctly different ways. Statistics show that colonial women did, but a comparable set of figures has yet to be collected and analyzed for the period following the American Revolution and into the nineteenth century. But the gendered ideology in each period did reinforce different ideals for women. In the circumstances of capture it is likely that these ideologies and the methods for dealing with Indian encounter each indicated were drawn upon as potential solutions for women and their families. In each era different devices were suggested for coping with the problems at hand. Certainly colonial mores and Puritan dictums endorsed faith, prayer, belief, and inner strength. The revolutionary era demanded unquestioned patriotism, fortitude, and, if necessary, willingness to fight. Nineteenth-century values and sentimental fiction encouraged dependence, weakness, cleanliness, and racial superiority. Rather than self-reliance and negotiation, some narratives suggested waiting for salvation from white men on horseback.

Women from the seventeenth century onward had difficulty as captives. But the cult of domesticity, the acceptance by many of doctrines of racial inferiority, their disgust with the body, their preoccupation with cleanliness, and their refusal to take responsibility for their actions appear to have turned some nineteenth-century women into Frail Flowers and added to the misery of their condition, perhaps leading some to an early death. At least in their writings, these women sound paralyzed and unable to adapt. Certainly it was acceptable if not popular to publish and illustrate frail women in the antebellum period as it had been unusual to do so before the nineteenth century.

It is difficult to draw a line between art and life in analyzing this literature. The three types, Survivor, Amazon, and Frail Flower, persist even to the present in films and stories about captives. Perhaps the important message is that male and female shapers of culture adapt in art and in life. Certainly not all nineteenth-century white female captives succumbed to fainting spells. It also appears that west of the Mississippi some white women were physically and sexually mistreated whereas for the colonial period there is little evidence of abuse and numerous testimonials to Indian men's respect for their captives. But even if only a small number of women were physically and sexually abused, rumors of rape were common. Glenda Riley finds that accumulated fears and stereotypes, some perpetuated by captivity stories, increased women's dread and could account for some of their responses. Certainly stories like Rachel Plummer's were terrifying enough.[57]

Beginning with Mary Rowlandson's opening paragraphs, the story of the female captive placed a Christian, European woman at the center of a profound battle in her community's history. In Rowlandson's and later accounts, women were at the mercy of others. Her narrative proved that a woman could find ways to gain control over her life and the lives of at least some of her

...

48

White
Actors
on a
Field
of Red

children. She could find her way out of racial and cultural violence and personal loss. She could muster religious, physical, social, and psychological resources on her own. Such a message opened possibilities for personal survival linked with accommodation for the most vulnerable members of white society and thus offered the suggestion for the rest of the society as well. By the nineteenth century, gendered messages in narratives by and about women generally worked to fuel racial hatred. The preponderance of the later captivity materials placed women at the center of a national tableau. They used white women's alleged strengths and weaknesses as weapons that threatened the lives and esteem of both the women and the Indian peoples who were the ultimate captives of a hostile national policy.

White Men
Held Captive

Smith they conducted to a long house, where
thirtie or fortie tall fellowes did guard him; and ere long more
bread and venison was brought him then would haue served
twentie men.
—John Smith

We are glad to see the prospect of your filling the place of a great
man, in whose room you were adopted. . . . Brother,—Your
conduct on this occasion hath pleased us much.
—Colonel James Smith's Delaware brother

Should the child be a boy, this period is to the mother peculiarly
interesting; because she now takes it with her in all her visits. . . .
[On returning home there] commences a very extraordinary
discipline. . . . She strikes him with her hand, pulls his hair, &c.
which her now hopeful boy retaliates in a spiteful and becoming
manner. Some time having passed in this way, by which her
pupil has learned to bear pain without dread, she takes him
again on a visit, and I have never known an instance of a second
disappointment in these trials of courage.
—John Dunn Hunter

...
50
White
Actors
on a
Field
of Red

In the first and most famous captive story of an Englishman on the North American continent, Captain John Smith spent a month among the native people of tidewater Virginia. Admitting to some difficulties, Smith wrote of his experiences: "Yet hee so demeaned himselfe amongst them, as he not only diverted them from surprising the Fort: but procured his owne liberty, and got himself and his company such estimation amongst them, that those Savages admired him as a demi-God."[1]

Were men's experiences, behavior, perceptions, and storytelling style on the various American frontiers different from women's? The answer is yes. On the New England frontier, many more males than females were captured. Of captives taken by French, by Indian and French, and by Indian forces between 1675 and 1763, 771 were males and 270 were females. Men were also at risk because, as in most of human history, men made up the fighting forces. Men were the warriors and the shock troops. They were the leaders of the onslaught onto Indian lands. The codes for prisoners of native capture differed, but a male at adolescence or older might be subject to torture, death, or a combination of the two. Of 1,187 known male captives of French, Indians, and French-Indians in the various New England hostilities between 1675 and 1763, 132 (11 percent) of the male captive population died of all causes; of 392 women, only 16 (4.1 percent) died. Yet 18 males (1.5 percent) were killed as were 33 females (8.4 percent). For infants and children to age six, there was little numerical differentiation between the sexes for those who died or were killed by Indians. For adult males over fifteen, 119 (10 percent) died and 9 were killed; only 12 women (3 percent) died, while 14 (3.5 percent) were killed.[2]

The white male experience ranged from one extreme of torture and death to the other of adoption and acceptance. Torture was nearly always reserved for men, but accounts of torture are also related to religion and ethnicity. The most horrific spectacles of torture were reported by French Catholics. Father Isaac Jogues, a Jesuit, was captured with a group of Hurons and three other Frenchmen by the Mohawks in Quebec in 1642. Three were killed and twenty-two marched south through three Iroquois towns on the Mohawk River. Jogues's report is filled with the burning, biting, and ripping off of flesh; running gauntlet after gauntlet; nails being plucked out; thumbs and fingers cut and bitten off; and ashes and live coals thrown at French captives. The Huron chief and French convert Ahatsistari (Eustace) suffered the worst abuse, "burned in almost every part of his body and then beheaded." On being rescued by the Dutch at Rensselaerswyck, Jogues wrote his observations back to Paris. Unfortunately, he returned to his mission in 1646 and was killed.[3]

There is certainly no lack of torture stories among the English and Americans of the new republic; which are true and which exaggerated is hard to know. The worst tortures seem to have occurred in times of war. The French reports appear to contain the most brutality, and one wonders whether the Catholic ideal of martyrdom or the need for continual financial support from the orders back home for further missionary activity might not account for the brutality detailed in the Jesuit sources. Certainly, men able to stand up under torture won both sympathy and heroic, if not martyr, status.[4]

White male behavior in captivity was not uniform. Age, time, place, and capturing Indian group were significant determinants. Surveying the captivity literature from the period 1608–1870 reveals two critical factors that shaped white male captives: the length of their stay among native people and their age at capture.[5] As was true for women, the younger the age and the longer the stay with the Indians, the more likely it was that the male captive would become a "white Indian." For some men and boys, adoption meant discovering a new world and new ways of understanding themselves, but to gain these perspectives, one was subjected to harsh tests.

The range of experience and the plight of male captives is reflected in the accounts of John Gyles, Quentin Stockwell, and James Smith. The first two were late seventeenth-century New England captives. Gyles was ten years old when he was captured along with his father, mother, and three other siblings at Pemaquid, Maine, in August 1689. He was held prisoner for nine years—six among the Abenakis, three with the French. When his brother James (held captive for three years) was caught deserting with an Englishman, both were recaptured "and carried back to Penobscot Fort, where they were both tortured at a stake by fire for some time; then their noses and ears were cut off and

...

52

*White
Actors
on a
Field
of Red*

they were made to eat them, after which they were burned to death at the stake." When captives were taken or deserters re-taken, Gyles saw the Indians dance and "torture the unhappy people who fall into their hands." Gyles himself was beaten with an ax and forced to dance around fellow captive James Alexander, "a Jersey man who was taken from Falmouth in Casco Bay." In the third winter of his captivity Gyles watched as John Evans, a "most intimate and dear companion," was given "a heavy burden . . . even though he was extreme[ly] weak with long fasting." While walking, Evans broke through the ice, cut his knee, and was eventually left to freeze to death.[6]

Unlike Gyles's firsthand account, Quentin Stockwell's story entered the colonial war and propaganda literature in reports from Increase Mather. Captured at Deerfield September 19, 1677, Stockwell described being brought together with a group of Hatfield captives. He and they were "pinioned and led away in the night over the mountains in dark and hideous ways about four miles further before we took up our place for rest. . . . We were kept bound all that night." They were spread out on their backs. "Our arms and legs stretched out were staked fast down and a cord about our necks so that we could stir no ways." He was told that it was the custom to fasten captives for the first nine nights of travel to prevent their escape. Over the northern New England winter, Stockwell, like Mary Rowlandson, had his taste of bear's foot and horse meat. He nearly died of frostbite before being cured by a French surgeon; he finally escaped.[7] Robert Rogers, a captive from Salmon Falls, New Hampshire, in 1690, was not so lucky. He was tortured and burned to death.[8]

Along with death, torture, and escape, adoption was a common experience, especially for young male captives. The first favorable account of this experience appeared after the close of the French and Indian wars. Colonel James Smith (ca. 1737–1814) was captured in Bedford, Pennsylvania, in 1755 and kept journals during his nearly six years of captivity. Smith observed that male captives, whether white or Indian, could undergo identical perils or ultimate good fortune. Smith was eighteen and on a road-building expedition in western Pennsylvania for General Edward Braddock just before the Battle of the Wilderness. He and other Indian enemies of the French were captured by Caughnawagas (Mohawks). Marched back to the Indian village, he was forced to run the gauntlet, flogged, had sand thrown in his eyes, and was beaten. He was then adopted and treated like a son.[9]

The violence and torture inflicted on male captives contrasts sharply with the experience of women. In the Northeast some women appear to have been tormented, and women and children were forced to march over miles of rough terrain and were tied down. But with the exception of a few reported cases in the seventeenth century, women were seldom killed except at the time of attack or occasionally, as in the case of John Williams's wife, Eunice, if they were sick and unable to make the required trek.[10] Several captivity stories, however, tell of women or small children carried by Indian men. John Dunn Hunter indicates that the pattern of saving women and children and torturing men continued into the early nineteenth century in the central and western states. In his experience, women and children were "treated well," but "the warriors, who were so unfortunate as not to fall in battle, were nearly all tortured to death" unless they were thought to be very brave, in which case they were allowed to live with their captors. Hunter and others discuss the socialization process that tried to mold stoic boys who, if captured, would go to their death singing, even if hot coals were applied to their genitals and skin stripped from their bodies.[11]

In general, in the captivity literature for the period 1608 to 1870 white Anglo-American males appear to fall into two categories: the Hero and the White Indian.

The Heroic Mode

. . . . . .

Male captives in the Heroic Mode came to the frontier to spread "civilization." They were there to uplift "mankind," bring the true God to the heathen, help the empire or the nation, and protect white women. Rarely, if ever, did they dwell on the advantages of their quest for their own personal gain; still, their exploits usually brought them the benefits of fame, fortune, and gratitude. Out of their capture by and contact with native peoples came a recognition of their own historic mission. Amusement, disdain, or contempt often accompanied the contact of these men with Indians; little appreciation or understanding of the other resulted.

...

54

White

Actors

on a

Field

of Red

"Heroes" of this type further subdivide into those who were inspired by God and those for whom empire, country, or "civilization" were the motivating force—along with occasionally saving women in distress. Captives in the Heroic Mode include Father Isaac Jogues, John Williams, Captain John Smith, Daniel Boone, and their dime novel spin-offs.

HEROES FOR GOD

The first Heroes for God in the North American wilderness were the Black Robes—Jesuit priests who moved through Quebec and New France and into New York and the Mississippi Valley. In the eyes of men like Father Isaac Jogues, no suffering was too great for himself or others to sustain for the glory of God. When the Hurons and fellow Frenchmen in his party were captured by the Iroquois (1642) one Frenchman was "stripped naked, all his nails torn out, his very fingers gnawed, and a broad-sword driven through his right hand." Jogues wrote to his superior: "Mindful of the wounds of our Lord Jesus Christ, he bore, as he afterward told me, this pain, though most acute, with great joy." Suffering blows to his own person, Jogues was no less willing to serve his God: when he entered a second Iroquois village gauntlet, "blows were not spared." Even though they were struck "constantly on the shins to our exquisite pain," Jogues comforted himself with a comparison between the work of the French Catholics and that of God's "apostle, who glories that he was thrice beaten with rods." In the worst of times Jogues saw his mission keenly. Rather than escape torture and misery, he was happy to serve the French captives. To do so might inspire "the christened Huron of his duties." Jogues found it "a peculiar interposition of divine goodness" to have "fallen into the hands of these Indians." During his stay he "baptized seventy, children, young and old, of five different nations and languages, that of every tribe, and people, and tongue, they might stand in the sight of the Lamb." [12]

Father Louis Hennepin, a Franciscan, was one of many French priests to go among the North American Indians. In April 1680, he and two other Frenchmen were captured by

Mdewakanton Dakotas, probably on the Mississippi near the junction of the Illinois River. The recollect found it especially difficult to say his breviary and was told by one of the other Frenchmen to watch out or they would all be killed. He tried going into the woods, but the Indians followed him. "I chanted the Litany of the Blessed Virgin in the canoe, my book opened." He got away with it because the Dakotas thought the breviary "a spirit which taught me to sing for their diversion, for these people are naturally fond of singing." Hennepin was luckier than Jogues on several counts. First, though full of his mission to God, he could see his captors. They in turn gave him a large robe made of beaver skins and trimmed with porcupine quills. When he was sick, they fed him fish and brought him naked into a sweat lodge with four Indians. There in the "cabin covered with buffalo skins" around red-hot stones the Dakotas sang and placed their hands on him, "rubbing me while they wept bitterly." He continued this regimen of sweats three times a week and soon "felt as strong as ever." Finally, he was rescued by explorer Sieur Duluth not long after his capture. Duluth saw the treatment of Hennepin in a more negative light than apparently the recollect himself, whose memoirs some say underestimated his cruel treatment as "a captive and a slave." Duluth says he told the recollect they must leave or else hurt the French nation "to suffer insult of this sort without showing resentment of it." [13] Hennepin, although a Hero for God, did not altogether spurn the Indian life, having something in common with both adventurous heroes for empire and White Indians.

Not so John Williams, an English Hero for God. Queen Anne's War began in the colonies in 1703 with an attack on Wells, Maine. Soon the two-hundred-mile area from Maine into western Massachusetts had become a battlefield. In late February 1704 a party of Abenaki and Caughnawaga Indians, with some Frenchmen, attacked Deerfield. John Williams (1664–1729) was minister of the Deerfield, Massachusetts, congregation, a Harvard College graduate (class of 1683), husband of Eunice Mather (niece of Increase), and father of ten children. During the attack, thirty-eight members of the Deerfield community were killed and about a hundred were captured. When the war party struck Deerfield, two of Williams's sons were killed. Williams and the rest of his family were among those taken prisoners. His wife died on the forced march to Canada.[14]

...

56

White
Actors
on a
Field
of Red

Williams's losses were considerable. Besides grieving over family deaths, he felt great anguish for his congregation. He tried to get protection for them before the attack, but the Massachusetts government ignored his pleas. After his nearly three-year captivity and return, he went back to Canada and worked to negotiate the release of captives from Deerfield and other New England towns. At the end of his narrative he gave thanks to God, "who has wrought deliverance for so many," and asked for prayers "to God for a door of escape to be opened for the great number yet behind," which amounted to nearly one hundred. He lamented that among the children, "not a few among the savages having lost the English tongue, will be lost and turn savages in a little time unless something extraordinary prevent." Among those children was his ten-year-old daughter, Eunice.[15]

Williams's narrative is in the heroic mold because he turns captivity into a religious trial and holy crusade. Captivity is a matter of Divine Providence. It has lessons to teach. Rowlandson's and Mather's narratives assume this. Williams goes one step further by turning the captivity into a jeremiad and a personal crusade. Williams's twin enemies were the Indians and the French. He feared "popish country." On the trek to Canada he was allowed to preach on the Sabbath, but on arrival in New France, he wrote, "we were forbidden praying one with another or joining together in the service of God," and some captives had their Bibles taken from them by the French priests "and never re-delivered to them, to their great grief and sorrow."[16]

Williams's heroism was most actively displayed in his struggles to get back his daughter Eunice and his son Samuel, the first from Indian, the second from Jesuit clutches. *The Redeemed Captive, Returning to Zion* (1707), Williams's narrative of the events, is given over to what today reads as esoteric religious debate. For Williams and the Puritan world, this debate was nothing if not a fight for the immortal souls of himself, his sons and daughter, and his flock. "All means," he wrote, "were used to seduce poor souls." Jesuits told him of wanting to baptize any of the unbaptized English, offering that, "if I would stay among them and be of their religion, I should have a great and honorable pension from the king every year." He would also get all his children back with " 'enough honorable maintenance for you and them.' " Again and again he rebuffed them, although he admitted that their efforts "to seduce" him "to popery were very exercising to me."[17]

More than a quarter of Williams's account consists of his correspondence with his son Samuel. Williams claimed that the boy was threatened continually by the priests, who sent him to school to learn French and then "struck him with a stick" when he would not cross himself. Williams "mourned" just thinking of this boy of fifteen or sixteen and a younger boy of six, both in Montreal being "turned to popery." One letter admonished Samuel and prayed that he might be "recovered out of the snare you are taken in." The father's letters were long and very specific on the subject of the apostles, the Virgin Mary, saints, and prayer. Repeatedly Williams declared that "the Romanists" answers were "a very fable and falsehood." The business of the letters is minute textual analysis, and in each Williams cites chapter and verse of the Scriptures. In one letter, after fourteen long paragraphs, Williams writes, "Again, if you consult Acts 15 where you have an account of the first synod or council, you will find. . . ." The father appears to overlook that Samuel was not a theological student but a *son* whose mother and two brothers had recently died. The rest of his family were in an unknown state and place. Now his father wanted him to follow a very complex line of theological debate. At the close of another letter, Williams momentarily realized he might be overwriting his case: "There are a great many other things in the letter [you sent] that deserve to be refuted, but I shall be too tedious in remarking all of them at once." But after a "yet" the minister continued in the same vein.[18] That Williams saw fit to print these personal letters filled with biblical citations shows that to him they were not just private writings to his son but part of a greater crusade against Catholicism.

Williams's narrative went through six editions between 1707 and 1795. *The Redeemed Captive, Returning to Zion* was first printed in Boston in 1707 and was issued four more times, including one by his son Stephen Williams, published in Northampton in 1853. John Williams's heroism in the service of God was widely read about and much admired in New England. A children's version, *The Deerfield Captive: An Indian Story, Being*

...
58

White
Actors
on a
Field
of Red

a Narrative of Facts for the Instruction of the Young, complete
with a print of the Deerfield house in flames on the title page,
went through several nineteenth-century editions.[19]

HEROES OF THE EMPIRE

John Williams, religious hero, was atypical of male captives
even in British colonial America; he was more typical perhaps
of some of his theological counterparts in New France and New
Spain. But Williams, like Mary Rowlandson, became a popular
and heroic figure to the Puritan community. Among the first
English settlers, the adventurous, death-defying hero predated
the religious one and is popular to our own day. As a swashbuck-
ling Elizabethan, a world traveler, a man who was patronized
by many women but married to none, an explorer, adventurer,
historian, scientist, and weaver of tales, John Smith still cuts a
heroic figure. It is to him that the heroic tradition of gunslinger,
Indian fighter, and twentieth-century western hero hark back.
He is a man alone, full of bravado, meeting with strange men
and exotic women.[20]

The text of Smith's work and the stories of his life are well
known. But let us begin by looking at the pictures. Following in the tradition of his earlier exploits in the Middle East,
Smith provides vivid illustrations of his North American exploits. His earlier works show knights jousting on horseback
and Smith killing a man by battering him over the head with
a club, whereas the six-part foldout of illustrations to *The Map
of Virginia* (1612) portrays Smith among the Indians. In the
top right and bottom left corners Smith is manfully confront-
ing individual Indian men. In one he has a gun, in the other
a large sword. In both cases *he* is taking Indians prisoner. In
both cases the Indian is a *big* Indian, at least a head taller than
the Elizabethan. In the two pictures that show him taken prisoner (bottom right and center left in the original) Smith is a
smaller figure among many Indians; they overpower him with
their numbers. These two renditions of his capture are much
less distinct and take up less space than those of his exploits.
"How they tooke him prisoner" is the smallest action shot of the
group.[21] "Their triumph about him" (top left) after he is cap-

tured is the same size as the drawing of him capturing Opechan-canough, the king of Pamunkey (or Pamunkee), which shows him "bound to a tree to be shott to death," but larger and more central is Smith surrounded by what appear to be dancing Indians, who, although carrying weapons, look more like figures out of Greek mythology. The top center picture shows Smith enjoying himself around a camp fire with several semiclad Indians, including a seated woman and a man wearing antlers. It all looks like a good deal of fun.[22]

In the top right picture of Smith taking the king captive, Smith points a gun at the Indian's head. Sunflowers are growing below Smith's "peece." Smith's left leg is close to the Indian's, almost in a fighting (or dance) pose. Each man has a long weapon pointing down and to the right, a sword in Smith's case, an arrow in the Indian's. The Indian's size and stature, plus his broad and seminaked physical frame, claim the center of the print. In comparison, Smith looks almost doll-like. He is pulling the king's braid, on one hand an ineffectual gesture, on the other one of mockery—something that a man might do to a woman, perhaps implying the "womanliness" of this tall, very masculine-looking bigger man. The "peece" becomes the great leveler. In the background, the English armies in two settings fire weapons at the Indians. In one case, the natives are wounded and run away; in the other, a few Englishmen fire on a larger number of Indians with many more in the background. The gun is thus an instrument of physical and sexual power. In the bottom right frame, we see how "Pokahontas beggs his life."

From the first, Smith wants us to see him "admired" as a "demi-God." Traditional Indian practice has something to do with his success, but the true causes for their hospitality escape him. In *A True Relation* (1608), he gives more detail but is hardly more modest. First, he traveled upriver with a barge, two of his men, and two Indian guides. They stopped to eat. He then headed off with one Indian to test soil. Within fifteen minutes he heard "a loud cry, and a hollowing of Indians." Figuring the Indian guide "betraid us," he grabbed him and bound his arms, his pistol "ready bent to be revenged on him." Smith was then hit in the right thigh with an arrow but was not hurt. So began a tradition in American literature, later picked up in film: a white

C. Smith bound to a tree to be shott to death (1607), "A reprint, with variations of the First Part of the Map of Virginia" *(1612). Courtesy of the Newberry Library*

man is in the wild with his men and an untrustworthy Indian, and he gets hurt. Some other men may die, but the Hero is fine—he can make it through. Smith spied two Indians "drawing their bowes" but made short work of them by "discharging a french pistoll." He then fired again. (Where was the rest of his party?) After a moment twenty or thirty arrows flew toward

C. Smith taketh the King of Pamavnkee prisoner 1608

37

The Countrey wee now call Virginia beginneth at Cape Henry distant
from Roanoack 60 miles, where was S.ʳ Walter Raleigh's plantation:
and because the people differ very little from them of Powhatan in any
thing, I have inserted those figures in this place because of the conveniency.

C. Smith taketh the king of Pamavnkee prisoner (1607), "A
reprint, with variations of the First Part of the Map of Virginia *"*
(1612). Courtesy of the Newberry Library

. . .

62

White

Actors

on a

Field

of Red

him. Miraculously, they all fell short! He was then surrounded by the "king of Pamaunch" and two hundred men, who drew their bows but then laid them on the ground—the scene referred to in the illustration of dancing Indians with bows and arrows. The Indians demanded his arms and told him his other men were dead: only him "they would reserve: The Indian importuned me not to shott." The Indian in question was the same one Smith had aimed a gun at and taken prisoner.[23]

Once captured, Smith turned on the charm—or as he would say, "I resolved to trie their mercies," hoping to buy his way to freedom by presenting the chief "with a compasse daill." He then gave the man "a discourse on the roundness of the earth" with a discussion of the stars and the moon—no doubt one of the first English science lessons in the New World.[24]

In Smith's subsequent travels though the wondrous kingdoms of Virginia, he charms us with complete descriptions of his captive but (according to him) honored guest status. The intercession by a young Indian princess and the lavish treatment he received will be discussed later, but his descriptions of men with "white Beads over their shoulders," of emperors sitting upon "tenne or twelve Mattes" with chains of pearls around their necks and covered with raccoon skin furs, of men who "have as many weomen as they will," must have tantalized the Elizabethans. They strike a twentieth-century reader as fare for movie moguls. Smith's captivity is the first big western without the silver screen.[25]

It is too bad that no Chesapeake natives wrote down their stories of Smith's escapades. Certainly self-aggrandizement helped the captain to construct the most abiding captivity narrative, which, significantly, is not recalled as a captivity narrative at all. Smith's expert storytelling gives his European and later American audiences all they want to hear: an exotic but primitive culture meets the European representative, is completely awestruck by him, and falls at his feet. There are many adventures with new food, drink, women, and battle, and there are harrowing experiences, but in the end, he wins and there are few real losses, no reconsideration of the worth of the colonizing project, and no thoughts of what might be the personal consequences for the other.

A second figure among male captive heroes for the empire is Daniel Boone. Both Smith and Boone are well-recog-
nized American folk heroes, but neither is known as a captive. Richard Slotkin has documented the impact of the Boone
legend on shaping the American mythic hero. Boone's origins,
however, appear to be well grounded in the English adventure
traditions personified by Smith, and Boone's significance as folk
hero, like Smith's, involves his three stints as an Indian captive.
There he outsmarts the enemy and "opens" the continent west
of the Appalachians. In two instances, Boone himself was captured; in a third, one of his daughters was captured and then
rescued by Boone.[26]

Between his introduction in 1784 as a bit player in the appendix of John Filson's *Discovery, Settlement and Present State of
Kentucke . . . The Adventures of Col. Daniel Boon*, to his 1856
starring role in Timothy Flint's *First White Man of the West, or
the Life and Exploits of Col. Dan'l. Boone*, the persona of Boone
undergoes a transformation. Its effect is important for showing
how male and female roles on the frontier became more stereotyped in the nineteenth-century captivity literature than they
had been in the colonial period.[27] Of the thirty-two pages devoted to Boone in Filson's account, one long paragraph, taking
up about a page of print, gives the first account of Boone's capture and escape in May 1769. Four pages are devoted to Boone's
second capture and escape from February to July 1778 and following. Boone's daughter's captivity on July 14, 1776, gets one-
half of one paragraph. Each of these exploits forms a chapter in
Flint's account seventy years later.[28]

In Filson's account of the first escape, Boone and friends
were enjoying the wonders of nature and admiring "a variety
of flowers and fruits" when, late in the day, near the Kentucky
River, "a number of Indians rushed out of a thick cane-brake
upon us, and made us prisoners. The time of our sorrow was
now arrived. . . . The Indians plundered of us what we had, and
kept us in confinement for seven days, treating us with common
savage usage." Because they did not seem anxious to escape,
the Indians were "less suspicious of us" and so "in the dead
of night, as we lay in a thick cane-brake by a large fire, when
sleep had locked up their senses, my situation not disposing me

to rest, I touched my companion and gently awoke him." They escaped. Escape and capture are not presented as major issues. One gets captured, undergoes some minor problems, uses one's wits, and outsmarts the "savages" to obtain freedom.[29]

The second capture was more difficult as Boone was taken, according to this account, by "a party of one hundred and two Indians, and two Frenchmen, on their march against Boonsborough." The similarity to the vast numbers who confronted John Smith is not accidental. How could a "hero" go into a second captivity out of stupidity or oversight? Apparently, only overwhelming odds could convince the reader of his undisputable prowess and the inferiority of "savage" tactics. Boone became the adoptee of a Shawnee family and was introduced to Indian ways. This second capture lasted from February 7 to July 15, 1778. It began the lore of Boone's out-Indianizing the Indians. Culturally, Boone became a White Indian, with the emphasis on the *White* because Boone—like Colonel James Smith, Caughnawaga captive of the 1750s—wanted to learn Indian ways for military purposes, to use them to wipe out Indians.[30]

Besides being a hero for empire, Boone begins the romantic tradition of savior hero. Filson's account gives us the following information about Boone's rescue of his daughter Jemima from captivity: "On the fourteenth day July, 1776, two of Col. Calloway's daughters, and one of mine, were taken prisoners near the fort. I immediately pursued the Indians, with only eight men, and on the fifteenth overtook them, killed two of the party, and recovered the girls."[31] In the mid-nineteenth century, this story of paternal rescue became a popular tale of female weakness and white male prowess. In John Frost's *Daring and Heroic Deeds of American Women . . . among the Pioneer Mothers of the Western Country*, this one-sentence recapture gets the frontispiece illustration and another illustration in a related chapter—noteworthy in the context of a book about women who escaped trouble on the frontier by their own wits.

In Frost's Boone account, he first praised the father of Kentucky for his "hardihood," ability to surmount "all perils," boldness, and the like: "But whatever praise we concede to Boone, we must remember that his wife and daughters also deserve our eulogy." Why? Because he "was a bold and skillful Indian fighter, and accustomed to scenes of danger and death. They

*Daniel Boone rescuing his daughter Jemima, from the
frontispiece from John Frost,* Pioneer Mothers of the West
(1869). Courtesy of the Newberry Library

belonged to what is commonly called a 'weaker sex,' were much
unaccustomed to the wilderness, and to constant alarms of savage warfare," but they went onto the frontier anyway.[32] Of the
triple capture of Jemima Boone and the Calloway girls, Flint
notes that all three friends, "if we may take the portraits of the
rustic time," were "patterns of youthful loveliness, inexpressibly
dear to their parents." But as girls will "imprudently" do, they
wandered into the woods too far from the protection of "their
habitations, to gather flowers with which to adorn their rustic fire-places. They were suddenly surrounded by a half-dozen
Indians. Their shrieks and efforts to flee were alike unavailing.
They were dragged rapidly beyond the power of making themselves heard." Once among the Indians, however, they were
treated with "the utmost indulgence and decorum."[33]

Apparently, the author would not want anyone to believe that
anything bad happened to these fair maidens. Flint followed
with a paragraph assuring his reader that this is always the case
with Indians: after their "demonic" cries and wild fighting an-
tics they "are universally seen to treat captive women with a
decorous forbearance." Why is this so, he asks? "This strange

...
66
White
Actors
on a
Field
of Red

trait, so little in keeping with other parts of their character, has been attributed by some to their want of the sensibilities and passions of our race." Translation: the reason for this unusual characteristic of not raping women during or after battle is that Indians are not as sexual or masculine as white males.[34]

When the parents missed their wayward daughters, Boone declares, "By the Eternal Power that made me a father, if my daughter lives, and is found, I will either bring her back, or spill my life blood." At this point, "every individual of the males crowded round Boone and repeated it." "Seven selected persons were admitted to the oath," and the rescue mission was on. The next day a few free men came to the camp, firing their rifles, "cutting down two savages at the first shot," and sending the rest running away. In a moment, the daughters were in their fathers' arms and "in the unutterable joy of conquest and deliverance, were on their way homewards."[35]

In sum, by the Flint account of 1856, Boone was not only a great Indian fighter, scout, and hero of the future American empire but a savior of white womanhood. According to nineteenth-century norms, women needed to be saved because they were weak. Men had a sacred duty to protect them. It was an especially sacred duty for the man of the family to try to save his daughter or wife. Boone's several experiences with captivity all resulted in benefits to him and to society because they showed his agility in escaping or in mobilizing escape parties. They resulted in his befriending the Indians to learn survival skills, which proved him to be smarter than they were, tougher than they were, and able to use their own tools against them as he moved across the Appalachians and into the Northwest and South. But the importance of the Boone narratives and accompanying pictures is their assertion of a father's power as savior and preserver of the frontier family and the basic insecurity of the family without the white male protector. From Rowlandson's and Williams's dependence on the protection of God to save souls, the main lines of protection move with the Smith and Boone traditions to dependence upon weapons, "smarts," and masculine prowess to save one's self and family.

By the mid-eighteenth century the religious figure faded as the clever, rough, and tough hero which Smith set, combined with the alleged "civilizing" and "rescuing" qualities of both Williams and Boone, emerged as the family figure that dominated the nineteenth-century male narratives of the Heroic Mode. These heroes "save" and protect the "weaker sex" and the patriarchal family. The evolution of this figure by the late nineteenth century can be observed in dime novel creations such as Edwin Eastman's narrative, *Seven and Nine Years among the Camanches and Apaches* (1873), one of many popular romantic savior stories, in which, after the capture of Eastman and his wife, the hero moves from a "consciousness" that he was "powerless to snatch her from her relentless captors" to organizing a rescue party and lifting "the curtain of dressed buffalo hide" and, after trembling "like an aspen" before his sleeping wife, "awakened the sleeper" and in "an instant" wrapped her in a robe, headed for the mountains, and was soon with the party "in full gallop down the valley." [36]

The combination of Smith and Boone themes, "pseudo–White Indian," "hero," and "savior of white womanhood," was exaggerated in dime novels and mid- to late nineteenth-century accounts. The center of the American pantheon changed gradually but definitively. The strengthening of the male hero came at the expense of and concomitantly with the waning power of the female figure. That this shift occurred in a period that idealized the weak woman and the angel of the bourgeois household and stressed male assertiveness and national expansion is not a surprise. But why is the female heroine nearly obliterated, and how is this accomplished? Why and how does the western frontier become the ground of female trivialization and male supremacy? Certainly the unsettling nature of the process of westering itself is important here, but so is the potential challenge of others, women and Indians, who might challenge the direction of gender and national hegemony.[37]

The dime novels' mass-market approach set the mode of the rough, tough, protector, rescuer male frontier figure packaged for an ever-widening audience. Erastus Beadle picked up where the Boston firm of Gleason and Ballou had begun in midcentury. The nickel and dime stories' novelty was in their characteristic packaging, advertising, and tendency to western themes. In the words of Henry Nash Smith, there were quite a few "subliterary" writers in the dime pool. Yet these works tended "to become an objectified mass dream, like the moving pictures, the soap operas, or the comic books that are the present-day equivalents of the Beadle stories. The individual writer abandons his own personality and identifies himself with the reveries of his readers. It is the presumably close fidelity of the Beadle stories to the dream life of a vast inarticulate public that renders them valuable to the social historian and the historian of ideas."[38] Early dime novels repackaged the themes and dreams of frontier capture and rescue and sold them for big profits. *Seth Jones*, Edward S. Ellis's best-seller of the 1860s and 1870s, became the newest forum for an old frontier hero, creating a popular heroic figure as part-time captive and full-time savior of white womanhood and protector of advancing "civilization."[39]

Ellis was a twenty-year-old teacher in Red Bank, New Jersey, when he was called to New York to make the deal on the book. In a later interview he recalled that the success of the novel was based on its marketing. It was with Seth, he said, that the Beadle series really began. "It was not the merit of the book. . . . It was the ingenious way in which it was advertised."[40] The technique was to print "a rush of posters" and "painted inscriptions" all over the country asking, "Who is Seth Jones?" Ellis claimed, "Everywhere you went this query met you. It glared at you in staring letters on the sidewalks. . . . In the country, the trees and rocks and the sides of roofs of barns all clamored with stentorian demands to know who Seth Jones was." When everyone was just about fed up with the question, the answer was presented in the form of "big and little posters bearing a lithographic portrait of a stalwart, heroic-looking hunter of the Fenimore Cooper type, coon-skin cap, rifle and all. And above or below this imposing figure in large type were the words: 'I am Seth Jones.'" The book was published on October 2, 1860. When soldiers went to the front, the Beadles sent them novels by the tens of thousands.[41]

Seth Jones is a "civilizer," savior of white womanhood, and easterner turned frontiersman. The work shows how the me-

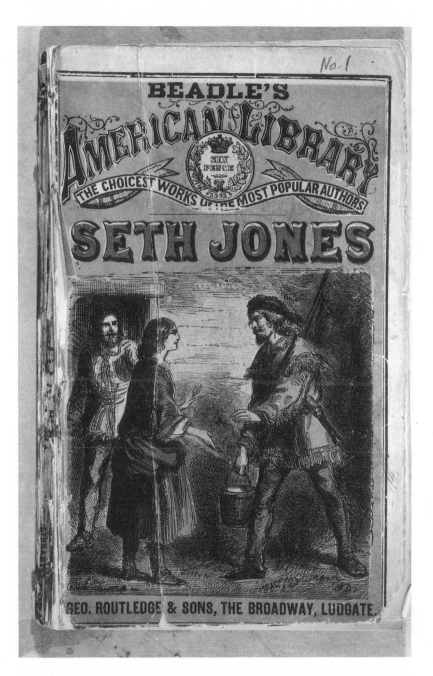

Cover from Edward Ellis, Seth Jones *(ca. 1878). Courtesy of the Newberry Library*

...
70
White
Actors
on a
Field
of Red

dium may change, but the message lingers on. As Seth's story begins, we hear the sounds of an ax and see "an athletic man" swinging it, "burying his glittering blade deep in the heart of the mighty kings of the wood." The settler's cabin is soon attacked and his "beautiful blue-eyed maiden" daughter stolen from him by "dusky beings." To the rescue comes Seth Jones, mysterious woodsman, to save "that purity daughter."[42] In a comic Boone-like replay, Seth out-Indians the Indians and amuses his captors as well. As with John Smith, his "air of conscious superiority" wins the day. He escapes, returns to the white territory to organize a rescue party, and rescues the maiden.[43] In this gendered, nineteenth-century way of looking at capture, the brave, smart, and tough American white male beats out the Indians. By contrast, the frail, childlike white female must wait for her father, husband, frontier hero, or some combination of white men to save her from misery. In the triumph of the romantic savior, nineteenth-century cultural frontier history thus juxtaposes the ascendancy of white male supremacy from the mountain to the prairie, while simultaneously depicting a weak, infantilized female needing male protection against the evil of Indian wildness.

White Indians

If the fictional models for the heroic figure in the captivities go back to the adventuring Odysseus and on to the "real" world of Captain Smith, those of the White Indian probably go back to the children raised by wolves in prehistoric Rome. Fortunately, the raising of white children by North American Indians is more easily documented. There are several narratives of adoptees who became White Indians. Those who assimilated rarely returned to write memoirs, but some did, and others recounted or dictated their stories.

Unlike the stolid, singular, and tough figures that came down in the heroic Boone and Leatherstocking lore, the male captives who lived among the Indians from an early age did not define their manhood by singularity and individual prowess but, not surprisingly, rather more in an Indian context of interrelationship. In many cases, that interrelationship was a bond between (Indian) mother and (white adopted) son. This was the case in two of the longest nineteenth-century captivities of white boys captured at a young age. Other elements that differentiated males in the White Indian mode from their "heroic" brothers (or fathers) was their sympathy for Indian ways and, even when they were not adopted as young children, their ability to see the group in which they found themselves, not as monsters but as people like themselves. Still another feature of these men and boys was the way in which they observed, respected, and became part of the natural world.

John Gyles became a White Indian. He was captured at about age ten on August 2, 1689, in Pemaquid, Maine, along with both of his parents and three siblings. Like many other white male captives, he experienced a good deal of beating and observed the death and torture of other white captives, both French and English. He admitted his fears; after all, he was a child. He mentioned whippings, the tossing of hot embers onto captives' chests, and the death of his brother. The difference between Gyles and almost all the female captives of the seventeenth and early eighteenth centuries was his occasional understanding of why captives were badly treated or even killed. He explained that captive James Alexander was treated badly to "revenge" the Indians "having lost some friends." This did not make Gyles happier or less fearful when they beat him, but at least he recognized the emotional intensity of the nature of war in any culture.[44]

Shortly after his capture, when he underwent some torment, a little girl took him "by the hand" and led him out of the captive circle, and an older Indian gave him a pipe to smoke. He thought he would be killed, but this was the first of many protective gestures shown him. When a plague fell upon the Abenakis, "Indians applied red ochre to my sores which by God's blessing cured me." And later, "an old squaw who was kind to captives" gave him hints as to what to beware of when watching male ceremonials and how to avoid the demons of the woods. After he watched one ceremony and came back to her, she "was glad that I returned without hurt."[45]

Gyles's approach was different from Williams's or Smith's. His writing shows an awareness of Indian humanity and an

. . .

72

White

Actors

on a

Field

of Red

alternative way of looking at the earth. He explained how his Eastern Abenaki (Maliseet) family protected him by having him run off when he was in danger; they told him not to return until they said it would be safe. A young Indian girl jumped in the river to save him when the Indian men forced him to swim even though they knew he could not. Another time, when he suffered with severe frostbite, these Abenakis helped him. (He was about thirteen at the time.) Gyles's lengthy stay in the wilderness made him a keen observer of flora and fauna. He probably wrote his memoirs many years after his release, when he was in his late forties, and revised them in his early fifties after living with the French and becoming a hunter. Still, the earlier years affected him. He called the moose "a fine lofty creature about eight feet high with a long head and a nose like a horse, with horns very large and strong." He included detailed descriptions of the beaver, the wolverine, the hedgehog, the tortoise, and the life of the salmon.[46] He described the ceremonies of the Indians of northern Maine from marriage to mourning and threw in a myth or two. For a seventeenth-century child of the Puritans, his openness to Abenaki ways and his lack of invocation of God and Providence are atypical of Puritan men and women alike. Gyles might well be called the prototype for the White Indian: a young captive living with Indians for many years, protected and cared for by them, especially by Indian women, learning to understand and appreciate the world around him. He was not a nineteenth-century figure and did not see his captors as noble. He would call them devil worshipers. He certainly expressed no interest in staying with them even though six of his first sixteen years of life were spent with them.[47]

The two most famous White Indians of the nineteenth century were captured as children and raised as Indians. John Dunn Hunter was captured at a young age by the Kickapoo along with two other white children. He eventually wound up with (Plains) Kansas Indians and was adopted by a woman who had lost a son in a war with the Pawnees. He found that the Kansas treated him "with regard and tenderness" and that women and children captives were treated well "while every imaginable indignity was practiced on the [adult male] prisoners." In such situations, women who lost a relative were joined by children. At the defeat of the Pawnee, Hunter said children "whipped the prisoners with green briars, and hazel switches, and threw firebrands, clubs, and stones at them as they ran between their ranks, to the painted post of safety." In this particular instance, all the male Indian captives died with the exception of two Mandan chiefs. The opposing chief expected to be tortured and gave the following speech: " 'I am a man: the fate of war is against me:—I die like a warrior.' "[48]

Hunter was adopted by several mothers. When he was among the Kansas, he felt a most "painful loss" when his mother drowned one day while collecting driftwood.

> I sincerely and deeply felt the bereavement; and cannot even at this late day, reflect on her maternal conduct to me, from the time I was taken prisoner by the Kansas, to her death, without the association of feelings, to which, in other respects I am a stranger. She was indeed a mother to me; and I feel my bosom dilate with gratitude at the recollection of her goodness, and care of me during this helpless period of my life. This, to those who have been bred in refinement and ease, under the fond and watchful guardianship of parents, may appear gross and incongruous. If, however, the imagination allowed scope, and a lad ten or twelve years of age, without kindred or name, or any knowledge by which he could arrive at an acquaintance with any of the circumstances connected with his being, be supposed in the central wilds of North America, nearly a thousand miles from any white settlement, a prisoner or sojourner among a people, on whom he had not the slightest claim, and with whose language, habits and character, he was wholly unacquainted; but, who nevertheless treated him kindly; and it will appear not only natural but rational, that he should return such kindness with gratitude and affection. Such nearly was my situation. . . . I have no hope of seeing happier days than I experienced at this early period of my life, while sojourning with the Kansas nation, on the Kansas river, some hundred miles above its confluence with the Missouri.[49]

Despite his grief, Hunter said he could not show his feelings because Indians "regard tears, or any expression of grief, as a mark of weakness in males, and unworthy of the character of a warrior."[50] Hunter's spirits were revived, however, when he

Drawn by C.R.Leslie.   Printed by C.Hullmandel

JOHN, D. HUNTER.

London. Published by Longman & C.ᵒ Paternoster Row. 1824.

Frontispiece of John Dunn Hunter from his Memoirs of a
Captivity among the Indians of North America *(1824). Courtesy
of the Newberry Library*

was adopted again, this time in Osage territory by the family of Shen-thweeh, whose wife, Hunk-hah, adopted him for her lost son and "took every opportunity . . . to engage my affections and esteem. She used to weep over me, tell me how good her son had been, how much she loved him, and how much she mourned his loss. 'You must be good . . . and you shall be my son, and I will be your mother.' " The daughter of the family was equally attentive to his needs: "The greatest care was taken to supply my wants with the choicest things they had in their power to bestow." Although he was still a boy, she made him ornamented moccasins, leggings, a beaver hat, a buffalo robe, and other clothes reserved for men. When he was wounded in a battle some time later, the "skill of our physicians and the kind attentions of my Indian mother and sister" cured him. At another point he could have returned to the Kansas but felt more kinship with his Osage "mother and sister, who were dear to me, and who loved me in return."[51] But though Hunter received much love and affection from Kansas and Osage mothers and sisters, his Kansas father showed him "little or no regard or tenderness."[52]

Hunter, like all white captive boys, was required to learn the meaning of manhood in the Indian context. The mother who was central to his care and comfort was the same woman who showed him the basic road to becoming a man and a warrior. His account shows the complex nature of the mother-son bond in those native societies in which he lived. He describes how boys at an early age were trained to withstand and inflict pain. In her rounds with the boy, the mother deliberately started fights with him, then took him home and, "placing a rod in his hand," helped him to beat up the dog "or any thing else that may come in his way." She also "teases and vexes him, creates an irritable temper, submits to the rod, and flees before him with great dread." Afterward, she beat him and pulled his hair and he responded by hitting her back, "by which her pupil has learned to bear pain without dread." These "trials of courage" were required by the mother before her son was allowed again to play with his friends.[53]

Hunter was given his name for his hunting prowess. He was neither shy nor modest. His feats included a sixteen-month trip across the plains and the Rockies and back. He compared his life to Daniel Boone's and boasted of an acquaintance with him, saying they "became strongly attached to each other."[54] But Hunter, like Gyles, demonstrates that living with the Indians helped some Euro-American men and boys find alternative ways of seeing their role as men in relation to women and living on the earth. In works like Hunter's, readers could see another way of living.

The life and work of John Tanner presents yet another example of a White Indian whose Indian mother reshaped the direction of his life. Tanner's father was a Virginia clergyman who settled on the Ohio River in Kentucky. Tanner's mother died when he was two. The family moved onto the edge of Shawnee territory, where his father's brother, with some other white men, killed and scalped an Indian. The family moved again after the father's remarriage, this time past Cincinnati "to the mouth of the Big Miami." As Tanner told the story, "The earliest event of my life, which I distinctly remember is the death of my mother. This happened when I was two years old, and many of the attending circumstances made so deep an impression, that they are still fresh in my memory." His clergyman father soon "removed to a place called Elk Horn." The boy was expected to take care of younger siblings and at one point was beaten for not doing so. "From that time, my father's house was less like home to me, and I often thought and said, 'I wish I could go and live among the Indians.' "[55] Shawnees captured him in 1785.

Tanner was first adopted by an old woman known as " 'the Otter woman,' the otter being her *totem*." She treated him well, but he was happier when he was readopted over her strong objections. His second Indian mother was chief of the Ottawa "notwithstanding her sex." Her name was Net-no-kwa. She was able to use her status and "considerable whiskey" to get the young Tanner. He thought she was younger and "of a more pleasing aspect than my former mother. She took me by the hand after she had completed the negotiation with my former possessors, and led me to her own lodge which stood near." He soon learned that she would indulge him a good deal. She fed him, gave him "good clothes," and told him to play with her children. They went past Mackinac and when the corn was ripe arrived in Ottawa territory in northern Michigan. Net-no-kwa's husband was seventeen years her junior and an Ojibwa

Frontispiece of John Tanner from Edwin James, A Narrative of the Captivity and Adventures of John Tanner *(1830). Courtesy of the Newberry Library*

who treated Tanner "like an equal, rather than as a dependent." Net-no-kwa led an Ottawa band at Arbre Croche on the northern part of the lower peninsula.[56] Tanner said he never met an Indian of either sex "who had so much authority as Net-no-kwa."[57] He respected her understanding of the world of nature and her ability to interpret dreams. Tanner, however, was a braggart. He told of every bear and elk he killed and probably a good number he never saw. He claimed to have killed twenty-four bear and ten moose in one month and at another point, twenty moose and elk and forty-two beaver in a ten-day period.

...

78

White
Actors
on a
Field
of Red

Although he had many words of love for his mother, he could say little good about his mother-in-law, whom he claimed tried to kill him. His marriages failed one after another. He complained constantly about his Ojibwa brother. No true sibling ever met a worse rival. Tanner spent more pages trying to tell how much better he was than his brother than John Williams did on the evils of popery.[58]

Tanner lived with the Ottawa-Ojibwas for nearly thirty years. Born in 1780 and captured in 1789 by Saginaw Ojibwas, he returned with his white brother to Kentucky in about 1817. After his return, he lived in emotional turmoil, later settling in northern Michigan Territory around Sault Ste. Marie. He is thought to have married four times. Between 1837 and 1846 he was arrested several times for killing livestock, was in jail, had confrontations with various northern Michigan whites, and had his house set on fire. He became more and more disturbed and reclusive after the failure of his third marriage to an Ojibwa woman, was accused of murder, and finally disappeared and was never heard from again.[59]

A nineteenth-century captive boy who remained with the Senecas was also deeply touched and shaped by his Indian mother. Renamed White Chief, he had been taken from the Susquehanna during the French and Indian War, at the age of four. He remembered losing his mother and finding himself in an Indian woman's lap. "Looking kindly down into my face she smiled on me, and gave me some dried deer's meat and maple sugar. From that hour I believe she loved me as a mother. I am sure I returned to her the affection of a son. . . . I always had a warm place at the fire, and slept in her arms. I was fed with the best food the wigwam could afford." The boy learned to compete with the other Seneca boys with the bow "my Indian mother put into my hands." He shot birds and squirrels, which she promised to cook. "I often gave her much pleasure by bringing her game and demanding the fulfillment of her promise. She never disappointed me."[60]

Stories of white male captives point out the necessity of dealing with a new culture. Adapting demanded a reassessment of all aspects of a boy's or a man's life: male behavior, family relations, and gender relations. In redefining or at least reassessing the "normal" behavior from which they came, men and boys were confronted with contrasting or perhaps more exaggerated (in their eyes) forms of male behavior. They were not to cry, not to show pain or fear, even under torture. Some were subjected to racial and ethnic taunts. Hunter's first memory is of a little girl captive being killed for crying. Tanner remembered Indian boys taunting captives with racial and sexual slurs. They "upbraided me with being *white,* and with the whites all being *squaws;* a reproachful term used generally among the Indians, in contradistinction to that of *warrior.*"[61] This new view of cultures did not always bring an easier life. Some nineteenth-century White Indians, like Hunter and Tanner, suffered severe marital and personal difficulties when they returned to Anglo-American life.

Mathew Brayton was a child captive who, as an adult, searched for and found his brother and other family members. He went from Anglo-American childhood to Indian manhood only to rediscover his original identity. In the end, he found his white family, but in the process abandoned his Indian wife and two children, along with the extended family and tribe that raised him. These contradictions are not stated in the happy ending of his narrative, a story told by another because he could neither write nor speak English fluently. One guesses that the next chapter of Brayton's life, like that of some captives who changed cultures and crossed sexual boundaries, did not have a happy ending.[62]

The captive experience forced both men and women to confront what they had thought were roles given by God and nature. For male captives it challenged their masculine definitions of strength and endurance. It required them to use

...

80

*White
Actors
on a
Field
of Red*

every method available to withstand violence against them and against friends and family. It forced them to assume responsibilities for the women and children in their families, which tested them both physically and psychologically. It forced them to live in new ways and in relationship to other men and other women, which, in every century, challenged their society's conceptions of men, women, family, and sexuality. There were variations in men's and boys' individual behaviors and responses, for males of different ages, between French and Anglo-Americans, and over time. Although the religious hero is a seventeenth- and early eighteenth-century phenomenon, and the adventure hero evolves from Smith to empire-building hero Boone and later dime novel romantic savior descendants, of the fourteen men discussed (and the one fictive captive), the basic typology of Hero and White Indian is more persistent than changes over time.

As is true for their female counterparts, the juxtaposition of the white male captive on a field of red brought out certain adaptive reactions based on extreme circumstances. For both men and women, age of capture was an indicator of adaptation, with younger captives being more malleable and more open to seeing the other. In both cases, however, gender and attitudes toward the Indian other were critical as well. For women, the separation from their families, homes, and traditional male "protectors" and the dangers to themselves and their children put them in touch with their vulnerability but forced them to confront their own inner resources. For most women in the centuries under consideration, capture proved a prolonged test of faith, endurance, and self-reliance. Not underestimating the ways in which many Indian societies facilitated the integration of captives into their societies, these women were, at least for the first days, weeks, and months, and for Mary Jemison, years, subject to feelings of deep loneliness. It appears that the tests for male captives were more on the battlefield of prowess, religious or physical, and that even when other tests presented themselves, these were the ways in which many defined the task of their captivity.

The mode of writing shaped the story told by both men and women. From the earliest accounts, style was shaped by period, by religious or secular orientation, and by the particular audience reading the materials. But again, gender left its mark, as has been evident. In her study of pardon tales in sixteenth-century France, Natalie Zemon Davis reports that in both style and content, women's and men's attempts to gain pardon for crimes by appeal before French kings and magistrates differed.[63] The same is true of captivity narratives and writings. With the exception of Mary Rowlandson, women in the seventeenth and much of the eighteenth centuries told their stories to others, and others wrote them. Women's written stories differ in style and content from men's (and from men's renditions of women's stories). The telling differs in the way it appeals to the reader, its emotion, its language, and its subjects. For men, adventure, trials, physical pain, and the resistance to pain, learning from, outsmarting, or becoming Indian are at the center of the accounts. This bifurcation of sentiment versus adventure was most pronounced in the period from 1830 to the end of the nineteenth century and was shaped largely by the demands of the market, along with the emerging ideology of separate spheres.[64]

But there were also physical and social realities that made capture different for each sex. For women there was the question of their physical vulnerability, the question of whether they had the stamina to go on, the mention of forced marriage to Indians, the fear of rape, and familial and psychic vulnerability. What will happen to the children? How will the woman, usually a wife and a mother, stand up under the stress? These are common questions beneath the plot and move the narration from the seventeenth century onward. Women are able to survive, though in some nineteenth-century cases they appear to revel in their frailty and vulnerability. In the Amazon stories, from Dustan and on through the nineteenth-century recountings, a few escape stories are told by these women themselves, but no violent stories or adventure narratives are written by them about their experiences. Similar stories of male prowess, from Smith to Eastman, are all written by the men themselves.

Why was this the case? To the extent that this literature served as nation-building propaganda, white male weakness always had to be both masked and overcome. Men who were too weak or could not outsmart the enemy would die. For men like Father Jogues, death meant martyrdom and the ultimate victory of

...

82

*White
Actors
on a
Field
of Red*

Christ; for Englishmen and men of the new American nation, it meant defeat of the founding mission and of the westward expansion of that mission through the perpetuation of new families. Powerful figures of women and children could be used as backups against the Indians and fortify the courage of all. But they were also symbols of the growth and vigor of a new Zion and later a new republic.

What changes occurred over time? Female vulnerability was more salable in the nineteenth century than earlier, as were protective male heroics. The markets for fiction and nonfiction were not very different when it came to reports about the frontier.[65] But female vulnerability is a constant, a continuity embedded in all the captivity genres, even those in which women strike back. Women's generally more diminutive physical stature and role as childbearer and nurturer is used as a sign of personal and social vulnerability to evoke sympathetic response. An injured, raped, or unprotected woman (or child) calls out for help. Captive stories of women and children pointed out the vulnerability of the family and social fabric on the frontier. These stories served as cautionary tales. If mothers and children could disappear from a homestead, near a frontier fort, en route west, or in an uprising, "civilization" was precarious indeed.

Charles Johnston returned to Virginia in 1790 after five weeks with Shawnees. His family thought him dead. "The anxiety of the neighborhood, to hear the details of my capture, and of all my way-faring, brought them in great numbers, day after day, to my mother's house, and subjected me to narrations, which I was compelled so often to repeat, and which begat in me so many unpleasant recollections, that I almost dreaded the return of each succeeding day."[66]

From the earliest accounts of Smith, Rowlandson, Dustan, and Williams, Anglo-American colonists identified with the variety of struggles men and women faced on the frontiers of the New World. Their epic stories challenged listeners and readers to put themselves in the place of the captive, to ask themselves what they would have done. These stories asked, Who are you? Who might you become? What might this land become? Their answers contend that you cannot know what man you are, what woman you are, what child you are until you have seen another way, have become vulnerable, crossed boundaries. In that other land, you encounter dangers of every sort. The very social experiment of the New World is brought to the test. You will see a different world, a different self, and in the process you will reevaluate the society of which you are a part.

Exploring Sexual Boundaries

"What was it like, Papa, when you were a little boy and used to hunt with the Indians?"

"I don't know," Nick was startled. He had not even noticed the boy was awake. . . . "We used to go all day to hunt black squirrels. . . . I went with a boy named Billy Gilby and his sister Trudy. We used to go out nearly every day all one summer. . . ."

"But tell me what they were like."

"They were Ojibways," Nick said. Could you say she did first what no one had ever done better and mention plump brown legs, flat belly, hard little breasts, well holding arms, quick searching tongue, the flat eyes, the good taste of the mouth . . .

—Ernest Hemingway, "Fathers and Sons"

> I can charm the man
> He is completely fascinated
> by me.
> Niwawin'gawia'. . .
>   Eni'niwa'. . .
>   —Love-charm Song, Ojibwa (Chippewa)

He was a snake with the power of a young hunter.
She would become the mother of all of the Black Snakes
he appeared to her on the surface of a lake
  —The Myth of Atois, Abenaki

> *we want what is real*
> *we want what is real*
> *don't deceive us!*
>   *—Song of the Bald Eagle, Crow*

In 1614 John Rolfe wrote a letter to Sir Thomas Dale, the deputy governor of Virginia Colony, asking forgiveness for wanting to marry Pocahontas. Rolfe assured Dale that he had no lustful intent and justified his request on the grounds that he would "save" her through conversion. He wished to be "no way led . . . with the unbridled desire of carnall affection: but for the good of this plantation, for the honour of our countrie, for the glory of God, for my owne salvation, and for the converting to the true knowledge of God and Jesus Christ, an unbeleeving creature, named Pokahuntas." Pocahontas and Rolfe were wed, but unlike the Catholic church in New France and New Spain, the Anglican church made less effort to convert the natives or to encourage or accept marriages between Indians and Englishmen.[1]

Pocahontas, Indian captive and rescuer of Captain John Smith, became the first native of Virginia to cross the cultural and sexual boundary by marrying an Englishman. From the earliest colonial encounters of Smith and Pocahontas to the later fantasies of the Indian Princess dime novels, from Mary Rowlandson's meeting with Metacomet to Mary Barber's with Squatting Bear, captivities confront their readers with real and potential sexual relationships across racial and cultural lines. Readers of frontier accounts, like Nick's child, wanted to know "what it was like." As in Nick's case, the sources are only partially forthcoming. But they suggest fear and fascination with the other—a combination of trepidation and wonder. The materials of white captivity begin to lift a veil along the ethnic sexual boundary—a land of forbidden intimacies.

Although Anglo-American men and women approached many things differently, they had much in common. That com-

...

86

White
Actors
on a
Field
of Red

monality was based on language, religion, culture, history, and what the last two centuries have labeled race. This common heritage—what will be called here ethnicity—was brought with successive migrations to new frontiers. How did these Anglo-American captives view their Indian captors' sexuality? Did they see them as possible mates? Did their views change over time? Were these views influenced by gender? And most important for these popular materials, what was the function of the attitudes and images produced?

Sexual attitudes and practices are hard to assess in any age. The materials for the seventeenth through the mid-nineteenth centuries are scarce at best. The captivity materials offer a spotty, exaggerated, and sometimes fabricated, yet available medium. With them we can attempt to gauge the perceptions (and occasionally the realities) of these Europeans and their American descendants.

From the Pocahontas story onward, the ambiguity of love and lust, of rejection and acceptance was part of the Euro-American attitude toward the Indian. Gary Nash has pointed out that from the beginning the Indian was viewed as having a dual nature: noble and savage. Rayna Green has suggested "exotic" 'as a third quality of Indian nature as perceived by Europeans. Along with the noble, the brutal, and the exotic, there is also the erotic. These four attributes have stimulated Euro-American interest but also ambivalence. Captivity materials offer a body of work which depicts Indian-white relations on the sexual frontier as exciting, dangerous, potentially disastrous, sometimes fun, occasionally romantic.[2] We will track the variations and continuities of these themes in the colonial period (1607–1763), the eras of the Revolution and the early republic (1764–1820), and the era of expansion (1821–70). For all three periods, the highly charged nature of eroticism will serve as the focus of the exploration.

The Colonial World, 1607–1763

. . . . . .

Englishmen found Indians irresistible. James Axtell says they had "unreserved admiration for the Indian physique," although Native Americans were seen as "young, wild, passionate, and alluring, but somehow tainted in the blood—as dark beauty is often portrayed in literary convention. . . . Succumb they did" to "intercultural dalliance."[3] Men in early Virginia and in most settlements outside New England had limited opportunities for white female companionship. The first Virginia settlers were white males. In Virginia, women arrived from England the same year as African captives, in 1619. The Jamestown settlement began in 1607. The number of white women remained low in the entire Chesapeake region until about 1700.[4] But whether in Puritan New England or Anglican Virginia, apparently few Englishmen married Indian women. In British, French, and Spanish settlements of the early years, with the exception of Puritan settlements, men greatly outnumbered women. In both French North America and Spanish and Portuguese South America, only religion barred colonizers from marrying native peoples. Neither the French nor the Spanish church was averse to converting Indians, many of whom married Latin Catholics. Only the English refused to welcome these unions, viewing them, as Axtell points out, "with an unmerciful eye." Intermarriage was not an issue for northeastern Indians. Tribes that adopted French, English, or other native peoples of rival tribes aimed at the full integration of those adoptees.[5]

From Winthrop Jordan's study of English attitudes toward Africans, we learn that religion was not the only difference in attitude between the English and their Latin counterparts in their assessment of native peoples. In the English view, blackness and the African body were spoken of and viewed negatively. Although there is evidence that the earliest Englishmen did not see Indians as "red"—this racialist color epithet was a late eighteenth- and nineteenth-century usage—early Englishmen were not color-blind to Indians. Their color sense for Indians may not have been as constantly negative as it was for black and blackness, and yet Captain John Smith referred to Powhatan as "more like a devill then a man," visiting him "with some two hundred more as blacke as himself," and Cotton Mather called New England enemies in one breath "Wolves," "Bears," and "furious Tawnies."[6] This mix of derogatory views toward Indian religion and color, along with positive responses to their physical attributes, created an ambivalent reaction to

Indian men and women from the first. The concoction of the noble, the wild, and the exotic appeared to whet the English sexual appetite, at the same time inspiring trepidation among several white captives.

...

88

*White
Actors
on a
Field
of Red*

In his *True Relation* (1608), Captain John Smith tells us of his meeting with several women, including "Queene of Agamatack," who "kindely treated us." His first story of capture tells how he was met every morning by three women who "presented me three great platters of fine bread" and enough venison for ten men. His impressions of ten-year-old Pocahontas mentioned that her "countenance, and proportion, much exceedith any of the rest of his people," and he extolled her "for wit and spirit" as well. In *The Map of Virginia* (1611) she was pictured saving him. In 1624, when he rewrote or added the story of her saving him, she "got his head in her armes, and laid her owne upon" him to save his life. Whether Smith had more intimate relations with the young girl, the queen, or any of the other women along the way, like nearly all the subsequent Englishmen and women of the settlement period narratives, he never clearly said. The Heroic Mode in which Smith wrote, however, allows the reader to read in intimacies, especially when he tells us that native men "have as many women as they will." One guesses that Smith enjoyed himself.[7]

But along with the lure of Indian women for Englishmen, accounts indicate possible harm to Englishwomen. One month after the first two English of the Puritan colony were captured at Wethersfield, Connecticut, in 1638, between three and seven hundred Pequot men, women, and children were killed, their village burned, and expeditions sent out by the English "to harry and destroy the miserable refugees fleeing into the wilderness." John Underhill's account of the April raid on Wethersfield, which resulted in the women's capture, used the word *bravado* to describe the way the Indians came by the Englishmen on shore, showing off their English prisoners with "English mens and womens shirts and smocks, in stead of sayles" on "poles in their Conoos." Had the women been stripped of their clothing? Perhaps just the taunt that the natives could "steal" "their women" was an inflammatory act and sexual provocation to the Englishmen.[8]

By the time of King Philip's War there was more than innuendo in at least one popular epic poem, *New England's Crisis* (1676). Although not one report even implied any truth to sexual misconduct among New England tribes, Benjamin Thompson wrote:

> They round our skirts, they pare, they fleece, they kill,
> And to our bordering towns do what they will . . .
> Will she or nill the chastest turtle must
> Taste of the pangs of their unbridled lust.
> From farms to farms, from towns to towns they post,
> They strip, they bind, they ravish, flay, and roast.[9]

The "wild" or "savage" Indian, even when he did not strike or make sexual overtures to Anglo-American women, became one who ravishes—a fearful part of the colonial imagination. The seeds of sexual fear then emerged in early New England. In these circumstances of war, rumor, and suspicion, these women were forcibly moved by their Indian captors across the Northeast landscape and slept in their dwellings.

There is little evidence either in the documents or in ethnohistorical scholarship for the rape of any white women in early New England. Both white women captives and men reported that sexual abuse of women did not occur. A combination of the Algonquian rules of war and the practice of adoption, which would bring incest taboos to bear, appears to be the reason. There is the suggestion that women would not report their dishonor. How to factor in the absence of reporting is problematic at best. By contrast, in the French records a report from Father Paul Le Jeune (for eastern Canada and New York) claimed that a group of young Indian captive girls among the Iroquois who were not married into the society were "constantly exposed to the danger of losing their honors or their lives through brutal lechery or cruelty of the Masters or Mistresses."[10]

Mary Rowlandson thanked God for bringing her through the captive experience: "I have been in the midst of roaring Lions, and Salvage Bears, that feared neither God, nor Man, nor the Devil, by night and by day, alone and in company, sleeping all sorts together, and yet not one of them ever offered the least abuse of unchastity to me in word or action."[11] Rowlandson's fears of rape were heightened by being thrown in the same "weetoo" with others, that is, "sleeping all sorts together." Sev-

...
90
White
Actors
on a
Field
of Red

eral of her male contemporaries felt similar discomfort. Massasoit asked several Plymouth Colony men to spend an evening at the Wampanoag sachem's encampment. Neal Salisbury tells us that those who accepted "slept on a plank bed with the chief, his wife, and two other men." They were asked to stay another evening but graciously declined, wanting to get back home to keep the Sabbath and complaining about lack of sleep because of lice, fleas, mosquitoes, "bad lodging," and "the savages' barbarous singing." With another sleepless night they were afraid they might not make it home for "want of strength," which Salisbury interpreted as "psychic discomfort . . . felt in the crowded presence of so many people who seemed free of the Puritans' obsession with self-control." During her weeks in captivity, Rowlandson went from one weetoo to another, at times with Metacomet (King Philip), with whom she developed a close friendship. With over twenty "removes" and the variety of changes in lodging that were acceptable Algonquian practice, Rowlandson might well have been anxious to discover who might be in what tent. Elizabeth Hanson writes that she was sent out of her master's tent because of disagreements and was accepted hospitably into the weetoo of another. The question of where one would sleep, with whom, and what would go on must have been upsetting to Puritan women and girls, as it was to men and boys as well. It is understandable that in winter among enemies, and in strange places, women might feel some trepidation when sexual closeness was imposed in their sleeping quarters.[12]

And what of the sexual relations or at least snuggling they must have seen? Certainly the Puritan settlers lived in close quarters; parents, children, and servants often shared the same room. But if this was accepted as natural in one's own community, within one's own household, it must have been uncomfortable and anxiety-provoking in the middle of another's weetoo. Rowlandson, Hanson, and others certainly saw and heard unsettling and shocking things "sleeping all sorts together."[13] In such situations, English meetings on the frontier with the "enemy," the "Savage," the "Tawney," raised questions of sexuality, morality, temptation, and fantasy.

Besides the perceptions and experiences of one's own sexual feelings and others' sexual practice, ethnic mixing had political, cultural, and religious implications. As Axtell has written, the French and Indians "took special pains to capture, acculturate, and convert English settlers, and they succeeded at a rate mortifying to English ministers and officials."[14] The most famous case of crossing ethnic sexual boundaries was that of Eunice Williams, daughter of John Williams. After his "redemption," Williams trekked across New England to bring Eunice back from Canada. After some negotiation, he spoke with the seven-year-old for an hour and found she "had not forgotten her catechism" but was coming under Catholic influence among the Caughnawagas. He "told her she must pray to God for His grace every day." By October 1706, Williams was able to get Massachusetts to negotiate with Quebec for the return of fifty-seven of the Deerfield captives, including his two boys, who arrived in Boston in November. But Williams closed his narrative confiding, "I have yet a daughter of ten years of age and many neighbors whose case bespeaks your compassion and prayers to God to gather them, being outcasts ready to perish."[15]

Eunice remained in Canada, converted to Catholicism, and married a Caughnawaga Indian. She refused to come back and thereby became a popular legend. A former captive and her brother, Reverend Stephen Williams, met with her, her Indian husband, and their two daughters at Longmeadow, Massachusetts, in 1743. He noted that Eunice preferred "the Indian mode of life and the haunts of the Indians, to the unutterable grief of her father and friends."[16] In the continuing legend of Eunice, New Englanders read and listened with simultaneous awe and horror as the Indianized Eunice refused to return to "civilization," refused to give up Catholicism for her Protestant birthright, lost her use of English, preferred the apple orchard to the bed inside her brother's house, and wore only native dress.[17] Eunice became a symbol for what could happen. The sexual bond created by her Indian marriage formalized her acculturation, permanently separating her and transforming her culturally into "them." She was no longer fully "us."[18] The power of a new culture along with those bonds was strong enough to cut her off from her ethnic origins and her own family. The marital bond kept a number of other New England captives from returning.[19] Apparently marriage could be as powerful a bond as baptism. One could break religious vows more easily than part from one's husband and children. Such a sexual liaison was not just a personal choice; a sexual union sanctioned by a marriage was a religious, cultural, and political threat.

Along with John Smith's promising first messages about Indian women, colonial accounts by and about white women indicated some causes for anxiety. The possibilities that crossing the political boundaries might mean crossing sexual boundaries, marrying and remaining Indian (pagan), or Catholic, added an ethnic and political dimension to such possible unions.

The Revolutionary Era and the Early Republic, 1764–1820

. . . . . .

Themes of exotica, savagery, and nobility continue into the revolutionary era and the early republic. By the 1790s exotica, sexual allure, and wildness become more explicit. In *An Account of the Remarkable Occurrences in the Life and Travels of Colonel James Smith* (1799), Smith's adoption by the Caughnawagas in 1755 after his capture at the time of the Battle of the Wilderness includes his first encounters with young Indian women. First, his hair was pulled out (with the exception of three or four inches on the crown). Holes were made in his nose and ears and rings and nose jewels placed through them. He was dressed in a breechcloth, his body and face painted "in various colors." Wampum was arranged on his neck and silver bands in his hands. The chief then called in a group of Delawares, and a speech was given. Smith was then handed over "to three young squaws, who led me by the hand down the bank into the river." He feared that they were going to drown him, but it turned out to be something of a splash party. The women bathed him and brought him back to finish the ceremony. The chief then announced: "My son, you are now flesh of our flesh." The picture of Smith among the young Indian maidens was one of a few foldouts in Joseph Pritts's popular family book *Incidents of Border Life* (1841).[20]

Male captives such as John and James Smith were not alone in enjoying the company of the ethnic other in early America. A female narrative with sexual overtones was written about

Squaws Dunking Col. Smith from Joseph Pritts, Mirror of
Olden Time Border Life *(1849). Courtesy of the Newberry
Library*

Jemima Howe of Hinsdale, New Hampshire. Significantly,
Howe's account was first published in Boston in 1792, and at
least nine more printings occurred in Philadelphia, London,
Boston, Rutland, and Watertown, Massachusetts, between 1803
and 1846. Howe's second husband was killed and she and her
seven children taken prisoner and marched to Canada in July
1755. She returned to New England about five years later after
living with both Canadian Indians and the French. When she
heard that her daughter Mary was about to be married to an
Indian, she was distressed and requested that the girl be placed
in a nunnery with another daughter. Howe strongly preferred
Catholicism to potential Indian marriage and was more interested in Frenchmen than Indians. In her own adventures we
see the first somewhat coy and flirtatious captive who might
have had a little fun (at least according to Reverend Bunker
Gray, who took down her story).[21] Jemima Howe was taken
from the "cruel hands of the Indians" and placed in a French
household, where, to hide her from her occasionally drunk and
abusive Indian master, she was "secreted in an upper cham-
ber" and "carefully guarded." In this household she underwent

...

94

White
Actors
on a
Field
of Red

"trials," which required "a large stock of prudence." Both the master of the house, a French army officer, and his "warm and resolute son" became "excessively fond of my company so that between these two rivals, the father and the son, I found myself in a very critical situation indeed . . . hardly knowing many times how to behave in such a manner as at once to secure my own virtue." [22] Howe's dalliances were with Frenchmen—more acceptable lovers for New England women perhaps than Abenakis or Iroquois. But once the literature opened the door for possibilities with Frenchmen, Indians would not be far behind.

Sexual explicitness, indeed erotica mixed with sadomasochism, reached new dimensions in the closing years of the eighteenth century with a key fictive captivity pamphlet that viewed the threat of sexual contact by an Indian as permission for white women to murder and dismember Indian males rather than "submitting" sexually. [23] In both historical and fictionalized accounts of captivities, social sanctions approved of the most "unwomanly" behavior, rather than allowing a woman to give in to sexual demands (and, perhaps, temptations). Between 1787 and 1812, twenty-four different printings and several editions of a highly popular narrative were published in a collection of New England cities and towns—in Windsor, Putney, and Rutland, Vermont; August and Fryeberg, Maine; Leominster, Brookfield, Amherst, Greenfield, and Springfield, Massachusetts; Jaffrey, New Hampshire; and New Haven, Connecticut. The sexual, and in the context of its day, close to pornographic nature of this fictional account gives us a better sense of the "New England mind" than of much of what actually took place on the American frontier. The first extant edition appeared in 1785 and was reprinted in an almanac in 1787. It was entitled *A Surprising Account of the Discovery of a Lady Who Was Taken by the Indians in the Year 1777, and after making her escape, She retired to a lonely Cave, where she lived nine years.* The second Windsor edition of 1794 (the eighth known printed edition) became *A Very Surprising Narrative of a Young Woman, Discovered in a Rocky-Cave; after having been taken by the Savage Indians of the Wilderness, in the year 1777, and seeing no human being for the space of nine years. In a Letter from a Gentleman to his Friend.* The narrative was credited to one "Abraham Panther," whose name appeared as a signature ending the text's "letter." [24]

The writer, walking in the woods with a male friend in the "Western Wilderness," is reported to have heard a voice. Turning to find where it came from, he "beheld a beautiful young lady, sitting near the mouth of the cave." After some talking, the "lady" began to tell her story. She was born in Albany in 1760, and when she was aged fifteen a clerk employed by her father "conceived an unfortunate passion" for her. One night they were in the garden together when her father came upon them and forbade her to see him again. They ran off together. The father searched for them, but she knew she could not "calm my father's rage" and they left the area. On the fourth day of their elopement, they were surrounded by Indians who "barbarously murdered my lover! cutting and mangling him in the most inhuman manner" after having tied him to a stake and burned him. All the time "they ran around, singing and dancing! rejoicing in their brutal cruelty! . . . I fainted away and lay some time motionless on the ground." When she awoke she was surrounded "on all sides with danger, I knew not what to do, without a guide to direct, or friend to protect me."[25] Somehow she became transformed into an Amazonian figure and wandered for fourteen days in the eternal American garden. At night the ground was her "couch," and by day the earth produced food for her. She tells her gentlemen "saviors" of her Amazonian transformation.

> "I was surprised at seeing an Indian, of a gigantic figure, walking toward me: to run I knew would be in vain, and no less vain would be to attempt to hide. . . . [He] accosted me in a language which I did not understand and after surveying me for some time, he took me by the hand, and led me to his cave; having entered, pointed to a stone seat on which he sat down; he then gave me to eat some nuts and some Indian cake, after which he stretched himself out on a long stone, covered with skins which he used as a bed, and several times motioned me to lay myself beside him. I declined his offer, and at length he *rose* in a passion, and went to another apartment of the cave, and brought forth a sword and a hatchet. He then motioned to me that I must either accept of his bed, or expect death for my obstinacy. I still declined his offer, and was resolved to die rather than comply with his desire."[26]

It is significant that by this, the 1799 edition, the heroine saw an "Indian." In the 1785 and 1794 editions and even in the Brookfield 1800 edition, she was "surprised at seeing a man, of a gigantic figure."[27] After he had tied her up and gone to sleep, she bit her way through the bark to which she was tied, using her teeth as "the means to liberate" herself. She saw this as her "only opportunity" to free herself from the "violence" he would use on her when he awoke. She then grabbed his hatchet "and summoning resolution, I with three blows, effectually put an end to his existence." Not good enough. "Then I cut off his head, and next day, having cut him in quarters, drew him out of the cave, about half mile distance; when after covering him with leaves and bushes returned to his place." She continued her story of how she had lived miraculously in the cave for nine years with her "faithful Dog," raising Indian corn from seeds she found there.[28]

The potential rape, the victim forced to turn murderer, and the dismemberment of the Indian are all central to the story. These elements give white women sanction to use violence and license in the wild when white men are not around to protect them from the savage other. At the end of the story the heroine is led by the "gentlemen" away from the wilderness and from her own Amazonian wildness, her threatening independence, and her castrating sexuality. She can again become "a lady."

Like the Panther narrative, other early republican publications signaled more explicit, although still often veiled, relationships between New England women and Indians. In the highly fictionalized piece by K. White (1809), she (or he) was captured by unknown Indians and taken to an uncertain spot. K. claimed she was "sorely bruised and lacerated; my arms were cut almost to the bone, from the withes I was tied with," but was rescued by a "kind Indian" who aided her escape. Her freedom, bringing together the elements of the savage, the noble, and the erotic, was as tinged with sexual promise as James Smith's adoption.

One night after I was retired to rest, I felt some person draw me by the hand, half awakened by the intrusion, I changed my position, but the drawing was repeated. I looked around and being moonlight, I discovered thro the crannies of the hut where I laid, an Indian standing near me. I rose in some

...

96

White

Actors

on a

Field

of Red

trepidation; he bade me "make no noise," his voice was familiar to me, and I at length found it was my Indian friend. He
bade me take my blanket round me and follow him. I did not
want a second invitation but followed him out of the hut.[29]

In several pieces of early republican writing, erotic motifs occur
within the captivity literature, extending the possibilities of
sexual encounters across racial, ethnic, and cultural lines. Tit-
illation and eroticism are apparent, "fact" and "fiction" are
blurred, for white women, Indian brutality is reported as being
more explicitly against them, and what is claimed as retaliatory
violence against Indians (in the Dustan mode) is sanctioned.

The Era of Expansion, 1821–1870

.   .   .   .   .   .

If the long-term image of Indians in relation to whites
was unchanging, there would be little need for the assertion
of brutality that became ever stronger, ever more sexual in the
nineteenth century. But whites' expansion onto Indian lands
brought a proximity between whites and Indians requiring caution and the withdrawing of cultural boundaries. Variations on
the colonial and revolutionary themes of the "lost" daughter,
taken from Eunice Williams and Jemima Boone, are expanded
in nineteenth-century fiction, biography, history, and art with
ever greater concern regarding sexual unions between whites
and Indians. Like stories of the tragic mulatto, the tales carry a
cautionary message. The basic theme is that Indian and white
unions are bad business and can come to no good for Anglo-
American society, the individual participants, or their mixed-
blood children. James Fenimore Cooper used the love theme
between a noble savage and a colonial white woman at least
twice, first in *Last of the Mohicans* (1826) and again in *Wept of
Wish-ton-Wish* (1829)—with tragic consequences both times.[30]
But some captivity stories and the illustrations accompanying
them and their dime novel spin-offs indicate that marrying or
having a love affair with an Indian might have some allure.
These appear to be subversive or alternative readings of life
in the woods, which is all the more reason that these affairs

are increasingly shown to come to no good. James E. Seaver's as-told-to biography of Mary Jemison shared popularity with the novel *Hobomok* by Lydia Maria Child (1824). Hobomok, a noble savage, married a New England captive woman in a nineteenth-century update of the Eunice Williams story.[31]

...

98

White

Actors

on a

Field

of Red

According to Mary Jemison, when she was about age sixteen, "my sisters told me that I must go and live with one of them, whose name was She-nin-jee." As she told Seaver in 1823, "Not daring to cross them or disobey their commands with a great degree of reluctance I went; and Sheninjee and I were married according to Indian custom." But what began as a forced marriage turned into a love match. Jemison described her husband as

> a noble man; large in stature; elegant in his appearance; generous in his conduct; courteous in war; a friend to peace, and a great lover of justice. He supported a degree of dignity far above his rank, and merited and received the confidence and friendship of all the tribes with whom he was acquainted. Yet, Sheninjee was an Indian. The idea of spending my days with him at first seemed perfectly irreconcilable to my feelings; but his good nature, generosity, tenderness, and friendship toward me, soon gained my affection; and strange as it may seem, I loved him!—To me he was ever kind in sickness, and always treated me with gentleness; in fact, he was an agreeable husband and a comfortable companion. We lived happily together till the time of our final separation, which happened two or three years after our marriage.[32]

Her husband's death after a brief marriage "was a heavy and unexpected blow."[33] When her son was about three or four she married again. Her new husband, Hiokatoo (Big Lance), remained her mate for about fifty years. The 1856 edition of her narrative added material that showed him as a vicious murderer, who from his earliest years "showed signs of thirst for blood," and who, at Braddock's defeat, allegedly took "two white prisoners, and burnt them alive in a fire of his own kindling." In Northumberland County, Pennsylvania, he reportedly aided the British by tomahawking "every wounded American." Jemison countered that she had lived with the man for fifty years and "received, according to Indian customs, all the kindness and attention that was my due as a wife. Although war was his trade from his youth till old age and decrepitude stopped his career, he uniformly treated me with tenderness, and never offered an insult." Rather than letting Jemison tell her own story, first Seaver, then later editors inserted material that made him appear more brutal, as if to counter Jemison's testimony of her loving marriage with Sheninjee and her second companionate marriage with Hiokatoo.[34]

What function did these attempts to turn Indians into beasts serve? The rise of racial ideology along with continuing and violent warfare seems to have made accounts of brutal rape and forced marriage to horrible Indians more acceptable and prevalent in accounts of capture after 1830. Nineteenth-century anthropology increasingly argued for superior and inferior races and rejected earlier ideas of a single humanity. Reginald Horsman argues that the evolution of racial thought in both America and Europe was directly related to "the need to jus-tify exploitation and destruction."[35] Certainly beastly men did not deserve to keep American land. The inclusion of popular family anthologies like John Frost's of two romantic pictures of women being taken away and one presumably being returned by a handsome Indian was all the more reason to publish ac-counts of brutalized and unhappy white captives. Along with the will to take over Indian lands there appears to have been a covert anxiety that Indian men could indeed serve as attractive and companionate sexual partners.

Female accounts, especially the Frail Flower narratives, deny the existence of sexual attraction and companionship. Rather, they are filled with forced marriages, dirt, and brutality. The writing is laced with fear of and hatred for Indian men. Caroline Harris and Clarissa Plummer were both captured and made Indian wives in the 1830s after their husbands were murdered. Harris was "clasped with an iron grip," "doomed," "compelled to co-habit with a barbarous and blood-thirsty savage." Clarissa Plummer watched while her husband, trying to defend her, was killed. She fainted "as one never to rise again" and was later "conveyed in the arms of one of the savages present to the hut occupied by the old sachem who had been the principal cause of the death of my poor husband." She was brought to a "filthy bed of leaves and moss" in his "miserable hovel."[36]

· · ·

100

White

Actors

on a

Field

of Red

Miss Lockhart carried away by the Camanche Chief from John Frost, Thrilling Adventures among the Indians *(1850). Courtesy of the Newberry Library*

Colonial women were repulsed by native food; mid- to late nineteenth-century women were repulsed by dirt. Their faint-heartedness was matched by what they saw as their profound sexual mistreatment. Plummer suffered starvation and brutalization "for no other reason than because I declined gratifying a savage brute in his unreasonable and wicked request." Har-

The Rescue, from John Frost, Thrilling Adventures among the
Indians *(1850). Courtesy of the Newberry Library*

ris preferred death to "becoming the companion, and yielding
to the fulsome embraces of a detestable Savage!—Alas! however revolting the idea, such, indeed, was my fate!" She described her marriage as "a mock ceremony" in which she was
"led, like a lamb to the slaughter," and later was "led, or rather
dragged . . . where I was doomed to spend eleven months in a
state of bondage and misery that beggars description! being not
only compelled to cohabit, but to yield to the beastly will of a
Savage brute!"[37]

More recently uncovered reminiscences of capture not packaged or sold show that forced marriage and fear were very real
for two women in Kansas. Sarah White and Anna Brewster Morgan were both captured on the Kansas frontier in 1868. Sarah
White was seventeen years old when she witnessed the death
of her father and an attack on her mother and six other children. Anna Brewster Morgan was a new bride whose husband
left her one day to work in the fields. She took a horse and a
gun to find him but en route was captured by Sioux who bound

...

102

White

Actors

on a

Field

of Red

her to her horse and carried her until they met up with another band, which had Sarah White. Both women were brought to a village, guarded, and made to do "menial work." They plotted an escape but were recaptured. Morgan "fought hard and said I would not go back. But they took me by main force and whipped me and bound me onto the pony. They took us back to the Indian village and they were more strict with us, giving us no privileges whatever." When an "Indian chief" proposed to Morgan, she "married him, thereby choosing the lesser of two evils." She immediately gained in status and had other Indian women to bring wood for her. Later the two women were exchanged for five chiefs held captive by the federal government.[38]

"There were many things that I have not spoken of," Morgan wrote. "After I came back, the road seemed rough, and I often wished that they had never found me." Two months after her return to white society, she gave birth to a son, conceived during her captivity. The boy died at age two. She became an object of curiosity, and writers and photographers came to find out more. According to a later account, the blond, blue-eyed woman with beautiful skin "died in an asylum." Unlike the evidence for colonial New England, at least some white women experienced humiliating sexual treatment on the plains. How common Morgan's experience was is unclear.[39]

Whatever the reality, midcentury white women suffering from Indian male brutality were commonly depicted in popular culture. Violent pictures of Indian men and white women and their sexual subtext dotted the dimes. The dime novel heroine Laura Hautville was held captive by Cunning Serpent. Laura was the white captive turned Indian princess who later turned white again. White Lily (Laura) dressed like an Ojibwa woman "in fawn skin." On the cover of this 1873 thriller a huge Indian aims a long and bloody knife almost at the crotch of the fainted maiden draped over his shoulder. Three tiny white men pursue.[40] These nineteenth-century stories created the need for a larger-than-life male hero to conquer the increasingly sexualized big Indian. In another dime novel, Mary Barber warned young girls to forget ideas about "the noble red men and relinquish all thoughts of going among them, for any purpose whatsoever."[41] The lurid pictures that accompanied her story reinforced her point.

Much as Mary Barber wanted to warn young women to watch out for Indian men, historical documents of captivity by White Indians show that sexual liaisons in the woods were equally disastrous for white men, although for different reasons. The published accounts of male captives in mid- to late nineteenth-century literature warned the western adventurer and would-be White Indian against sexual wanderlust. John Dunn Hunter never mentioned a wife or beloved Indian woman. John Tanner had two Indian and one white marriages; all three failed. In the first case, he indicated that Indian mores accepted a courtship in which he and the women he eventually married slept together before the marriage. But once married, the wife was not good for him and her mother tried to murder him. Nor did his next Indian marriage work.[42] Another midcentury narrative of a fictive white hunter named David C. Butterfield sounded a warning to men who roamed on the frontier and married Indian women. The subtitle told the story: *A Northern Pioneer, for the Last Twenty Years: Who Was Taken When Young by the Indians and Bound by the Strong Chains of a Squaw, for Ten Long Years.*[43]

The tragic fate of men who crossed the sexual divide and engaged in forbidden intimacies came into the dime novel market with the first (and one of the best-selling) dimes—*Malaeska: The Indian Wife of the White Hunter*. Its author, Ann Sophia Stephens, was a popular writer of her day. *Malaeska* first appeared in serial form in the *Ladies' Companion*. In its first year the book sold three hundred thousand copies. *Malaeska* featured an Indian maiden who lived with and had a son by a white hunter. Malaeska was Indian, but she was not like other Indian women. She wore no paint on her face, and "the embroidered moccasins laced over her feet, were the only Indian ornament about her." But she was Indian enough that her forbidden intimacy with Danforth must prove tragic. The hero was not a true hero; otherwise why did he father a half-breed child? Danforth was eventually killed by Indians. Malaeska tried to protect him by covering him with furs, but he did not live past the first few chapters.[44] Malaeska took the child to Manhattan to find the boy's grandparents. They hired her as a maid. She raised the child, but he was not told of his Indian mother's identity. The boy rejected her and later tried to marry a white woman on the

...
104
White
Actors
on a
Field
of Red

frontier. When he discovered his true identity, he jumped off a cliff into a river and drowned. Malaeska died the "heart broken victim of an unnatural marriage."[45]

Fiction mirrored fact in Malaeska. Approximately two decades earlier child captive Matthew Brayton lived with Canadian Indians, was sold to Sioux, then to the Snakes, and finally to a group he called the Copper Heads. His white identity slowly emerged, but he did not discover it until Chief O-wash-kah-ke-naw married him to his lovely daughter Tefronia, or Tame Deer. When his white identity was finally and reluctantly revealed by his Indian family, he was granted a year's leave of absence on his promise to return. He left in search of his white relatives and apparently never returned to his wife, son, and daughter.[46] Despite the reunion with his long-lost white family at the narrative's end, one wonders whether he missed Tame Deer. Apparently, earlier family and racial ties superseded his love in the woods.

Other frontier romances have happy endings but only when the mate-to-be, who appears to be an Indian, turns out to be white. On the frontispiece of one of the first editions of Edward S. Ellis's *Frontier Angel: A Romance of Kentucky Rangers' Life* stands a dark fairy-princess-like Indian maiden. She is graceful. A bracelet is around her left arm. On her head are feathers flowing down her long hair. Her lover sits next to her on a stump, Boone-like, complete with coonskin cap, rifle in repose. When we first read of the heroine we are told she was a "mystery to all" and might even be white because her language was like frontiersmen's speech. She was always alone, and the "whole object of her life seemed to be that of befriending the settlers." She frequently "saved scores of whites from the fury of the savages." Later, when white heroes came to her rescue, a physician noticed through the fading paint that the "lady" was actually Marion Abbot, "lost to white society many years earlier after Indian capture." Her rescuer turned out to be Marion's former beau, and she now married him. The climax of life for the rescuing romantic hero was not John Smith's continuing adventure but the dream of finding the dark woman of his dreams, who was a kind of white girl next door with whom to settle down and love happily ever after.[47]

The theme of forbidden intimacies—an Indian running off

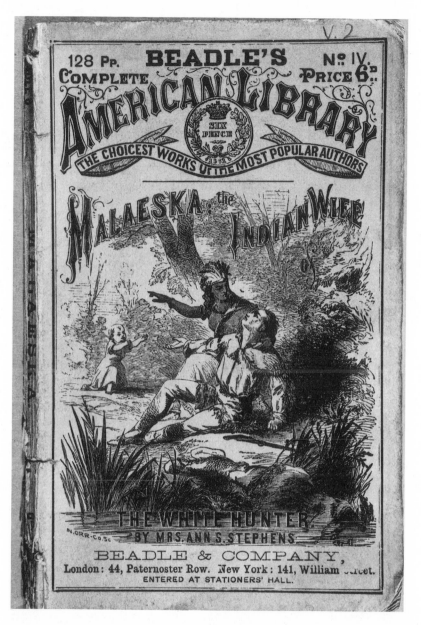

Cover from Mrs. Ann S. Stephens, Malaeska: The Indian Wife of the White Hunter *(1861). Courtesy of the Newberry Library*

...

106

White

Actors

on a

Field

of Red

with a white woman or a white man with an Indian woman—
was also explored in several nineteenth-century artworks. As
in fictional and historical literature, erotic and brutal elements
are in evidence, but romance seems to be favored over brutality.
On the brutal side, the capture of Jemima Boone was depicted
in a lithograph and in several oil paintings. In G. W. Fassel's
lithograph (1851), father Boone steps on the Indian while re-
capturing his daughter. Here the brutality is on the white side
but in the Heroic Mode, in the service of rescuing the daughter from a sexual and racial fate "worse than death." A somewhat incestuous picture emerges as Boone's hand is around the
young woman's waist. In Charles (Carl) Wimar's oil painting
(1853), a distraught Jemima lifts her hands in prayer as three
"wild" looking Indians, one with a rifle, head out (or return) in a
canoe. These Indians are not so much brutal as "wild," and they
are taking her off to who knows where? In another oil painting on the same subject (1855), Wimar has Jemima looking on,
frightened, during her abduction. All these works depict wild,
potentially brutal Indians and helpless white women awaiting
or praying for imminent rescue. There is also *White Captive*
(1858), Erastus Dow Palmer's sculpture in white marble of a
nubile and naked captive girl standing with arms tied behind
her back, a tear in her eye.[48] But there are other works of the
same period portraying the noble (in bearing) and highly erotic
Indian.[49]

In Charles Wimar's highly eroticized mid-nineteenth-century painting *The Abduction of Daniel Boone's Daughter* (ca.
1850), a frail and limp Jemima Boone is placed in the arms of a
dashing young Indian. The Indian is stripped to the waist, with
hair and feathers flying behind him. His legs are astride a rust-
colored horse. The woman's head is drooping, almost resting
on his chest. The horse, rider, and landscape are rusts, russets,
reds, and browns; she is set off, white on this field of red, by
a long cream-colored dress. The horse and its two riders move
across a spacious western landscape in a world not of Kentucky but of the imagination, where the horse enters a stream.
Her wrists are bound, but she does not appear to be otherwise
constrained. Captured in 1776, this daughter of the man who
"opened" the new West looks momentarily unhappy, but like
the horse entering a stream, she might be headed toward a re-

freshing independence. If there were Indians who looked like this one, no wonder there was a need for stories of tragic sexual unions.[50]

Chauncy B. Ives's *Willing Captive* (first produced in 1862, carved in marble in 1868, and cast in bronze in 1886) drives the point home.[51] An erect Indian towers over a diminutive young white maiden. She clings to him, and his arm draws her to his side. Her mother is on her knees beseeching the girl to return or perhaps pleading with the Indian to send her home. Is this a depiction of Jemima Howe? Is it a scene from the return of captives after the Seven Years' War, when some women refused to leave their Indian husbands and families? Or is it a symbolic representation of a fear that young women would prefer the noble bearing and indeed the sexual and physical superiority of Indian men to their white counterparts?[52]

Why were these clear sets of cultural instructions on love on the frontier necessary? For two reasons. The appeal of the Indian male and female to the Euro-American had a long history. The physical stature of both sexes was celebrated in American painting and sculpture, which consistently depicted Indian males as Adonis-like creatures with appearances close to those of the Greek gods and Indian women as lithe and often naked. Art historian William H. Gerdts finds that especially toward midcentury sculptures appeared using "powerful idealization, even erotization, of the Indian brave . . . [with] a conflation of images of the Classical god and the noble savage of Romanticism."[53] Love in the woods and its staying power became ever more popular from the 1830s to midcentury as mountain men and trappers moved onto the frontier. Statistical findings point to the frequency of these liaisons, especially between white men, especially French but also American, and Indian women. Many of these couplings were permanent. The derogatory term *squaw-man* points to the common feature of a couple consisting of a white man and Indian woman.[54]

But continued interest in the captivity narratives and other Americana in the possibilities of white-Indian love, romance, marriage, rape, and illicit sex requires additional explanation. Projections of barbarity and sexual fantasy onto other racial and ethnic groups is not new. Racial fears of mongrelization and

Charles Wimar, The Abduction of Daniel Boone's Daughter *(ca. 1850) Oil on canvas. Collection of E. R. Minshall, Jr., Tulsa, Oklahoma*

other animalistic projections fueled notions of blacks as rapists of white women in the nineteenth century.[55] In a recent study, David K. Shipler charts the sexual fears and fantasies of Israeli Jews in relation to the "violent, craven Arab" and "the primitive exotic Arab." He senses "the specter of seduction" as a major theme of right-wing Jewish forces. Behind such anxieties he senses the fear of "dilution and assimilation."[56]

The possibility of crossing sexual boundaries on the North American frontier was very real. The observations and fantasies of Anglo-American men and women between 1607 and 1870 had to do with ideology, politics, and culture. To cross these boundaries was to enter into a world of forbidden intimacies, whether in fact or in the imagination of the reader or viewer. The lure began early with the drawings and writings of John Smith's adventures and even earlier with the first writings and drawings of the New World. Smith's Elizabethan adventures with Amerindian women are the stuff of continuing folklore and began the tradition of the exotic Indian maiden.[57] The first signs of relationship, both threatening and companionate, for Anglo-American women date to the early Indian wars in New England and to Mary Rowlandson's friendship with Metacomet. Overt brutality and sexuality of Indian men toward white women in captivity literature first appeared in the seventeenth century but became more common in the late eighteenth century. From the early republic to the 1820s we find an occasional coy allusion to women's sexual interest in "others," stories of love affairs and happy marriages with Indians, but also stories of threatening and brutal Indian males. In John Vanderlyn's *Death of Jane McCrea* (ca. 1804), the Indian served as a prototype man-beast who might capture, sexually assault, and murder women on the frontier (see Chapter 4).[58] In the early 1830s, the overland journey narratives like Harris's and Plummer's continued to depict the Indian as a sexual beast. Much iconography of the period presented suffering, battered, and mutilated (tattooed) women as victims of Indian lust and mistreatment. Nineteenth-century captivity materials offered mixed messages for women: excitement, possible romantic bliss, but the chance of sexual harassment. The big, dark Indian was pictured simultaneously as a thrill and a sexual threat to white women and consequently a competitive sexual threat to white men. The erotic power of

Indian men was undercut by some women's accounts of them as dirty and disgusting.

...

110

White

Actors

on a

Field

of Red

White Indians like Tanner and Hunter praised the Indian mother and sister over the Indian wife or sexual partner. Just how noble or ignoble the "savage" male or female was as a mate for a white American was then not predictable. The mixture of the images and literature portray an erotic but also a potentially dangerous, disgusting, or tragic liaison.

There are two other models in the Americas of sexual relationships across racial and cultural lines which should be looked to for comparison with those of Anglo-Americans and Indians in North America. The first comes from the Spanish conquest in Mexico, the second from the African-American experience in North America. Cortés's successful conquest of Mexico was eased by his liaison with Malinche, a Mexican woman renamed by the Spanish, Doña Marina. Traveling with Malinche gave Cortés the convenience of a cultural and linguistic translator as well as the comforts of sexual contact. Malinche later bore him a son. But despite the Catholic presence and practice among his troops, he never honored her with the sacrament of marriage. In *The Labyrinth of Solitude*, the Mexican poet and essayist Octavio Paz finds this relationship between Spanish conquistador and Indian woman a defining one for the history of Mexico. As a result, Mexicans call themselves *hijos de la chingada*, roughly, sons of the fucked one. Out of this mixing of the races, half accepted, half coerced, a new Mexico was born.[59]

Rather than the story of a conqueror with a mistress by his side, the North American materials most usually give us an Indian man running off with a reluctant and terrified white woman. Alternatively, we have a white man taken captive, who from John and James Smith to Hemingway's Nick enjoys sensuous moments of sexual freedom in the woods. The offspring of these unions are rarely discussed as new people of the Americas.[60]

In the African-American example, from the Elizabethan period, Winthrop Jordan has traced the origins in words and images of English disdain for Africans. It manifested itself in a contempt for blackness along with a publicly disguised lust to possess African-American women while projecting onto African-Americans the attributes of perverse sexuality.[61]

Unlike attitudes and practice with African-Americans, captivity materials of Indians do not present a uniform or continuous picture of sexual hatred, fear, and projection. Strains of sexual fear and projection exist. They become more common characterizations of Indian men in the mid- to late nineteenth-century dime novels. Indians are portrayed as rapist/murderers as when Cunning Serpent, with the fainted body of heroine Laura Hautville flung across his shoulder, holds a knife poised near her crotch on the cover of *Moccasin Bill*.[62] There are obvious parallels with the presumption of black men as rapists of pure white women. (Laura as White Lily is a reverse of Lily White.) There is a merger in sexual race hatred of blacks and Indians related to the racial sentiment and theory of the period. Similarly, white women were placed on a pedestal and at risk when black women and Indian women were experiencing sexual abuse at the hands of white males on the plantation and on the frontier. Clearly there was an unwillingness to see who was most at risk from male sexual aggression and who was the aggressor.[63]

To continue with the comparisons and contrasts, African-American images were popular in the same years that Anglo-America made war on American Indians, the same years that Nat Turner, John Brown, and the abolitionist movement worked to free slaves. The fear of "miscegenation" was also used to suppress potential sexual unions between whites and blacks. Daniel Aaron has traced fears of sexual interaction between blacks and whites. He found that the word *miscegenation* was invented in 1863 and first published in a book in 1864 by an anonymous author. In the same period a poem by Morris Thompson called "Voodoo Prophecies" spoke of racial mixing as the "inky curse." White southern defeat especially raised fears and associations of defeat with race mixing.[64] Indian and white competition for land and hegemony was always more equal than black and white competition. A clear defeat and domination of the various native groups was not certain until the late nineteenth century. Although fear of sexual relations with Indians or Indianization alarmed whites, it was not seen as unnatural, as were sexual relations between whites and blacks, which were linked to the creation of "mongrel" races. Forbidden intimacies with Indians were apparently more acceptable for white Americans to

. . .

112

White

Actors

on a

Field

of Red

think about than were those with blacks, and in the first wave of white migration, including the fur trade, they were common. At least reading about Indians of the opposite sex and looking at pictures was not taboo. Through reading and viewing, white Americans of both sexes certainly might rethink who they were and who they might become by choice or by accident.[65] If the Indian was totally brutal and savage, there would be no need to worry about his (or her) sexual appeal, only the force needed for conquest. But if, as in the painting of Wimar's Indian and white woman on horseback, the big Indian of Ives's *Willing Captive*, and John Smith's and other captives' reports, the Indian was noble and erotic, there might be something to worry about. The overtly erotic elements in captivity materials from popular culture and "high" art recognized the power and beauty of the Indian and offered fantasies and possibilities to Anglo-Americans of both sexes.

Alfred Jacob Miller's painting *The Trapper's Bride* (1845) is about the erotic appeal of crossing sexual boundaries. Rather than depicting a situation of capture, a young, handsome trapper sits love-struck at the feet of a shyly beautiful, exotic, and erotic Indian maiden. She is being given away with the blessings of father and chief. The maiden is at the center of the canvas. Light radiates from her buckskin dress as if it were white satin. The two reach out for each other's hands. Others, including a sensuous, partly clad young Indian woman, look on.[66] With Indian men and women like these, there was always the possibility that the sons, like the trapper, would stay in the woods, like never-returning "captives" of their own heart's choice. The daughters might not all be distressed to be a young woman on horseback, riding into the western country with such men, but choose, like Eunice Williams or Mary Jemison, to stay with their Indian husbands. Once the sexual boundary was crossed, a political boundary was crossed as well. The fate of the next American generation, in fact the fate of America's mission on the frontier was at risk.

Part Two

Women in Times
of Change

Part I surveyed a wide range of literature and images of white actors on a field of red. As we move from this broader picture to focus on three white captive women, some words are in order about the shift from general topics to specific cases and the materials and methods employed in the larger quest. After looking at white women, white men, and the world of sexual boundaries in a framework of over 250 years, it is appropriate to examine several cases in more detail. The three women chosen are highly popular, published, or represented figures. Jane McCrea appeared in paintings, lithographs, etchings, plays, fictionalized accounts, and a myriad of local and national histories. Mary Jemison's story found its way into more than twenty reprintings, into children's books, plays, and as a statue in a state park. Sarah Wakefield did not become a national or local heroine, but her book was issued in two editions and her story was well known in Minnesota. Her actions and views were not well received, and her history after capture largely disappeared from the public record. These factors make her case merit further consideration.

The cases chosen do not represent unequivocally the prototypes laid out in Chapter 1. Nor do they fit neatly into the three periods designated as helping to explain the transformations of the captive story. Jane McCrea's story extends from her life in the revolutionary period to her legend, which persists to the present day but was memorialized in the nineteenth century. Mary Jemison lived nearly a century, from the 1740s to the 1830s. Her life, too, was the subject of legends and folklore in both the nineteenth and twentieth centuries. Wakefield's story fits squarely into the mid- to late nineteenth century, but its implications are still with us. The categories of Survivors, Amazons, and Frail Flowers, like any typology, have both explanatory power and limits. With greater depth and under closer scrutiny, categories often lose their simplicity—human life and the legends we create around them are more complex.

Examining these three captives makes it possible to observe the dynamics of gender and ethnicity at closer range. It enables movement from how the white culture constructed and reconstructed captive stories to an attempt to uncover more accurate accounts, along with a deeper understanding of particular women's experiences across cultures. In the case of Jane McCrea (Chapter 4), the "real" story appears so hopelessly embedded in retelling and reimagining that I have left the "historic" Jane behind to focus on Jane the cultural construction. For Mary Jemison (Chapter 5) I first trace the remaking of her story through James Seaver's narrative and its subsequent editions, then inquire into her life cycle as a woman, and finally, her life as a Seneca woman. The three facets together bring us closer to the real Jemison along with a sense of the missed opportunities for Indian and white relations which her story represents.

An artist must choose materials carefully before painting a canvas. So must a historian. In each era greater or fewer are available from which to choose. These in turn force the writer's hand or lure the scholar off in a variety of directions and ultimately shape the work. In answering the questions of longevity, power, and popularity of the captive story and in trying to discover the connections between gender and ethnicity, the exploration of sources in this section moves from the cultural, to the ethnographic, and finally to social and political history. Geographically, I have chosen a Turnerian path, beginning due west of New England on the upper Hudson during the revolutionary era, into Pennsylvania, the Appalachian and Ohio country, and into central and western New York. With Sarah Wakefield (Chapter 6), the focus becomes the Minnesota frontier in the first years of the Civil War. In all three cases, women are at the center. Although both men and women were the subjects of captivity and captivity stories, these three women point to the power of the woman's story, especially in the nineteenth century. In the last two cases, women and their children are constantly in view—white fiancés, fathers, and husbands recede in importance, and Indian men move into central roles. In these nineteenth-century renderings, what women do determines a small part of the national fate. The woman captive's story is an American counterpart of the diva's in Italian opera. It is the woman at the center for whom we feel and with whom we suffer. But ultimately, in this American medium, she provides a clearer view of both Indian and Anglo-American life.

Jane McCrea and the American Revolution

Jane McCrea's is a strange story. In 1777 a young orphaned daughter of a Presbyterian minister was living with her prorevolutionary brother John in Argyle, on the upper Hudson near present-day Glens Falls, New York. There she met and fell in love with David Jones, a loyalist. In the midst of their courtship and in the growing turmoil of the Revolution, Jones left for Canada to become an officer in General John Burgoyne's army. Not wishing to leave his beloved behind, he forged a plan whereby the two would meet and marry when Burgoyne's troops came down through the Hudson Valley. Jane never made it to her lover's arms. According to American legend and popular history, while en route from Fort Edward she was captured, scalped, and killed by Indians allied with British forces. General Horatio Gates used the story of her capture and death and her alleged scalping and murder to drum up support among New Yorkers and New Englanders for the revolutionary cause at Saratoga. When the result was a victory for the rebel side and the turning point in the war, a woman who had run off with a Tory soldier was transformed into a martyred revolutionary heroine.

So much for the facts of the story, many of which remain in dispute to this day. Since 1777, McCrea's misfortunes have appeared in poem, song, play, newspaper account, dedication and rededication at centennial and bicentennial events, in paintings and etchings by John Vanderlyn, Asher B. Durand, and Nathaniel Currier, and on a battle monument relief at Saratoga. She was recently reburied, complete with a rededicated tombstone. The variety and longevity of her story's popularity point to a cultural obsession with the role of women and independence in the early years of the republic. The story of Jane McCrea (ca. 1752–77) was well known in her day and into the nineteenth century. It was "an event which drew tears from every eye" and a "tragedy" that "at once drew the attention of all America." One writer claimed that it was "familiar to all readers of American history." Others said it was well known in Europe and "celebrated wherever the English language is spoken." Early republican bard Joel Barlow called for "Eternal ages" to "trace it with a tear." For over a century its dramatic impact and patriotic function were widely recognized. An officer in Burgoyne's army wrote that Jane's murder upset the general's forces. Some said that her capture and murder contributed to the flight of settlers in the Hudson Valley and the mass mustering of New England and New York troops against the British.[1]

The political and propaganda function of McCrea's death was evident to Generals Horatio Gates and George Washington, both of whom cited it to remind New Yorkers and New Englanders that the British could not be trusted. The revolutionary papers spread word of the murder even before the young woman's name was known.[2] Until the 1970s almost every writer born in the United States who wrote about it interpreted McCrea's story as evidence of the political and military misuse of power by John Burgoyne's Indian allies and an act of English duplicity, if not stupidity.[3] The message was that Englishmen would not protect even their own. To follow their lead would be to put one's life and the lives of one's family in danger. Burgoyne had told his Indian allies of the complex set of loyalties of upstate New Yorkers, many of whom were on his side. He warned these Indians to be careful not to hurt friends of the British cause. But the stories of the Allen family, members of whom were killed the day before Jane in the same neighborhood, and of Jane herself demonstrated that the word of Burgoyne held no power over "his" Indians.[4] The murders inflamed northern colonial men and solidified an otherwise divided northeastern New York behind the revolutionary cause. At the Saratoga battlefield in October 1777, the tide of the war was turned with a colossal and humiliating British defeat. According to some, the name of Jane McCrea was on many a patriot's lips going into battle. Saratoga assured McCrea's place in the revolutionary pantheon.

One hundred years after her death, a Washington County, New York, historian noted that the power of the story did not lie in Jane's murder: "Thousands of men, women, and children have been massacred during the wars between the Indians and the colonists, thousands more during the old French wars, and still other thousands during the Revolution and subsequent conflicts, but not another case among them all has attracted so much attention as that of lovely Jane McCrea." He attributed the import and popularity of her story to "the youth, beauty, and social position of the victim" and even more to "the romance that mingled with the tragedy."[5] Her first biographer, David Wilson, bemoaned the increasing search for the truth of her story by writers who, "as if to atone for the errors of their predecessors, have endeavored to divest the story of all that romantic interest which actually belongs to it."[6]

Two interpretations have predominated from the eighteenth century to the present; the first is political and patriotic, the second is cultural, related to sentiment and romance. Jane is a folk heroine. Her story involves issues of politics and culture. The cultural interpretation of the McCrea story's popularity stated first by David Wilson and Chrisfield Johnson has been updated by Jay Fliegelman. Like Michael Kammen, Fliegelman sees the Revolution as a cultural turning point and recognizes how the rebellion of a youthful set of colonies against an aging monarchy functioned as a vital piece in the cultural and psychodynamic picture. Fliegelman calls McCrea "the new nation's first folk heroine." Jane, dressed for her marriage vows, lay dead at the hands of villains. "Here was the great scene of sentimental fiction horribly come alive." Burgoyne was "the tyrannical parent sending his ferocious minister to deny his child, his loyal Tory child, the sacred nuptial rites."[7] But a third position, which I will present, is based on politics and culture as they relate to gender. The perpetuation of the story reflects the persistence of ambivalent attitudes toward women's independence.

Female independence in the McCrea story has three aspects. First, the narrative is a discourse on female choice. In the era of republicanism, following a war in which women were forced to assume positions of independence, the story raises questions about the perils of granting them wider freedom. How would young women of the emerging nation make use of the independence of mate choice available to them, and what would be the potential impact of this freedom on the social and political body?[8] Second, it is a study of a young woman whose fate was determined by powerful men, and other female figures are either absent or of dubious merit. There is an especially negative attitude toward older women and their role in helping young women as they enter marriage, their most important rite of passage in the late eighteenth to late nineteenth centuries. Again, women's decision-making abilities come into question. Third, McCrea's story is highly sexualized. Her struggle to determine her sexual fate occurred in an arena in which her body was the prize; she ultimately had no control over the contest. Men representing a variety of ethnic and political positions— patriot, loyalist, American, British, or Indian—did battle over her. The message reinforces the notion that women in the face of violence are defenseless in controlling their own bodies and therefore unable to make the correct choices as to what to do with their lives. They must depend on and put their faith in white male protection and are at the mercy of "savages" when that protection fails them.

Jane's Choice

. . . . . .

The alleged decisions Jane McCrea made continued to be noteworthy subjects of history, literature, and art between 1780 and 1930. A late eighteenth-century novel, a nineteenth-century biography, and an early twentieth-century play questioned Jane's choice. Historians have characterized the late eighteenth and early nineteenth centuries as a time of transition from an agrarian to a more industrial age. A variety of long-term changes were creating new roles for women. The Revolution forced autonomy on women of all ages and classes while husbands, fathers, and brothers were away at war. Demographically, there were a higher proportion of white women to men in the population than in the colonial period. In the Northeast, there was beginning to be a percentage of women who did not marry and women who in substantial numbers were limiting their family size. In an examination of adolescence in this period, John Demos argues that the transition to adulthood "became increasingly disjunctive and problematic." For males it involved student unrest and even rioting on several campuses, economic fears, questions of religious conversion, dependence, and independence. The recent "factor of *choice*" gave young men and women greater power over who would be lovers and future mates.[9] For women such an exercise of autonomy virtually determined their destiny, but personal choices were also social ones that could determine the nature of the American family and, by extension, the new nation itself.

Jane McCrea's story is one of female independence in the realm of love, but it is a story of female independence run amok—a story in which independence is ultimately punished and female freedom is seen as an example of *mis*choice at a critical time both in her life and the emerging republic's. According to most renditions, Jane deliberately did not go with her brother's family to fight for the rebel cause but chose instead her lover, David, and thus the Tory side. The fiction, histories, and biographies of Jane give mixed messages regarding her decision to desert her patriot brother (or father) for her loyalist lover. In Michel René Hilliard-d'Auberteuil's patriotic novel *Miss McCrea: A Novel of the American Revolution* (1784), Jane is a bad daughter, her choice both unfilial and unpatriotic. The title page of the novel's first edition claims that it was published in Philadelphia in 1784, but the first edition was probably published in Brussels; the second was Continental as well. According to Lewis Leary, "*Miss McCrea* is the first book-length prose narrative to deal wholly with a national American incident and with America as the entire scene of action." Its French republican writer visited America during the Revolution and may have been at Fort Edward when Burgoyne and his forces were marching south.[10] As the novel opens, Jane McCrea is living in Manhattan, the dutiful daughter of a patriot father. The Revolution is on and troops stationed on the island become engaged in fighting. An English officer, Captain Belton, is injured. (Hilliard changed David Jones's name to Captain Belton and his native land to England.)[11] Jane comes to his aid, nurses him, falls in love, and is immediately at odds with her patriot father, Nathaniel McCrea. (Reverend James McCrea, Jane's actual father, died in 1769, eight years before.)

> In her eagerness [to help Belton] she did not wait for the return of her servant to fetch the necessary bandages, but tore in pieces the kerchief that covered her fair bosom, which had been heaving violently for some moments. Belton opened his eyes and saw her in this charming disarray. Her eyes met his, she became disconcerted, her hand trembled, she could not finish. He fell at her feet; respect, gratitude, and love overwhelmed all his senses. Jane raised him up and was supporting this dangerous enemy's head on her breast in order to bandage his wound, when Nathaniel McCrea, her father, entered the room.[12]

Father McCrea is shocked at his daughter's behavior and lack of political understanding. " 'Jane, what is this I see?' he cried. 'Has not the horror which the soldiers of George III, instruments of our enslavement, should inspire been able to suppress in your heart the sentiment of mercy? Come to my arms daughter.' " McCrea, a trader with land on the Hudson, is planning to leave New York as soon as possible, and he urges Jane to hurry and run from the "vile agents of European tyranny." When Belton tells the father he is there to serve his king, Nathaniel replies with anger: " 'You renounce man's most precious rights, liberty and justice; and you want to make us slaves like you! Permit me—permit me to save my daughter, or take my life!' " After Belton leaves, the father remains distressed; "liberty, oppression, and natural rights occupied his thoughts." When Jane tells him she wants to marry the man, and Belton's politics do not

change, he forbids his daughter to see him. But it is too late—
"love had spoken." [13]

After the father and daughter move to the upper Hudson,
father McCrea decides to join the patriot cause to the south. He
mobilizes three hundred men and says good-bye to his daughter, asking her to promise to "renounce the mother country forever," boycott its products, and not deal with or marry anyone
who wished to remain a British subject. Jane refuses, saying,
" 'Alas, father, . . . I love Belton.' " Even worse, she holds Belton
up as a symbol of those qualities her father has taught her to
admire and repudiates the Revolution and the ideal of American independence. " 'I find in him the model of virtues that you
taught me to desire in the one who would be my husband. . . .
Ah, father, if you had seen him commanding his troops, you
would have been convinced that the English are bound to triumph over us. . . . Give up, father, give up an unfortunate
rebellion.' " Her words send her father into shock, dismay, and
tears, but he recovers, grabs "his saber and rifle," and goes off
to rejoin his men. [14]

The first part of the novel shows a clear conflict between
father and daughter over the choice of a suitor. Unlike *Clarissa*,
the romantic and popular eighteenth-century English novel by
Samuel Richardson in which a father's unjust demands inter-
fere with true love, Jane renounces all that is sacred for an
unworthy man. For her own "selfish" independence, she even
renounces political liberty. As the novel moves on, the daughter
continues her independent course. Jane again unsuccessfully
seeks her father's approval for the marriage and then leaves to
find Belton with the help of her servant Betsy. Belton (Jones)
turns out to be a scoundrel, an aristocratic Englishman of the
worst type. He has fine manners and style but at heart is no
good. In his brief return to England, he seduced and abandoned
a young English girl, Emilia Fairlove, who has followed him to
North America and is found by Jane wandering in the woods
in a wretched state of collapse. Jane nurses her back to health.
Despite discovering the cause of the woman's misery, she continues to look for Belton. When they meet, he cares for her not
at all but in "his senses relished her voluptuousness" and tries to
seduce her. Jane fights to preserve her honor but, blinded by love

and willing to believe him, sets herself up to become a victim of a ghastly murder. She has betrayed father and country for a no-good Tory. The message is that pretty women, even smart ones, cannot be trusted by the revolutionary generation. Their actions and alliances are unpredictable, unreasoned, destabilizing, and dangerous to the republic.[15]

Unlike the French novelist Hilliard-d'Auberteuil, historians and writers on this side of the Atlantic disagreed with Jones's politics, but few would criticize his character or potential devotion to Jane. One poet proclaimed that Jane's "lover's heart was true / True he was; nor did forget, / As he marched the wild woods through."[16]

The attempt to view Jane more sympathetically and David more gallantly coincided with the rise in popularity in the new republic of sentimental fiction (roughly between 1820 and 1850) and its merging with historical fiction and, indeed, with history. This shift from the political arena, in which women were presumed deficient, to the private sphere where, at least in the nineteenth-century middle-class world, they had more control, allowed for the recasting of Jane as a romantic heroine. The McCrea story fills several bills here by combining patriotism, romance, the popular captivity genre, and made-to-order savages. One such version lauds Jane's choice of David. When David asked her to leave with him, "Far from discrediting the sincerity of him who could not deceive her, she heroically refused to follow the flying [patriot] villagers [to New England]. . . . It was enough her lover was her friend. She considered herself protected by the love and voluntary assurances of her youthful hero."[17] Here Jane's choice is correct. The blame for her fate is clear from the book's title, *Indian Atrocities!*. This short mid-nineteenth-century version of the McCrea story contains the seeds of a shift toward a greater trust of woman's choices but also the notion that female choice alone is not the decisive force against life's vicissitudes.

The Life of Jane McCrea, with an Account of Burgoyne's Expedition in 1777 (1853), a biography by David Wilson, finds Jones not only interested in a wedding and loyal to the end but, after her death, despondent for the rest of his life. Rather than seeing her choice of Jones as a foolish one, Wilson found it natural. He traced their growing affection. Their common childhood friendship in New Jersey continued and matured once both families settled on the Hudson. Later testimonials to Jones's faithfulness indicated that Jane was not stupid but (understandably) in love and caught in a dilemma. From Wilson's perspective, although Jones and his family were "conspicuous tories," Jones was a reasonable choice for Jane's future mate. David Jones was a man "well calculated to attract attention. Besides a handsome and manly form, he possessed an easy affability and grace of manner." Jane herself was no fool but was more privileged and knowledgeable than most women of her day. She was "a young lady of fine accomplishments, great personal attraction, and remarkable sweetness of disposition." Her father's library and "devotion to literary pursuits" gave her "the means of gratifying a natural taste for reading, not enjoyed by many of her age in those early times." She was held in high regard and was "spoken of in the language of admiration." But Jane was a filial daughter from the start. Her brother John, a patriot land speculator, would not tolerate a Tory courting his sister. Jane's independence became the center of a growing family feud.[18]

Wilson's biography was a combination of historical fact and romantic fiction. But his message was more sentimental than historical: Jane's (rightful) emotion in her woman's heart was stronger than reason. Although no letters between the two are extant, Wilson says that when Jones joined Burgoyne's armies and headed south toward Fort Edward, love letters flowed to her. One alleged letter in particular arrived. Wilson tells us that, though no such note survives, Mrs. Sarah McNeil (whose story he otherwise discounts) was a source of accurate information, and through her "the substance of its contents has been preserved."[19] The author takes care of the rest, dating it July 11, 1777.

Dear Jenny, I do not forget you, though much there is to distract in these days, and hope I am remembered by you as formerly. In a few days we march to Ft Edward, for which I am anxious, where I shall have the happiness to meet you, after long absence. I hear . . . that the people on the river are moving to Albany. I hope if your brother John goes, you will not go with him, but stay at Mrs. McNeils. . . . There I will join you. My dear Jenny, these are sad times, but I think the war will end this year, as the rebels cannot hold out and will see their error. . . . Believe me yours aff'tly till death.

DAVID JONES[20]

As British troops were about to descend, John and other Whig families readied to escape. For Jane, "there was a contest between duty and affection," but she was ultimately drawn to the "long, sweet dream of her youth." Jane, "unexpectedly placed" in a dilemma and overly "confiding" in the first place, is finally "distracted." She does not make a conscious choice but, like a true sentimental heroine, is swept away by emotion.[21] She is a lovely, charming, but rather weak character, a woman torn between two loyalties who exercises her independence in an indirect way and seals her own fate in a state of distraction during her nation's most dramatic moment. Jane's choice is for love, which leads to her doom.

Wilson's work is a testimonial of ambivalence toward Jane's independence. Romantically she is not wrong to go with Jones, but politically she makes an unpardonable move; the Indians do the rest. From Wilson's sentimentally Whiggish perspective, her martyr's death rallies the American forces and makes independence for the nation a possibility. "Indeed, it would seem that Providence had selected the betrothed maiden on the shore of the Hudson, as a sacrifice to the drooping spirit of Liberty."[22] Balancing romance and patriotism, Wilson turns Jane's understandable mischoice into a precondition for revolutionary victory, thus softening the havoc and betrayal suggested by the earlier interpretation by Hilliard-d'Auberteuil. By first presuming the woman's "natural" propensity to think with her heart but ultimately minimizing the intelligence of that romantic choice, Wilson produces a tragic romantic heroine.

Even 150 years after the death of Jane McCrea, the legend of the tragically martyred romantic heroine persisted. Philip Henry Carroll's play *Jane McCrea: A Tragedy in Five Acts* (1927) was written and presented as part of the Jane McCrea Sesquicentennial Celebration in the Saratoga area. In this production the conflict over the young woman's choice is between John, a patriotic older brother, and Jane, a younger sister, whose patriotism is far from secure. As in Hilliard-d'Auberteuil's version, David Jones, although not a romantic villain, serves as the fall guy for deceptive and unpatriotic behavior.[23] His love for Jane is true, but she is still faulted for bad judgment in leaving her patriotic brother and thus putting herself in harm's way, even if the outcome is nationalistic martyrdom. Carroll uses Wilson's themes of family feud and Jane's dilemma, but it is her brother John who is the mainstay of the play's action. When there is conflict between David and John, David is told to leave. Jane disagrees with her brother's actions, but all she can do is to follow stage directions and drop *"to her knees."* For the moment she abides by her older brother's wishes, saying "sadly" (according to the script's directions) "Good-bye, good-bye David." John tries to make plain the important lesson about David, saying "(*with dignity*). A man who is false to his country cannot be true to any girl." [24] Jane drops to her knees again and prays for peace.

As Burgoyne's armies approach, John forbids his sister to stay in Sarah McNeil's Tory household. When a shouting match ensues, McNeil says she will stay with her, but John says no, "She will go home with me." Jane, rather than asserting her wishes, is passive. The stage notes say she *"is nervous and sad"* and add, *"What will she do? A sweet girl struggling between love and duty."* Carroll's play shows David Jones to be, if politically marred, nonetheless a true love, but the play shows a woman in a difficult position who lacks inner direction. While Jane prays, sighs, and kneels, John acts. He assumes a patriarchal and custodial role. He objects to his sister's intent to marry and calls her "A coward bride!" He threatens to commit suicide if Jane goes off with Jones. Ashamed of his threat, he relents, rededicating his life to his country.[25] As in the earlier versions of the story, Jane's disregard for a man of the family's wishes is unpatriotic, causes everyone trouble, and leads to her own demise.

In the nearly 150 years of writing about Jane McCrea, the authors of major and minor fictional and historical versions of her story have seemed uncomfortable with the choice she made. In Hilliard-d'Auberteuil's novel, she picks a man portrayed as both politically and morally bankrupt. In Wilson's biography, she is in a family dilemma but accepts the call of romance, which brings her to a tragic end. In Carroll's play, she is a weak second best to a patriotic brother whom she should have followed if she were smart and wanted to stay out of trouble.

Among the molders of culture these and other works indicate uncertainty about a woman's independent use of choice in both the public and private realms. This popular but ambiguous heroine of the Revolution can do hardly anything right.

The Other Women

. . . . . .

The novels, plays, and histories that tell Jane McCrea's story are dominated by forceful military figures like Gentleman Johnny Burgoyne and General Horatio Gates, patriotic ones like her brother John McCrea and her father, devoted ones like David Jones, and vicious ones like the Indian Wyandott Panther. In both earlier and later versions of her story, Jane is a backdrop to the strong military figures of Gates and Burgoyne and the hideous "savage" figures of Indians. With the exception of Wilson's romantic biography, in their portrayals of the Revolution writers seem unwilling to place a female figure at center stage. They are uncertain about how much visibility women deserve. As late as Philip Henry Carroll's play (1927), John McCrea rather than Jane is the centerpiece. Jane's death is not the important moment of the play; the climax is a duel between John McCrea and David Jones at Saratoga.[26]

If Jane is an uncertain leading figure among men, in various forms of the printed legend other women play an even lesser role. In the historical record, her mother, Mary Graham McCrea, died in 1753 when Jane was in her first years. She was of Scottish descent and came to America at age seventeen. She married Reverend James McCrea, also from Scotland and a former resident of northern Ireland. They had seven children, Jane being one of two daughters. Her name is not even mentioned in most of the general histories, although many discuss the lives of James and John McCrea at length.[27]

Two other women are present in the written accounts: David Jones's mother, known as the "widow Jones," and Mrs. Campbell, remarried and also called Mrs. McNeil. In the McCrea accounts, both women are without husbands.[28] Even the names of these women are vague; one cannot find first or maiden names without combing the records. The parts these women are given to play lend additional evidence to the case that the McCrea story demonstrates uncertainty about women's independent role in the early republic.

The widow Jones is the mother of six Jones sons who amassed a large and profitable share of Hudson Valley land. And yet in the accounts in which she appears, the widow Jones is a somewhat shadowy figure whose main part in the McCrea-Jones liaison is to provide a stopover for Jane on her way to Mrs. Campbell/McNeil and, in one account, to provide a dressing room for Jane as she attires herself in her bridal robes on the way to meet her betrothed. According to local lore, "his mother must have conveyed word to Miss McCrea, to come to her house that night, prepared to go to the camp the next day." Then she "passed from Mrs. Jones' to Mrs. Campbell's above the Fort, in which a small body of American troops remained."[29]

Sarah Fraser Campbell/McNeil's role is more complex, but like the widow Jones, she is the head of a loyalist home. Both homes are places where Jane can meet with and wait for David. They serve as potential training grounds from which she might join the loyalist side. Neither woman is given much importance or credence as a serious villain like Burgoyne or the Indians, but both women are on the wrong side, by implication the womanish side—the side of the crown. In widow Jones's case, this is demonstrated by her raising loyalist sons instead of republican ones. In Wolfgang Amadeus Mozart's *Magic Flute* (1791) Pamina is taken away from her mother, the Queen of the Night. When her savior Tamino wins his beloved, they live in the halls of the patriarchal kingdom. As in Jane's case, older, motherly women are not to be trusted and various Queens of the Night are dangerous characters. The young woman must be won by the appropriate male; the nubile maiden, like Persephone, must leave the world of the mothers.[30] Here, in a contemporary female rite of passage, the young woman is assisted by two older women; the outcome suggests that women do not give right direction. Such a profoundly rebellious act with the assistance from women indicates female complicity and alliance with the antirevolutionary forces.

In the story of McCrea's capture by Indians, Sarah Campbell (McNeil) plays a more central role, for she also is captured. But she could not protect Jane, nor could she save her. She is depicted as a comic character, a fat blabbermouth whose word cannot be taken seriously. Nineteenth-century accounts call her a bright, well-traveled woman of means, who "was more re-

markable perhaps for extreme corpulency, than for any particular characteristic." According to one popular version of the capture, while Jane and she were waiting for news from David Jones, the two women heard Indians and ran for the cellar, "the former being aged and very corpulent, and the latter young and agile, Jenny reached the trap-door first."[31] Some accounts have Campbell being captured by being pulled out of a cellar by her hair.[32] The Indians then dragged out Jane. Mary Gillespie Bain, only seven at the time and living three miles from the Allen house, talked to Asa Fitch some sixty years after the event and claimed to recall Sarah Campbell's words: "I have heard her [say] she was in bed when the alarm was given, lieing there with nothing on but her *chamise*. She jumped through the trap door into the cellar with Miss McCrea. . . . And I will give you her very expression, with regard to being taken out of the cellar. Said 'Big and heavy as my arse is, my hair was stout enough to sustain the weight—' meaning she was lifted out by the hair of her head."[33]

They then tried to place the older woman onto a horse, but she "was too heavy to be lifted on the horse easily." She was just too "fleshy and heavy." According to one county historian, she was so fat that when the Indians put her on a horse she fell off. In an account told some years later to Asa Fitch, Robert Blake said Indians grabbed the woman's arms: "Mrs. McNeil did not ride. I have repeatedly heard her tell how the Indian hold of her arms made her run, they running like gray-hounds, & dragging her along, & that she was tired all but to death ere she got to the camp."[34]

Along with providing comic relief by being fat and unwieldy, McNeil appears to have had trouble keeping her clothes on. In accounts in which Jane is allegedly stripped it is a clear violation, but in the case of Mrs. McNeil it is a joke. As the stories go, Jane was taken by one set of Indians, while McNeil, being unable to mount a horse, walked and ran alongside another group of Indians. She was "stripped by her captors" and was in a "half-denuded state" when she came into the British camp. There she was delivered to her cousin, General Simon Fraser, "in a state of perfect nudity with the exception of her *chamise*." Fraser "was much perplexed and embarrassed to provide a suitable robe for so corpulent a lady."[35] And so "the ladies in camp ransacked their baggage, but among the wardrobes of them all, there was not a gown of sufficient vast dimensions to inclose her expansive figure. She was under the necessity, therefore, of using the general's camp coat for a garment, and his pocket handkerchief as a substitute for a cap."[36]

Besides the historic figures, which are minimized and trivialized, writer Hilliard-d'Auberteuil, in his novel *Miss McCrea*, finds two women of different ethnic origins on which to blame some of the maid's problems. One is Betsy, an Irish woman and former criminal who had been shipped to America. At some point she slips a note to Belton (Jones) telling him that the McCrea family has money and offering to help "bring about your marriage" for financial gain. Later, when Jane plans a rendezvous with Belton, debating whether to leave her father, "the pitiless Betsy kept watch, and she tore her from her swooning father's arms. All was in readiness, and Betsy, followed by a valet whom she had employed in Belton's interest, set the horses into a gallop toward Burgoyne's army."[37]

The second unsavory, non-Anglo-Saxon woman is a "Jewess," in whose home Jane and Belton were to have their illicit meeting. "There in the center of a dense forest on the side of the hill, Rachel Rideworld, weary of moving in fashionable society where she had been known for her love affairs, had chosen her retreat. . . . An old friend of Betsy's, Rachel was industrious and thrifty, but the influences of vices acquired in her girlhood could still overcome her at the age of fifty."[38]

This is almost the entire cast of female characters in more than 150 years of writing. Very little positive is said about any of these figures. In the McCrea legend, the roles of other women in the creation of the republic and the ushering of young women through their important rites of passage is either destructive or insignificant. In the era following the Revolution, as Linda Kerber tells us, republican ideology cast women in the roles of republican mothers, whose main responsibility was to raise republican sons.[39] Presumably, such mothers would give right direction to daughters, who in turn would become republican mothers. A part of the McCrea legend, then, not only uses the captive theme to point out Indian savagery and to denigrate one young woman's independent decision making, but also cautions both daughters and mothers to look to patriotic male authority in matters of both love and politics. By questioning the roles of these auxiliary women involved in McCrea's fate, the writers of history and literature covertly question the extension of rights for women as open to misuse by unpatriotic or frivolous females. In these tales, capture and murder by Indians are only the final, if tragic, implication of too much female independence.

Jane's Body/Jane's Hair

. . . . . .

Not only do Jane's ambiguous choice and a strong contingent of men with a dubious contingent of women hover over the McCrea legacy, but the body and hair of McCrea are powerful centers of violence in visual and written materials. As early as the year following her death, in a poem titled "A Tragical Death of Miss Jane M'Crea," Reverend Wheeler Case imagined himself walking along a New York road and discovering McCrea's body, "struggling there with death," a "cursed *Indian* knife" in her scalp. The poem leaves little to the imagination— her body with blood "gushing forth from all her veins," "her scalp torn from her head." The poet asks, "Is this that blooming fair? Is this McCrea? / This was appointed for her nuptial day . . . / "Oh, cruel savages! What hearts of steel! / O cruel Britons! who no pity feel!" In Joel Barlow's *Columbiad* (1807), after the defeat at Saratoga, her lover runs "Swift thro the wood paths frenetic springs" calling her name while Mohawks "Drive the descending ax" through her face. His contemporary Philip Freneau (1809) seals the image of the maiden "all breathless, cold and pale, / Drenched in her gore."[40]

It is no surprise to find Indians the bloody means by which Jane's body is mutilated. Which Indians are to blame is not at all clear. Early republican poets define them only as "cruel Indians," "wildmen," "skulkers," "kindred cannibals," "yelling fiends," who "Howl" and "Scalp."[41] Some accounts feature Winnebagos, others say the Saint Regis tribe of Mohawks, a recent account includes these along with "Ottawas, Chippewas, and Menominies." Wyandots (Hurons) are also popular. Some merely say Canadian Indians or western Canadian Indians, while most just speak of "Indians."[42]

Indians play the role of abductors, rapists, scalpers, and murderers in nearly all the written accounts. In the artistic renderings, one after another shows Jane's body pulled, dragged, or thrown from horseback and pushed to the ground by two or more Indians. It appears that they often take turns stabbing or mutilating her with knives and tomahawks. Some of these are paintings on canvas, others, like John Warner Barber's *Murder of Miss McCrea* (1847) and Robert Sears's *Murder of Miss Jane McCrea* (1847) come from etchings in history books. These popular representations contrast Jane's body—young, white, female, innocent, and unprotected—against those of dark, violent, Indian "savages." Each works as a reminder of enemy brutality, female weakness, and the need to restrict women's choice for their own good. Jane is almost always alone and unprotected. Asher B. Durand's *Murder of Miss McCrea* (1839) indicates members of the other party, but they are in the distance, unable to help. Usually Jane is at the mercy of "savages."[43]

In critic Samuel Y. Edgerton's analysis, a variety of visual works about McCrea note the frequency of "poor, pitiable, vainly imploring Jane with her head thrown back and arms outstretched" embodying "the tradition of shrinking Victorian womanhood," along with a "formula" with "racial overtones" which shows "villainous Indians" pulling Jane's hair on either side. "The popularity of this image persisted despite the facts —and even legends—which stated that many Indians were present and that the girl was first shot dead while seated on her horse."[44]

Visual representations of Jane McCrea highlight her hair and the violent domination of her body. John Vanderlyn's famous painting *Death of Jane McCrea* (ca. 1804) is a classic depiction of Indian horror wreaked upon white womanhood. Shocking and striking in its day, it was originally commissioned by Connecticut poet Joel Barlow for a set of illustrations to his epic poem *The Columbiad*. Vanderlyn (1775–1852) was a member of a Dutch family of artists and limners working along the Hudson. He was a recognized American artist and studied with various neoclassical masters on the Continent. At the time of his

John Vanderlyn, Death of Jane McCrea *(ca. 1804) Oil on
canvas. Courtesy of the Wadsworth Atheneum, Hartford,
Connecticut*

McCrea commission, he was in Paris. The painting, which he
called "the Picture of the Mohawks," was his first attempt at historical painting and combined contemporary European artistic
styles with a home-grown American theme—Indian captivity.[45]
According to William T. Oedel, Vanderlyn "was America's fore-
most neoclassical painter." Born at the time when America was
looking "for a monumental and specifically American art" to
"create a national mythology" and "express the uniqueness of

the American experience," Vanderlyn in his painting depicted a frontier woman frustrated by the designs of evil Indians.[46] The painting "won academic approval" and was "the first indigenous American history piece ever accepted."[47] Thus in the new nation the McCrea story provided both the first fictional work and one of the first major works of art. According to Richard Drinnon, the painting "set the pattern for an endless series of pictorial indictments of Jefferson's 'merciless Indian Savages.' Always the epic contrast was between dusky evil and fair innocence, between maddened red cruelty and helpless white virtue."[48]

Besides the propaganda effect and the use of good and evil prototypes, it is worth further examining the image of a white woman assaulted by Indians for the ethnic and gendered messages transmitted. In *Death of Jane McCrea*, Jane is on one knee, while an Indian pulls on her right arm. He holds a tomahawk in his hand in order to scalp her, while Jane's left arm tries to remove a second Indian's grip from her long, light brown hair. This Indian also carries a tomahawk. The focus of the painting, because of Jane's pale skin and her clothes compared to the darkness of the Indians, is on Jane, especially her breasts and face, but also her hair. As he pulls her hair, the Indian's arm creates a line from his shoulder to her hair, bringing the viewer's focus directly to that point. Jane's left arm reaches up to loosen his grip.[49]

Jane's hair is light brown with glinting blond highlights. In her kneeling posture, it nearly brushes the forest floor. Along with her breasts, it is her most feminine, exposed, and vulnerable feature. The Indian's clasp on her hair serves to imprison her. It is by this feature of her sexuality that the Indian enemy binds her and seals her doom. Here she is depicted as a large woman with strong arms and ample legs. She is nonetheless overwhelmed. Her hair becomes a snare; its power attracts the "savage" and entraps her. Because of it she is rendered helpless. Her hair becomes a trophy and a symbol of evil Indian male power over good white women, the most lovely, most cherished members of the colonizing society.

When the painting is viewed from a distance, the attack dominates. The arms of the two Indians set up a nearly parallel track of light in the forest. Behind the three figures, serving as a contrasting backdrop, is a huge dark tree. Jane is not passive. Though a victim, there is tension in both her arms; one being pulled from her to bare her chest, the other trying to loose the hand pulling her hair. The faces and figures overwhelm the viewer. Jane's face is filled with terror—she, a sacrifice, is a strange dramatic reworking of Abraham's attempt to sacrifice Isaac, with no God intervening. The Indians are vicious; their bodies, according to one critic, are "reminiscent of Hellenistic sculpture."[50] Both men are naked above the waist. Jane is kneeling, and her ample thighs ground her. But she is under attack. The nipple of her right breast is exposed. Her ripped bodice frames it in white lace and slate-blue satin.

But immediate retaliation is not to be. A white male coming to the rescue is a dark figure about one and a half inches high— about half the size of the Indian's upper arm from elbow to shoulder—a thin, almost invisible figure. Is it David Jones? A British officer? The only red clothing indicating a possible British presence is a tiny plume on the man's hat. He is carrying a gun but appears more like a pixie in the woods than a rescuing hero—certainly not a Boone-like figure and certainly too little and too late. Vanderlyn's iconographic rendering martyred Jane publicly. His work signals graphically the dangers to white women on the frontier; it cries out for retaliation. Jane symbolizes the white woman of her era, a potential mother of the new republic. Her gown is a variation on red (more like rose), white, and blue.[51] Her fiancé (if it is him) presents an American (or perhaps a European) manhood impotent before the tides of savagism and darkness. The images in Vanderlyn, Durand, and other popular lithographs and etchings of McCrea conjure up the *Rape of Europa*, the *Rape of the Sabine Women*, and other classical and neoclassical favorites of ravished womanhood subdued by sexual force during moments of cultural and national struggle.

A more recent presentation of bodily violence toward McCrea appears in an oil painting by F. C. Yohn called *Capture of Jane McCrea*, which was popularized in a calendar by Glens Falls Insurance in 1912 and was reproduced in the 1930s. Again, Jane's body, this time heavily clothed (taking directions from the folklore that she was all dressed up for her wedding) is the center of the painting. Jane, on horseback (with the horse's knowing eye looking at the viewer), is surrounded by at least twelve Indians, several leering at her, one nearby with a tomahawk, another further back but shirtless with loose long hair and lunging forward with a rifle, others with guns and hatchets, and all in war paint. It is as if an entire war was to be waged around this fair Victorian maiden alone and in distress. Her expression is melancholy and resigned rather than horrified as in the Vanderlyn.[52]

Jane's age and appearance are hard to determine from the eighteenth- and nineteenth-century accounts, but she was apparently somewhere between seventeen and twenty-five years old and "a pleasing person." General Horatio Gates called her "a young lady lovely to the sight, of virtuous character and amiable disposition."[53] Some mention her youth and charm, but almost all accounts and paintings highlight her hair. There is no doubt that her hair was her most notable attribute. It is interesting to examine how her hair was presented in the hundred or more years in which the story and its artistic representations flourished. In these Jane's hair had three aspects: color, texture, and length.

Jane's hair, like her story, has many variations; it is blond, black, and almost every shade in between. The poet H. W. Herbert writes that David Jones recognized Jane's scalp when it was brought to the British camp: "Oh! he knew that yellow hair!" A county historian says she had "blond complexion" and "golden brown" hair. A more recent source claims the hair and scalp were "red-gold," and a justice of the peace examining her remains in the 1840s said the scalp had short hair, "red like horse hair." David Wilson writes that Mrs. Neilson, a friend of Jane's, remembers her "dark hair." The poet Alfred B. Street called the hair "black as midnight."[54]

There is more agreement about the hair's texture and quality, variously called "silken," "glossy," "glorious," "uncommonly beautiful," "luxuriant," and "ample." By all accounts it is long, but not merely long—according to one historian, it measured a yard and a quarter. Another suggested a yard and a half. A third, less precise, suggested that it "trailed on the floor upon which she walked."[55]

Clearly, hair is a central symbol in the story of Jane's captivity and death. It is first an effect, beautiful and sexual. Then it is brutally and gorily discarded, evoking dismay and grief. Jane's hair is significant, but what has it to do with independence? Her hair and scalp are powerful symbols of the mind and body, both her rational and sexual features. It was her desire to take both her rational and her sexual powers with her to join her Tory lover. But in all of the stories and depictions, it is obvious that Jane's independent wishes are not under her control. Not only are her hair and her life at the command of Indians, they are controlled after her death (according to legend) first by David Jones and then (in fact) by the various committees at Fort Edward who buried and reburied her and investigated her body and her head. A woman who did not succeed in effecting her own independence in life had even less control in death. Her mischoice left her out of control even at her end. By making the wrong political choice and by choosing a "hazardous love," a woman can lose the little freedom she has.[56] But this is not all. To choose the wrong side, even in love, is to put oneself in the hands of barbarians. The McCrea story uses a woman's hair to demonstrate this loss of control over one's body to the forces of evil.

Again, Indians are to blame. Whatever the tribal membership, Indian desecration of Jane's locks accompanies her death. In a volume celebrating the revolutionary centennial of New York (1879), Alfred B. Street mourns her fate:

> Ah, savage heart! he aims—she falls! the sweep
> Of glorious tresses, black as midnight, heap
> The wampum belt! ah, lovely, lovely head,
> By the unsparing knife so foully shred. . . .
> Another fierce savage, as demon-like, shred
> The long glossy-locks from her beautiful head.[57]

Jane's scalp was "*torn* off." According to David Wilson (1853), the Iroquois leader Le Loup (the Wolf) killed her, his "accursed fingers" wrapped around her hair. He then tore her dress. Once she was killed, her Indian "captors" "scalped her and carried her glossy tresses into the camp." The scalp was waved about on the road back to the British camp, "her long, luxuriant hair . . . [a] ghastly trophy." Jane's hair is continually described as an Indian trophy.[58] The British-allied Indians then allegedly took the scalp from her head and, entering the British camp, threw it down in front of General Fraser and Lieutenant Jones. Jones first expressed his "grief over her bloody tresses."[59] Some say he then went on to fight madly, but without conviction, at Saratoga. But Benson J. Lossing, popular nineteenth-century historian of New York, says he left for Canada before the battle, "carrying with him the precious locks of his affianced."[60]

The focus on McCrea's hair continued into the twentieth century. In the Philip Henry Carroll play of the 1920s, the good Indian Duluth sadly arrives at the ceremony for the wedding and with tears in his eyes has to indicate that Jane won't make it. The script gives Duluth directions to turn slowly in the direction of the scalp on the ground. Continuing in such *great distress*," he can only try to point. David Jones looks, "*recognizes the hair of* Jane McCrea. *He shudders. He looks lovingly at the scalp. He is sadness personified. He attempts again and again to touch it.*"[61]

In the early 1970s, as part of a wider feminist critique of the uses of women's bodies, Germaine Greer brought a heightened attention to women's body parts, including their hair. She indicated that the pressure for women to shave the body and depilate body hair is a way of desexualizing women. Ancient and modern Western men and women have seen hair as an attribute of power, especially of sexual power, and as far back in the Bible as Samson, cutting an enemy's hair was a symbolic and actual act of domination. In several of the captivity accounts of Jane McCrea and Sarah Campbell, one, the other, or both are pulled out of the cellar by their hair. For women, hair is power and enticement.[62] That Indians could kill Jane and gain her power through her hair was certainly a possibility. Scalping was a sacred and powerful part of ritual practice. But stories of the death of Jane McCrea are so confused and so various, with such an array of weapons and cross fire, with bodies being dug up and little being obvious, that we will probably never know the true story.[63] Whether in fact Indians scalped her, shot her, or cared at all for her hair, we may never know.[64] In the Anglo-American world, by taking Jane's hair, the Indians had taken her and could do with her what they wished. The sexual and violent poses of the Indians and the shockingly exposed breast of the Vanderlyn painting suggest not only murder but rape. Jane's body, strong, full, and voluptuous, potentially a body for bearing children of the republic, is struck down and desecrated, calling out for protection against savage rape and brutality. Her purportedly lurid death encoded a clear message to white women to play it straight, avoid the savage enemy and his royal representatives, and accept the new (actually traditional) male authority of the postrevolutionary era. Nineteenth-century stories and pictures of rape and mutilation endorsed greater military force against Indians. For women, these cautionary pieces urged an acceptance of constraints and deference in exchange for white male protection.

The story of Jane McCrea might well have passed into immediate obscurity as one more death on the frontier during the Revolution. That it did not and that it became a combination of captivity lore, romantic fiction, artistic expression, monumental statuary, and local fetish tells us something less about the elusive Jane McCrea herself than about the role of women in American culture. In this case, politics, romance, and notions of gender and the other intersect, all verifying women as potentially undutiful and uncontrollable forces.

The battle for the Hudson Valley and Appalachian frontier during the Revolution was real and bloody. But how to represent it, and what of women's roles? Linda Kerber has argued that the place of women during and immediately after the Revolution was ambiguous at best. The Founding Fathers did not quite know what to do with the female patriot. After the Revolution, women were expected to be republican mothers to nurture and guide republican sons. During the Revolution itself, women's position was more problematic. Whereas men served in the military, women had to find other means of expressing patriotic fervor. Politics, said one woman in her correspondence, "is not our sphere." Nevertheless, in a world in which politics was vital, women who used petitions and broadsides forged "historical role models" and "contemporary female martyrs" based on biblical and classical predecessors. One such broadside depicted McCrea's plight.[65]

While some women saw McCrea as a martyr, the male patriot world more often depicted her as a victim of murderous Indians supported by Burgoyne's duplicity. Jane's story was a cautionary tale—a warning against the dangers of female autonomy and misdirected emotion. From the beginning, the story of Jane McCrea was about the ambivalence toward white women in the new republic. After all, only the daughters of the republic, daughters like Jane, had the reproductive power to give birth to the next generation on the frontier. If they misused their sexual energies, chose the wrong mates, or unwittingly fell prey to the wild forces within themselves or in the forest, the American family, and through it the republican experiment, might be in jeopardy.

Historians have debated whether women's roles were changed by the Revolution in any dramatic way.[66] Jane McCrea answers the cultural side of the question—how have women of the Revolution been portrayed and why? How do these portrayals fit white women into the broader national story? Beginning as a revolutionary victim (1777), McCrea is fashioned first into Hilliard-d'Auberteuil's problem child (1784), then into Vanderlyn's (and other artists') sacrificial martyr (ca. 1804), Wilson's ambiguous romantic heroine (1853), romantic historians' and artists' murdered sweetheart, Carroll's supporting cast for male heroes (1927), and Fort Edward's nineteenth- and twentieth-century reigning saint.

The histories of the revolutionary period are totally dominated by male heroic figures. We know much about the Founding Fathers but rarely hear of the Founding Mothers and Daughters. With the exception of Martha Washington, Abigail Adams, and perhaps Mercy Warren, few women are found in the popular representations.[67] In the wake of the war and its rhetoric, questions about equality of men and women were raised. In this framework, Jane McCrea served as a female figure representing a combination of frontier settlers' fears and general anxieties about the possible loss of the Revolution and possible political and perhaps sexual conquest by the Indian enemy. Her story indicates fears that the daughters might not come over to the republican camp of their brothers and fathers but instead might choose to go with the mother country or even follow the ideas of nonrepublican mothers. She represents women's vulnerability and their unpredictable political and sexual choices. These fears originated in the early years of the republic, expressing a perhaps warranted apprehension in a period of profound change. But the popularity of Jane's story demonstrates the American nation's continuing uncertainty and unease with women's bodies, women's choices, alliances with other women, encounters with the other, and women's roles as helpmate in colonial conquest.

In the mid-nineteenth century, the McCrea legend was perpetuated in a multiplicity of local and national histories, illustrations, and other works of art. It merged domestic, political, sentimental, and gothic elements of earlier pieces, and it became increasingly romantic and decreasingly political. It then became a marginalized piece of the wider revolutionary panorama. By her centennial (1877), and even more so by her sesquicentennial (1927), the legend became a local rather than a national story. Of fifty-six articles on Jane McCrea in U.S. newspapers published between 1822 and 1913 (sixteen between 1901 and 1913) forty-nine were published in Fort Edward, the Washington County area, and Glens Falls, with a few in Troy and Albany.[68] Carroll's play was a local production, dedicated "To the Jane McCrea Chapter, Daughters of the American Revolution, Fort Edward, N.Y." A house in the town claims to be McCrea's. Today, a DAR marker is found across the street from the high school and another a few miles downriver, along with the new grave site in the Fort Edward cemetery near the local McDonald's. Jane is something of a local patron saint.[69] Were it not for Vanderlyn's painting, she would be largely forgotten. But the fascination with Vanderlyn's painting, unlike the written accounts of Jane's story, has hardly faded. According to records at the Wadsworth Atheneum in Hartford, which has housed the work since its acquisition in 1855, requests for the painting for exhibits and reproduction rights for books and articles have been frequent for the past forty years.[70] Why is it so popular? Aside from Vanderlyn's classical craftsmanship, the painting has symbolized the threat of violence from Indians on the American frontier. The powerfully crafted image of a white woman attacked by Indians rather than Jane herself sustains its popularity. In its contemporary setting at the Wadsworth Atheneum, the painting hangs among a collection of idyllic scenes of the early American countryside, suggesting a darker side to the early republican idyll.[71]

Clifford Geertz reminds us that a people's culture "is an ensemble of texts, themselves ensembles," which can "open up the possibility of an analysis which attends to their substance rather than to reductive formulas professing to account for them." [72] Jane McCrea's story demonstrates the need of elite male producers of culture and history to find roles for women as martyrs and victims. The ensemble tells us something of early fears in the republic. There, where the entire Appalachian area and the Northwest were opening to settlement, women's "weakness" was portrayed as a source of national concern and ethnocentric anxiety. Women's perceived sexual and reproductive vulnerability and the inability of men to protect "their" women, perhaps even gain their active political support, left a most vulnerable frontier indeed.

McCrea had no direct part in the scripting or visual representation of her experience. Other women on the frontier, even female captives, had a role in their own presentations. Their stories, like McCrea's, portrayed the dilemmas of women alone and in mortal danger. But unlike hers, other narrative traditions showed a variety of means by which women could use their own resources, protect themselves and their children, and emerge alive and with dignity, thus creating a literature of women's capacity to endure and enlisting them in the efforts of nation building. The McCrea story, alternatively, shows a woman as an untrustworthy and destabilizing influence, potentially forfeiting republican goals for "selfish" desire, thereby bringing on her own death.

According to Lynn Hunt, "When the French Revolution challenged the political authority of the Old Regime, it therefore also called into question its cultural frame." It asked, "Where was the new center of society, and how could it be represented?" Hunt suggests that "the experience of the Revolution showed for the first time that politics was shaped by culture . . . and, most important, that the members of society could invent culture and politics for themselves." [73] The Revolution in North America, like the Revolution in France, threw up a variety of challenges to the old order and created social and cultural dilemmas for the new one. In an answer to a letter from his wife, Abigail, asking him to "Remember the Ladies" in the new government, John Adams complained that "our Struggle has loosened the bands of Government everywhere" "stirring up," among others, Negroes, Indians, and Roman Catholics. Calling his wife's request "saucy," he somewhat jokingly resisted relinquishing any additional male prerogatives, "which would compleatly subject Us to the Despotism of the Peticoat." [74]

The construction of Jane McCrea's legend helped to define the role of white women in American life after the Revolution. New creators of culture devised the mytho-poetic victim Jane became, centered her in a compelling plot, transformed her into a romantic legend, and finally left her as both a local legend and a victim of "savages" in need of protection and direction— a national image of female vulnerability in an expanding republic. By so doing, like John Adams, they rejected women's demands for a more serious role in both politics and culture and indicated a distrust of female power and sexuality which reasserted female dependence. In this way, the pieces of the McCrea legend, however contradictory, contributed to the construction of an ideology of womanhood in the republic which reinforced notions of Indian savagery and also contributed to the legitimization of white male hegemony immediately after the Revolution and for generations to come.

Mary Jemison: The Evolution of One Captive's Story

In November 1823, a slight woman of about eighty years, escorted by a younger man, walked four miles from her home in south-central New York on the Genesee River to a small cabin. There she remained for three days, telling the story of her life. Captured at about age fourteen, she spent most of the rest of her years living with the Senecas in western New York State. She had blue eyes and a pale complexion. Her once light brown hair was now gray and slightly curly. Her face was expressive, with high cheekbones. When she talked, she held her head down in an Indian manner of humility, "peeping from under her eyebrows." Her clothes, like her life, her demeanor, and her speech, were a blend of cultures: buckskin moccasins, an Indian blanket, a brown flannel gown, a petticoat, and a bonnet. She spoke clearly, with "a little of the Irish emphasis" of her origins still recognizable in her voice. Her memory appeared clear to James E. Seaver, who listened to her account. At times, as she spoke of her experiences, tears came to her eyes.[1]

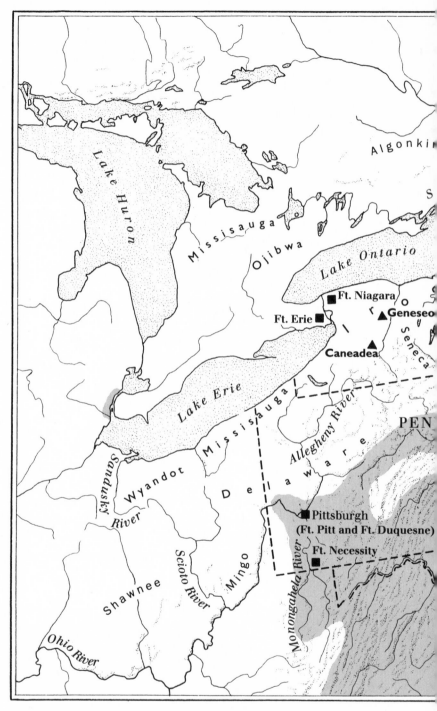

New York and Indian Country, 1755–1780

CANADA

● Montreal

Lake Champlain

NEW YORK

● Burlington

NEW ENGLAND

Lake George

Mohawk

■ Ft. William Henry

■ Ft. Edward

● Saratoga

Ft. Stanwix ■ *Mohawk River*

● Boston

Oneida

Onondaga

Cayuga

Cherry Valley ● Albany

● Springfield

Connecticut River

Hudson River

● Hartford

SYLVANIA

New York ●

Susquehanna River

Philadelphia ●

ATLANTIC OCEAN

Lawrence River

▲	Indian village
●	White settlement
■	Fort
▨	White Population

The story she told was one of a survivor, an adapter, and a keen observer.

When Jemison sat down with Seaver in 1823, she was continuing an old captivity narrative tradition. Just as Hannah Dustan had sat before Cotton Mather in the late seventeenth century and by telling her story had become a famous figure in her time, so too Mary Jemison's story was retold, this time not in sermon form but in a narrative edition published in Canandaigua, New York, in 1824. The book was printed in twenty editions between then and 1918. Jemison was further memorialized in bronze in an upstate New York park in 1910. By 1969 the children's book *Indian Captive: The Story of Mary Jemison* had appeared in more than twenty printings. In 1986, the transmission of Jemison's legend changed from the printed word back to the oral tradition. A group of about thirty gathered around the Jemison statue while a park historian gave his weekly recounting of her story and her place in the Indian life of the region. Children of five to adults of seventy-five listened closely for over an hour; few left, although it was a clear summer day and the park had other amusements.[2]

Between 1763 and the decades following the Revolution, slow but relentless moves by white settlers and land speculators had pushed white settlement from the Atlantic coast into the North American forests, mountains, and meadows east of the Mississippi. As white families moved onto the frontier of western Pennsylvania, Maryland, and Virginia, farms and small villages were attacked, and along with the hardship of the new frontier, there was occasional death or capture. Some white captives never returned to white society; some stayed with Indians by their own choice. Mary Jemison was one such white captive.

Born on shipboard, she was the daughter of Thomas Jemison and Jane Erwin Jemison, Scotch-Irish immigrants who left Ireland in 1742 or 1743. The family settled in south-central Pennsylvania, about ten miles north of what later became the Gettysburg area.[3] She was the second daughter of six Jemison children. On April 5, 1758, the Jemison family and visiting friends were attacked by six Shawnee Indians and four Frenchmen. Her older brothers Thomas and John were in the barn and escaped, but Mary's parents, two brothers and a sister, and the visitors were captured, then killed. Only she and the friends' young boy were spared.[4]

Why has the Jemison legend had such longevity? Folklore and many of the Jemison editions call her "The White Woman," and "The White Woman of the Genesee." Mary was seen by some as The *White* Woman, putting stress on her race, her color, and all they represented to the white world. But in the nineteenth century, when the Jemison narratives were most popular, her romantic story might well have been followed closely by those most ardent readers of fiction: women. Many must have seen in her story "The White *Woman*," a historic and heroic representative of their sex. A third perspective is that of Jemison as an Indian woman. From the first edition, Jemison narratives, sculpture, and children's books had an Indian imprint. Seaver added an appendix claiming to explain Indian ways. Following his lead, subsequent editions looked for Indian "experts" to provide information on customs, folkways, and Indian names. New editions offered Jemison's supposed Indian name. In the mid- to late nineteenth century, illustrations showing Iroquois clothing, weapons, and tools were added. Sculptor H. K. Bush-Brown traveled to national museums to study Indian clothing for his Jemison statue (1910).[5] Anthropologists and historians have seen her narrative as a window into the life of Indian society, and contemporary scholars frequently cite her as a good source on the life of Indian women.[6] The Iroquois certainly saw her as one of their own and still do. Her descendants and Iroquois people are quick to remind those who study her that Jemison never returned to white society but chose to remain with her Indian family. Each facet of her life—the white, the female, and the Indian, along with their subtle blends—extended her popularity and the fascination she held for a wide audience. Studies of the *White* Woman and the White *Woman* give a clear sense of the evolution of the Jemison legend. Tracking the Indian woman connects Jemison to a new cross-cultural American family on the frontier and suggests possibilities for cooperation rather than conquest.

The *White* Woman

. . . . . .
. . .

The Jemison story's white, female, and Indian aspects all contributed to its longevity, but its white aspect and the perceived persistence of the woman's white traits were of prime interest to an Anglo-Saxon world that believed in the triumph of "civilization," Christianity, and what it believed was a superior society over "savagery."[7] What would happen to a white child in a "savage" world? Would whiteness and the higher "civil" virtues win out? Jemison had become an Indian. In doing so would she inevitably move backward into a more primitive and savage state, preferring a more uncivilized society? The Jemison legend was used into the twentieth century to assert racial, religious, and ethnic supremacy. Much like Rudyard Kipling's story of Mowgli (the boy raised by wolves) and Edgar Rice Burroughs's tale of Tarzan (raised by apes), the introductions to and commentaries on the Jemison narrative were attempts to investigate whether the "civilized" and "inherited" traits of a white woman would prevail in "barbarous" circumstances.[8]

In the nineteenth century, Jemison's story evolved with the narratives of her life that were published. In the twentieth century, artistic representations and children's books became the main means of communicating her story. All these forms have their white, female, and Indian components.

First I will trace the cultural history of the Jemison legend as it evolved between 1824 and 1969. The prime constructors of Jemison's story were James E. Seaver and his brother William Seaver, Ebenezer Mix, Laura Wright, William Prior Letchworth, H. K. Bush-Brown, Arthur C. Parker, Charles Delamater Vail, and Lois Lenski. There was more than a single, simple motivation for most of this work, but in all versions of the story, the *White* Woman was an important figure.

THE SEAVERS' JEMISON

Although born a white child, Mary lived and died in an Indian world. As is true for most Indian women, the story of her life did not come to us directly. Rather, as Gretchen M. Bataille and Kathleen Mullen Sands point out, such stories are often filtered through one or many people. They are "as-told-to" stories. Like Indian women's autobiographies, these accounts "tend to be retrospective rather than introspective" and develop through a process involving both teller and editor in "selection and recollection, structuring, and expression." The "possibilities of error are great, and distortion and misrepresentation are confronted at every moment because two creators are at work simultaneously. But where this creative collaboration is careful, and at least occasionally inspired, the form and content merge, and the work admits a nontribal audience into the life and ways of an individual Indian woman within her culture in a mode that is dramatic and stylistically satisfying." The Jemison narrative also follows in the tradition of writing about ethnic women in which, as Mary V. Dearborn notes, it is difficult to find a clear sense of the ethnic woman's authorship because another author "translates, transcribes, and annotates" in a process Dearborn calls "midwiving," in a birth that is not always successful.[9] Jemison's "white" narrative, then, follows an ethnic and Indian as well as a captivity tradition—putting her life in another's hands. Those hands first belonged to James Everett Seaver, a doctor from western New York State who became her first and most important interpreter.

Little is known of James Everett Seaver's life. The Seaver clan traces its ancestry to Robert Seaver, who arrived in Roxbury, Massachusetts, in 1634 and remained in the Boston area until James's father, William, left. James's mother, Mary Everett, was a first cousin of Edward Everett. Born in 1787, James was the first of four sons. He became a physician and moved to Darien (then Pembroke), New York, in 1816, married, and had four children.[10] According to local history, he came to town nearly broke, "with a stock of medicine in his pill bags," bought a bushel of wheat, and because of "overwork and exposure became ill and had to give up work." Seaver was a pioneer of sorts and the first practicing doctor in Darien.[11]

No copy of Seaver's original notes survives nor did he record why or how he proceeded with his meeting and interviewing. What he asked, what he left out, the order Jemison chose to tell her story, which words are hers and which his, and how she felt about her interviewer cannot be known for sure. But Seaver rewrote her story, using a combination of her words, his words, and a language common to female literature of the day. From the first he added pieces to the story, along with an extensive appendix in which he purported to tell the public something of Iroquois and Seneca life and to recount some of the events of the Revolution in western New York. In 1824, one year after their meeting, *A Narrative of the Life of Mrs. Mary Jemison, Who was taken by the Indians, in the year 1755, when only about twelve years of age, and has continued to reside amongst them to the present time* was published in Canandaigua, a small town in central upstate New York. Within the next 105 years it went through twenty-seven printings and twenty-three editions ranging from 32 to 483 pages. Beginning as an oddity of local history known only to residents of western and central New York, the books and booklets soon were in second and third printings in Howden and London, England. The book was printed in New York cities and towns including Batavia, Auburn, Westfield, Rochester, and Buffalo and in New York City for three printings just before the Civil War. In the late nineteenth century it was printed three times by G. P. Putnam's Sons of London. Thus a remote frontier event became a nationally, indeed internationally, known story.[12]

The first edition of the book was an instant success, selling over one hundred thousand copies in its first year. According to Charles Delamater Vail, "readers of the period literally wore out the copies of the little 16 mo which were frequently carried in the pocket, and more frequently passed from hand to hand so that only a few have survived the intensive use to which they were put."[13]

In the opening paragraphs of his introduction to Jemison's narrative, James Seaver tells us that in the early nineteenth century, "the richness and fertility of the soil" in western New York "excited emigration." Many settlers moved to the state, "settled down and commenced improvements in the country which had recently been the property of the aborigines. Those who settled near the Genesee river, soon became acquainted with 'The White Woman,' as Mrs. Jemison is called, whose history they anxiously sought, both as a matter of interest and curiosity."[14]

At the start of the Jemison narrative we are introduced to a frontier family of Christian faith. Mary's Christian life included

A NARRATIVE

OF THE LIFE OF

MRS. MARY JEMISON,

Who was taken by the Indians, in the year 1755,
when only about twelve years of age, and
has continued to reside amongst
them to the present time.

CONTAINING

An Account of the Murder of her Father and his
Family; her sufferings; her marriage to two Indians;
her troubles with her Children; barbarities of the
Indians in the French and Revolutionary Wars; the
life of her last Husband, &c.; and many Historical
Facts never before published.
Carefully taken from her own words, Nov. 29th, 1823.

TO WHICH IS ADDED,

An APPENDIX, containing an account of the tragedy
at the Devil's Hole, in 1763, and of Sullivan's Expedition; the Traditions, Manners, Customs, &c. of
the Indians, as believed and practised at the present
day, and since Mrs. Jemison's captivity; together
with some Anecdotes, and other entertaining matter.

BY JAMES E. SEAVER.

CANANDAIGUA:

PRINTED BY J. D. BEMIS AND CO.

1824.

Title page from James E. Seaver, A Narrative of the Life of
Mrs. Mary Jemison *(1824). Courtesy of the Newberry Library*

a daily round of "morning and evening" prayers by her father in the family setting. At school she learned to read small amounts of the Bible. She also learned the catechism and repeated it to her parents often, along with prayers in front of her mother at bedtime. After the family's capture, just before she was separated from her mother, the mother told the child that her life "will be spared." In that new life she should remember all of the family names and her "English tongue" and should not try to escape. Finally, in a section labeled "Mother's Farewell Address," the child was told, "Don't forget, my little daughter, the prayers that I have learned you—say them often; be a good child, and God will bless you. May God bless you my child, and make you comfortable and happy." [15]

At the time the narrative appeared, it is not surprising that the mother was the conduit of religious piety. [16] The pairing of mother love and direction with the world of purity, family, and white settlement is a setting from which Mary's adventure moves in the first and all subsequent versions of her narrative.

Although Seaver had great respect for Jemison, his respect did not extend to the Seneca people with whom she chose to live. Admitting that Jemison had become almost fully Indian, Seaver in the introduction to the narrative explains her dress, her way of eating, and her home: "Her habits, are those of the Indians— she sleeps on skins without a bedstead, sits upon the floor or on a bench, holds her victuals on her lap, or in her hands. . . . The doctrines taught in the Christian religion, she is a stranger to." He also says she was "sensible of her ignorance of the manners of the white people" and would not "say something that would be injurious to herself or family. . . . The vices of the Indians, she appeared disposed not to aggravate, and seemed to take pride in extolling their virtues." For these reasons, Seaver found it necessary to go to Mary's "cousin" George Jemison to find out about her second husband, the Seneca warrior Hiokatoo. [17] Thus the negative information on Hiokatoo and the so-called biography of him that were inserted into Jemison's text did not come from Jemison herself.

> In early life, Hiokatoo showed signs of thirst for blood, by attending only to the art of war, in the use of the tomahawk and scalping knife; and in practicing cruelties upon every

thing that chanced to fall into his hands, which was suscep-
tible of pain. In that way he learned to use his implements of
war effectively, and at the same time blunted all those fine
feelings and tender sympathies that are naturally excited, by
hearing or seeing, a fellow being in distress. He could inflict
the most excruciating tortures upon his enemies, and prided
himself upon his fortitude, in having performed the most barbarous ceremonies and tortures, without the least degree of
pity or remorse. Thus qualified, when very young he was initiated into scenes of carnage, by being engaged in the wars
that prevailed amongst the Indian tribes.[18]

The intent in this section, which goes on for several pages, is
to present a barbaric man from a barbaric society and to contrast him with the white woman with whom he lived. There is
no recognition of Seneca values, and it is assumed that Jemison
always opposed the Iroquois warrior codes, although all Seaver's
versions include her reports of siding with the Senecas during
the Revolution. Generally, Jemison's account does not accept
the warlike tactics of either side.

Anthony Wallace's study of the Senecas demonstrates that
men were raised to protect their society. Their status was gained
from a personality type he calls "the ideal of autonomous responsibility." A man with these qualities could practice and
withstand torture.[19] Jemison would not tell Seaver what her husband did so Seaver emphasized her whiteness and purity over
his darkness and evildoing. He accomplished this structurally
and rhetorically by placing allegedly biographical material on
Hiokatoo within the story of the woman herself and then, in the
introduction, presuming her feelings toward Hiokatoo: "The
thoughts of his deeds, probably chilled her old heart, and made
her dread to rehearse them, at the same time she well knew they
were no secret." [20]

Following James Seaver's death in 1827, and in light of his
narrative's promising sales figures, his brother William was
reluctant to let a good thing die. He therefore published the
first major revision of his brother's work. In contrast to James,
who died at forty a virtual unknown, William was a business-
man and public figure in western New York. Born in 1789, two
years after his brother, he lived for eighty-two years, fifty of

them in Genesee County, where he headed "a large drug, book and printing establishment." According to one county gazetteer, "his influence was hardly second to any one in Genesee County." He edited the *Batavia Spirit of the Times* and occupied such diverse local offices as postmaster, captain and chief engineer of the fire department, president of the village, and senior warden of St. James's Episcopal Church.[21] William Seaver's new editions were first published in Batavia, New York (1842 and 1844), then in London (1847). In them, an Indian name and the words "white woman" appear together in bold type on the title page: *DEH-HE-WÄ-MIS or A Narrative of the Life of Mary Jemison: Otherwise Called THE WHITE WOMAN . . .* , highlighting the persistence of white in a world of red.[22] William Seaver was also the first of many publishers to enlist "experts" on the Jemison case and to add Indian material. Ebenezer Mix's new additions *in text* to the Jemison narrative, like Seaver's earlier insert on Hiokatoo, have a "white" intent. They contrast the Anglo-American Christian with the "pagan" way and attempt to demonstrate the ultimate victory of the white woman's ways over those of the baser world of "barbaric" Indians with whom she lived.

In an attempt to improve on his brother's work and, no doubt, to sell more copies, William Seaver changed the original. His new edition underscored the ways in which the white and Indian parts of Jemison's life were used by others for their own ends. It contributed to a sense of white superiority and entitlement in an era marked by the displacement of native peoples. In a "Publisher's Notice," William explains the alterations he is introducing to his brother's text and why they should improve it. He begins by dedicating his work to his "deceased brother" and tells his reader that while at work on the narrative, James Seaver was "laboring under a painful chronic disease." Working on the book shortened his life and resulted in "the defects of the first edition, both in style and arrangement," thus "the publishers have felt at liberty . . . to make such corrections, revisions, and additions, as seemed necessary and proper" to create what the first editor "originally intended it should be; a faithful, interesting, and instructive history of the subject and events to which it relates." To do all this, Seaver brought in Ebenezer Mix, Esq., who, he says, had a knowledge of western New York "not surpassed, if equalled, by any person now living." The result of this collaboration is that Seaver and Mix "transposed, divided, consolidated, and re-arranged, various chapters and parts of chapters, in order to give a more clear and connected view of the subjects under consideration, and yet carefully preserving all the facts as originally narrated by Mrs. Jemison." In reality, they duped the reader by various sleights of hand.[23]

Mix was a mason by trade, but after teaching school for some years he became a lawyer. He was a central figure in the arrangement of the Holland Purchase, which divided up former Seneca lands in western New York. He was especially renowned for his knowledge of New York geography, boundaries, and land allotments.[24] But Mix was hardly an objective observer of Indian culture and land claims. Nor was he or Seaver much of an editor. Their collaboration created confusion: a text that is supposed to be Jemison's account of her life and yet includes an unannounced series of treatises on the geography and history of western New York in the late eighteenth and early nineteenth centuries, along with disparagements of Indian life and testimonials to Anglo-Saxon Protestantism (called Christianity). Mix's work replaced Indian place names in chapter 5 with English ones because he felt Indian languages were "fast fading from among us."[25]

The push to Christianize Jemison began with the Seaver/Mix English and American editions. The publisher of the Devon and London printings suggests that reading the book will give one "a clearer view of the necessity of an adoption of the gospel of Christ to render either nations or individuals truly happy."[26] In both printings, Mix claims that the "white woman" changed back from a "pagan" to a Christian, her true virtues remaining constant. And the Seaver/Mix editions are the first to tell of Jemison's alleged reconversion. Mix begins by saying that Jemison was generous to "white and red" alike, "practicing this most exalted of Christian virtues, charity, in feelings as well as in actions." He claims that in 1833 Jemison "seceded from the pagan party of her nation, and joined the Christian party"; repudiating "paganism," she "embraced the Christian religion," with the help of Reverend Asher Wright, and was given a Christian burial.[27]

In addition to emphasizing the triumph of Christian principles, the Seaver/Mix editions present the continued "progress" of industrialism in western New York over the more "backward" Iroquois, who "would have accepted with joy" government removal.[28] To strengthen his case, Mix conveniently omitted a paragraph from the Jemison text that recounted how the daughter of frontiersman Ebenezer Allen and his Indian wife made a claim to land which Allen had sold, a claim that was decided in favor of land developers. Mix closes with the nineteenth-century canard of the vanishing savage race: New York will soon see "the last of the Mingoes *wending* his *way* toward the setting sun."[29]

In even worse distortions, Mix's addition, "General Sullivan's Expedition to Western New York," reverses the Jemison narrative. Mix praises the fall 1779 invasion of Iroquois country by the revolutionary armies. Jemison lived through the terror and told Seaver:

> At the time I had three children who went with me on foot, one who rode on horse back, and one whom I carried on my back.
>
> Our corn was good that year; a part of which we had gathered and secured for winter. In one or two days after the skirmish at Connissius lake, Sullivan and his army arrived at Genesee river, where they destroyed every article of the food kind that they could lay their hands on. A part of our corn they burnt, and threw the remainder in the river. They burnt our houses, killed what few cattle and horses they could find, destroyed our fruit trees, and left nothing but the bare soil and timber.

After foraging and hunting, Jemison and the Senecas returned to their village to find "not a mouthful of any kind of sustenance left, not even enough to keep a child one day from perishing with hunger."[30] Mix's revision describes, rather joyously, the revenge the revolutionary forces unleashed on the Seneca people, the shooting and scalping of two Indians, and the destruction of their cornfields.[31]

The Seaver brothers' first editions (1824–47) were important if somewhat distorted accounts of the Jemison story. James Seaver's edition of Jemison's narrative appeared one year after James Fenimore Cooper's *Pioneers* (1823) and two years before *The Last of the Mohicans* (1826).[32] White captives such as Jemison must have appeared to be something like the Japanese fighter who stumbles out of a cave on a Pacific Island to tell his story of World War II—a reminder of an earlier set of battles and beliefs. As white settlement moved into the new West and the frontier world of the Anglo-American frontier settlers receded, the need to remember that older world emerged as part of the cultural process of forging a new American identity.[33] The Seavers wished to frame the past to show the march of progress—of rising Anglo-American dominance, domesticity, industrial expansion, and Christian piety over a savage but receding Indian presence.

BUSINESSMAN AND ARTIST

Although he was interested in the Indian side of Jemison's life, the exploration of the white elements of the Mary Jemison story were perpetuated beyond their antebellum origins by businessman William Prior Letchworth. Unlike William Seaver and Ebenezer Mix, Letchworth was not an Indian hater; he thought himself rather a patron of Indians, taking a paternal approach to them and other "downtrodden" groups. Letchworth was born in Brownsville, New York, in 1823, the same year Seaver interviewed Mary Jemison. His Quaker family moved from Philadelphia to New York in the early part of the nineteenth century. Letchworth went into business in the Buffalo area between 1848 and 1869 and with Pascal P. and Samuel F. Pratt founded Pratt & Letchworth Ironworks in Black Rock, New York.[34] The business was highly successful, and Letchworth became a multimillionaire. In 1859 he purchased seven hundred acres of land along both sides of the Genesee River. The Genesee Valley is known to some as the eastern Grand Canyon, with gorges up to 350 feet deep. The land and waterways of the area were used by Indians for thousands of years. The Letchworth purchase included the river's upper, middle, and lower falls with drops of 70, 110, and 90 feet, along with major portage points. Resident Indians had long believed the falls areas to be the homes of Iroquoian spirits. The land was admired by whites as well. Writer Edward Hagaman Hall said Letchworth's Glen Iris estate was a home Emerson or Thoreau would have loved but was the home "not of a dreaming poet, but of a man with a poet's soul united into a practical and executive mind which has been devoted for more than the length of an average generation to the welfare of his fellow men."[35]

Hagaman Hall was right on both counts. After his retirement in 1869, Letchworth threw himself into an array of charitable and philanthropic projects involving New York people and land. He became the prototypical late nineteenth-century business-man turned public servant and philanthropist. A Quaker up-bringing left its mark; his charitable interests focused on the poor, the sick, the insane, the young, and the Indian. He helped organize a county workhouse. It was his custom annually to "entertain a large number of poor city children on his spacious estate." In 1873 he was appointed commissioner of the State Board of Charities, a position he held for twenty-two years. He researched and wrote two books, one on the treatment of the in-sane, the other, *Care and Treatment of Epileptics*, and founded a colony for the treatment of epileptics near Glen Iris.[36]

Along with his philanthropic work, Letchworth developed a genuine and abiding interest in local Indian life and the life of Mary Jemison in particular. In 1872 he organized the last Indian Council in the valley on his estate and moved the old Seneca council house from Caneadea. His friendship with the Senecas resulted in their honorary adoption of him. They named him Hai-wa-ye-is-tah, meaning "The man who always does the right thing." When he died, the *Washington Post* announced in a headline, "Friend of Indian Is Dead."[37]

Letchworth was responsible for a new look in the Jemison edi-tions. Reflecting the growing interest of readers in illustrations and the new ease of their reproduction, the five Letchworth edi-tions included drawings of Iroquois clothing, tools, and weapons from Lewis Henry Morgan's plates in *League of the Ho-dé-no-sau-nee of Iroquois*. Four printings of Seaver's narrative were published under his direction (1877, 1880, 1898, and 1910), and his revisions remained in print after his death in 1910.[38]

Besides adding illustrations, Letchworth began documenting Jemison's life. One important "finding" was a continuation of the path broken by the Mix/Seaver editions to verify the return of the "white woman" to Christianity in her dying days. In a letter Laura Wright (wife of Reverend Asher Wright) wrote to

Letchworth, she claimed that she had met Jemison after coming to Buffalo Creek in 1833. "I had often heard of her history, I felt a desire to see her." Laura Wright went with an interpreter who had told her that Mary wanted to see a missionary. "I had been told that she had never been interested in any efforts made to give her religious instruction, and that in fact she was as strong a pagan as any of the Indians, and was strongly prejudiced against the Christian religion." As soon as Wright arrived and Jemison understood her mission, the old woman told her of her mother's last wish that she "never forget the prayer which you have always repeated with your little brothers and sisters" and that she say it "every day as long as you live." Wright reported that she found Jemison distraught, having spent sleepless nights worrying; she was sobbing, her voice almost "inaudible." For many years she had said the prayer, but as time passed she had forgotten it. When Wright told her she need not worry and re-peated the Lord's Prayer, "suddenly it was evident a chord had been touched which vibrated into the far distant past, and awak-ened memories both sweet and painful."[39] Jemison died soon after this meeting, a meeting which Wright and others inter-preted as Jemison's moment of permanent return and reconver-sion to Christianity. Wright's report of her meeting contributed to Jemison's Christian legend and linked it to the "civilizing" powers of maternal values so frequently expressed in American ideology in the nineteenth century.[40]

In Letchworth's plan to set aside land on his considerable Glen Iris estate for a major state park, he added a significant Jemison component; he moved her old home from Gardow (or Gardeau) Flats, below a canyon on the west side of the river, into the park. He also found her daughter Nancy's house and moved it to Glen Iris. All these acts were an attempt to collect, order, and memorialize this pioneer woman at a time when pioneer life had become history. His most lasting contribution to the white element of the Jemison legend, however, is the statue he commissioned from H. K. Bush-Brown, cast in bronze and dedicated in 1910, right before its patron's death.

Letchworth took more than a cursory interest in the creation of this Jemison likeness, as did Bush-Brown. Henry Kirke Bush-Brown, the man commissioned to do the piece, was a famous sculptor in his time. Born in Ogdensburg, New York, in 1857, he studied in Philadelphia at the National Academy of Design, in Paris at the Academie Julien, and in Italy. Before the Jemison statue his major work included equestrian statues of Generals George G. Meade and John F. Reynolds installed at the National Military Park at Gettysburg, along with a statue of General Anthony Wayne at Valley Forge, a Lincoln Memorial also at Gettysburg, and a work titled *Buffalo Indian Hunt* for the 1893 Chicago Exposition. Bush-Brown favored bronze but also worked in granite and marble.[41]

Letchworth and Bush-Brown had a long and detailed correspondence regarding the design of the Jemison sculpture. Letters began in November 1906 and continued for four years until Letchworth's death. Bush-Brown was invited to Glen Iris so the two men could discuss the ongoing work. In July 1907 the sculptor and his wife took the train to Portage, near the Letchworth estate. In October he wrote his patron, saying that sketches would be on the way. The sculptor wanted to create an "authentic" statue of Jemison and worked hard on the Indian aspects of the woman's figure. For the white elements, he found a young woman of Scotch-Irish background to pose for the statue. In March 1908 a second visit to Portage was planned in which Bush-Brown promised to bring his sketches. Letters continued between the two men for the next two years, during which time photographs were given to Letchworth of the plaster work in progress in Bush-Brown's studio.[42]

Bush-Brown undertook a systematic study of Iroquoian artifacts and dress to satisfy his patron's desire that the White Woman be dressed in the most accurate renditions of Indian clothing. In November 1907 he went to Harvard University's Peabody Museum to discuss Indian "costume" with the head of its collections. A month later he wrote Letchworth of his visit to the Field Museum in Chicago for a similar consultation with its director. He visited the New York State Museum at Albany, the New York Museum of Natural History, and the National Museum (known today as the National Museum of Natural History at the Smithsonian Institution).[43] Despite the authenticity achieved in the Jemison statue, including moccasins and cradle board copied from Lewis Henry Morgan's Iroquois collections, it remains strikingly clear that the figure depicted is a solitary white woman, a mother carrying her child. The artist presents a woman alone on her journey from the Ohio country to New York, complete with braids, moccasins, cradle board, and buckskin. The more than six-hundred-mile trek was not made alone, however, and could not have been made at all without the direction and protection of Mary's Indian brothers, not just on foot but by canoe and on horseback.[44] By creating and dedicating this statue to the White Woman (although they placed an Indian name at her feet), Letchworth and Bush-Brown celebrated the white and Euro-American values they saw Jemison representing: individuality, perseverance, the need to go it alone—values of late Victorian capitalist America, which would persist even when confronted by "savage" life.

Bush-Brown's imprint is worthy of note: whoever the model was, the final statue looks like a Nordic woman dressed Indian-style. Jemison's left arm shown holding the burden strap for the cradle board with the baby on her back is strong. To Bush-Brown's credit, he has Jemison moving; Letchworth had wanted her standing still—a perfect testament to late nineteenth-century white womanhood. The bronze statue projects a strength which Jemison undoubtedly had, and it is physical as well as moral. Accounts, including Seaver's and Laura Wright's, emphasize her tiny size; they say she was less than five feet tall. Perhaps biographers underestimated her size to keep her in the ideal petite, frail, early nineteenth-century mode and then suggest that her faith and her mother's values saved her.[45] The statue's strength is memorialized in the White Woman, a braided young pioneer mother of the West in buckskin.

The statue of Jemison was Letchworth's last project. As part of a plan to turn over his land to the American Scenic and Historic Preservation Society dating from the time in 1874 when he brought Jemison's remains from their burial place in Buffalo and reburied her next to the Indian council house, Letchworth saw "my purpose to complete the monument . . . by placing [on the marble base] a bronze statue of this unfortunate and heroic woman." Four months before his death, he had watched the dedication of the Jemison statue "in memory of the White Woman."[46]

*H. K. Bush-Brown's statue of Mary Jemison (Bronze) (1910),
Letchworth State Park, New York. Photograph by June Namias*

H. K. Bush-Brown's statue of Mary Jemison (Bronze) (1910),
Letchworth State Park, New York. Photograph by June Namias

Along with doctors, lawyers, businessmen, missionaries, and artists, Mary Jemison captured the hearts of bibliophiles, anthropologists, and writers of children's books. Lewis Henry Morgan, the father of anthropology, edited the 1856 edition of her narrative.[47] Arthur C. Parker followed. Parker was born in 1881 as a Seneca on his father's side and a New England Yankee on his mother's and was trained in anthropology at Columbia with Franz Boas and Frank G. Speck. Parker was a keeper of the Jemison flame and was called upon to address a commemorative speech to the White Woman held at Letchworth State Park in September 1933 on the one hundredth anniversary of her death. "From the teachings and culture of the Scottish-Irish pioneers of our frontier," he said, Jemison "was at once plunged into the environment of another people. . . . The test is whether the inherent qualities of the white woman as derived from teaching and heredity would or could endure after 80 years of submersion."[48] When he rightly praised Jemison as a survivor, Parker compared her not with humanity in general or with Indian women but with an ideal white pioneer mother. "Taken by cruel hands at random, this woman was to be an example, as it were, of the kind of womanhood that formed this pioneer race of ours, and if that race has any glory, it is because of such as she."[49] That in Parker's case the "pioneer race" was both Yankee Protestant and Seneca was overlooked. In his professionalization and scholarship, Parker sustained Jemison's mythic qualities under the banner of white female sensibility.

The white Jemison legend can be said to have evolved in four stages. The first was from 1824 to 1847, when the James and William Seaver editions of the narrative appeared. The second was the period 1877 to 1910, when William Prior Letchworth, with the help of Laura Wright and H. K. Bush-Brown, reshaped the legend. A third falls between 1918 and 1933, when, under the aegis of Charles D. Vail and Arthur Parker, an attempt was made to find a more scholarly base while continuing the Jemison legend. The fourth, from 1941 to 1969, was under the direction of Lois Lenski, who removed the story from the adult realm, placing it squarely in the world of childhood. In doing so, she retained much of its nineteenth-century romanticism, adventure, and ethnic biases but also restored its authenticity, freshness, and appeal to an understanding of Jemison's female and Indian worlds. Lois Lenski was a popular writer and illustrator of juvenile books. She wrote *Indian Captive: The Story of Mary Jemison*. Lenski's book appeared in close to twenty printings in several U.S. and foreign imprints. It probably did more to bring the life of Jemison into the consciousness of twentieth-century readers than any of the Seaver volumes. Lenski was born in 1893 in Springfield, Ohio, to a Lutheran minister father and a schoolteacher mother. After obtaining degrees in education and art, she wrote and illustrated nearly one hundred children's books, which were published in Europe, the Americas, Asia, and Africa, and by 1970 her works were available in fourteen languages. At the time of her death in 1974, she had won awards and honors from five colleges and universities along with numerous book awards. Her books are known for their outstanding sense of place and for giving children a better view of other ways of life. Lenski has been called a pioneer of children's realism; her book *Strawberry Girl* has been favorably compared with *Tom Sawyer*.[50]

Lenski decided to write about Jemison after she had published more than twenty children's books. The suggestion for the book came from the literary editor of the Cleveland Press; encouragement and direction came from R. W. G. Vail, New York State historian and bibliographer of captivity narratives. Lenski spent more than three years researching the book and became known as one of the first author-illustrators of children's books to use primary sources. Because of the quality of its research and its sympathetic view of Indians, the book won the prestigious Newberry Honor Book award in 1942. It was called "the most distinguished piece of children's literature published in 1941." Between 1950 and 1969, *Indian Captive* was reissued four more times on both sides of the Atlantic.[51]

Lenski's story depicts the journey of a white girl as she becomes an Indian woman, and for its time, its words and illustrations generally bring the white child into sympathy with Indian culture. In an introduction to the book, Arthur Parker, then director of the Rochester Museum of Arts and Sciences, wrote that Lenski's version contained elements that many scholarly versions lacked because she had visited Indians and relatives of Jemison along with checking historical and Seneca sources. Lenski's story deals with that period of Jemison's life from childhood and capture to early womanhood. She changes the girl's name to Molly. Molly's whiteness is emphasized in the first part of the story when her trial is made more intense by nasty Indian women. There is a double-page illustration of a cross woman kicking her and Molly rushing off in surprise and haste. No negative tales of Indian women appear in Jemison's narrative.[52] Lenski also emphasizes an aspect of Jemison's appearance which, as in the case of Jane McCrea, arrested the attention of nineteenth-century authors: her hair. James Seaver says that originally Jemison's hair had been "light chestnut brown," but when he spoke with her it was "quite grey, a little curled, of middling length and tied in a bunch behind." But folklore and Laura Wright, who saw Mary when Mary was ninety years old, claimed it had been blond.[53] The centerpiece of Mary's whiteness in Lenski's work is her hair. Lenski creates a scene at Fort Duquesne that is not in the original and resembles other captive stories such as James Smith's.[54] An old "friendly" Indian tries to clean up the captive children and takes out a "crude comb," "painstakingly" combing "their blond hair" free of briars and tangles, then shaving the boys' heads. But "Molly's hair he leaves hanging loose and free about her shoulders, a shower of shining gold." The children captives' faces are then painted.

> " 'All we need now is black hair!' said Davy bitterly.
> 'And black hearts!' added Nicholas, with a flash of insight."[55]

During Molly's adoption by her Indian sisters and the other Seneca women, "It was her hair that pleased them most. It made them think of blooming corn-stalks, of soft, fresh corn-silk, of pale yellow ripened corn—the dearest things in life. So when they gave her a name, there was only one they could think of. They called her Corn Tassel that day and for many a day thereafter."[56] When the boy Little Turtle, also a Lenski creation, intercedes for Molly, he is drawn to her by her sadness but also her name: "Corn Tassel! Her name was as beautiful as her hair! If only she could be happy."[57] In all the illustrations in the Lenski book Molly appears in long blond braids, the only blond among dark people with black hair. On the cover there is a pink-white and pubescent Jemison with bright blond braids picking corn with similarly colored yellow tassels. She is pictured alone, a white girl in Indian garb, a basket on her back, in buckskin skirt, leggings, and moccasins, stripped to the waist. Almost all of the illustrations, indoors and out, contrast Iroquois existence with that of the white frontier culture. Many of these make the Indian life palpable, friendly, and communal. But throughout, there are illustrations of a white girl, looking always like something out of *Heidi*, so white that she never even gets a tan, an incarnation of purity from another world.

Lenski uses the girl's hair and her name to signal a transformation which is positive. Unlike the doctors, lawyers, businessmen, and anthropologists who preceded her, she does not see Jemison's life as successful only because she maintained her whiteness, her Christianity, and her "better" Anglo-American ethnicity. At the end of the story, when Mary decides to stay with the Senecas, Chief Burning Sky renames her in front of the tribe. He says at first she was called Corn Tassel " 'because your hair is the color of the tassel on the corn. But now you have earned your real name. . . . By your willingness to become an Indian Woman, you have earned the name, *Little-Woman-of-Great-Courage*. Cherish this name, and do not tarnish it. . . . You are now a woman, and the women of our tribe will welcome you as one of themselves. Welcome to the Seneca, Little-Woman-of-Great-Courage.' "[58]

Lenski also shows Jemison's mother not as Laura Wright would have us see her—chastising Mary for leaving Christianity—but rather as being pleased that her daughter remained true to another directive, to be courageous. The closing illustration portrays the white/Indian girl happily lifting an Indian baby in the air. In the story it is the child of a white trapper who befriends Molly and marries an Indian woman, but it is easy to deduce that Molly herself will have such a baby. These features of whiteness, womanhood, and Indian life are brought together at the end of Lenski's work.

Although Morgan, Letchworth, Bush-Brown, and Lenski all recognized the Indian impact on Jemison's life, in the cultural evolution of her legend, they and others placed a strong emphasis on the white part of her life, as if to remind their European and North American audiences that even in a competing world

Frontispiece from Lois Lenski, Indian Captive: The Story of
Mary Jemison *(1941). Courtesy of the Newberry Library*

of dark-skinned and non-Christian people, the ultimate superiority of whiteness and Christianity would survive and prevail. Only Lenski hints at the positive rather than the exotic features of her merging with her Seneca world.

The White *Woman*

. . . .

What was the fascination of Mary Jemison for the nineteenth-century public? Dawn Lander Gherman recognized that Jemison's was one of a series of captivity narratives emphasizing the connections between native men and white women. She argued that, far from corroborating women's fears of the frontier and of the American Indian, especially the male Indian, the popularity of these works suggests the fascination with and indeed identification of many female readers with life, not just on the frontier, but in the tepee. "Would I not make a nice squaw?" was the implied and sometimes stated question she perceived readers to be asking of work like Jemison's in which white women chose to remain with Indians.[59]

But the story of Mary Jemison was popular also because it is a nineteenth-century *Pilgrim's Progress* that spans the critical years of the early history and birth of the republic. It is an epic story setting a woman at the center of a New World cosmic drama. Beginning at the edge of the Appalachian forest when a young girl is captured by an alien enemy, it proceeds as she matures in the fires of the Revolution, albeit on the "wrong side," and ends as an old grandmother watches the Age of Industrialization and white "civilization" move in on her. In it, a child becomes a woman estranged from her own people and enters a strange, "savage" world. Here, in less than ideal circumstances, she finds her own, her children's, and her new people's humanity. She finds the strength to marry twice, raise seven children, and live through grave personal crises and major social and political changes.

Mary's story is a woman's story, and from the beginning it addresses itself to a woman's life course—the development from childhood through old age.[60] Although the story hinges on the *white* part of the White Woman, the *woman* is also a critical component. Just as the story of Daniel Boone emphasizes Boone's maleness and his heroic character in facing adversity, Mary's story emphasizes her femaleness, her capture, and her heroic character.

In recent years, new theories have addressed the reasons for the popularity of literary works. However these theories disagree, there appears to be a consensus among critics on the need to analyze two categories to comprehend such books. The first is termed *authorship* and represents an inquiry into who wrote the book, under what conditions, and with what intent. The second category of analysis, *readership*, explores the question of how the reader is being addressed by the author.[61] Feminist critics are looking for gender-related clues as to how and why books are written and read. In moving away from the New Criticism of the 1950s, recent scholars demonstrate a respect for the text itself but argue that it is important to attend to that text's place in a particular historical, social, and cultural context, taking note of its relation to other works, to period conventions, and to the ways it addresses particular readers. The following explication of Jemison's as a woman's story is informed by this recent discourse, although historical methods and assumptions have guided the analysis.[62]

Although Jemison's story comes to us through the words of a white male author, in fact several male authors, going back to the original edition of *A Narrative of the Life of Mrs. Mary Jemison* one is struck by its structure, plot, and language as a work tracing the story of a White *Woman* and one appealing directly as a woman's story. From the outset, Mary Jemison is presented as a young girl and a victim. The structure of the narrative moves her from a setting found frequently in the captivity genre—the family idyll. The dissolution of this idyll begins with an attack on it, as seen through the victim's eyes, and incorporates her personal experience of grave violence and destruction of that earlier world. Through a series of subsequent events, Jemison creates a new vision of her own power and goes on to reconstitute, albeit through extreme hardship and more family turmoil, personal triumph and a new family idyll. Seaver has her describing the Jemison farm in southwestern Pennsylvania before her victimization: "Our mansion was a little paradise." But as is standard in many of the captivity narratives, there follows the destruction of an earlier familial peace: "But alas! how transitory are all human affairs!" First comes the death of a neighbor, then the capture of the family, the separation from those not captured, the escape of two brothers. Next there is the separation from those also captured, mother, father, two brothers and a sister, and the women and three children of visiting friends. Finally, there is the horror of recognizing the scalp of her mother being cleaned, then placed on a hoop and waved in the breeze of the canoe in front of her as she is brought down the Ohio.[63] From family destruction, the victim Jemison reemerges, first with a new Indian family and later with her children and grandchildren, her own Indian family. Within the structure of this narrative we have the prototype of the successful female survivor, whether inside or outside Indian society. This woman successfully overcomes adversity and functions as a mother and a person in her own right. Thus even in its overall narrative structure, Jemison's is a woman's story.

The story itself is built around the traditional female life cycle. As a child, Mary was weak and small. Her family seems almost passively to have awaited capture. Once captured, it was her mother rather than her father who sustained her. "Mother, from the time we were taken, had manifested a great degree of fortitude, and encouraged us to support our troubles without complaining; and by her conversation seemed to make the distance and time shorter, and the way more smooth. But father lost all ambition in the beginning of our trouble, and continued apparently lost to every care—absorbed in melancholy. Here, as before, she insisted on the necessity of our eating; and we obeyed her, but it was done with heavy hearts."[64] When her mother saw the Indians placing moccasins on Mary's feet, she knew this meant her child would be saved, the rest of the family killed. At this point she took Mary aside and in a heartrending soliloquy said good-bye to her daughter: " 'My dear little Mary, I fear that the time has arrived when we must be parted forever. Your life, my child, I think will be spared; but we shall probably be tomahawked here in this lonesome place by the Indians. O! how can I part with you my darling? What will become of my sweet little Mary!' "[65]

Mary and a small boy were then separated from the rest of the other captives. At first she was despondent.

It is impossible for any one to form a correct idea of what my feelings were at the sight of those savages, whom I supposed had murdered my parents and brothers, sister, and friends, and left them in the swamp to be devoured by beasts! But what could I do? A poor little defenceless girl; without the power or means of escaping; without a home to go to, even if I could be liberated; without a knowledge of the direction or distance to my former place of residence; and without a living friend to whom to fly for protection, I felt a kind of horror, anxiety, and dread, that to me, seemed insupportable. . . . My only relief was in silent stifled sobs.[66]

The next change in her life and the initial end to her sadness came when, after she was taken by canoe down the Ohio to Fort Duquesne, "two pleasant looking squaws of the Seneca tribe" came to look her over and, after a few minutes, claim her. After separating from the Shawnees and heading off down the river behind them, she was in a small canoe with the two women, passing all kinds of war horrors unscathed, somehow already in a new state of protection.

When they arrived at the Seneca encampment, the women left her, but only for a moment, to get her "a suit of Indian clothing, all new, and very clean and nice." These replaced her old clothes, "now torn in pieces, so that I was almost naked."[67] She describes her adoption ceremony as attended only by women: Mary, a young girl, surrounded and protected, then accepted by grieving Seneca women. Like all captives among the Iroquois, Mary was claimed by bereaved women who would decide her fate. Arriving at their village, she was washed, cleaned, and dressed "Indian style." The two Seneca sisters had lost their brother in battle the year before. As Mary sat with them, many women of the village came into the wigwam to mourn.[68] Then, "all the Squaws in the town came to see me. I was soon surrounded by them, and they immediately set up a most dismal howling, crying bitterly, and wringing their hands in all the agonies of grief for a deceased relative."[69]

Then one stepped forward and, "in a voice somewhat between speaking and singing," recounted the life of the lost brother, his qualities, the situation of his death, and the fate of his spirit now "in the land of his fathers." Mary soon became the focus of their attention and their joy. They renamed her and substituted her for the lost brother. By virtue of this ritual adoption she "was ever considered and treated by them as a real sister, the same as though I had been born of their mother." With this new family, she began to be restored. When Seneca warriors brought home captives and she was invited to attend the ceremonies and watch the tortures, her Indian mother objected and protected her by telling her sisters: " 'Oh! how can you think of making her bleed at the wounds which now are but partially healed? The recollection of her former troubles would deprive us of Dickewamis, and she would depart to the fields of the blessed, where fighting has ceased, and the corn needs no tending—where hunting is easy, the forests delightful, the summers are pleasant, and the winters are mild!' " [70]

The women of this new family and particularly her Indian mother assured her that she would be accepted and protected. They made sure she was not returned to British authorities during peace negotiations, working out strategies to ensure that she would never be sent back into the British colonial world. Her sisters and the women of the village taught her their language and the economic skills of planting and caring for skins. As other Indian children coming of age were taught, the same-sex parent or siblings showed the way into the adult world. [71]

When it came time for her to marry, her sisters arranged the match to the Delaware, Sheninjee. When Mary looked back on the quality of that marriage, she partially credited their wisdom and the wisdom of customary Seneca marriage patterns for the success and love it brought. Thus in a short time a young woman had moved from defeat and despondency to acceptance and love and from weakness to a "famous feat"—a nearly seven-hundred-mile journey from southern Ohio to west-central New York State, "an arduous 600-mile wilderness trek to join her adopted sisters in the Genesee River country." [72]

Following the death of her husband, she remarried. Here the story reveals the problems of woman as wife. Her second husband, Hiokatoo, was fifty years her senior and held a powerful leadership position in Seneca society. If the reader missed or overlooked Seaver's notes on George Jemison on Hiokatoo's brutality, the discussion of the second husband may be read as one might guess many married woman readers would read it—as the life of a husband with whose values one cannot fully concur. Several other factors support a reading which gives less than full credibility to Seaver's presentation of Jemison's distaste for her husband's "savage" nature; first, Jemison would not have been likely to criticize her husband in public or to a stranger. Second, if one's husband was out in the world, one did not have total control over his behavior. In the rapidly industrializing period between 1820 and 1880, when the first editions of Jemison's narrative appeared, there must have been a considerable number of middle- and upper-class female readers in England and America who had little control over their husbands' work, whether in manufacturing, on plantations, or in battle. In her analysis of romance literature, Janice Radway posits that women who read contemporary romances are interested in men who are strong but gentle and loving. Their nineteenth-century counterparts may have felt the same. Perhaps Hiokatoo was such a man. Jemison gives us few clues.[73]

Mary's difficulty as a mother and her ultimately tragic experiences with her sons constitute an arresting if harrowing tale for any mother. Her eldest son, Thomas, was the child with whom she had traveled on her six-hundred-mile journey. Later, in 1811, when he was fifty-two, a long-standing hatred between him and his younger brother John erupted into an argument. John was forty-eight and Mary's son by Hiokatoo. Thomas had come to the house drunk. A fight ensued, and John killed his half-brother. A year later John killed his younger brother Jesse in another alcohol-induced brawl. Such a frightening fate for one's sons might easily evoke the sympathy of other mothers. Jemison (or Seaver) expected that the reader could "imagine what my feelings were. . . . My darling son, my youngest child, him on whom I depended, was dead; and I in my old age left destitute of a helping hand!"[74]

Some of Seaver's language here seems deliberately sentimental and contrived; not that the situations are not difficult, but one assumes he was influenced by the growing sentimental trends in literature of his day.[75] On the conflicts between her children and the pain they caused Jemison, Seaver's text reads: "No one can conceive of the constant trouble that I daily endured on the account of my two oldest sons whom I loved equally, and with all the feelings and affection of a tender mother, stimulated by an anxious concern for their fate. Parents, mothers especially, will love their children, though ever so unkind and disobedient. Their eyes of compassion, of real sentimental affection, will be involuntarily extended after them."[76]

Seaver uses the language of sentiment, appealing to the mother-child bond, which the middle-class white world increasingly idealized in the nineteenth century. But given the facts of Jemison's family life, the feelings she must have had, if not Seaver's diction, seem genuine. These would be well known to women with children. In the years of the first edition, the average number of children borne by white women was seven; by 1900, it was between three and four.[77]

Along with the agonies of motherhood, Jemison relishes its benefits, its generativity. She talks about her grandchild going to Dartmouth College in 1816, what a good student he was, and how he was planning to be a doctor.[78] In recapitulating her life she counts her children and her grandchildren, much as any Jewish, Chinese, or in this case, Indian grandmother might. She tells Seaver, "I have been the mother of eight children; three of whom are now living, and I have at this time thirty-nine grand children, and fourteen great-grand children, all living in the neighborhood of Genesee River, and at Buffalo."[79]

Jemison was twice widowed, first as a young woman with a new baby. Of her first loss she says: "This was a heavy and unexpected blow. I was now in my youthful days left a widow, with one son, and entirely dependent on myself for his and my support."[80] As a widow again in her later years, her experience was different. Her husband lived to be over one hundred, but he had been much older than she to begin with. After the Treaty of Big Tree (1797), she was awarded a huge tract of nearly eighteen thousand acres. During these actions, Jemison was naturalized by an act of the New York State legislature and with the assent of the Seneca chiefs awarded a tract of two miles. But within the next thirty years she went from wealth to near poverty by signing the land away to white buyers. After her dealings with whites she was left with a small piece of land, about two acres along either side of the river, a minuscule portion of what had been the Gardow Flats.[81]

Despite the extraordinary circumstances of her life, it is its sharing of the pattern common to any ordinary woman's life cycle that makes it compelling. In an age of a burgeoning press, with an ever-growing female readership and a market for female fiction, this "true" story of struggle in a woman's life in a strange world allowed its female readers to identify with a heroic figure who was small and appeared weak yet who accomplished much, both in dealing with others and in summoning her own strength. In her childhood victimization, her sisterhood with other women, her marriage, her childbearing, her mothering, her violent loss of her sons, her continuing commitment to family and community life, her widowhood, and her sense of the meaning of life, Mary Jemison's story had strong appeal for nineteenth-century female readers.[82]

Summing up her life to James Seaver, she said:

> My strength has been great for a woman of my size; otherwise I must long ago have died under the burdens which I was obliged to carry. I learned to carry loads on my back, supported by a strap placed across my forehead, soon after my captivity; and continue to carry the same way. Upward of thirty years ago and with the help of my young children, I backed all the boards that were used about my house from Allen's mill at the outlet of Silver Lake, a distance of five miles. I have planted, hoed, and harvested corn every season but one since I was taken prisoner. Even this present fall, 1823, I have husked my corn and backed it into the house.[83]

Mary Jemison was a survivor. She was a woman who outlived two Indian husbands, bore eight children, lived through the violent deaths of her parents, siblings, one husband, and two sons, two major wars, a revolution, and the beginnings of the Industrial Revolution. She met with and knew the leaders of her people: Joseph Brant, Red Jacket (Sa-go-wat-ha), and Cornplanter. More than a *white* woman or a white *woman*, through her own work and the power of her story, Mary Jemison became a heroine in her own right.

Indian Woman

. . . . . .

There were special beings on the other side of the sky. In
the center of their village stood the chief's lodge. Here he lived
with his family: a wife and a girl child. It happened, however,
that he became lonesome. The Ancient One was thin, and his
bones were dry. The child did not make him happy; in fact, it
was thought that his state was caused by jealousy. His condition
persisted, and he wanted to find its cause. The other beings assembled to find out through dreams what the problem was; in
this way they sought the reason for his disturbance. Much time
passed. Finally, one of the beings said, "I think I understand the
true nature of our chief's problem. He needs to have the tree
standing near his lodge uprooted."

"That is it," said the chief, "Thank you."

Now the other man-beings came together and said, "We will
all work together to uproot the tree. There must be some on
each root." So they pulled it up and placed it somewhere else.
A wide opening was left in the sky-earth, and the male beings
regarded it. Each one looked down and saw only green. Then
the chief said to his wife, "Come and let us both look at it. She
put her child on her back to do this. The chief walked slowly
and with difficulty, and the two of them arrived at the abyss.
He looked at it, then was tired. Turning to her he said, "Now,
you look at it." "Ah," she said, "I fear it." And she hung back.
"Come on," he urged, "look at it." First, she put the edges of
her shawl in her mouth so as to hold the child securely and then
rested her body on her right side with her hand beneath her.
She leaned over to look into the abyss below her, but both her
hands gripped tightly the ground beneath her. Then she looked.
But as she bent over, her husband grabbed her leg and pushed
her into the great hole.

Beneath the sky-world floated the body of the white Fire-
dragon—the true cause of the ancient chief's jealousy. As the
woman fell, the Fire-dragon took an ear of corn and gave it to
her. He then gave her a mortar and a pestle and took from his
chest a small pot. Last, he gave her a bone and said, "Here is
what you will continue to eat."

Below this sky world of the ancients lived all other beings, including the Wind and the Thick Night. These assembled and held a council. At first they expressed reluctance, saying, "It is probably not possible for us to help this woman falling from the sky toward us." But then each one spoke and said, "I could help her." The Black Bass said, "Perhaps I could help," but others thought he had too little intelligence. The Pickerel then said, "Maybe I could do it." But the others said, "No, you are too much of a glutton." Next it was the Turtle's turn. "Perhaps I could help the woman-being." They all agreed he could. And so it was Turtle who swam to the place where the woman's body was falling, and it was on his back that she came to rest.

But once at rest she sat, and she began to cry. She cried for a long time. It was only then she remembered that in her hands she held some of the sky-soil. She opened each hand and scattered it over Turtle's back. As she moved it there was more room to walk, and the earth grew. She became conscious of how, by her actions, she formed this new earth. She moved great distances over Turtle's back, enlarging it. Soon shrubs and grasses and reeds of every kind grew and vines of wild potato. She saw this all happen before her.

She stood up and said, "Now light will be present, and it will make day; early each morning a globe of light will appear, and it will move through the day until it sets." Then she stood up again and said, "Next in the order of things comes a star, and there will be many in the sky." It happened. She pointed her finger as she said it, and many stars appeared. Moving her hand in the direction where cold comes she said, "Those will be called the stars pursuing the Bear," and "Here will be a large star before the daylight which will be called, it-brings-the-day." Turning toward a group of stars she pronounced, "They will be called the cluster. With them one will know if the year is on course. They are dancing. Next in order is a woman sitting. She will accompany the cluster. The-Beaver-whose-skin-is-spread-out is what all of these together will be called. As one travels at night one will watch all of these."

Then, the she one spoke again saying over and over, "All of these will dwell far from all human beings in a place were a stream is always present." And it all happened thus, the cause of it being the She Master, the Ancient One.[84]

The story of the woman who fell from the sky and landed on Turtle's back has many versions. In nearly all, the fall of Sky Woman, the mobilization of the animal kingdom to help humans, the growth of food on the earth, and the birth of children are the result of the fall and arrival of a woman on the earth. Animals cooperate and share; they are friends and co-workers in creation.[85] What did the Indian world depicted in such an account of the world's origins mean to Mary Jemison, a woman who chose to remain a part of it for so much of her life? It is certainly possible that Seaver did not hear the Iroquois version of how life began from Mary. It is unlikely that she had not heard it. Besides her social and economic experiences with the Seneca community, she must have been exposed to a spiritual community as well.[86] Being brought up as a Christian girl, Mary must have found the contrast to the Creation she knew striking. What a different Fall of Man—the fall of a woman, making all life possible, a fall in which animals do not tempt and deceive, bring sin or exile, but rather provide and nurture.

How does one enter into another world, and what is it that one first sees? After a year or two, if the opportunity arises to leave, why would one decide to stay on? And as one's life moves through its course, much as the yearly cycle moves through its course, with birth, growth, maturation, aging, and death, what would make a woman, a man, a child, raised in one place, with one people, stay on in another, with a very different family, a very different people?

Jemison's story suggests some answers. To know more of the actual nature of her life as an Indian woman, we need a further investigation into her Seneca life. First, we need to return to the Jemison narrative itself to analyze the distinctive references to an Indian woman's life which are found scattered through it. Second, we must briefly reexamine two views of Jemison's Indianness as developed by two of her interpreters, James Seaver and Lewis Henry Morgan. Finally, we need to investigate other sources that will bring us closer to Indian life: history, material culture, anthropological fieldwork, ethnohistorical works on the Seneca nation, and available reports of Senecas or Iroquois themselves.

A careful reading of the Jemison story reveals that she became an Indian woman by learning to work in Seneca society, by receiving the benefits and returning the obligations of Senecas, by careful observation and comparison between the white frontier society from which she came and the Seneca society of which she became a part, and then by identifying with and choosing the Indian world over the emerging American one.

In both her work and her social relations, Jemison was well on her way toward "Indianization" within the first four years of her captivity. She was brought into the Seneca family that adopted her, she learned their language, and she participated in every aspect of a Seneca woman's work. In the spring of her fourth year of captivity, when her son Thomas (her first surviving child and son of Sheninjee) was "three or four moons old," she participated in the fur trade. Senecas with whom she lived on the southern Ohio River moved from their winter camp of Sciota to their summer camp of Wiishto, and from there up the Ohio to Fort Pitt to sell "our fur and skins that we had taken in the winter, and procure some necessary articles for the use of our family."[87]

Looking back on the four years that had passed, Jemison reflects on the work of this Indian world and says, "Our labor was not severe," one year being much like the next "without that endless variety that is to be observed in the common labor of the white people."[88] As to the stereotypes of Indian women as beasts of burden, she assures Seaver this was not the case: "My situation was easy; I had no particular hardships to endure." She observes:

> Notwithstanding the Indian women have all the fuel and bread to procure, and the cooking to perform, their task is probably not harder than that of white women, who have those articles provided for them; and their cares certainly are not half as numerous, nor as great. In the summer season, we planted, tended and harvested our corn, and generally had all our children with us; but had no master to oversee or drive us, so that we could work as leisurely as we pleased. We had no plough on the Ohio; but performed the whole process of

planting and hoeing with a small tool that resembled, in some respects, a hoe with a very short handle.[89]

She learned to preserve meat, to "prepare or dress the skins," and to use deerskin to make clothing. She learned how to cook by pounding corn "into samp or hommany, boiling the hommany, making now and then a cake and baking it in the ashes, and in boiling or roasting our venison."[90]

She experienced the mutual benefits and obligations of the Seneca world almost at once. Her sisters adopted her, protected her, and taught her the ways of her new world. The care and protection they provided her brought obligations resulting in her marriage to Sheninjee, the Delaware Indian they brought for her mate. Her sisters told her, "I must go and live with one of them, [the Delawares] whose name was She-nin-jee. Not to cross them, or disobey their commands, with a great degree of reluctance I went; and Sheninjee and I were married according to Indian custom."[91] When her child was due they assisted her in the dangers of childbirth. At the time "the kernels of the corn first appeared on the cob" she was taken "to a small shed, on the bank of the river, which was made of boughs." There her sisters stayed with her until, on the second day of her confinement, she gave birth. The baby died, but her husband, Sheninjee, took care of her when she came home. He and her family helped care for her during her long recovery.[92] About two years later, she was asked to take her new baby and travel with her two Seneca brothers from their place along the southern Ohio back to their home on the Genesee in west-central New York.[93] Her husband consented to the move and began the journey with Jemison, the baby, Thomas, and her brothers but brought along "fur and skins which he had on hand" and spent the winter hunting with his friends, planning to meet her the following spring.[94]

During the Revolution, Mary pounded samp "from sun-set till sun-rise" for Colonel John Butler, "Mohawk Valley Loyalist," and Joseph Brant (Thayendanegea), Mohawk leader of the Indian resistance, when they came through her area on the Genesee. Jemison was not a passive onlooker in the Revolution. She supported and identified with the Iroquois people and their British and loyalist allies and was proud to tell Seaver how she had provided food and hospitality to these men, thus moving beyond family and clan obligations to tribal loyalty.[95]

Throughout her story Jemison observes and compares Indian and white life. She tells Seaver that both liquor and the attempts "to civilize and christianize" have hurt Indians. Each "constantly made them worse and worse; increased their vices, and robbed them of many of their virtues; and will ultimately produce their extermination." She also criticizes "education" and white culture's presumption that by taking Indian children away from their parents it can make them into whites. Later she says, "No people can live more happy than the Indians did in times of peace, before the introduction of spiritous liquors among them. Their lives were a continual round of pleasures. Their wants were few, and easily satisfied; and their cares were only for to-day. . . . If peace ever dwelt with men, it was in former times, in the recesses from war, amongst what are now termed barbarians."[96] Although critical of the brutality of certain aspects of Seneca warfare, Jemison continually testifies to the positive aspects of Indian life and the destructive nature of white encroachments.

Jemison had several opportunities to leave the Seneca nation. She did not. At the end of the Seven Years' War, when she was to be returned with other war prisoners, Jemison chose to stay. Later, she was to be taken by a Dutchman to Niagara, where he would be given a bounty for her return. "I was notified of his intention; but I was as fully determined not to be redeemed at that time, especially with his assistance." Again, after the Revolution, her Indian brother Kau-jises-tau-ge-au (Black Coals) told her she could return to white society. Her son Thomas wanted her to go and said he would come with her to help her with her young children. Senecas saw in Thomas a potential warrior and would not allow him to leave. For two reasons Jemison decided to stay: "To go myself, and leave him, was more than I felt able to do. . . . But another [reason], more powerful, if possible, was that I had got a large family of Indian children, that I must take with me; and that if I should be so fortunate as to find my relatives, they would despise them, if not myself; and treat us as enemies; or, at least with a degree of cold indifference, which I thought I could not endure." At this point (depending on which year it was), she had between three and five children, and of course her husband, Hiokatoo, to whom she had been married since about 1765. This realization of potential and ongoing white hostility toward her and her children led her to tell her brother "that it was my choice to stay and spend the remainder of my days with my Indian friends, and live with my family as I had heretofore done."[97]

The treaties following the Revolution ended traditional life and began what Anthony F. C. Wallace called "slums in the wilderness." According to Wallace, before 1797 most of "Iroquois territory east of the Genesee River had already been sold." At the Treaty of Big Tree (Geneseo, September 15, 1797), all the land "west of the Genesee River was sold for $100,000" in exchange for future annuities for individual tribal members. There were 310 square miles left, four large reservations and six small ones. Revolutionary financier Robert Morris, in debt and in control of the land at the time, was instrumental in turning it over to the Dutch bankers of the Holland Land Company. Several chiefs and important Seneca leaders, including Red Jacket and Cornplanter, were able to get these smaller one- to two-square-mile plots.[98] Jemison's Indian brother Kau-jises-tau-ge-au negotiated land for her over the objections of Red Jacket. Jemison marked off the land she wanted, including the Gardow Flats. The Gardow Tract was 17,927 acres of prime river property along the Genesee near Castile. Years later, on April 9, 1817, the legislature of New York passed an act naturalizing Mary Jemison and giving her title to the land and solidifying her land claim.[99] Mary lived with her family when the Seneca nation was displaced, lost its rights to the land, and was forced onto reservations in the western and southwestern part of the state.[100] Because of the special status granted her by naturalization and land, Jemison, her aging husband, Hiokatoo, and her sons and daughters lived between the encroaching white world and the beleaguered Indian one. Her land at Gardeau remained in her hands until the mid-1820s.

In the early 1820s a man claiming the name of George Jemison appeared in the Gardeau area saying he was Jemison's cousin on her father's side. She believed him and lent him the use of some of her land. He proceeded to act in devious ways to get her to sign away a large tract to him. She did not know how to read English. She gave him what she thought was forty acres.

After signing the document, she found that the figure was over four hundred acres, which was soon sold to someone else. This was the same George Jemison whom Seaver used as his prime source on Hiokatoo and in a note tells the reader, "Mrs. Jemison is now confident that George Jemison is not her cousin." [101]

Shortly before she spoke with Seaver, on September 3, 1823, two white men to whom she leased all of her land except for four thousand acres, persuaded her, with the consent of the Seneca council, to sell all the rest of the Gardeau reservation. She would keep a two-mile tract along the river and would receive $300 per year. In less than three years her last two miles became part of a package sold by the Senecas for $28,260, along with nine other tracts of varying sizes on the Seneca reservation land in Caneadea, Squawky Hill, Tonawanda, and Cattaraugus. In one more way, then, Mary Jemison became an Indian woman. Though she lived on the margins of white society and acquired rights to the Gardeau land, the legalization of her rights was a setup for speculators to buy what had been prime Indian land. She was cheated out of her land by these white men, and her children were deprived of their due by "legal" and illegal deeds.[102]

From Jemison's narrative we find that work, a system of mutual obligations, family relationships, white prejudice, and her experiences with land bound her to the Seneca community, defining her as an Indian woman.

SEAVER'S AND MORGAN'S INDIAN WOMAN

In interpreting her story, there is the inherent problem of extricating Jemison from Seaver, of trying to figure out what he asked and what she offered to tell him without questions. We would also like to know what he left out about her Indian life, but to date, no trace of Seaver's notes has been found. In such an encounter, answers generally depend on the relationship forged between what we would call the interviewer and his subject and the questions asked. In early nineteenth-century American society, few men of Seaver's class would have been able to get highly personal information even from Euro-American women. Barring the real possibility that sensitive matters were brought up by Jemison and deliberately left out of the final narrative, it appears that either Seaver did not ask some of the right questions or Jemison was loath to give him the answers. It is unlikely that a white man would be given access to much basic information about Seneca women's lives even if Seaver had been trained to understand Seneca life, which he certainly was not.[103] Besides having the right questions, one who ventures into the deeper places of another's life must know when not to ask questions and when to accept silences. The listener must transmit his or her faith that the speaker has a story worth telling, a story worth listening to.[104] Seaver knew that Jemison was in many ways a Seneca, but he appears not to have asked questions that would reveal what this meant on a daily or annual basis. Nor did he seem to have asked questions that would uncover the personal meaning of Jemison's political, spiritual, familial, or clan life as a Seneca woman.[105]

Beginning with a substantial climb up the steep canyon from her house along the river, eighty-year-old Jemison walked four miles to see Seaver. The climb alone takes fifteen- to twenty-five-minutes on a nice summer day. The river view is beautiful, but there are good chances to slip and slide.[106] Jemison was attended by Thomas Clute, a white neighbor, whom Seaver said she saw as "her protector." Clearly she would not have traveled that distance at her age if she did not want to tell her story. Seaver spent three days with her, but his preface indicates that they were not alone. They met at the house of Jannet Whaley in Castile, "in company with the publisher" and lawyer Daniel W. Banister, who had "procured the interesting subject . . . to come to that place."[107] Does this mean that the three men were there all the time or only off and on? Did Whaley come by to feed them? Did both Seaver and Jemison stay at the Whaleys' overnight? Certainly it is likely that people came and went. The meeting could not always have been the private one depicted in the frontispiece of the 1856 edition. We do not know if the two spent time alone together. Nothing is said of an Indian interpreter. Jemison knew English, and Seaver reports that a hint of her Irish accent was still noticeable, but after having spoken Seneca as a first language most of her life, one wonders if there were things she said in English that would have had a different meaning if said in Seneca. Despite these problems of culture, gender, age, language, and privacy, Seaver learned a great deal about Jemison. He was probably a good listener. Other men had chosen him for this task. But we do not know what he left out, how he arranged his notes, or what she left out.

Jemison tells us that she entered the Indian world by her feet. Shawnees "stripped the shoes and stockings from the little boy that belonged to the woman who was taken with us and put moccasins on his feet, as they had done before on mine."[108] What did she think of these new feet, this new feel of the earth beneath them, her other new clothes? Although eastern Indian clothing in the eighteenth and early nineteenth centuries sometimes borrowed from white style and fabric, much was reformed and adapted.[109] Besides clothing and utensils, what was her life like in the longhouse or log cabin? Which stories did she hear? What daily and seasonal rituals did she observe and join?[110] What were the wider obligations of her life as defined by Seneca kinship? Was she a member of the Wolf clan or was she a Turtle, a Beaver, or a Heron? Did she have the full power of a native-born woman of this clan, or did she and her children have less power because of their foreign origins?

Seaver gives us more than we would otherwise know, but he goes only so far. He seems to have realized this himself because he added an appendix of some thirty-eight pages to the first edition of the narrative in which ten of the entries deal with his understanding of Indian life. The appendix provides the reader more with a sense of Seaver's views than of Seneca and Iroquois life.[111] Although there appear to be no papers attesting to Lewis Henry Morgan's work on it, nor does his name appear as a revisor or editor anywhere in the text, several scholars have credited him with work on the 1856 edition, and some of the additions to the text indicate his hand. In his own copy, at the close of the preface he signed, "Morgan."[112] Lewis Henry Morgan's work on the Iroquois confederacy appeared in 1851 and has since become a classic in the field. In that work Morgan, assisted by the Seneca Ely S. Parker, detailed and illustrated the life of the Iroquois. How heavily the hand of Morgan fell on the Jemison legend is hard to decipher, but some of his additions lent his considerable authority as an Indian expert to the Seneca life of Jemison, the Indian woman. A few sections, such as the extensive listing of Iroquois place names, simply transferred information from Morgan's earlier work on the Iroquois to the new Jemison edition. But from the first page, where Ely Parker gives a testimonial to the authenticity of the narrative, there is a stronger Indian cast to this edition. The "Publisher's Note" follows with a clear statement—the first since the book's first publication—that Jemison became an Indian woman: "The life of Mary Jemison was one of singular vicissitude and trial. . . . Trained in the wilderness to the ordinary duties of the Indian female, she became imbued with their sentiments, and transformed essentially into one of their number." As a result, "it was her sad destiny to become lost to the race from which she had sprung, and affiliated with the one which she had every reason to abhor. This transformation, the reverse of the order of nature, was perfected by her becoming the wife of an Indian, and the mother of Indian children." Jemison "found friends among her Seneca kindred, and was ever treated by them with consideration and kindness." At the end of her life, "she was forced to fulfill her destiny by dying, as she had lived, a Seneca woman."[113] Some aspects of the 1824 and 1856 editions, then, begin to open their readers to Jemison's Indian life.

JEMISON'S SENECA LIFE

The best estimates of chronology in Mary Jemison's life and death place her birth in 1743, her capture in April 1758, her death in 1833—a life span of ninety years.[114] In North America those years saw a major political transformation of the continent. At the time of Mary's birth and capture, France and Spain controlled vast empires and Britain's colonies hugged a narrow strip of the Atlantic shore. Much of the Ohio Valley, the upper Mississippi Valley, and what is now northeastern Canada was claimed by France but was homeland of the five nations of the League of the Iroquois, along with Shawnees, Miamis, Ojibwas, Hurons, Lakotas, and other native peoples. In the Southwest, Spain claimed Florida, the areas along the Gulf Coast, and west of the Mississippi including all of Mexico. Here again, north of Mexico, European powers were in the minority while Comanches, Apaches, and other Indians they were unable to control held sway.[115] By the time Jemison was twenty, the political map of North America was radically changed.

With the defeat of the French by British forces in Quebec

in 1763, the French missions, traders, forts, and communities came under British control or suffered British toleration. British colonial settlement began to move across the Appalachian frontier. With the Proclamation of 1763, Britain tried to keep its promises to its Iroquois and other former Indian allies in the French and Indian War while restricting settlement to east of the Appalachians. This policy failed. At the close of the Revolution, white settlement moved into Kentucky, the Ohio Valley, and western New York and Pennsylvania. The men of Sullivan's campaign were given Iroquois and other Indian lands by the new government, and land fever seized the New England countryside. By 1824 New York, which since the sixteenth century had been dominated by the League of the Iroquois, gave way to the transforming powers of canals, state roads, market agriculture, new townships, cities, industry, and millennial religion.[116]

What could these changes have meant to those native peoples whose ancestors had lived on this land? What could they have meant to Jemison herself, who, although born an immigrant child from a frontier family, lived seventy-five years among these people? Contrary to the lore, popular fiction, and film, Iroquois peoples were not continually running through the forest carrying hatchets. The Ho-de-no-sau-nee is the name the five nations gave to themselves. Each was an independent and powerful nation in its own right. According to their traditions, around the 1600s, so they could live peacefully together, a leader came into their midst and traveled all over what is now New York trying to bind up the nations' wounds. His name was Dekanawidah, and he forged an alliance of the five nations under a tree of peace. The five nations began where the sun rose in the east with the Mohawks along the Hudson Valley and into the Adirondacks, moved to the Oneidas, the Onondagas and the Cayugas in central New York and around the Finger Lakes. The Senecas called themselves Nun-Da-Wah O-No-Ga, the People of the Western Door. Their lands were the most extensive of the Five Nations and included the area along the great lakes Ontario and Erie and south to the Allegheny River.[117]

The Senecas were a matrilineal, agriculturally based people. They lived in settlements in the southwestern part of what is now New York State and southwest into the Ohio region. Their lives were dictated by seasonal cycles. Their sense of time ran not by the clock but by a lunar calendar according to which the name of each moon foretold the nature of the earth. The spring month was Planting Moon, followed by summer's Strawberry Moon, Thunder Moon, and Moon of Green Corn. Fall months were Corn Harvest Moon or Moon of the Changing Leaves, followed by Moon of the Falling Leaves, while winter months were Freezing or Ice-forming Moon, Moon of Long Nights, Big Spirit Moon, and Starving Moon. With the thaw came Maple Moon and Frog Moon.[118] Jemison remembered her first years along the Ohio. In springtime through late fall, her village lived along the river. After harvest, they moved inland, where the men would hunt and trap beaver. In the spring they would move back to the Ohio to sell pelts and plant corn.

The matrilineality and the centrality of corn to Seneca existence meant that women had extensive powers among them. Politically, economically, and socially women's powers, women's words, and the works of their hands were respected. These powers diminished in the years of Jemison's life because of the losses from disease and warfare, the impact of liquor, the ascendancy of the new United States, and the coming of a Seneca millennialism. Still, the powers of Seneca women remained formidable in her lifetime. These included the "power of life and death over prisoners of war"; the designation of male members to sit in the councils of war to the point of control over a declaration of war; the power to unseat such representatives; the selection of leaders of spiritual life, many of whom were women; the passing of property and titles through the female line; the arrangement of marriages; and the authority over the extended and extensive household, the longhouse.[119]

Longhouse living centered around the lives of mothers and their sisters. Men were often on long missions of war and diplomacy. Sometimes they were out hunting. Anthony Wallace even suggests that they might have been away for as long as they were to avoid the overpowering presence of female authority. When they returned, husbands could find themselves displaced by new lovers, over whom they had little control. They would then have to pick up their things and find some other home.[120]

The longhouse itself, like the houses of Indians east of the Mississippi, was constructed of poles and bark. It was a physical structure which incorporated a particular social structure. Houses could range from twenty up to one hundred feet long and from fifteen to twenty feet wide, and they were roughly twenty feet to the rafters. Extending the rafters was like building on an addition for a new family. The fireplace would be in the center of a small house and, in the case of a several-family dwelling, in a row down the center, with each grouping around its central fire. Holes in the roof allowed smoke to escape. Platforms for sleeping hugged the sides of the house, layered with bark and then furs for warmth and comfort. There were poles to mark off sections and skins for dividers. Platforms above the sleeping areas were used for storage, while food such as corn could be extended from strings to dry. Storage space could also be made by digging below the sleeping quarters. Socializing and cooking took place around the fires. Warmth was retained in the lodging by insulating the outside with elm bark. Sheets of elm up to six feet long and four feet wide were peeled from trees in the spring and early summer and sometimes soaked for seasoning, then flattened out with heavy rocks and extended lengthwise along the house.[121]

The longhouse mirrored the wider social structure. Throughout Iroquoia there were clans—Wolf, Bear, Heron, Deer, Snipe, Turtle, and others. The clan included the larger extended family. There were members of the Bear clan in the Seneca, Mohawk, Oneida, and all of the other five and later six nations. A child was born into his or her mother's clan. Longhouses might have the clan symbol on the doorpost or over the doorway. Members of Wolf, Heron, or Snipe visiting the village from another part of Iroquoia were accepted and welcomed in all longhouses of their clansmen wherever they might travel.[122] When a daughter married, she brought her new husband to her mother's household. The husband maintained his mother's clan despite his new home. Lineage and residence kept both the daughter and her children within the maternal family perpetually.

When Jemison was first adopted, Senecas still lived in longhouses, but the transition to log cabins was moving fast. By the postrevolutionary and reservation eras, log cabins were the common houses of Indians along the northeastern frontier. Even so, the traditions of the central fire and the bedsteads close to the walls were maintained. The social structure, too, changed but remained basically intact to the extent that even today, Iroquois identify themselves as Turtles, Herons, and the like. The clan Jemison belonged to is uncertain. One relative claimed she was a Turtle, but Arthur Parker said her Indian name was common among the Heron clan.[123]

Seneca men hunted and fished and were involved in far-flung organizations of diplomacy and warfare, ranging north into what is today eastern and central Canada and south into Virginia and the Carolinas. Their power was great, but it was shared with women. Labor, often cited as being rigidly divided between Indian men and women, was not. Jemison speaks of how as a young girl she went out on the hunt. She had the job of cleaning skins and bringing them back to the village.[124] Seneca women had considerable economic power; their planting, gathering, harvesting, and storage determined survival. Seneca women planted in the late spring with their children near them but had no master overseeing them, working "as leisurely as we pleased," with short-handled hoelike tools.[125] "In order to expedite their business, and at the same time enjoy each other's company, they all work together in one field, or at whatever job they may have at hand. In the spring, they choose an old active squaw to be their driver and overseer, when at labor, for the ensuing year. She accepts the honor, and they consider themselves bound to obey her."[126]

Corn, beans, and rice, "the three sisters" seen as gifts of the Ancients, were all critical to Seneca diet. More than sixty types of beans, nearly twenty varieties of corn, more than thirty wild fruits, many nuts, edible roots, leaf and bark, drinks, maple syrup, more than twenty animals, and many types of birds, fish, and a few shellfish were all part of the Iroquois diet.[127] But corn was central; its importance is indicated by the many words in Iroquoian languages for the various parts of the corn plant and the state in which it is found. Corn itself came in all varieties and colors. F. W. Waugh counted eight Seneca varieties, including two types of white, two types of yellow, purple, black, and popcorn. In western New York, the snow may come early, and the winters can be long and severe. In deep snows it was often difficult to hunt. Crops gathered and stored for the winter were a more predictable part of the diet from December to March than food gathered from hunting.[128]

That corn was such a central determinant of tribal existence was noted by the early French explorers. On Hochelaga Island, an Iroquois village along the St. Lawrence, Jacques Cartier saw cornfields and noticed storage bins on top of the houses. Seventeenth- and eighteenth-century sources show the great admiration of men from Champlain onward for the Iroquois's fields of grain. Both the French empire builders and the American revolutionaries tried to decimate Iroquois power less on the battlefield than on the cornfield. In 1687, New France's governor-general Marquis de Denonville "deemed it our best policy to employ ourselves laying the Indian corn which is in vast abundance in the fields, rather than to follow a flying enemy to a distance and excite our troops to catch only some straggling fugitives." In four Seneca villages, the French burned caches of corn, and corn in the fields "computed according to the estimate afterwards made at 400 thousand minots (about 1,200,000 bushels) of Indian corn." [129]

When Mary Jemison was in her thirties, the tactic of burning cornfields was taken up by Washington's army in western New York. In a September 16, 1779, report to General Washington regarding an attack on Seneca farms along the Allegheny, Daniel Brodhead wrote that the "troops remained on the ground three whole days destroying the Towns & Corn Fields." Later that month, an officer of Major General John Sullivan's invading army wrote of his success with this policy. In a letter to John Jay (September 30, 1779), Lieutenant Colonel William Butler boasted that along with burning five major towns in Cayuga country, on the eastern side of Cayuga Lake, he "destroyed two hundred acres of excellent corn with a number of orchards one of which had in it 1500 fruit trees." Besides laying waste another forty towns, the Sullivan expedition destroyed corn amounting to 160,000 bushels "at a modest computation" "along with a vast quantity of vegetables of every kind." Continued Butler, "I flatter myself that the orders with which I was entrusted are fully executed, as we have not left a single settlement or a field of corn in the country of the Five Nations." [130] It was the success of this policy that led to the breaking up of Iroquois villages. After experiencing this destruction and the starvation that followed, Mary Jemison and her family moved south onto Genesee River land, where they made their way separate from the Senecas moving west.

Despite the fortunes of history (or perhaps because of them), the Seneca world maintained a close connection to seasonal cycles and close contact with the animal world of ceremony. Order and connection were created by the use of ritual, song, and dance. In 1791 a white visitor on an important mission was told that all negotiations must stop because pigeons were plentiful and catching them was the pressing matter at hand.[131]

Women's roles in planting supported their political clout. Jemison was in her early fifties when the visitor mentioned above entered Seneca country. In early March 1791, fifty-two-year-old Thomas Proctor was sent by Secretary of War Henry Knox as a U.S. government commissioner to the Indians. From Pennsylvania, Proctor traveled west and north toward Seneca country. His mission was to meet with Seneca leader Cornplanter (also known as Captain O'Beel). Proctor was not entirely new to the area, having been part of General Sullivan's expedition "against the savages" in 1779 in which he commanded six thousand men. Nor was he without personal stakes in the project of peacemaking with the Indians along the newly evolving frontier. Going into western Pennsylvania, he was told he was near one twelve-hundred-acre tract and another twenty-five separate tracts of land never seen by white men. In a diary kept for Knox he repeatedly noted the land of western New York as "fine," "extraordinary rich," "a most beautiful country and excellent land." The new government wanted him to keep the Senecas divorced from the more hostile Shawnees and Miamis, who were attacking settlements in the Ohio country.[132] To assist in his diplomatic task, Proctor paid for the services of former white captive turned interpreter Horatio Jones. After much difficulty with weather, horses, rheumatism, and Indian doctors, and without much awareness of the complicated rifts in Iroquois country, both north and south of the border, Proctor continued on to meet with Cornplanter only to find that the Six Nations did not negotiate with a single leader.[133] When he finally arrived in Buffalo, council meetings began.

Although the new republic's representative was anxious to

get on with negotiations, Proctor was told that "the Indians are not like the white men; for they must think a great while."[134] Along with the growing number of participants to be consulted, the Senecas had to check with the British at Fort Niagara and Joseph Brant (the Mohawk leader who after the Revolution brought many Iroquois into Canada). And there was yet another group with whom he had to contend before any of the Iroquois could go with him to face down the Indians to the south and west.

On May 15 Proctor recorded the following:

Early this morning the elders of the Indian women resorted to my hut, (present a number of chiefs.) Having heard the general conversation that took place between me and the Young King [Cornplanter] the evening before, addressed me in the following manner:

"BROTHER:—The Lord has spared us until a new day to talk together; for, since you came here from General Washington, you, and our uncles the sachems, have been counselling together. Moreover, your sisters, the women have taken the same into great consideration, because that you and our sachems have said so much upon it. Now, that is the reason why we have come to say something to you, and to tell you that the great Spirit hath preserved you, and you ought to hear and listen to what we women shall speak, as well as to the sachems; for we are the owners of this land and it is ours; for it is we that plant it for our and for their use. Hear us, therefore, for we speak of things that concern us and our children, and you must not think hard of us while our men shall say more to you; for we have told them."[135]

Proctor says he "acceded" to the women's request that he listen to "their sachems in the council this day," that is, "the women's speaker, the young prince of the Turtle tribe, (Red Jacket)."[136] These women soon fired off a gun, which signaled the men to come to a council. Proctor was brought into the council by a Seneca man and described the scene as follows: "Being arrived, the first matter unusual that presented itself, were the elders of the women seated near their chiefs. When, after a short silence, the speech of the women was continued by Red Jacket . . . as follows: '. . . we are left to answer for our women, who are to conclude what ought to be done by both sachems and warriors. So hear what is their conclusion.' [which he discusses]. . . . And this is the words of our women to you, and the sachems and warriors who shall go with you. And now we shall name them." Proctor was pleased at the meeting's results and on May 17 entered into his journal for Knox that along with having given Indians in the various towns "something to drink," he also "desired that the women should be attended to particularly, for their valuable conduct in the last great council." [137]

Mary Jemison does not mention Proctor's visit in her narrative. She was living on Gardow Flats at this time and did not move to Buffalo Creek until the mid-1820s. She also tells us she did not attend Indian "frolics." But the rights of Seneca women over their land and in diplomacy must have been known to her. Even though she was an adopted Seneca, her son could be appointed a sachem. Such was the case of one white woman captive. In a town close to Gardeau in the village of Nondas [Nunda], Proctor stayed at the house of a white woman who had been with the Indians "from her infancy" and had nine children by an Indian husband: "Her second son had lately been adopted a sachem and styled the promoter of peace." [138] It is unclear whether adopted women could sit on the council of women, but Jemison's Seneca contemporaries certainly did: "For we are the owners of this land and it is ours; for it is we that plant it for our and for their use. Hear us, therefore, for we speak of things that concern us and our children." The protection of their community's resources and the life of future generations formed the basis of women's concerns and women's rightful authority even as the Seneca world was being torn apart.

The world in which Jemison had arrived as a young girl in 1758 changed dramatically by 1800. But from the culture that survives and the objects that remain one can feel and see the richness and texture of that world and imagine the power it could hold over someone entering it.

Along with the musical instruments, tools, weapons, clothing, and toys, any child or adult would have been exposed to the taste of its food, the sound of its music, the rhythm of its dance. Even today the Seneca people have many dances called "social dances" in which men and women move in a variety of patterns in a large circle, from east to west, retracing the daily path of the sun. There were and are also ceremonial dances and songs that punctuate the year, bring the community together, and allow the body to feel connection with itself, the earth, and its creatures, the old, the young, and one's contemporaries. Midwinter dream and medicine rites include Bear Dance, Dance for the Dead, Masked Dance, Eagle Dance, and others. Dances that have come down to the present have names such as Duck Dance, Fish Dance, Raccoon Dance, and Chicken Dance.[139] Spring dances called Food Spirit dances centrally involve women. Recent fieldwork among Canadian Grand River Iroquois of four longhouses suggests that "women are the sole singers and dancers in their spring and fall ritual." Two older women officiate by singing a series of songs, corresponding to a male song. In the Corn Dance, the songs are "among the most melodious of Iroquois tunes," and these are performed by the lead women, who accompany themselves with horn rattles. There are early twentieth-century Seneca drawings of women leaders carrying armfuls of corn and tortoise shell rattles and walking in front of a group of women in a circle dance. A late eighteenth-century white guest reported two women with tortoise shells leading a ceremony.[140] Dancing and singing were often described in captivity narratives as frightening and savage. Jemison's narrative has no mention of it. Either she did not talk about it with Seaver or he excised her comments.

From the close of the Revolution there was heated competition between Quakers and Presbyterians for Seneca souls. The year Seaver spoke with Jemison, many New Yorkers were wrapped up in the Second Great Awakening. This evangelical movement expressed the Protestant world's need for more palpable spiritual experiences. The earlier revivals of 1799 swept Geneva, Victor, Onondaga, Cayuga Village, and other once Iroquois towns.[141] It is possible that Seaver might not have thought that Seneca (as opposed to similar Protestant) activities were significant religious experiences for the old woman before him. But no one who has spent any time in a culture in which movement is a means of both release and connection can minimize the power of music and dance.[142] Jemison could be no exception.

The world of cycles framed the ongoing continuity of Seneca

life. In the spring of the year the Seneca people gathered (and still gather) for the Green Corn Festival. On the first day of that festival an incantation is made to the Great Spirit. Thanks are given for preserving the people and for the ceremony itself. "This institution has descended to us from our fathers. . . . Great Spirit, continue to listen: We thank thee for thy great goodness in causing our mother, the earth, again to bring forth her fruits. We thank thee that thou has caused Our Supporters to yield abundantly. Great Spirit, our words still continue to flow towards thee. (Throwing on tobacco). Preserve us from all danger. Preserve our aged men. Preserve our mothers. Preserve our warriors. Preserve our children." [143] Both mothers and fathers, in the principles of maleness and femaleness, are recognized here. J. N. B. Hewitt, who lived and worked among the Iroquois at the turn of this century, noted "a dualism running through all public assemblies of the Iroquois people." He felt that this was part of "the motive to dramatize two dominant principles which appear to pervade and energize" Iroquois life. The male and female each pass on a mythic sense of life and ways of perpetuating it—a basic need to create "tribal organic unity." "It was deemed imperative," he said, "to recognize the male and female principles of the biotic world and all that such recognition implies." Equally valued are both "fatherhood and motherhood and the duties and obligations arising from these states." The earliest ancients, "prophet-statesmen" of the league, were thought to have been of both sexes, and the league itself was conceived of as "an animate being." Hewitt tells us that in major rituals, not only of the harvest but of politics and mourning, both sexes are recognized, "the father and the mother sides." By representing both mother and father, a "union" "for the promotion of the life force and welfare of the community" was made manifest.[144] Such a balance of power and recognition of both principles shows respect for each. Jemison herself remembered both the male and female in her own family, naming the children after her father, her mother, her sisters, and her brothers. Still, the balance and wholeness of this society were of a different order than that of the frontier Scotch-Irish tradition of Pennsylvania in the mid- to late eighteenth century. Not only were women's powers in perpetuating food paid homage, but their political and economic control over land, in governing councils, and in family matters far exceeded that of their contemporary Euro-American sisters.[145]

Besides ceremony, family, politics, economics, song, and dance, any cursory examination of the clothing and items of use in Iroquois day-to-day life from the mid-eighteenth into the first few decades of the nineteenth century cannot help but inspire awe. If the Iroquois were not interested in such things as moccasins, pouches, and beaded bags, brooches, sashes, knife holders, and the like as objets d'art, they certainly took pride in the careful crafting of such work. During this period, John Tanner, a captive among the Ojibwas, made a point of writing how pleased he was with the care his mothers and sisters took in making his clothing. It was a sign of devotion and care for a woman to cut and sew deerskin moccasins. Even simple moccasin designs with little or no decoration were graceful and soft. On long raids Indians took along multiple pairs to substitute during times of wear and tear.[146] There was also quill work, studded belts, tobacco pouches, and knife holders. Porcupine quills preceded European glass beads. After porcupines were hunted down, killed, skinned, and their quills carefully pulled out by the men, these were sorted and the long, coarse ones saved. Women dyed the quills one of six colors. A bag, sash, or pouch might have blue, orange, and yellow quills in geometric and then semicircular patterns. One tobacco pouch depicted a pair of thunderbirds with three little birds around their shoulders. Besides quill beading, a belt or a knife holder might, after white contact, have "tin jinglers." During Mary's lifetime, Iroquois silver brooches in heart-shaped patterns, in florid squares, and with crowns were copied from Scottish "Luckenbooth" brooches. A visitor to Cattaraugus after the Revolution commented on women being loaded down with silver. A design was certainly a thing of joy and of play, as on the occasion when a carefree, perhaps dancing figure was quilled onto a black skin pouch with two lines of quill beads beneath its feet.[147] Even corn provided not only food but playthings and baskets for storage. Cornhusk dolls were easily made and hard-to-break toys, and every size basket with complex weaves provided aesthetic and practical means for carrying produce.[148]

Certainly daily and yearly life wedded Jemison, and perhaps other nonreturning white captives like her, to Indian society.

Like the woman who fell onto Turtle's back, gave birth to new life, and planted a new world around herself, she found a new family, abundance, and new powers. The agricultural routine was similar to that of her early life on the Pennsylvania frontier, but it offered new and joyous ways of celebrating the earth's cycles, along with its own finery and richness.

Was Jemison the *White* woman, the White *woman*, or the *Indian Woman*? The Jemison narrative diverges from the standard captivity story in which a woman is captured, undergoes difficulty, and comes home to white America. At the beginning of this inquiry I asked, Why has the Jemison legend had such longevity? Following various aspects of the legend, the white, the female, and the Indian, demonstrates how each appealed to particular interpreters and readers. Perhaps the story itself is like a triangular crystal prism. Each side offers a way of looking through the object. In the case of the prism, each side is identical; in Jemison's case, each side gives a different perspective. The *White* Woman aspects emphasized boundaries—Jemison's fall from grace into the world of mixture, "mixed-bloods," the pagan, the savage, and the primitive—with only her mother's and father's Christianity to guide her, her basic whiteness to help her through her life's trials. But her experience as a woman, from childhood to old age, along with her life as a Seneca, showed her other ways of looking at life. The combinations explain how Jemison became a survivor, and a fuller view of her life points to strategies for coexistence. The three facets together offer an answer to the question of why this woman's story and those of others who never returned have had such an enduring hold on generations of Americans. For some there is "proof" of savagery and of white and Christian superiority. For some there is evidence of female endurance. For still others (and, of course, these may not be three distinct groups) there is the chance to learn about and perhaps sympathize with a close but alien world.

If the journey to find Mary Jemison has been a difficult and circuitous one, it is because, despite her popularity, her life has been hidden. Why? Why, even in the cases of the most well-known captives, is it so hard to figure out the real story of those who move between cultures, those who live in two worlds, learning from each? The answer appears to be (to change metaphors) that the lives of women such as Jemison are used by others as playing pieces on a larger board in a game that pits white America against Indian America. Even though there may be no one "white America," no one "Indian America," these are the terms in which the match is described. Which society, Indian or Anglo-American, is better? Whose women are more womanly, whose men more manly? In this battle for gender and ethnic points, Jemison's and other captivity stories (whether in the form of narrative, sermon, local news story, painting, illustration, dime novel, or contemporary film) offer strategic weapons as white and dark queens and pawns are moved about. The difference between the Jemison narrative and most others is that Jemison, after her capture, chose to remain with Indians. She never really returned to white society. By 1800 she and her family were on the margins of the ever-encroaching white settlements of New York, and by the time she sat long enough to tell her story, that society was on her doorstep. She chose to tell it to one from whose midst she originally came, but even then others obstructed the telling. Why? There was too much at stake. Those stakes were *us* versus *them*. For "us" it is "our" women versus "their" women, "our" men versus "their" men, our maleness and femaleness versus theirs.

The *White* Woman of the Genesee? The White *Woman* of the Genesee? The Indian Woman? The White-Indian Woman? Such confusion and mixture in a society that wished for racial and sexual absolutes did not allow for easy understanding of those who differed. Although offering the reader or the viewer diversion, such crossovers were hard to categorize, hard to figure out, hard to tolerate. A study of Jemison uncovers the fear and fascination of white America with its national and sexual identity.

The prizes in the game of ethnic, moral, and cultural superiority are more easily won than the understanding one might gain with a clearer but more complex vision. They allow a dismissal of the other, a takeover of the other, retrenchment and self-assurance in one's own sexuality and superior nationality. The alternative, that clearer vision, requires a reconsideration of frontiers, both sexual and national. Such a re-visioning might mean sharing the prize.

Mary Jemison had much in common with the woman who was pushed from the sky and fell onto Turtle's back. Forced to enter a new world, separated from her family and the home she knew, she was a stranger. She suffered losses but was greeted by human (rather than animal) friends and built a new and ongoing family. A wider understanding of her life as a white woman's and an Indian woman's story argues for the need to accept the other, an attempt to understand the other. It expresses a desire for accommodation and a disdain for bloodshed in an increasingly diverse and expanding American society. Jemison survived, served as a mediator, judged the bad, and commended the good in both cultures. As a young girl alone, as a woman in a new world surrounded by a strange society, as a wife to men vastly different from herself, as a mother of a large family who had to mediate and fend for her children—this is what she had to do. Her work, suffering, and pride offered and still offer successive generations an alternative to extermination and bloodshed.

6

Sarah Wakefield and the Dakota War

Coming into the Country

It was a Sunday in June when the Wakefields entered "Indian Country." A steamboat brought them down the Minnesota River from their home in Shakopee to Redwood Ferry. Shakopee, a town twenty-two miles south of Minneapolis, was over one hundred miles north and east of the Lower Agency. On the first step of their journey, the family stayed the night on agency property, five to seven hundred feet above the river looking out on what seemed to the doctor's wife "a high prairie" of "vacant space." The following day they traveled northwest in a train of seven wagons carrying women, children, and $160,000 in gold.[1]

When Dr. John L. Wakefield left his practice in Shakopee for a tour of duty on the Minnesota frontier, he was moving one step farther away from his Connecticut origins. Following Abraham Lincoln's election as president in the spring of 1861, new appointments were made on both the national and regional levels, bringing Thomas J. Galbraith in as Indian agent for the Minnesota region of the Northern Superintendency.[2] In June,

Galbraith called on Wakefield to act as doctor for the Yellow Medicine Upper Agency and surrounding Indian community. Wakefield, a graduate of the Yale Medical School, was one of a small and elite corps of eastern doctors on the frontier. Married for several years when called, the thirty-eight-year-old Wakefield was accompanied on his new mission by his wife, Sarah, and their two children, three-year-old James Orin and six-month-old Lucy.[3]

Born in 1823, John Luman Wakefield was from an old English family with several lines in colonial America. His father, Luman Wakefield, was a doctor with an interest in politics who was twice elected representative to the Connecticut General Assembly. His mother, Betsey Rockwell, was also from a politically active Connecticut family. He graduated from Yale Medical School in 1847. His eight-page "Dissertation on Cynanche Trachealis," written in his own hand, was one of the longer, better organized, and more substantial of the twenty-four dissertations in his year.[4] Dr. Wakefield first practiced medicine in Winstead, Connecticut. In 1849 he moved to the California goldfields, where he treated patients until 1854, when he contracted cholera and returned to Winstead. His younger brother James Beach Wakefield had by then finished attending Trinity College and studying law in Painesville, Ohio. In April 1854 the two brothers came together again in Shakopee, Minnesota, where John became the town's second physician. In June 1858, in a battle between the Dakotas and the Ojibwas, Dr. Wakefield treated many Dakota wounded.[5]

Shakopee (pronounced Shock'-o-pee) was founded on the site of a major Indian village, in this case the Mdewakanton village of Shu'k pay. A coach ran to St. Paul every Monday, Wednesday, and Friday; there was a daily steamboat to St. Paul as well. A new Republican newspaper was on its way, with the promise that "true grit is about to be started" in Shakopee. Here was a good place for both a lawyer and a physician to locate.[6] The 1857 city census listed the village population at 800, Scott County's at 5,331. A year later the town had 1,500 people, three churches, a new Thespian Society, and a Masonic Lodge in which Wakefield became senior warden and Thomas J. Galbraith its secretary.[7]

At thirty-one years old, Sarah F. Wakefield was seven years

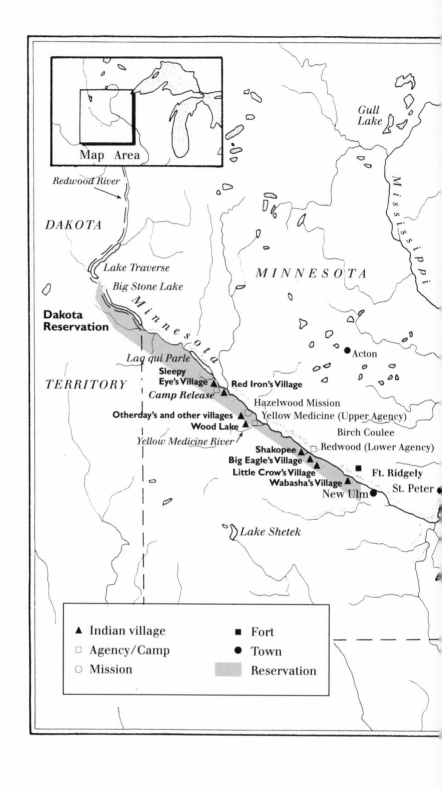

Map Area

Gull
Lake

Mississippi

Redwood River

DAKOTA

MINNESOTA

Lake Traverse

Big Stone Lake

**Dakota
Reservation**

Minnesota

Laq qui Parle

• Acton

**Sleepy
Eye's Village** ▲   **Red Iron's Village**

TERRITORY   *Camp Release*

Hazelwood Mission

Otherday's and other villages ▲   Yellow Medicine (Upper Agency)

Wood Lake ▲   Birch Coulee

Yellow Medicine River   **Shakopee** ▲ □ Redwood (Lower Agency)

Big Eagle's Village ▲

Little Crow's Village ▲   ■ **Ft. Ridgely**

Wabasha's Village ▲   St. Peter

New Ulm ●

Lake Shetek

▲ Indian village	■ Fort
□ Agency/Camp	● Town
○ Mission	▨ Reservation

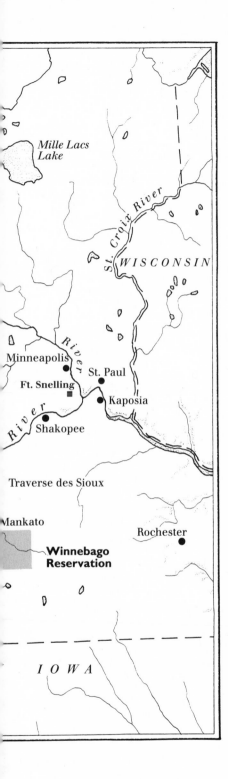

Mille Lacs
Lake

St. Croix River

WISCONSIN

River

Minneapolis

St. Paul

Ft. Snelling

Kaposia

River

Shakopee

Traverse des Sioux

Mankato

Rochester

**Winnebago
Reservation**

IOWA

Minnesota in 1862

her husband's junior when she moved from Shakopee to Yellow Medicine. Sarah Brown was born the youngest of three children on September 29, 1829, a native of Kingston (or Kingstown), Rhode Island. Her life before her marriage is difficult to reconstruct. The Brown family background and status, how they educated their daughter, and her interests and experiences before her marriage are unknown. Whether she knew her future husband from family connections in the East and then went to Minnesota to marry him, or whether she alone or with her family first migrated to Minnesota where they then met is unclear. The records tell us only that John and Sarah married in 1856 and first lived together in Blue Earth near the Iowa border, about forty miles south of Mankato.[8]

Sarah was a tall woman with light brown hair; she weighed close to two hundred pounds. Although not frail in form, she dressed in the smartest finery of the day. Her wardrobe was replete with silk, cashmere, linen, and chenille dresses, lace and embroidered collars, silk- and velvet-trimmed aprons, kid and beaver gloves, an otter muff and cuffs, and a green velvet hat with feathers. Her cultural tastes required many books and the latest in manners, fiction, and fashion from contemporary eastern magazines.[9]

Writing of her most recent move about two years later, she first expressed fear that she "had really got out of civilization," but as the wagons moved along she began to enjoy the ride "for a more beautiful sight than that prairie, I have never seen. It was literally covered with flowers of all descriptions; the tall grass was waving in the breeze, and it reminded me of a beautiful panorama."[10]

As they passed through Little Crow's Mdewakanton village at the Redwood River, all remarked on the region's beauty. "Very high hills enclose the stream, while huge rocks are thrown around in the valley, giving grandeur to the scene." The early June sun beat down harshly on the open wagons as they passed an ancient Indian burial mound. Then, after roughly thirty-five more miles, they arrived at the junction of the Yellow Medicine and Minnesota rivers. Flags were flying from many buildings to honor their arrival. The Wakefields were in their new home.[11]

The night of their arrival a less idyllic picture emerged. Sarah Wakefield later described it as "one of horror to all." Not under-

standing Dakota song and dance, she thought "they were singing our death-song." The next morning brought a racket in
front of the house, which turned out to be loose horses standing on a platform to get away from mosquitoes. A more serious
incident occurred a month later on July 4, 1861, one month
after the Wakefields' arrival. Agent Galbraith was away when
Indians arrived at the agency en masse complaining of having
been cheated by local white traders. It was a tense day. When
"festivities resumed" later that afternoon, Indians restricted the
movement of whites, not allowing them to walk about "without questioning them." Sarah Wakefield expected to be shot.
The women tried to cool the situation by inviting "some of
the Chiefs" for ice cream, apparently a first for them, which
"seemed to calm them down." They stayed and watched "our
dance with great pleasure." [12]

The next morning the Dakotas returned for a council to
present the reasons for their actions. The first was hunger, the
second, traders' cheating; the two were related. The Indians
needed food and were angry that the "Farmer, or Christian
Indians" were given food every week though they got it only
once a year. The Upper Agency Indians, like all of the Dakota
who were involved in the Treaty of 1851, were entitled to an annuity. This money was distributed at the agency and was used
to buy food from agency traders. Traders were on hand when
money was distributed and snapped it up, claiming it was owed
them for credit extended during the year. As Mrs. Wakefield
saw the situation, the four trading houses at the Yellow Medicine Agency "kept groceries and dry goods . . . cheating the
creatures very much." The Indians did not keep accounts, and
the traders gave them goods on credit. When Indians arrived to
get their nine-dollar annuity, "the Traders surround them, saying, you owe me so much for flour. Another says you owe me so
much for sugar, &c. and the Indian gives it up, never knowing
whether it is right or not. Many Indians pay before the payment
with furs, still they are caught up by these Traders, and very seldom a man passes away with his money. I saw a poor fellow one
day swallow his money. I wondered he did not choke to death,
but he said, 'They will not have mine, for I do not owe them.' I
was surprised that they would allow such cheating without retaliation." [13] Mrs. Wakefield noted that these traders were the

root of "evil habits," including swearing and the sexual abuse of native women. They took Dakota wives, "would raise several children with them, and then after living with them a number of years would turn them off." She knew some retribution would occur, "all in God's own time." [14]

On the morning of July 5, Upper Agency Indians fired their guns in the air and beat on the doors acting "very saucy." Flour was promised by Galbraith, who had by then returned, and additional flour arrived, all of which was taken.[15] The disturbance subsided.

This tension between being on the verge of chaos and living in paradise continued for Sarah Wakefield. But despite unsettling incidents, soon after her arrival she began to explore her new world. Feeling a sense of adventure and independence, she took the family mare and rode "unprotected" through the woods with her young son. The landscape and its people overwhelmed her with their pristine beauty and wildness: "The scenery around Rush Brook was grand. Enormous hills—almost mountains—were on every side of this stream, and when a person was at the top and commenced descending, they would tremble with fear for awhile, but at last they would entirely forget all danger, while looking at the beauties of the scene. Away down between the hills, among the brush, could be seen these wild men roaming in pursuit of game, while their wives, and children bathed in the stream: and from the top of the bluff they looked like babes, the distance was so great." [16]

On these rides she first met Dakota women. On her way home at dusk she often stopped by their village and asked "to take a puff from their pipe." She enjoyed such moments, joining the women as they sat cooking, mixing bread or baking it, and smoking their long-stemmed pipes, "about two feet in length," "resting on the ground, the end in their mouths." [17]

The Dakotas, Santees, or eastern Sioux were made up of four divisions: Sissetons, Wahpetons, Wahpekutas, and Mdewakantons. The Mdewakantons, or people of the lakes, were divided into eight bands. The Lower Agency Dakotas were primarily Mdewakantons. In 1851 Mdewakanton villages ranged along Minnesota's rivers from Wabasha's village in the southeast, below Lake Pipin, to Little Crow's at Kaposia south of St. Paul, to Shakopee's village south and west of St. Paul. But following the treaty of 1851, the Dakotas were slowly forced to settle on a reservation located ten miles on either side of the Minnesota River from north of New Ulm diagonally north and west past Lac qui Parle, Big Stone Lake, and on to Lake Traverse in Dakota Territory. Mdewakanton villages were then restricted to the strip of river land and dotted the Minnesota in the lower part of the reservation, from just north of the Redwood River south to the Little Rock River.

There were about two thousand Mdewakanton. Little Crow's (Taoyteduta or His Red Nation), Shakopee's (Little Six), and Wabasha's were the three most powerful bands.[18] The Upper Agency Dakotas were predominantly members of the Sisseton and Wahpeton bands. Samuel Pond, a missionary with an interest in ethnography, claimed that the Dakotas were so intermingled that it was "impossible to ascertain their exact numbers" but that an 1862 census enumerated close to four thousand. At her Upper Agency home Mrs. Wakefield employed local Dakota women to sew for her and other native women and men to help with her work. She says she soon "began to love and respect them as well as if they were whites" and became "accustomed to them and their ways."[19]

The Upper Agency had five to seven buildings along with a jail for "unruly Indians." Among these were the agent's residence and warehouse and a brick duplex building that housed agency employees and served as a workshop and Indian school, as well as a barn, a hotel, and a house. Nearby were two missionary stations. Dr. Thomas S. Williamson's had come twenty-seven years before; his Dakota Church was three miles from the agency. Stephen Return Riggs's mission was two miles farther away in Hazelwood.[20]

The Wakefields' house was next to the agent's quarters and warehouse building. It contained five rooms: a parlor, "family room" (or bedroom), dining room, kitchen, "help's room," a storeroom, a substantial closet, and an outhouse. Within a year after their arrival, the Wakefields settled in, surrounding themselves with the comforts to which they were accustomed. A parlor was carpeted and furnished with matching walnut center table, rocker, sewing chair, and cabinet. There were many more mahogany furnishings, a green damask sofa, kerosene lamps, paintings, a pair of vases, bound books, and assorted collections of eastern magazines of culture and feminine advice such as *Harper's*, *Peterson's*, *Eclectic*, *Mothers*, and *Godey's Lady's Book*. The dining room had two bird cages, each with three canaries, sheet music, *Riggs' Dakotah* and *Webster's Dictionary*, the family Bible and hymnbook, songbooks, grammar, geography, and other books.[21]

The house was well stocked for lavish entertaining. For big crowds there were six- and ten-quart porcelain pots and glassware and dishes for twelve with glass goblets, egg glasses, tumblers, breakfast, dinner, and tea plates, two sets of silver, large damask tablecloths, and a carving set for roasts and poultry. Pounds of coffee and brown and green tea were on hand, with a fifteen-quart brass tea kettle and sixteen-quart coffee kettle for boiling the water or brewing the coffee. The kitchen was well equipped, the closet and outhouse were filled with the appropriate wares for hosting substantial dinners, and the larder was well stocked with such staples as pork, dried beef, ham, codfish, mackerel, cheese, crackers, sardines, rice, butter, lard, eggs, sugar (crushed, brown, and powdered), salt, pepper, syrup, vinegar, coffee, tea, and flour (regular and buckwheat). Gallon and quart jars were filled with raspberries, gooseberries, strawberries, rhubarb, blackberries, pickles (mixed, sweet, muskmelon, and grape). The contents of dozens of cans of peaches, pears, and quinces could help sweeten the winter months and brighten the family or company table. In the summer of 1862, when food was scarce for Dakota families in Minnesota, the Wakefields claimed to have 100 pounds of pork, 75 pounds of dried beef, 150 pounds of ham, 50 pounds of codfish, a keg of mackerel, 45 pounds of cheese, 50 pounds of crackers, 75 pounds of rice, 100 pounds of butter, and 10 dozen eggs. They had thirty-nine hens, a pig, and a mare with a harness.[22]

Such a comfortable, tasteful, and plentiful world of goods, with ample supplies and closets full of fancy clothes for every member of the family, was unusual in the remote Indian agency skirting the edge of Dakota Territory. It contrasted sharply with the world of local white farmers, agency employees, and missionaries, not to mention the world of Indian farmers and those more traditional Indians who still hunted and many of whom were close to starvation.[23]

In the year after the Wakefields' arrival problems of hunger, traders, and annuity payments continued to worsen for the Dakotas. These problems rarely seemed to be of concern to most whites in the Minnesota River valley. Between 1850 and 1860, they were interested in growth and settlement. In 1850, the territory's white population stood at a mere 6,000. By 1860 it was 172,000. Almost all of this growth was in the Minneapolis–St. Paul area or in the river valley. Dakota treaty negotiations had opened up southern Minnesota for settlement, and thousands of Germans, Scandinavians, English, Irish, and northeasterners were moving into river counties south and west of the twin cities.[24]

To newly settled American whites and immigrants Indians were less a concern than local growth and imminent national events. In 1862, the Civil War was moving into its second year. News of it dominated the daily newspapers and affected the life of every young man in the state.[25] From the first, the new thirty-second, strongly Republican state of Minnesota threw its full support behind the war effort. The First Regiment of Minnesota Volunteers left Fort Snelling in late June 1861 and fought at Bull Run in July; the Third spent the early spring of 1862 in Murfreesboro, Tennessee; the Fourth was dispatched in October to St. Louis, where the men fell in droves from typhoid.[26]

The week before trouble struck again at the Upper Agency, President Lincoln sent a private and confidential telegram to Governor Alexander Ramsey asking for fifty thousand "additional troops now." "I believe I could substantially close the war in two weeks," he wired, "but time is Everything, and if I get fifty thousand (50,000) new men in a month, I shall have lost twenty thousand (20,000) old ones during the same month. . . . The quicker you send, the fewer you will have to send—Time is everything—Please act in view of this." [27] The population in Minnesota, according to the 1860 census, was 172,123.[28] To meet Lincoln's call for fifty thousand men would place almost a third of the state's white population in battle.

The significance of the rapid depopulation of young men in the state was not lost on local Indians. Harvest for the 1861 crops was poor and mass starvation growing among the Dakotas when spring annuity payments came due. Men, women, and children waited in the fields around the Upper Agency eating unripe fruit from the trees, waiting for food money that should have arrived between late June and early July. At an early August council with Indians, the Dakotas pleaded for more food. A trader named Andrew Myrick laughed and told them they could eat grass. The comment was widely circulated. On August 17 in the rural village of Acton, three young Dakotas goaded a fourth over whether he was brave enough to steal an egg from a white farmer. The incident ended when the Indians called out Robinson Jones for target practice and then shot him, his wife, and three guests. The four Indians returned to their soldiers' lodge at Rice Creek near Shakopee's village. Continuing anger about starvation and the overdue annuity blended with the realization that such payment would not be given unless the murderers were surrendered. The next morning, more than a hundred warriors from the Rice Creek and Shakopee villages came downriver to the camp of Little Crow. They challenged him to reverse the indignities his people were suffering. Lodges of the Mdewakanton were hastily brought together. Much division was expressed. Many of the Dakotas thought war would be folly. Divisions remained, but a fatal decision was reached.[29]

On the sunny early Monday morning of August 18, 1862, Dakotas struck the Lower Agency, pinpointing the stores and those who worked there, whether white or Indian.[30] Several men were killed, barns seized, guns and supplies taken. The Dakotas fanned out around the agency with plans to attack white settlements north and south along the Minnesota River. A new war was on.

"A Most Terrible and Exciting Indian War"

▪ ▪ ▪ ▪ ▪ ▪

On the morning of August 18, 1862, John Wakefield heard ominous reports. He arranged for Sarah and the children to leave that afternoon with George Gleason, an Upper Agency clerk. Mrs. Wakefield "grew unusually sad" and went about "from room to room." Others in the area were blind to impending danger. Samuel J. Brown, the son of former Indian agent

Major Joseph R. Brown and part-Sisseton Susan Frenier Brown, was on his way to the Upper Agency from his family's house about seven miles away when he was told by a local Dakota that the Lower Agency Indians were on the attack. He did not believe it. At noon, Gleason told Samuel Brown of his plans to drive Mrs. Wakefield and the children east that day to Fort Ridgely.[31]

Gleason had the loan of Wakefield's horse and open wagon. A trunk of clothes packed, the three left that afternoon around two o'clock. Gleason sat directly in front of Mrs. Wakefield; she she was behind him with four-year-old James Orin on her right and baby Lucy on her lap. As they started off, they paused to talk with the Upper Agency traders and were told the Indians were killing people in the area of Big Woods and were in council planning another attack. Sarah was frightened and asked Gleason if he had a gun. He was joking and evasive. Retracing the Wakefields' earlier journey, they passed no one on a road that usually had many travelers. She became more fearful and asked to go back. When they reached the Indian mound, the halfway point between the agencies, she could see smoke rising from burning buildings miles across the prairie. She jumped out of the wagon, then started to cry. Gleason told her she must "not act so hysterical," although he himself was acting manic, laughing and speaking loudly to allay his own fears. It was quarter after six by his watch as they approached Old Joe's house—two hours away from Fort Ridgely.[32]

Of the next events, we have only two firsthand accounts. Wakefield says that two Indians approached them. Rather than move ahead, Gleason drew in the lines and stopped the wagon. At that moment a man called Hapa fired his gun, hitting Gleason in the right shoulder. His body was thrown back into Wakefield's lap, crushing the baby against her. Hapa's second shot hit Gleason in the abdomen, flipping him off the wagon on his face.[33]

While the horses went wild, Hapa reloaded his gun. The mother feared she and her children would be next and begged for mercy. The second Indian, Chaska, quieted the horses. He recognized her and asked if she was "the doctor's wife." When she said she was, he warned her that Hapa was drunk and not to be trusted. Hapa shot Gleason a third time. He then came toward the wagon and aimed a gun at Mrs. Wakefield's head, but Chaska struck it out of his hands. She says Hapa tried to kill her several times, but Chaska told Hapa of "little acts of kindness my husband or myself had shown them in years gone by." After an hour of dispute, the two men jumped into the wagon and drove it several miles to the Shakopee encampment. When they arrived, Wakefield found herself among the same Mdewakanton band she knew from their old winter encampment near her Shakopee home. Gleason's body was left on the prairie.[34]

On Thursday, August 21, in the second year of the Civil War, a terse and urgent telegram was mailed by the governor of Minnesota to Secretary of War Edwin M. Stanton: "The Sioux Indians on our western border have risen, and are murdering men, women and children. . . . Telegraph at once."[35] The new state of Minnesota, barely out of its territorial infancy, woke up in the late days of August to find its white settlement community under attack all up and down the southwestern corner of the state and on both sides of the Minnesota River. The shock of this series of attacks reverberated through the neighboring new states and territories of the Mississippi Valley and out onto the northern plains for weeks and months thereafter. One August in Virginia thirty-one years earlier, a similar set of shock waves had flared across the South when a black slave preacher, Nat Turner, took up arms, killing fifty-seven whites in Southampton County. The uprising of eastern Dakotas in Minnesota, like that earlier attack, called up the most profound fears of white settlers on the frontier: Indian attack, family murder, rape, and carnage.

Two days after Governor Alexander Ramsey's message arrived, word came again to Stanton, this time from Brigadier General James Craig in Laramie, Wyoming: "Indians, from Minnesota to Pike's Peak, and from Salt Lake to near Fort Kearney, committing many depredations." If the five hundred troops guarding telegraph and mail lines were to be used against Indians, they would be unprotected and perhaps destroyed.[36] In the midst of the most profound, divisive, and punishing war in American history, the War Department in Washington, reeling from huge casualties and defeats in Virginia, was beseeched by messages from the West. Governor Ramsey, claiming that panic among the people had "depopulated whole counties," could not wait for the promised but still uncertain return of the Third Minnesota Regiment and again wired Stanton that he was sending the Sixth Regiment along with a thousand horsemen to shore up the "distracted condition of the country." The following evening he wired President Lincoln regarding his requests that Minnesota's call for draftees be postponed. "Half the population of the State are fugitives. . . . No one not here can conceive the panic in the State." The next day, three Minnesota congressmen wrote to the president, claiming, "We are in the midst of a most terrible and exciting Indian war . . . a wild panic prevails in nearly one-half of the State." Lincoln replied to the governor: "—attend to the Indians—if the draft *cannot* proceed of course it *will not* proceed—necessity knows no law. The government cannot extend the time."[37]

The panic continued to spread. John G. Nicolay, Lincoln's private secretary, wrote to Stanton from St. Paul, repeating warnings that rather than a local uprising, the Northwest had a major Indian war on its hands. Not only were Sioux attacking, but Chippewas and Winnebagos were also "turbulent," "threatening," and "hostile." As an appropriate response, he called for over one thousand cavalry, from five thousand to six thousand guns with five hundred thousand cartridges, enough medical supplies for three regiments, and blankets for three thousand men. Rather than a restrained attempt to end the outburst, he wrote, "As against the Sioux it must be a war of extermination."[38]

Minnesota officials were not the only ones who projected the danger of a red menace on the western frontier. Reports flooded Washington from Fort Laramie, Wyoming, warning of dangers from Snake, Blackfeet, and Utes near Denver and from Dakota Territory, where Governor William Jayne wrote of Yankton threats and "our defenseless condition." "A general alarm pervades all our settlements." He warned that "a few thousand people" were "at the mercy of 50,000 Indians should they see proper to fall upon us," and he predicted that without immediate help "our Territory will be depopulated." Five days later, the governor of Iowa pleaded, "The danger is imminent, and nothing but prompt action can stop the terrible massacre."[39]

Earlier that summer, news in the Minnesota press had been almost entirely about the War of the Rebellion, with little mention of Indians. There was a sense of vulnerability, but it was the vulnerability of raw recruits being taken, young volunteers being solicited all over the state, for an urgent conflict back east in Virginia and south in Mississippi. There was little sense of a personal or territorial threat, little sense of being on a frontier. But with the Sioux outbreak, the enemy was suddenly on one's own doorstep, and the defense of the Union would have to be fought on all sides.

From August 18 to September 28, 1862, eastern Dakotas captured more than a hundred members of Minnesota's new white communities. Minnesota had been first to heed the call to the colors of the new president. A year and a half after Fort Sumter, the men of the Third Minnesota Regiment, suffering considerable losses from the bloody and punishing Virginia campaigns, were being called back home. There would be no time for rest or shelter, mourning or accolade. A newly homesteaded farm, a small-town plot, acres of speculated land might be under attack and perhaps lost to native inhabitants. Here was another enemy. In the eyes of some western officials, this new/old enemy threatened frontier existence. The Confederacy to the South, along with a feared confederacy of Plains Indians coalescing in the West, could mean a very different country than either the one of small towns and farms conceived by Thomas Jefferson or the one of growing manufacturing cities desired by Alexander Hamilton. They could mean an America of three and maybe many more nations: the United States of America, the Confederate States of America, and perhaps the Confederate Indian Lands of America. This was the dark prospect faced by western military and civilian authorities, who were frantically calling for troops for the Northwest. Wires flooded Washington offices from Wyoming, Nebraska, Colorado, the Dakotas, and Iowa. Alexander Ramsey was not alone when at 5 A.M. on September 6 he wired President Lincoln. "This is not our war; it is a national war. . . . More than 500 whites have been murdered by the Indians." Officials in Washington concurred. That very day the secretary of war gave orders to Major General John Pope, barely recovering from Virginia defeats, to take command of the Department of the Northwest, establishing its headquarters in St. Paul. His mission was "to quell the hostilities" using "whatever force may be necessary."[40]

The Trials of Autumn

. . . .

Between the outbreak of the Dakota War at the Lower Agency in August and the release of the Dakotas' 269 captives six weeks later at Camp Release in September, a series of battles were fought. There was an attack on Fort Ridgely on August 20 and one on the German community of New Ulm on the twenty-third. As the Dakotas and their captives moved north and west up the Minnesota River there was a skirmish at Birch Coulee on September 2 and a final battle at Wood Lake on the twenty-third. Attacks also occurred north of the river in Acton, on white settlements north of Minneapolis, and at Fort Abercrombie. At the time, estimates of the white dead ran between five hundred and one thousand. Indian casualties were unknown.[41]

General John Pope was then in St. Paul. A substantial force of Minnesota troops under Colonel Henry Hastings Sibley, with help from internal conflicts among the Dakotas, would soon put an end to the shooting war. Sibley was a well-known force in Minnesota life and politics. An early settler in the territory and a former fur trader, he knew local Indians well. As a Minnesota legislator, newspaper owner, and first governor of Minnesota, he was an easy choice for leader of the Minnesota troops, conqueror and negotiator with Indians, and head of the rescue mission. The safe release of the captives was one of Sibley's paramount missions.

Divisions between Upper and Lower Agency Indians (basically, between Mdewakantons and Sissetons) and also between farmer Indians (sometimes called "cut hairs" because they had cut their hair) and "blanket" or traditional Indians were part of the wider conflict from the first. As the Lower Agency Indians moved north and west up the Minnesota River, many of their Dakota brethren did not join with them. By mid-September Sibley was on their trail, and letters of negotiation were going between the two camps. One group broke off from the main Dakota encampment, setting up a new camp and bringing captives with them into safety. Reverses at the battle of Wood Lake made it clear to those Dakotas still fighting that critical decisions had to be made, and many more captives were moved to the "friendly" camp, digging trenches and separating themselves even more from Little Crow's forces.

As letters went back and forth between the camps, on Wednesday, September 24, Little Crow told his men the time had come to make preparations with their families to escape into Dakota Territory. There was talk of killing the white captives. By Thursday captives still in Little Crow's hands were being turned over to the "friendlies." Early Friday morning the Little Crow contingent had broken camp and headed onto the plains.[42]

For the captives and the Dakotas who remained, there was the release and the surrender. "White rags were fastened to the tips of the tepee poles, to wagon wheels, cart wheels, to sticks and poles stuck in the ground, and every conceivable object." One Indian covered his black horse with a white blanket, wrapped himself in an American flag, then "mounted the horse and sat upon him in full view of the troops as they passed by."[43]

How would Sibley, the troops, and the U.S. government view these remaining Dakota people who had fought with Little Crow but had separated themselves off and had held both white and part-Indian captives? The answer came quickly. A ploy was devised to disarm the Indians. Men were promised money if they turned in their weapons. They did so and were then arrested.

After a Dakota prayer meeting, Chaska feared he would be arrested as two other Indians had been. That afternoon Sarah Wakefield was questioned by members of the commission and by Reverend Stephen Return Riggs. "They thought it very strange I had no complaints to make, but did not appear to believe me." When she saw Chaska, he looked "very pale and frightened." He told her that he knew the whites would not protect him but would kill him. She tried to convince him to leave and told him she would take care of his mother. He said, " 'No, I am not a coward, I am not afraid to die. All I care about is my poor old mother, she will be left alone.' " He should have left earlier; now he was "sorry" she had earlier convinced him to stay. His mother was "very angry" with her that this had happened. Wakefield tried to persuade him that everything would be all right. She was wrong. Soon after they finished talking, he was arrested.[44]

Captain Hiram P. Grant told Wakefield that seven of the "black devils" would be hanged before the next evening and that Chaska would be in a subsequent group meeting the same fate. She threatened to kill Grant. In a remark widely heard and, according to her, "reported throughout the State," she told him, " 'Capt. Grant, if you hang that man I will shoot you, if it is not in twenty years.' " In her narrative she tried to soften the power of her words, saying she then added, " 'But you must first teach me to shoot, for I am afraid of a gun, unloaded even.' " She further covered herself by admitting to a "violent impulsive disposition" and little patience.[45]

From September 28 to November 5, a military commission was hastily assembled to try, convict, and hang as many Dakotas as possible.[46] The commission was made up of Colonel William Crooks of the Sixth Regiment of Minnesota Infantry, Lieutenant Colonel William R. Marshall of the Seventh, Captain Hiram P. Grant of the Sixth, Captain Hiram S. Bailey of the Sixth, and First Lieutenant Rollin C. Olin of the Third. The judge advocate was Isaac V. D. Heard, a lawyer turned army private, turned judge, and soon to be a popular writer on the war.[47]

Nearly four hundred cases were tried in a little over a month, often at a rate of thirty or forty a day. Most of the accused had no chance to cross-examine the witnesses against them, no lawyers or witnesses for their defense, and no specific charges to answer.[48] Stephen Return Riggs, the missionary who cooperated with the commission as a translator, admitted later: "In the majority of instances, the trial was so brief and hurried, that the facts could not possibly be ascertained." The main principle was "that all participation in the outbreak was worthy of death," and "if a man present at a battle had a gun which was fired that too made him a condemned man." That " 'they are Indians' was regarded as sufficient justification for hasty and superficial trials." According to Riggs, over 400 "grown men" and 4 women testified before the commission "trusting that the innocent could make their innocency appear. This was a thing not possible in the case of the majority. . . . And more than three hundred were condemned to be hung." Isaac Heard defended these practices in the trials as "very monotonous" but fair, employing officers "well known to the community as respectable and humane gentlemen." Of the 393 men and 1 woman tried, 303 were sentenced to death and 18 to imprisonment. If many were condemned, said Heard, "Great also was the number of crimes of which they were accused."[49]

The case of the man Sarah Wakefield called Chaska came before the commission on the first day of hearings. The name given on his record is written "We-Chank-Wash-ta-don-pee." This name is a critical piece in his story. *Chaska* is common Dakota usage for firstborn male child; it is a name used by many Dakota males. Hapan (or Hapa), meaning second-born male child, was the name of the "bad Indian" whom both Wakefield and Chaska held responsible for her mistreatment and Gleason's death.[50] Between the cover and the six pages of the trial record, Chaska's name is spelled five different ways.

Case 3 began with the swearing in of the military commission.

> We=chank=wash, tu da pee a Sioux Indian was arraigned on the following charge and
> specification viz-charge
> Murder—
> Specification. In this that the said We=chank=to=do=pee, a Sioux Indian did, on or about the 18th day of August 1862, kill George H. Gleason, a white citizen of the United States, and has likewise committed sundry hostile acts against the whites between the said 18th day of August 1862, and the 28th day of Sept. 1862.—This near the Red Wood River, and at other places on the Minnesota frontier—[51]

The charge and verdict of this case and its vague references to place and time were typical of the 392 cases that came before the commission. The difference here was that it was one of the few with witnesses, in this case the unusually large number of two witnesses. Their names as signed on the record were Sarah Wakefield and Agnes Robertson. The case was more than six times longer than most of the others, its record coming to five and one-third pages of longhand on legal-sized paper with more than three and a half pages of testimony. Wakefield was the only woman to appear before the commission in defense of a Dakota man on trial.[52]

When called to testify in his own behalf, Chaska stated:

I plead not guilty of murder. The other Indian shot Gleason, and as he was falling over I aimed my gun at him but did not fire—I have had a white woman in [my] charge, but I could not take as good care of her as a white man because I am an indian—I kept her with the intention of giving her up—Don't know of any other bad act since Gleason was murdered—I moved up here with the indians—If I had done any bad act I should have gone off—I was present when the white man was killed. There were two in the war party who killed Gleason— The other indian was not a relative of mine. The other Indian fired twice. The other indian said "Brother in law let's shoot him." He had already shot at him. I aimed at him because I was told I must kill the whites to serve my self—I have been in three battles—I have not fired at any other white man— I wanted to prevent the other Indian from shooting—I prevented him from killing the women [sic] and children with Gleason—I snapped my gun at Gleason, but it failed to go off. The reason I attempted to shoot was that the other indian asked me if I was afraid to shoot—I don't know why the gun wouldn't go off. I shot over Gleason when he fell—This was the third shot. I afterwards snapped at him when he was dead on the ground.[53]

The testimony has several problems. Besides not being given before a jury of one's peers, the English facility of the witness is problematic. According to Sarah Wakefield, Chaska knew English. But in a life-or-death situation, more than simple knowledge was needed; nuances were critical. Chaska continually asserts his innocence. He admits he was at the scene of Gleason's death and aimed a gun at or above him three times but claims that it clicked or "snapped" but either did not fire or else fired over Gleason's head. Wakefield's testimony and both her narratives tell a similar story. She agrees that Chaska protected her and her children. She does not agree on Hapa's role, and she mentions no third Indian. Chaska says Hapa, Gleason's killer, was not his brother-in-law. Wakefield's narrative says he was. Apparently understanding of kinship terms differed.[54]

Sarah Wakefield then rose to Chaska's defense.

I was with Mr. Gleason when he was killed—Myself and two children were riding with him—There were two in the party who attacked us—The indians were coming up from the direction of the Lower Agency—The other man shot Mr. Gleason. This man tended the horses—When the shots were fired the horses ran and he caught them—The indian was near the wagon when he fired—He shot both barrels and loaded up while this indian ran after the horses—

When Mr. Gleason was in his death agony this indian snapped his gun at him—

He afterwards told me it was to put him out of his misery— I saw this indian endeavor to prevent the other indian from firing at me—He raised his gun twice to do it—He said he did not go into this thing willingly—The pipe I spoke of yesterday I have since heard belonged to a white man, who was killed, and that he (the prisoner) felt so bad about it, he didn't care whether he was killed or not, in this war, and that was why he was in it—Jo. Reynolds knows him very well and considers him a fine man—He is a farmer indian and spells a little— He had on leggins at the time Gleason was shot—When we got in, he took me from a tepee where it was cold, with my babes to one where there was a white woman—Since then he has saved my life three times.

When this indian prevented the other indian from killing me, the other wanted to kill my children, saying "they were no use" and this indian prevented it—I have never known him to go away but twice—He went only when he was freed to go and expressed great feeling for the whites.

His mother took me in the woods and kept me when my life was threatened. He saved my life once, when Shakopee the chief of his band tried to kill me—This indian has no plunder in his tent,

They are poor, he and his family—They have had to beg victuals for me and my children and gone without himself.

He is a very generous man. I have seen him give away his own shirt to indians.[55]

This is the basic story that Wakefield wanted to tell, needed to tell, and was willing to tell over and over again to the military and in her narrative to the public at large, neither of which was greatly interested in hearing anything good about Dakotas or any other Indians. It has three parts: first, Chaska is innocent and did not kill Gleason; second, he is a protector of white women and children; third, he is a "civilized" and "good" Indian—he does not steal, he wears leggings, not a breechcloth, he speaks English, and he has some English education. In sum, he is not out to harm white people; he is more "us" than "them." Whatever the merits or problems of her case, Wakefield put herself and her family on the line in a most remarkable set of circumstances. The state's white population was in a complete frenzy of Indian hatred. Accounts of rape were widely reported in the local and national press and were in keeping with what most white settlers presumed. "The revelations of the white women caused great indignation among our soldiers," wrote Riggs some time later, "to which must be added the outside pressure coming to our camp in letters from all parts of Minnesota,—a wail and a howl,—in many cases demanding the execution of every Indian coming into our hands." Yet Wakefield was determined to stay and defend Chaska. Three other women who remained for the trials were Margaret Cardinal; Mattie Williams, who testified against two Indians on charges of rape; and Harriet Valiant, who swore she was with Cardinal during the rape. In her narrative, Wakefield said, "I do not know of but two females that were abused by Indians."[56] Even if Wakefield did not join that chorus, there was no need for her to testify in Chaska's defense. She could have thanked him, taken her children in tow, and left with the vast majority of other women and children. Vouching for his protection of white womanhood was more than most Minnesotans could tolerate.

Colonel H. H. Sibley first wrote to his wife, Sarah Jane Steele Sibley, from St. Peter in late August. In a series of letters he described "poor people up here, who are being butchered by

the score, with the horrible accompaniments of fearful mutilation." Calling the Indians "fiends, the devils in human shape!"
he prepared "to begin my work upon them with fire and sword."
Echoing Cotton Mather, he wrote, "We are gradually closing
in upon the miserable hounds," adding the more contemporary
phrase, "and they are trying to skedaddle."[57]

On August 31 Sibley told his wife of a "woman with four small
children she has found in the woods," two of them struck by
tomahawks and being treated, and on September 4 he wrote of
the burial of seventy-one of his men. In late September victory
was his, and he described the surrender of "all the white prisoners," estimated at 100 to 150. They were "a pitiable sight,"
crying for joy with "their deliverance from loathsome bondage . . . suffering meantime nameless outrages at the hands of
their brutal captors. Most of them were young, and there were
a score or more of fine, lady-like appearance, notwithstanding
the ragged clothes they wore." Into this scene came "one rather
handsome woman," who "had become so infatuated with the
red skin who had taken her for his wife, that, although her white
husband was still living at some point below, and had been in
search of her, she declared that were it not for her children, she
would not leave her dusky paramour."[58]

On Friday, October 10, Sibley wrote to his wife: "I learn
that Mrs. —— of whom I wrote you, is displeased because I
did not call to see her more frequently, and will not interpose my
authority in behalf of her Indian *friend,* who stands a fair chance
of swinging." By October 11, General Pope ordered Sibley to
send the sixteen hundred Dakota men, women, and children not
accused of crimes to Fort Snelling on the Mississippi just south
of St. Paul. In a letter to his wife, Sibley admitted that such an
action would be "hard upon those who may be innocent," but
orders were orders.[59]

The fate of the remaining captured and accused Dakotas
moved back and forth between Washington and Minnesota. As
Sibley saw their trials roll forward, watching "all the proceedings," and realizing that the fate of more than three hundred
"human beings" was in his power, he told his wife, "it makes me
shudder." But his sense of duty and need for judgment of the
"red skins," despite "railings" of Dakota mothers, wives, and

daughters, helped him continue with his work. His discovery of a recently taken scalp of a young girl and numerous daguerreotypes brought from the Indian camp also helped. He looked forward to "the execution of the wretches who have murdered and ravished." How many would die? The number "will be sufficiently great to satisfy the longings of the most blood-thirsty." He added, "I see the press is very much concerned, lest I should prove too tender-hearted" but promised his wife he would not "harm the innocent." [60]

During this time when Sibley was hoping and planning for the rapid death of the remaining several hundred Dakota prisoners ("I shall execute the criminals at once"), the same woman appeared again. "The woman I wrote you of yesterday threatens that if *her* Indian, who is among those who have been seized should be hung, she will shoot those of us who have been instrumental in bringing him to the scaffold, and then go back away with the Indians. A pretty specimen of a white woman she is, truly!" [61]

Sibley presumed her "hysteria" must involve a "dusky paramour." The alternative, that Wakefield felt an overwhelming debt to a man and his kin who saved her life and the lives of her children, that her conscience required her to act, was more than he could believe.

When Wakefield appeared to testify at Camp Release for "We=chank-wash-tu=du=pee," those listening "thought it very strange that I could speak in favor of an Indian." She was angry to find "they considered my testimony of no account." She knew that if they believed her he would have been acquitted. Then and after "many false and slanderous stories" were "in circulation about me." Word spread about the camp that she and Chaska were lovers and that she preferred him to her husband. She called these "horrid, abominable reports." His case was decided. "We-chank-wash-ta-do-pe" was sentenced "to be hanged by the neck until he is dead." [62]

Two days before leaving Camp Release, Wakefield went to the Indian camp in search of Chaska's mother. The Dakota woman put her arms around her and cried out, "My boy! my boy! they will kill him! Why don't you save him? He saved your life many times. You have forgotten the Indians now your white friends have come." Wakefield says she was moved and tried to reassure her. The mother told Wakefield that she tried to carry bread to her son, but the soldiers would not allow it. Wakefield had not visited him or other prisoners, knowing it would make her feel guilty, "sad to see those who had been so kind to me tied together like beasts" and fearing their "reproach." In fact, when she went to see Chaska, he refused to shake hands with her and told her she had forgotten all the things he had done for her. She cried when he brought up the times he had slept without a blanket because he gave his to her children and how he sold his coat for flour to feed them. They finally came to an understanding, and she "convinced him that I was not to blame."[63]

Sibley continued to be concerned with sexual encounters between whites and Indians. In his letters to his wife he complained, "I find the greatest difficulty in keeping the men from the Indian women when the camps are close together." But he appeared less concerned about the possible dalliance between a white woman and an Indian. In the Wakefield case he need not have worried. Twenty-one of the prisoners were shackled together by their feet, and she could not get close to him; even so soldiers told stories about her. We-chank-wash-ta-do-pe and Sarah Wakefield shook hands. She never saw him again, "for I left very soon for my home."[64]

Before leaving, she checked with Captain Grant and was assured then that Chaska would not hang but would serve five years in prison. That comforted her. She left the Minnesota River that day and arrived at her Shakopee home a few days later.

Indian Captives

In mid-October the prisoners remained shut up in a huge hog pen, chained together in pairs. By late October the trials were winding down at the Lower Agency and the weather was growing cold. In early November, 193 people were buried by Sibley's forces; he estimated between 600 to 800 in all had died. He was tired and longed "for one good home meal." When the trials were finished, Riggs helped write up the results. Riggs admitted, "It almost made me sick to write off two rolls of *three hundred and ninety three men and one woman* and attach to three hundred and three of *them . . .* the penalty '*to be hung.*' Happy to write 'acquitted.' "[65]

On November 13 the uncondemned Dakotas finished their six-day trek from southwestern Minnesota and arrived at Fort Snelling. At times their train was four miles long with only a few wagons for some of the women and children. Thomas Smith Williamson, Yale Medical School graduate and minister to the Dakotas since 1835, noted that on arrival they were moved from the bluff where the fort was situated to the river bottom, just above the ferry stop. Guards protected them from possible attacks from whites. The sixteen hundred Dakotas stayed at Snelling through the winter.[66] The sixty-two-year-old Williamson then returned to his home in St. Peter. On November 15, the close to 360 Dakota men remaining in Camp Release were marched past New Ulm in chains en route to a camp just west of Mankato. About 20 Dakota women and their children stood by them and cooked for them, though there were too few pots to cook in. As the group marched south and east, Indian prisoners in wagons of 10 prisoners each, "flanked by a strong force of mounted men," were attacked by what Sibley characterized as "a crowd of women, who showered brickbuts and missiles upon the shackled wretches, seriously injuring some fifteen of the latter, and some of the guards." The white (mostly German) attackers were beaten back by "a bayonet charge," and fifteen or twenty men were arrested and reprimanded for insulting the flag. Insults were hurled by "their female associates." Sibley feared that if he fired he would kill women and children, but he thought of the avenging German women of New Ulm as "Dutch she devils—They were as fierce as tigresses."[67]

In the cold Minnesota days of November and December, various missionaries to the Indians saw a great opportunity. Dr. Williamson often walked the thirteen miles from St. Peter to Mankato "to preach to the condemned men the words of eternal life, which they were now eager to hear." As Riggs put it, "We passed through a great trial of faith." Episcopalian Samuel D. Hinman lived at Fort Snelling, and Bishop Henry Whipple visited and confirmed one hundred of the Dakotas there and visited prisoners at Mankato as well, recognizing three members of his church among the condemned. In mid-December,

Father Augustin Ravoux arrived at the Mankato prison from St. Paul.[68] Among the over three hundred Dakota prisoners at Mankato and the sixteen hundred at Fort Snelling, the churchmen doubled their efforts.

Though the war was over, the hysteria did not fade. In late November, Riggs wrote east to the American Board of Commissioners for Foreign Missions in Boston of the "great clamor all over the state" for a mass execution. Newspapers demanded annihilation and extermination. "You will understand," he continued, "that in such circumstances, when every body speaks against the Dakotas, it is hard to stand up for them."[69]

President Lincoln demanded that the trial transcripts be sent to Washington for review. With pressure from Bishop Henry B. Whipple and eastern reformers to protect the Dakotas on one hand, and Minnesota congressmen and press demanding mass execution on the other, Lincoln had members of his staff go through the trial records, reducing the more than three hundred death sentences to thirty-nine. On December 6, he sent the final list of the thirty-nine to be executed to Sibley. Well aware of the tensions in the state, he ordered that prisoners should be held "subject to further orders, taking care that they neither escape, nor are subjected to any unlawful violence." For weeks the more than three hundred prisoners were fastened to the brick floor by chains, talking, occasionally smoking. The great majority wore breechcloths, leggings, and blankets; some wore paint. Several of mixed Indian-white backgrounds wore white men's clothes.[70]

The Dakota War and the upcoming execution were no longer local stories. The *New York Times* and *Harper's Weekly* were among the papers from beyond Minnesota's borders that had been following these events at length and had reporters in the state. The first story on Minnesota appeared in the *New York Times* on August 23 on page 8 at the bottom of column 5. But Sunday headlines the next day read, "THE INDIAN MASSACRES Terrible Scenes of Death and Misery in Minnesota. Five Hundred Whites Supposed to be Murdered. The Sioux Bands United Against the Whites FORT RIDGELY IN DANGER." An editorial called the "Indian massacres in the vicinity of Fort Ridgely . . . the most terrible and heartrending character" and estimated that "at least five-hundred whites have already been murdered by savages." There were three more stories concerning the event during the next week. In September, *Harper's Weekly* ran a lurid cartoon reminiscent of the *Death of Jane McCrea* but including babies grabbed from their mothers' arms and dangled by the feet before readied Indian knives.[71]

While Lincoln evaluated the records of the accused, Minnesota politicians put on the heat. They capitalized on the hysteria focused around the issue of the white women captives. In a letter to Lincoln published both locally and nationally and entered into the Senate records, Minnesota congressmen demanded execution of all those accused of "wholesale robbery, *rape, murder.*"

There were nearly ninety female captives. They were the wives and daughters of our neighbors and friends.

They were intelligent and virtuous women; some of them were wives and mothers, others were young and interesting girls. These savages, to whom you purpose to extend your executive clemency, when the whole country was quiet, and the farmers were busily engaged in gathering their crops, arose with fearful violence, and, traveling from one farm-house to another, indiscriminately murdered all the men, boys, and little children they came to; and although they sometimes spared the lives of the mothers and daughters, they did so only to take them into a captivity which was *infinitely worse than death.*

The letter goes on to claim that "a girl of eighteen years of age," known to the congressmen "before and at the time of her capture," a girl "as refined and beautiful . . . as we had in the State," was taken, bound and tied, and "ravished by some eight or ten of these convicts before the cords were loosed from her limbs. . . . Without being more specific we will state that all or nearly all the women who were captured were violated in this way."[72]

In Minnesota's *Faribault Central Republican*, Senator M. S. Wilkinson warned that any decision to pardon "would only lead to riot and blood-shed." Labeling Lincoln's "misplaced clemency" toward "traitors, and rebels" as "chicken hearted," he implored, "in the name of the bereaved and the stricken by the arm of the savage murderers of wives, and children, the ravishers of our daughters" that all 303 accused Indians be executed to prevent "the horrors of mob law." [73]

On December 11 President Lincoln sent a message that was read before the United States Senate explaining his actions, which had "caused a careful examination of the records of the trials to be made." As to those "proved guilty of violating females," he concluded that, "contrary to my expectations, only two of this class were found." Attached to his statement was the order issued to now Brigadier General H. H. Sibley from the Executive Mansion on December 6 with a list of the names and numbers of the thirty-nine "Indians and half-breeds" to be executed.[74]

One week before the execution, the cover of *Harper's Weekly, Journal of Civilization*, depicted the "Identification of Indian Murderers in Minnesota by a Boy Survivor of the Massacre." The little boy stands before a uniformed federal guard. Clean, suited, and white, his right arm in a sling, he stands with his left arm extended, his finger pointing at a proud, erect Indian surrounded by dark, grotesque, witchlike figures crouching animal-like on the prison floor. The inside story, titled "The Indian Murderers in Minnesota" by the "gentleman who made the sketch," tells the reader that the number of dead came "to over one thousand. . . . There is no record of a massacre so thorough in detail in the history of our country." Comparing the Sioux with "the most blood-thirsty of their kind" around the world, the writer described those he saw in the prison as "the most hideous wretches that I have ever seen" and went on to report the story of the little boy "who had escaped after seeing the murder and outrage of his mother and sisters." [75] Such a tone set the climate for the mass hanging. During those last days before the execution, crowds poured into Mankato from all over the state.

When the president's list appeared in the local papers, Sarah Wakefield did not see Chaska's name or number. Chaska, We-chank-wash-ta-do-pe, Case 3, was not on the list of those meant to hang. She thought everything was fine. This, however, was not the case. The number stated to be hanged at Mankato was thirty-nine, changed to thirty-eight when Prisoner No. 1, "Godfrey, a Negro," was let off at the last minute for his role as a witness against many others in the trials. But Chaska would be one of the thirty-eight.[76]

The task of hanging was taken care of by Stephen Miller, a friend of Sibley's who got his commission in the army with Sibley's help. An extension of time was needed to get the right rope. Sibley obliged Miller by sending the "proper rope" so that he could "rig up a single gallows, splice the bed-cord, and hang the Indians, one at a time."[77]

If Miller took care of bodies, the missionaries continued to watch out for souls. In the days before the execution, Riggs and Williamson were inspired by Chaskay, a Christian Indian prisoner from Riggs's church at Yellow Medicine, renamed Robert Hopkins. He became the instrument through which the Holy Spirit seemed to speak. Prayer meetings began in the Mankato prison, and the missionaries came and spoke on Sabbath. Hopkins held prayer meetings through the week. The result was a harvest of souls. In one day, Samuel's brother, Reverend Gideon H. Pond, came and baptized three hundred Dakota men.[78]

On Monday, December 20, Colonel Miller told Father Ravoux that the condemned men would be separated out and told their sentence. At three that afternoon he, Williamson, Riggs, and Reverend M. Sommereisen, another Catholic priest, came to the prison. Two lists, a Protestant one and a Catholic one, were prepared; the thirty-nine condemned men were signed up for the confessors of their choice. Twenty-four preferred the Catholics, twelve asked for Protestants, two wanted neither. Ravoux expressed surprise that theirs was the longer list, given that both Riggs and Williamson "have a perfect knowledge of the Sioux language, and have been for twenty-five years amongst them." Despite the Protestants' "good service" at Mankato, the Indians still preferred the "black robes." "I know not," he wrote his superior, "unless it be the work of God, and the accomplishment of that promise of our Lord to His church and her ministers: 'Go teach all nations.'"[79] On Christmas Day, one day before the hanging, Father Ravoux "gave Holy Communion to the three mestizos" and thought they "were inexpressibly happy." He returned to the prison late that afternoon with Reverend M.

Sommereisen and then baptized thirty more of the condemned men, saving a total of thirty-three whom he referred to as "my little flock," "my Indians," "my dear neophytes." Three other Dakotas converted to Presbyterianism.[80]

That day, men who had earlier taken medicine from Williamson refused to do so, saying "they did not want to be separated from their relatives in the other world." Instead, they used his services to transmit letters to friends and family. One of the condemned, Rda-in-yan-ka (Rattling Runner), the son-in-law of Mdewakanton chief Wabasha, sent a statement that could well have expressed the mood of the Dakota prisoners in Mankato, especially those sentenced to die: "You have deceived me. You told me that if we followed the advice of General Sibley, and gave ourselves up to the whites, all would be well; no innocent man would be injured. I have not killed, wounded, or injured a white man, or any white persons. I have not participated in the plunder of their property; and yet to-day I am set apart for execution. . . . My wife and children are dear to me. Let them not grieve for me. Let them remember that the brave should be prepared to meet death; and I will do as becomes a Dakota."[81]

On the morning of December 26, Riggs went "to assist in identifying" prisoners, "lest some mistake should be made, and the wrong persons executed." He said it was not he but Joseph R. Brown "who, better than any other one man, knew all these condemned men" and whose work it was to select from the 303 those "who were named to be executed." When the execution was near, Colonel Miller told Joseph R. Brown to have the chaplains prepare the prisoners for death. He then had Riggs read the list of the condemned and pronounced them each guilty "of wantonly and wickedly murdering" the children of their "Great Father in Washington" and sinning against mankind so that they could only ask mercy from God. Looking back on these events less than a month later, Riggs wrote: "Communicating the death sentence to a whole room full of human beings— taking their confessions and pointing them to Jesus who could love the thief on the cross. How unlike other winters!"[82]

At 7:15 in the morning, the thirty-eight had their irons removed. Their elbows were tied behind their backs and their wrists tied in front of them. The men sang as they were tied and walked around the room shaking hands with reporters and soldiers. They then "stood up in a row," sang again, then "sat down solemnly." Father Ravoux came in and prayed in both Dakota and English. He, Riggs, Williamson, and Sommereisen stayed with the men until the last moment possible. Then long white muslin caps were rolled up and placed on each man's head and rolled down on his forehead. A reporter at the prison noted, "Chains and cords had not moved them—their wear was not considered dishonorable—but this covering of the head with a white cap was humiliating." The singing stopped. At ten o'clock the thirty-eight were marched "two abreast" through the line of soldiers to the scaffold.[83]

As they mounted the scaffold, they began once again to sing and keen. Each went to his assigned place. An "awful interest" was focused on the thirty-eight. One of the condemned continued smoking a cigar on the scaffold; one smoked a pipe. The baglike caps were rolled down to cover the men's faces. One St. Paul reporter noticed a moment in his death song when one Indian made "an indecent exposure of his person, in hideous mockery of the triumph of that justice whose sword was already falling on his head." A rope was placed around each neck without resistance, but continual wailing and mournful cries kept their own harmony. There were three drumbeats. William J. Daly was a man whose three children had been killed; his wife and two other children had been captured at Lake Shetek and were somewhere out on the high plains.[84] At 10:15 he stepped forward and cut the rope. The platform drop fell. A great cheer went up from the crowd. The bodies hung suspended, the men, with bound hands and arms still reaching out for one another, and "several in a row were hand in hand," their voices singing and calling each other's names.[85]

How did Chaska come to die? According to military commission recorder-turned-historian Isaac V. D. Heard, Riggs was the "grand jury" for the trials. Even if this was not the full story, Riggs had the most expert knowledge of the Dakota language among the whites. With this knowledge he set to work writing up Indian names on government documents. After the prisoners were marched downriver to Mankato, Riggs went to the prison almost daily, talked with the men, prayed with them, and tried to organize mass conversions with the help of the Christian Indian renamed Robert Hopkins. It was Riggs who,

on December 26, called the names of the thirty-eight sentenced to hang. It is no wonder that Sarah Wakefield contacted him when she heard of Chaska's death.[86]

Giving Riggs and the authorities the benefit of the doubt on the Chaska "mistake," one must acknowledge the similarities (to an English speaker) of the numerous Chaska-like names among the accused Dakotas. There were Case 121, Chaskay-don or Chaskay-etay, "Convicted of shooting and cutting open a woman who was with child"; Case 342, Chay-ton-hoon-ka, "Proved to have been one of a party that committed the massacres at Beaver creek"; and Case 359, Chan-ka-hda, "proven to have been of the party, and present when Patville was killed, and to have saved Mary Anderson (who had been wounded) from being killed, and to have taken her prisoner."[87]

Both publicly and privately, Riggs called Chaska's death "a mistake." In her narrative, Wakefield published a letter she claims he wrote to her on the matter. Each of her two editions has a slightly different text, and no original of the letter appears to exist. In the 1863 edition, Riggs's letter says: "We all felt a solemn responsibility, and a fear that some mistake would occur." The 1864 edition says "should occur." In both versions Riggs says that they realized there was a third Chaska but remembered only a second, the Christian Indian Robert Hopkins. "On that fatal morning we never thought of the third one."[88] In the second edition the Riggs letter reads:

Mrs. Wakefield—*Dear Madam:* In regard to the mistake by which Chaska was hung instead of another, I doubt whether I can satisfactorily explain it. We all felt a solemn responsibility and a fear that some mistake should occur. We had forgotten that he was condemned under the name We-chan-hpe-wash-tay-do-pe. We knew he was called Chaska in the prison, and had forgotten that any other except Robert Hopkins, who lived by Dr. Williamson, was so called. We never thought of the third one; so when the name Chaska was called in the prison on that fatal morning, your protector answered to it and walked out. I do not think any one was really to blame. We all regretted the mistake very much, &c.

—With kind respects, yours truly,
"S. R. RIGGS"[89]

Riggs tells us, "We had forgotten that he was condemned under the name of We-chan-hpe-wash-tay-do-pe."[90] Who was "we"? Wakefield claims that after she was "introduced to Sibley, Mr. Riggs, and the others, they requested me to point out the Indian who had saved me. He came forward and I called his name; and when I told them how kind he had been they shook hands with him, and made quite a hero of him for a short time." Riggs clearly knew the man in question. Reverends Riggs and Williamson and Father Ravoux were all at the prison often those days before the execution in Mankato. According to Ravoux, the names of the accused were given to the clergymen on the Monday before the execution.[91] Riggs himself was one of those who called the names. Riggs and the other clergy watched as the men walked to the scaffold for execution. Nor was the alleged lover of Wakefield a mystery man to the officers and the soldiers in charge.

There is yet one more problem with Riggs's "mistake." According to the *Mankato Independent* of December 26 (page 3), Riggs received and gave to the newspaper what it called the "condensed out-line of Confessions and statements of the condemned" from those about to hang. Under number twenty was "Chas kay dan," who said he had witnessed Gleason's murder and had protected Wakefield. "He saved Mrs. Wakefield and the children; and now he dies while she lives." The question arises, What was Riggs doing taking the "confession" of a pardoned man? Certainly he was complicit in this man's death. The sorry fate of Indian captives might well be pondered.

Sarah Wakefield's Story

. . . . . .

Sarah Wakefield's career as author and reporter of her own experience as a captive began shortly after the hangings at Mankato. Why did she write her book? What is its history and what does it tell us about this woman, the historical event in which she participated, and the role of conscience? Wakefield's decision to write her narrative was infused with her sense of guilt and her inability to overlook what appeared to her as a deliberate attempt to get rid of Chaska. In it she wrote, "Now I will never believe that all in authority at Mankato had forgotten what Chaska was condemned for, and I am sure, in my own mind, it was done intentionally." Which others in authority Wakefield held responsible, she only vaguely implied. As to her own role, her own conscience, she first wrote, "Now I will always feel that I am responsible for that man's murder, and will never know quietness again." She later changed the end of the sentence to read, "and will reproach myself for urging him to remain." [92]

Six Weeks in the Sioux Tepees: A Narrative of Indian Captivity first appeared in print within months after the release of Wakefield and her children. The printing history of this book was short; to date only two imprints are known, one in 1863, published in Minneapolis by the Atlas Printing Company, and the second, issued in Shakopee by Argus Book and Job Printing in 1864. Even in the print shop, Sarah Wakefield was "subjected to many embarrassments," including the "malice and gross carelessness of the printer," who produced a first edition with many "omissions and misprintings" and any number of misspelled Indian names. [93]

From the few extant copies of both editions, we can tell that Wakefield's was one of those captivities which, in the grand tradition, was read to pieces. The small pamphlets came with colored paper covers, printed on rough, inexpensive paper. They were made to sell fast, not to endure as classic literature. The second edition added a frontispiece with a picture of Little Crow. Its back cover announced:

AGENTS WANTED
Local Traveling Agents wanted in every section of this and adjoining States, to whom a liberal discount will be made.
Address

Mrs. SARAH F. WAKEFIELD,
Shakopee, Minnesota [94]

Besides the desire to sell the work, an examination of these editions uncovers their author's intent and her crisis of conscience. Those first printing errors were corrected, but other changes took place between the 1863 and 1864 editions, in both length and content. The 1863 edition had fifty-four pages, the 1864 edition, sixty-three. This nine-page addition might appear insignificant; quite the opposite is the case. Nine pages of tiny print in the 1860s would be closer to eighteen pages in today's more readable typefaces. The expansion of the booklet, even in its own day, adds nearly 18 percent new material to the original.

In the new, enlarged edition, with 50 lines to a page, a total of 653 lines were added. The new material falls into four categories, each adding greater detail and depth to the original story; they are the mother/survivor role, Chaska and Dakota life, the threatening nature of Indian life in captivity, and issues of conscience.

The sequences dealing with her as mother-survivor and with Chaska as protector of mother and children constitute a central plot and an expanded defense of Chaska. But the intervention of a heroic Indian figure in the position of rescuer of white womanhood and savior of helpless white children did not fit the mythic archetype for rescue of the maiden in distress from the dragon or animal-like man-beast. Her appeal here and elsewhere seems especially aimed at the female reader. She describes her actions as those of a virtuous mother defending her young with Chaska's help. The soldiers and others hold her virtue suspect. Along with themes of protection and virtue, Wakefield included threatening aspects of Indian life which mirrored the sentiment more typical of other Minnesota captives, earlier captivity stories, and the popular press. Such anti-Indian statements probably functioned to buy credibility with the Minnesota public, allowing Wakefield to attack the government and agency whites for bringing on the conflagration.

But despite traditional captivity elements, Wakefield's argument amounts to three indictments of the government: she assigns it responsibility first for the Dakotas' state of starvation and misery; second, for the hanging of an innocent man; and finally, for dispossessing the Dakotas and leaving them to die on the prairie. The combined impact of these charges elevates the original narrative from a white woman's defense of her own actions to a moral critique of the Minnesota and federal authorities. Their sins of commission, all deliberate, all avoidable, are delineated by her as an act of Christian conscience, a plea by a Christian mother for mercy in support of Minnesota's Indian community.

In the preface to both editions Sarah Wakefield tells the reader that the work was not intended for public consumption, but rather for the eyes of her children, and she continues: "I do not pretend to be a book-writer," warning the reader not to expect "much to please the mind's fancy." Apologies and disclaimers aside, in the second edition she persuasively sets up her story, tracing in the setting, the backdrop of the first night of fright, the first July 4 incident, the habits of the traders. This takes up six pages in the later edition, amplifying the plea for sympathy into the fuller context of a dramatic story. Rather than an anti-Indian tract we have a pro-Indian story, constructed with the realization that compassion can more easily flow from understanding and empathy.[95] In a metaphorical sense it is the story of a mother to her children but also of a mother in the wider community.

From the first page of the first edition, Wakefield is clear as to how she sees the Indian people with whom she found herself. After a single sentence about her husband's appointment to Yellow Medicine, she says of her relationship with the Dakotas: "I found them very kind, good people. The women sewed for me, and I have employed them in various ways around my house, and began to love them and respect them as if they were whites. I became so much accustomed to them and their ways that when I was thrown into their hands as a prisoner, I felt more easy and contented than any other white person among them, for I knew that not one of the Yellow Medicine Indians would see me and my children suffer as long as they could protect me."[96]

By August 1862, there had been "murders committed among them by the Chippewas," and the Dakotas came in for their annuities and "camped out" a mile from the agency buildings. "Here they remained many weeks, suffering hunger: every day expecting their pay so as to return to their homes."[97] Her sympathy for them in a time of starvation dominates her opening words. This is different from the second edition in which she writes a more romantic lead-in to the Wakefield family arrival.

But even here, one expects that the scenes coming into the pristine Dakota prairie prepare the reader for the violent events that ensue.

Through its discussion of the murder of George Gleason and her children's escape from death, Wakefield's narrative sets up the dichotomy of the good and the bad Indian, with Chaska taking the role of the good Indian and Hapa [Hapan] appearing as the "horrid, blood-thirsty wretch." Although she was arguing with a "dual vision" that dates back to early seventeenth-century America, she couched it in the language of the debate informing nineteenth-century white-Indian discourse. In this environmentalist view, Indians were inferior because of their lack of Christian religion and membership in an "inferior" racial group. But the missionaries and "liberal" whites of Wakefield's day thought that Christianization and civilization could change people. Chaska represented the potentially "civilized" Indian, as opposed to Hapa, who stood for the worst of the old Indian ways. In her text Wakefield sees the two as foils and says, "Here can be seen the good work of the Missionaries. The two men were vastly different, although they both belonged to one band and one family; but the difference was this: the teaching that Chaska had received; although he was not a Christian, he knew there was a God, and he had learned right from wrong." [98]

From the moment Wakefield and her children arrived in the Dakotas' camp she was treated with great respect. They recognized her as the woman they knew from their winter camp in Shakopee when they had come to her house and she had given them food. During fighting between the Dakotas and the Ojibwas in 1858, her husband had treated Dakota wounded, "and they often said he saved many of their lives." [99] Now they greeted each other as "old friends." She describes how, in exchange for these good works, "they would protect me and mine." The old women helped her down from the wagon, crying when they saw her and spreading carpets for her, giving her a pillow and asking her to rest herself. They made supper for her and her children and assured her she was safe. She was then told to go with Chaska and to trust him as a "good man." [100] She followed him and explains how she could survive by following along and not complaining. She laughed and joked with the Dakotas, helped prepare meat for the warriors by pounding it into leatherlike

241

Sarah Wakefield

strips they could wear around their waists into battle, painted blankets, and braided ribbons to ornament the horses. She explains how her behavior would "conciliate them, and a different course would have caused different treatment." [101]

Sarah Wakefield tells us that her main motive was to protect herself and her children. On Thursday, August 21, the Indians got up early to attack Fort Ridgely. Chaska explained that for her protection she and the children should go with him to his grandfather's, "who lived in a brick house about a mile away." His sister Winona "painted my cheeks and a part of my hair. She tied my hair (which was braided like a squaw's down my back) with several colored ribbons and ornamented me with fancy colored leggins, moccasins, etc. My children were painted in like manner. . . . Who would have known me to be a white woman?" [102] She disguised her boy James by rubbing dirt on him so that those Indians who she had heard would kill them would not know he was white. She tore the dress from baby Lucy to show her dark skin. When a Dakota woman warned her they would kill her and hold the children for ransom, she said she would rather see them dead and begged for a knife to kill her daughter. "What I suffered, let every mother imagine, when you think of my trying to cut my child's throat myself." In describing many of these trials of motherhood, she plays on the reader's sentiment to highlight her will to survive and protect her children. [103]

But some of the white captive women around her judged Wakefield's behavior to be too cooperative. Mary Schwandt remembered that "Mrs. Dr. Wakefield and Mrs. Adams were painted and decorated and dressed in full Indian costume, and seemed proud of it. They were usually in good spirits, laughing and joking, and appeared to enjoy their new life. The rest of us disliked their conduct, and would have but little to do with them." [104] In the second edition Wakefield adds piece after piece about her protective role as a mother and her willingness to sacrifice everything for her life and her children's: she worked, gave away, and changed clothing. "They asked me to take off my hoops, which I did. I think I should have cut off my right hand if I could have saved my life." [105]

After emphasizing motherhood, Wakefield turns pleas for sympathy into forums for describing how Chaska and his family saved her and the children. When she was about to kill her child, Chaska's mother came and took the baby on her back, gave her crackers and a cup, and urged Sarah and the boy to hurry to the woods. There the Indian mother told her they should hide themselves in the high grasses until morning. When danger threatened, Chaska carried her son James to his aunt's home.[106]

As a result of these experiences, Wakefield tries to convey the necessity and rightness of helping Indians in return: "I was anxious to do all I possibly could for them when they needed assistance." While others attribute her behavior to love and misdirected passion for Chaska, Wakefield places her actions on the field of conscience: "I could never love a savage, although I could respect any or all that might befriend me, and I would willingly do everything in my power to benefit those that were so kind to me in my great hour of need."[107] Her sense of duty to others is based on a Christian dictum: "Do unto others as you would have them do unto you." The civilization of a Christian woman could be no less generous than that of a newly Christianized Indian.

Along with its Christian impetus, perhaps her way of dealing with her grief and guilt was to transpose the personal story into a political one. Unlike the usual captivity narrative, Indian action and damage done have *causes* other than God's or the Devil's work or savagery or malevolence. As the Dakotas' forces and their captives moved miles up the river valley past the Upper Agency at Yellow Medicine and on past Lac qui Parle, Wakefield saw the destruction wreaked on Dr. T. S. Williamson's mission—an effort of over twenty years which Wakefield admired and respected. She ponders the rubble and Williamson's life work thus repaid after years among the Indians. Why had this happened?[108] "I could not think of any other cause than this— it may be right, it may be wrong; but such is my belief—: That our own people, not the Indians, were to blame. Had they not, for years, been cheated unmercifully, and now their money had been delayed; no troops were left to protect the frontier and their Agent, their 'father,' had left them without money, food or clothing, and gone off to the war."[109]

At the end of her narrative, in the second longest addition to the second edition, Wakefield expands the scope of her story.[110] She says that when H. H. Sibley arrived at Camp Release with the Minnesota military forces, many women changed their stories. One woman who used to complain that she was over-fed by the Indian women told the soldiers how she was nearly starved, going for days without food. Wakefield claimed such lies were made up to "excite the sympathy of the soldiers."[111] "My object was to excite sympathy for the Indians and in so doing, the soldiers lost all respect for me, and abused me shame-fully; but I had rather have my own conscience than that of those persons who turned against their protectors, those that were so kind to them in that time of great peril."[112] Her narrative closes with an attack on the contemporary state of affairs in Minne-sota. She refers to the members of the expeditions mounted in 1863 to capture those Dakotas who escaped onto the plains as profit mongers, not heroes. Describing the situation of the Dakotas in their new reservation on the South Dakota plains, she points out that thirty-six hundred Dakotas lived on poor land with alkali water, waiting for government food supplies and dying in great numbers. She is also concerned about the Winnebagos, former enemies of the Dakotas, who lived in the southern part of Minnesota and northern Iowa. Although they did not fight in the war, they were leaving Minnesota under threats of extermination and, according to Wakefield, risked death on the high plains at the hands of their enemies the Tetons and Brules.[113]

Sarah Wakefield felt guilt for Chaska's death but also sor-row for "my neighbors," who "lived like the white man; now they are wanderers, without home, or even a resting place." "Their reservation in this State was a portion of the most beau-tiful country that was ever known, and they had everything they wished to make them comfortable if they could have only stayed there; but a few evil men commenced their murderous work, and all has gone to ruin."[114]

Though more than two centuries away from Mary Rowland-son's narrative, like her predecessor, Sarah Wakefield closed her book by calling upon her maker to set things straight. She tells of an Indian family recently passing through Shakopee. Recog-nizing them, she ran down to talk and bring them food. "For this," she laments, "I have been blamed; but I could not help it. They were kind to me, and I will try and repay them, trust-

ing that in God's own time I will be righted and my conduct
understood, for with Him all things are plain." [115]

"Farewell Forever"

. . . . . .

"And now I will bid this subject farewell forever," wrote
Sarah F. Wakefield in the last line of her second edition.[116]

It is hard to know whether she was successful in her wish. The
paradox of wanting to forget and yet being forced to remember
the past may have been with Sarah Wakefield the rest of her
life. In a strange way, such memories bade her and her family
a farewell, and in other ways they seem to have followed them
like a spirit, perhaps the Dakota spirit of the eagle, to which I
will return.

Like Mary Rowlandson, Mary Jemison, John Tanner, and
others who had crossed over into the Indian world, Sarah Wakefield found the return neither complete nor easy. Besides the
social and psychological transformations Wakefield underwent,
there were physical ones as well. In the six weeks between her
late August capture and her early October release, her hair
turned completely white, and this tall and substantial woman of
close to two hundred pounds lost forty pounds. Such fear-filled
effects of captivity did not go unnoticed among her Minnesota
neighbors. Swiss immigrant Sophie Bost wrote to her in-laws in
November from Chaska, a town near Shakopee:

> You may well believe that many horrible or exciting incidents
> occurred during those days of terror. The wife of a doctor,
> formerly of Shakopee, seized by blind fear, was determined
> to leave Fort Ridgely. . . . She saw her guide killed beside her
> by an Indian. . . . [In captivity] she was continually threatened
> with death in every form, not to mention all the infamous out-
> rages to which all these poor creatures were subjected. She
> herself has told Ms. [sic] Maxwell how the Indians, finding
> whiskey in stores frequently came back to camp drunk, de-
> termined to kill all the captives, and how it was the squaws
> who hid them. Once the unfortunate woman of whom I'm

speaking was hidden in a swamp for a whole night while her two children, on another occasion, under a pile of hay where she had to smother her child, a little baby, so its crying would not be heard . . . no wonder this poor woman's hair turned white![117]

Nor did the events of the bloody Monday of August 18 leave Dr. John Wakefield unscathed. He and others at the Upper Agency got warnings of what was to come. That night, Dr. Wakefield, along with twenty men and forty-two women and children, took refuge in the warehouse. According to Parker Peirce, a young worker at the agency, several men stood by with rifles; others had shotguns. "The women were armed with knives and axes and appeared brave." "Bales of blankets" surrounded the windows, and "barrels and loads of stone" were braced at the top of the stairs to be "rolled down" on the heads of potential invaders. That night Dr. Wakefield believed his wife and children dead. From inside the warehouse he and the others watched flames rise from the traders' stores a half mile down the hill. They heard and saw the sounds and flashes of guns; they anticipated their own deaths as a bleeding trader stumbled in, begging for help. To their great good fortune, the rescue of the agency population was accomplished because of John Otherday, a Christian Dakota with a white wife, who with other Dakotas took the sixty-two across the Minnesota River and walked with them to the safety of the Wakefields' hometown of Shakopee.[118]

We have no record of Dr. Wakefield's life during the next six weeks. He must have presumed his wife and children dead; local and national papers were reporting the deaths of hundreds. On August 29, the *Mankato Independent* reported that Gleason and the Wakefield family "were all murdered." By the time Sibley's troops reached Camp Release, there was no way for Dr. Wakefield to have known if his family was dead or alive. Whether he heard of their survival before, during, or after Chaska's trial at Camp Release on September 28, we have no record. Whether he heard about Sarah's pleadings for Chaska's life, her threats, and her testimony is uncertain. Nor do we know what thoughts might have crossed his mind when word of his wife's defense of Chaska and intimations of a possible affair reached him. The combination of relief and joy—that his family was safe at a time when so many others had been killed and orphans were roaming about—along with humiliation, perhaps anger, and uncertainty about whether his wife had betrayed him could well have been on his mind. The possible impact of all of this publicity on his career must have affected him as well. We can only speculate as to his precise feelings. Years later, Lucy Bourke, the captive daughter of Sarah and John, burned the family letters. In the extant small collections of family papers that might shed some light here, there is only one relevant letter. Following the uprising, John's sister Elizabeth Wakefield sent from Winstead, Connecticut, words of sympathy to be relayed to the doctor's wife. There are no known copies of a reply.[119] It would be fair to say that in the best of marriages, the trauma of these events would have made an impact. A time of reconciliation and clarification would be needed before normal life of the family could be reconstituted.

In the years following the printing of *Six Weeks in the Sioux Tepees*, Sarah and John Wakefield effectively disappeared from the public record. This family with its prominent past is impossible to find outside the census records and city directories. From those sources we find that the couple remained in Shakopee and had two more children, Julia E. in 1866 and John Rockwell in 1868.[120] In the next decades, John's star fell as that of his brother James rose.

In 1856 James Beach Wakefield had moved from Shakopee to Blue Earth City, near the Iowa border. There, in Faribault County, he continued to build the real estate empire he had started in Scott County. Following the political propensities of his parents' families, after the war he built a political career on top of a land empire. He ran for state legislator from his district and was elected twice between 1863 and 1866. He was then elected to the state senate from 1867 through 1869. His statewide popularity gave him the lieutenant governorship in 1875 and again in 1877. His nearly perfectly round head and full mustache can be seen in the state legislatures' photographs of 1866. After this, James left state politics for Congress, where he served as a Republican for two terms, in 1884 and 1886, leaving at midterm to become head of the Winnebago land office. James Beach outlived both John and Sarah Wakefield. In August 1910, the *Mankato Daily Free Press* announced his death. A long and prominent obituary eulogized him as "one of the fathers of the state, a noble citizen and an elegant and courtly gentleman of the old school."[121]

From the family, court, and state records, we find a less complete and more disturbing record of the remainder of Dr. John Luman Wakefield's life. On February 19, 1874, an unusual obituary appeared in the *St. Paul Daily Pioneer*. It told of a Shakopee doctor, formerly of the Upper Agency and a graduate of Harvard, who had died of an overdose of opiates the previous Tuesday night. "It appears that he returned home, and shortly after retiring requested his wife to call him at a specified hour. A short time after, the attention of his wife was attracted by his breathing, and upon attempting to arouse him found herself unable to do so. Assistance was called, but to no avail, and he expired soon after."[122]

The *Shakopee Argus* mentioned no opiate but reported that he had been confined to his house with an illness since Saturday but not thought "dangerously sick." A doctor was called Monday night, but Wakefield died Tuesday morning before his arrival. The official death certificate stated the cause of death as "Gen.[eral] Debility." Perhaps the doctor died of a self-administered accidental overdose of the drug; perhaps his overdose was deliberate and the local paper wished to cover up such a shocking death in "the prime of life" of "one of our oldest and best known citizens."[123]

Wakefield died without leaving a notarized will, but among the surviving family papers is an unsigned, undated will, in pencil and in his hand. Beginning coherently, and ending with omissions, it left blocks of land and other goods to his wife, Sarah, and other pieces of property to his two eldest children, James Orin and Lucy. This document points to his own knowledge of an imminent demise. This and the request for Sarah's return indicate suicide and even perhaps Wakefield's deliberate attempt to leave his wife with his anger and his pain.[124]

Four years earlier, the 1870 census listed John L. Wakefield (age forty-seven), wife Sarah F. (forty) "Keeping House," and four children (James O., twelve, Lucy E., ten, Julia E., four, John R., two). The physician's real estate was valued at $4,500, his personal estate at $1,000.[125] But when funeral services were performed at the Methodist church that Friday in 1874 by Reverend Samuel W. Pond, although he provided his family with a cemetery plot in Shakopee, Dr. John Luman Wakefield was buried in an unmarked grave.[126]

When Dr. Wakefield's estate went through probate, nearly seventy-nine individuals and businesses came forward to lay claim to over $4,500 of an estate valued at $5,073. What happened to the entire estate cannot be determined from the records. Records do exist of the claims; these reveal something of Wakefield's last years in Shakopee and may provide some insight into his untimely death. The fifty-one-year-old Wakefield was a heavy drinker and a smoker. Three saloon keepers submitted total claims of slightly over $370, nearly $300 of which was allowed. Two of their records show that between 1868 and his death in 1874, Wakefield stopped into one or both establishments daily for several beers, a whiskey or two, and often a can of oysters. He also left substantial bills at one local grocer's, where he routinely picked up tobacco, whiskey, rum, and beer along with oysters, sardines, cheese, crackers, "treats," candy, and coffee. The largest outstanding bill was for drugs (over $200), perhaps a natural expense for a doctor, perhaps not.[127]

During those years Dr. Wakefield and his family had continued to satisfy their earlier tastes for the comfortable life. There were substantial bills for clothing, groceries, meat, and innumerable tracts of real estate all over Scott and nearby counties. There was also a bill of over $300 for livery; cash amounting to several hundred dollars owed to various creditors; and combined bills for wood, carpentry work, other labor, and music classes at St. Gertrude's Academy. A look at the inventory of the estate shows that $3,850 of the $5,073 appraised value was in real estate. The list of housewares is more modest for its place and time than the list of goods claimed lost in the Wakefield's Upper Agency claim. Perhaps at his death, an undervaluation was substituted for the earlier overvaluation of claims after the uprising. But there were still two horses, two cows, a sleigh, and a buggy along with the requisite sofas, dining room furniture, several carpets, three tables, three rockers, bureaus, beds, featherbeds, sets of dishes, pots and pans, washtubs, milk pails, and the usual accoutrements of middle-class life.[128] Perhaps it was the penchant for land and the trappings of leisure and bourgeois life, along with his love of beer and oysters, that sent

Dr. Wakefield into debt and caused his despondency. Perhaps such activities went along with the life of a once successful and prominent doctor whose reputation turned around amid rumors about his flamboyant, articulate, and reform-minded wife.

Whether Dr. Wakefield committed suicide or accidentally took an overdose of drugs is impossible to know for sure. In any case, the Shakopee debtors lost no time in deluging the courts with claims on the Wakefield properties. Of the $5,000 estate, $2,800 was awarded to creditors, leaving Sarah Wakefield with effects and land worth $2,273. In keeping with the physician's request, son James Orin (then sixteen) was rewarded with $850 worth of land lots in Blue Earth City, Faribault County. The location of the lots and the guardianship of the property under the direction of Eli T. Wilder both indicate the influence of James Beach. A Judge Ely T. Wilder was James Beach Wakefield's brother-in-law (originally from Painesville, Ohio), with whom he had studied law. There is no direct evidence of any communication between Sarah and her brother-in-law at any time after John's death. Daughter Lucy (called Nellie) was left some property; the other two children, Julia and John R., were left nearly nothing.[129]

Negotiating her husband's debts and trying to collect from his debtors to support four children was not easy. By December 1874, Mrs. Wakefield's expenses included $186.37 for her husband's burial, debts of $150 along with $50 for the children's schooling, $200 for their music lessons, $50 for schoolbooks, attorney's fees, household repairs, and other expenses totaling $220, and $1,251.66 for taxes. Sarah Wakefield auctioned off the hens, two cows, the buggy, the sleigh, tables, clocks, lamps, mirror, and other household effects to get $160 and collected about $380 owed to her husband. In her report she informed the court, "I found it extremely difficult to collect the accounts of the deceased" because of "the irresponsibility of many of the creditors, doubtful responsibility of many others," and so "found it necessary to commence many suit." In early March 1875, the widow Wakefield had her lawyer petition the court for an allowance to live on while the estate was being probated. The year's income amounted to $1,200.[130]

The vulturelike descent on the Wakefield estate might have

been the result of pure greed. One Wakefield descendant suggests that it was in the nature of an economic attack on a widow who had little ability to deal in a patriarchal court system and economy.[131] But such an attack might be interpreted as delayed retribution against this woman, perhaps for driving Wakefield to his grave, perhaps because she was "an Indian lover," or perhaps because she was simply too uppity for her own good. Maybe her persistent show of conscience was too Christian for most of her Minnesota neighbors to abide.

By 1876 Sarah and her four children had moved to the outskirts of St. Paul. There, for the next two decades, she gradually pulled together more money and bought a house at 110 St. Anthony Avenue in the Merriam Park district. Apparently she bought property in the downtown, for her grandson recalled stories by his father, John Rockwell, about how his mother sent him to the library for armfuls of books while she did business. She is also remembered as the guiding force in her children's education, urging them to take advantage of St. Paul's schools and sending Lucy to Macalester College.[132]

On May 27, 1899, St. Paul's headlines reported a new war on yet another frontier. The paper cautioned "No More Shilly-Shallying With the Filipinos." In the sports news, the home team, the Saints, "Gave the Game Away" to the Detroit Tigers, while in St. Louis the game with Brooklyn was called in the twelfth inning because of darkness. The fashion pages that week recommended "Delicate Silks and Fine Laces to Be Found in the Wardrobe of the Willowy Girl" and pictured a seated woman underneath which it advised, "Knickers for the Wheel Woman, to be Worn Under a Skirt." On Monday, May 29, next to an advertisement for Ivory Soap, the paper reported the May 27 death of Mrs. Sarah F. Wakefield, former Sioux captive, at age sixty-nine.[133]

There is little evidence to indicate that Sarah Wakefield and Chaska may have been involved in a romantic encounter, but anything is possible. The two slept in the same tepee for much of her capture. The desperation of her situation and his generosity may have brought her close to the man. During the trial, their testimonies, even their words, seem identical regarding Gleason's death and the gun "snapping."[134] That Sarah Wakefield

*Photograph of Sarah F. Wakefield (date unknown).
Courtesy of the* St. Paul Pioneer Press Dispatch *and
James Orin Wakefield II*

could have fallen in love with Chaska is not unreasonable from
her description of his qualities, her own state of mind, and an
examination of her husband's behavior.

In the first summer of Dr. Wakefield's tenure at the Upper
Agency, an editorial appeared in the St. Paul paper accusing
him of beating his wife. The headline asked, Why should the
government pay him to beat his wife? and demanded his dis-

missal. Commissioner Thomas Galbraith claimed he was away when the alleged incident took place but that he investigated charges and also spoke with Mrs. Wakefield. She and others denied that any such incident took place. The new Republican administration with its new personnel was under general attack by the older Democrats. Of course, the charge may have been true, and Mrs. Wakefield just covering for her husband.[135] Was John a drunken and abusive husband or was this a purely political charge?

But the power of Wakefield's story comes from her sense of duty to her "protector," her willingness to sacrifice for him because it is the right, Christian thing to do. When her narrative is examined, her indebtedness to both Chaska and his family for going out of their way to save her and her children from the disasters of war and intracamp hostility is evident. This sense of reciprocity, of owing, is wedded to a sense of fairness and conscience crucial to Wakefield's worldview. It is not purity or piety but a sense of rightness and fair-mindedness which keeps her in the fray until neither Chaska nor she can fight any more. But as in the case of Mary Rowlandson and Metacomet (King Philip), it was nearly impossible for some to believe that such a relationship could exist across both ethnic and gender lines. No one doubted, as Wakefield noted in her narrative, that another man named Chaska could save agency trader George Spencer and be his close friend. And no one doubted that a young Dakota woman named Snahna (Tinkling), later called Mrs. Maggie Brass, could heroically stand by the German girl Mary Schwandt, or that Mahkahta-Heiya-Win (Woman Who Goes on the Earth), later Mrs. Mary Crooks, a part-Mdewakanton, part-Winnebago woman, would save the life of Mrs. Urania S. White and her baby, Frank. Minnesota later added this woman's name to the monument of "good Indians." But an Indian man and a white woman seems to have been too hard to accept.[136] Mrs. Amos W. Huggins, a missionary to the Dakotas, was similarly protected with her two children by Walking Spirit and his wife and family, who walked her over eighty miles northwest of Camp Release to keep her safe and then placed her on a horse and went eighty miles to bring her back to Sibley at Camp Release.[137] Chaska's wife, however, was dead. Even if Sarah Wakefield loved Chaska, there is no evidence that she had sexual relations with him. But even if a sexual relationship is granted, it is still clear that a genuine gratefulness and respect, along with a personal code of duty and fairness, underlay her actions on the first day white soldiers "released" her, during the trials of October 1862, and through the two editions of her narrative in 1863 and 1864. Writing of her anguish at Camp Release on hearing he was in prison, she "felt as if the Indians, as well as myself had been deceived. All the solemn promises I had made to Chaska were as naught. What would he think of me? I could not eat or sleep, I was so excited about him. I felt as bad as if my brother had been in the same position." [138]

Of Dakotas and Eagles

. . . . . .

This discussion of Sarah Wakefield and the Dakota War began as an illustration of an unappreciated dimension of both the captivity narrative and the captivity story—the dimension of conscience. It is not that the Wakefield story lacks elements of the Indian stereotype. Her vision of the "good Indian" was probably a very limited conception of who the man We-chank-wash-ta-do-pe really was. It is certain that the real man was far more complex than the "protector" she described. When one compares a picture of the man with the group of Mdewakanton in Washington at the signing of the 1858 Treaty, there is a man who looks like "Chaska," labeled "His Bloody War Club." [139] His name remains something of a mystery, but it contains *war club* and was probably based on a powerful experience during his vision quest as a young man. Perhaps his initiation came during a time of war; perhaps he had to use his war club to kill an animal or an enemy. Wakefield, in an effort to defend the man, may have overly Christianized him, though it is certain that he, like most Minnesota Dakotas, was moving toward acculturation.

It is certainly possible that this man, earlier in his life, had been a Dakota warrior. As time changed on the Minnesota frontier, he, like Little Crow and others, may have realized the necessity of negotiation with whites. From the visual evidence it appears he was a more than passing figure. This may be another element in the "mistake" of his execution.

What about the Dakotas, and what about the man, We-chank-wash-ta-do-pe?

The events for which the Sioux are most remembered by non-Indians are Custer's Last Stand and Wounded Knee. But what then appeared to be "the last days of the Sioux nation" had begun not in Montana at the Little Bighorn, but earlier, along the Minnesota River and then in Mankato, Minnesota, on December 26, 1862.[140] The death of the thirty-eight did not end the Minnesota drama. A month later the "strange winter" brought more death. At the camp, prisoners and their families remained waiting for the government's next moves. In late January, Riggs wrote to the American Board of Commissioners for Foreign Missions in Boston: "It is a very sad place now. The crying hardly ever stops. From five to ten die daily." And a new, ultimate captivity ensued. "It is a state of captivity," he wrote. "They have nothing to do. They feel low spirited." Drinking became a common pastime.[141] By April 1863 Dakotas condemned at Mankato were sent to prison in Davenport, Iowa. Riggs saw the Dakotas' banishment onto the plains in biblical terms—"a kind of Israelite journey through the desert," where unfortunately about one-quarter of "the Dakotas of the Dispersion" died during the next three years. In the first months, according to Williamson, who traveled with them, men, women, and children died at a rate of about three or four per day. About six or seven hundred were dead by April 10.[142]

This was not all. On December 26, 1887, the twenty-fifth anniversary of the mass hanging, a letter arrived at the Minnesota Historical Society from J. F. Meagher of Mankato. Enclosed was the gift of a watch chain, or as Meagher called it, "a Relic of the time of the Sioux Execution."[143] Meagher had intended to send it to Gleason's friends or parents, "that they might know that the death of George Gleason was avenged by the Strong arm of the law administered by the Govrment." Instead, he mailed it to the society.

His letter, semiliterate and full of misspellings, accompanied the "Relic." He began by remembering Gleason as the man with a "Genial face" and a "hearty laugh" who first helped run the steamer *Frank Steel* or *Favorite* from 1858 to 1860. When Galbraith was appointed Indian agent, Gleason was chosen as his clerk. Continuing with the incidents surrounding Gleason's shooting, Meagher accuses "Chaska Don" (that is, Chaska or We-chank-wash-ta-do-pe) of Gleason's death. After dinner on the night of the execution, "a few well known men of that day accompanied by Dr La Bootilier with a team and Wagon" went to the shallow grave site of the newly buried Indians in Mankato, dug up the Dakotas, "and among those resurected was Chaska Don." Meagher continues:

> We all felt keenly the injury he had don in murdering our old friend Gleason, in cold blood. I cut off the Rope that bound his hands and feet, and cut off one Brade of his hair with the intention of sending them to Gleasons relatives should I hear of there whereabouts. I never herd of his friends, and so I had the hair made into a Watch chain by a Lady friend in St Paul. I wore it untill it was as you see about wore out, and now I send it to you thinking that some day it might be of interest with the other momentoes of those terible times and that great hanging Event.[144]

Looking back, he continued, much could be said of "that resoruction" and the "Strange Scines" of that day that now appeared "unchristian like." But the horrible "Bucheries" of the "Masacre" had "hardened" people. Meagher recalls the deaths of Jo LeBow and an Indian shot on a haystack in back of Fuller's store in New Ulm "and the way they were served by our boys." Of this violence he admits that "we were Steeled to it, by witnessing the indiscriminate massacre of men womon and children and *worse*. . . . Hopeing you will Deem this old chain worthey of a place in the Historical society I remain Yours Very Respct John F Meagher." It was so deemed. A note at the top of the society's typescript reads: "The hair watch chain made from the hair of Chaska Don, mentioned in this letter, is in the museum."[145]

But this is not the end of Chaska's story, nor the last of the Sioux nation, nor the end of Sarah Wakefield's exercise in conscience. There is still the spirit of the eagle.

The power and the memory of the executions are not lost on those Dakota people now living in Minnesota. Amos Owen, a Dakota spiritual leader, recently spoke to a reporter of "the 38" and the power of Mankato. There remains something ominous about the place. "Indians would go through there in the dead of night . . . headed west, or headed back there, but never stop." In 1972, Mankato sponsored a festival and some Minnesota Dakotas were asked to set up a powwow. No one came the night before, as is the usual practice, but the next day "that field was full." When people came to the ball field to dance, "we looked up and there were all these eagles up there. There were 38 eagles, and people ran around and said, 'What does this mean?' And we said, 'Why those are just our grandfathers.'" The eagles come back every year.[146]

Captive as Conscience

. . . . . .

"My object was to excite sympathy for the Indians and in so doing, the soldiers lost all respect for me, and abused me shamefully; but I had rather have my own conscience than that of those persons who turned against their protectors, those that were so kind to them in that time of great peril."[147] Perhaps there is much in Wakefield's story to excite sympathy for her own fate, to justify herself, and to have readers overlook her own moral shortcomings. Her anguish at Chaska's arrest at Fort Release, her own leaving, and then his subsequent death had a profound enough effect on her to galvanize her to write her story. She says that the night before she left, Captain Grant "gave me his word as a gentleman" that Chaska "would not be executed, but would be imprisoned for five years." At the time she says she "was very well contented, and troubled myself no further."[148] But why was she "contented" if he was to be imprisoned and she and her children went free? Why did she not stay longer, get assurances from others and in writing? Or is this expecting too much? Apparently, her own conscience, her own guilt that she was ineffective in saving a man who saved her came upon her after Chaska's death, and her own narrative, as much as it tries to clear her name, is a plea for conscience and an attempt to clear her conscience as well.

In the past, the genre of the captivity narrative has been examined as an original, perhaps quintessential American form often interpreted as functioning from the first as a mythic justification for Protestant Anglo-America's violent defeat of the infidel and "savage."[149] But a careful examination of Sarah Wakefield's narrative indicates that if it was used to help her own credibility, it was not written or used primarily as anti-Indian propaganda, a white-supremacist polemic, or an ethnographic work. On the contrary, it was the statement of one white woman's conscience and sympathy, and it tells us something of the complex nature of such conscience in the world of Indian-white relations.[150]

The narrative is important because it is one of the few to be written and published by a female captive almost immediately after the Dakota War of 1862. At least eight other narratives exist of or by white women, a few others by white men. Only one other was published by its author as a separate piece in the first years following the event.[151] Most were published as part of nineteenth-century white settler histories, some twenty, forty, or sixty years later in varying editions in Minnesota newspapers and local histories.[152] Wakefield's narrative, like Mary Jemison's, offers an alternative vision of Indian-white relations on the frontier.

The Dakota War was something of a civil war, in this case, an Indian-white communal war. Christian conversions, Indian acculturation, years of intermarriage, and the taking of part-Indian hostages had simultaneously blurred and sharpened cultural divisions along communal lines.[153] Along with land hunger and race hatred, a subtext of the war became sexual and racial fear, a fear of relations between white women and Indian men. Sarah Wakefield's story is remarkable for the unusual nature of the narrative itself, its author, and her relationship to the Dakotas who protected her and her family through the six weeks of the uprising and the man who likely died because of this relationship.

In an essay on Harriet Beecher Stowe's *Uncle Tom's Cabin*, Jane P. Tompkins urges us to look again at popular literature by women. She sees Stowe's work as a critique of American society, representing "a monumental effort to reorganize culture from the woman's point of view." The popularity of sentimental novels is a good reason "for paying close attention to them."[154]

Like Stowe's, Wakefield's work appealed to women's sense of justice. Both appeared in a world in which it was presumed that women had greater moral and spiritual power than men. Like Stowe, Wakefield was a New England woman who saw the lie behind white dealings with a people of color. She too wrote of duplicity, and her work called out for fairness. And she wrote in a popular genre, read by both men and women and, in the nineteenth century, often written by women. Unlike Stowe, the world she described came from her own experience and observation. And unlike Stowe, Wakefield's work did not ride a crest of feeling open to changing oppression, rather it appeared in a place and time that favored Indian extermination. Yet hers was not a work of Indian hatred but an act of conscience, posed in the wider framework of a woman who, in defense of her own self-interest, also recognized a set of wrongs against the other. Wakefield's life and work blended the genre of captivity with a Christian message of compassion. Hers was a woman's story, which included an attack on political and economic domination and an attempt to understand one who was like a brother. Like Stowe, she believed it to be her Christian duty to speak out against these evils. "They were kind to me, and I will try and repay them, trusting that in God's own time I will be righted and my conduct understood, for with Him all things are plain." [155] In the world in which she lived, her action and her writing were dangerous but, she felt, necessary.

The social relations between people of different races, classes, nations, sexes, and ethnic groups define us profoundly. Individuals can and do work for change, but the forces that maintain these systems of dominance are strong. Most of us think that if our country or community acted unjustly toward others we could stand up, protect those falsely accused, do the right thing. We hope we are not irrevocably bound to the social categories in which we were born and raised. Sarah Wakefield was put to such a test. Under the intense pressure of war, racism, and hysteria, under the immediate pressures of other captives and the commanding officers and soldiers at Camp Release, she was expected to keep to the party line, to say that Indians were fiends, worse than beasts—rapists and murderers. She was expected to consent to the nearly unanimous view of Minnesota whites that they should be exterminated, one and all, or at least banished from the state onto the prairie—the farther away the better. We can only guess that she may have been under unexpected pressure as well from her husband, who aside from having lost his books, his instruments, and his job and fearing the death of his wife and two children in the melee that was Minnesota, wanted to take his family by the hand and lead them away. Instead he found a wife whose life had taken an additional turn. She not only had rejected the story of savage Indians, she had become close to one of "them," in fact a whole family of "them." Who knew how close? She had responsibilities to her husband. She had not seen him. Given the rumors about her life, they needed a lot of time to clarify what had happened. And there were likely his expectations that as a mother with two children, who had undergone the traumas of war, she would want to protect them, be the "good mother," take them away to a safe place where they could put these weeks of murder, disruption, and parental separation behind them.

Part of her must have wanted to move away from the recriminations of other women prisoners and the men of the military as fast as possible. But this was not what the doctor's wife did. It was her clear intent to defy the common view of wife, mother, and Indian, not just privately but publicly. She would not just resume the protection of her husband's custody, take her children and go home. No, she would stay and publicly take the stand in Chaska's defense in a set of trials that saw next to no defense for nearly four hundred Dakotas.

Sarah Wakefield, woman of privilege, did not walk away from a man, a family, and a people who had saved her life and had made it as comfortable as possible under the circumstances. She was the recipient of a respect and appreciation she was seen as deserving based on the years of care she and her husband had dispensed to the Dakota community. Now she was intent upon showing reciprocity and a Christian woman's sense of compassion. First at the military commission trials, later with the publication of her narrative, the costs for this public stance were great. It is true, however, that she did not stay long enough. Why did she not stay longer? Could she have done more? She had no effect in reversing the verdict against the life of one Dakota man and against the ultimate fate of his family and his people.

Chaska died; his family was part of the Dakota community that was banished onto the prairie and died in droves on reservations in South Dakota and Nebraska. The "Indian problem" was moved on to a further frontier, the Indian people soon to experience another wave of decimation.

In the closing words of her narrative, Sarah Wakefield said she would "bid this subject farewell." It was not so easy then, nor is it easy now.

Conclusion: Women and Children First

My numerous progeny, often gather around me, to hear the sufferings once felt by their aunt or grandmother, and wonder at their magnitude. My daughter, Captive, still keeps the dress she appeared in, when brought to my bed side, by the French nurse, at the Ticonderoga hospital; and often refreshes my memory with past scenes, when showing it to her children. . . . And now reader, after sincerely wishing that your days may be as happy, as mine have been unfortunate, I bid you adieu.
   —Susannah Johnson (1796)

Almost one hundred years ago Frederick Jackson Turner announced the closing of the frontier. Since that time, the perpetuation of culture has largely passed from the world of small-town exchange, books, and newspapers, to radio, television, and film. The realities and exaggerated horrors of the earlier migrations, warfare, and settlement have been largely reimagined and repackaged into the western film. In that genre, six-foot-tall cowboys in ten-gallon hats have preempted contemporary understanding of western settlement, much as prototypes of dour Puritans dressed in black have taken over the popular view of the earliest settlement period. Only recently have historians reinstated white women and children on these frontiers in appropriate numbers even as on the screen some Indians have begun to speak their native languages.

From the first years of white settlement in Virginia and Massachusetts a tense and complex environment existed intermittently on successive American frontiers. Although by no means a daily occurrence, the possibility of Indian attack and capture was real. Rather than cowboy heroics, life on the frontier more typically involved what Susannah Johnson described as great "distance from friends and competent defense" and at times, the night songs and yells of Indians "awaken[ed] those keen apprehensions and anxieties which conception only can picture."[1]

In every colonial society from Australia, to South Africa, to Argentina, pioneer settlers have been lionized by their descendants. The memories and writings of the early white settlers in North America constitute a wide array of popular literature, high and low art, and an amazing documentary trail in the various public and private records. The diverse evidence from captivity sources shows some of this material to be hagiographic in nature. In it, generations reminded their contemporaries and then their children how difficult it was to build a new society in a new world. But from the beginning, gender constructed perceptions of "the wilderness" and the ways in which men and women wrote about and acted in it. The Heroic Mode exemplified by John Smith's account of his life among the Indians suggested a sense of superiority and a stance of bravado toward Indians. Mary Rowlandson, obviously shaped by her Puritan training but also by her life as a woman, described a more fearful, sorrow-filled set of encounters which revealed the nature of one's place in God's kingdom. Men's and women's accounts evolved from these beginnings, with both the heroic male and the suffering female witness coalescing into familiar archetypes. But from the colonial period, variations on Hannah Dustan's Amazonian behavior, and in the late eighteenth and nineteenth centuries, more extreme tales of woe gave rise to the Frail Flower and sentimental fictional renditions of capture. For men, the earlier recollections of John Gyles and James Smith developed in the nineteenth century into a growing number of accounts of White Indians and brave rescuers.

All of these accounts served the reader by transforming victims of historical circumstance into heroes and heroines. Moving onto land that belonged to or was contested by Indians and on which they were not entirely welcome, white settlers often placed themselves and their families in harm's way. Unlike contemporary western film, earlier accounts in narrative, newspaper, and art recognized the centrality of women and children in Anglo-American life on the frontier. From the earliest narratives in which white women were held captive, captive dramas shifted the usual focus of the frontier story away from the white male figure, the usual embodiment of the movement of European culture west, to otherwise marginal figures. White women and children, along with Indians, became the focus of attention to the reader, hearer, or viewer. In different eras, women as captives were scripted to fulfill differing archetypes; they were transformed and occasionally mythologized for political, economic, religious, and social purposes. The captive drama persistently took the peripheral event, the capture of a white woman and her children, a piece at the margins of European or American society, and forced it onto center stage. Why did this happen? In part, such representations recognized that women and children were necessarily the center of the family and the private world—the basic stuff of which any new society would be constructed. Another possibility suggested by the horrific nature of much of the captivity material is that murder, mutilation, and familial devastation were a cause of general anxiety of both sexes about an adventure in migration that could prove to be disastrous.[2] Because most visual and written presentations were produced by men, placing women and children at the center may have been a way of recognizing their worst anxieties of being unable to provide adequate protection without admitting to weakness or unwillingness to take on the "civilizing" mission.

There was and is a raw power in these gendered images. They prompted sympathy and identification with the white child and the white woman who became Indian captives. They also justified "heroic" white male rescue, from John Williams's aborted mission to save his daughter Eunice, to Daniel Boone's rescue of his daughter Jemima, H. H. Sibley's rescue of the Minnesota captives, Seth Eastman's rescue of Mrs. Eastman, and even Seth Jones's rescue of Ina. In the nineteenth century, these images were lifted from the page onto pedestal and canvas. Erastus Dow Palmer's marble sculpture *White Captive* (1858) depicted a young, naked woman, alone, without hope of rescue.

As in John Vanderlyn's *Death of Jane McCrea* (ca. 1804), Charles Wimar's *Abduction of Daniel Boone's Daughter* (ca. 1850), and John Mix Stanley's *Osage Scalp Dance* (1845), women and children along with Indian men become the center, while white men hopelessly occupy the periphery or are altogether absent.[3] Such a shift of the marginal to the center, such a flip in the "natural" order of things, and especially such a new, in some cases obsessive, focus with the frontier world, presents an anxious view of North American expansion. In it the main values and future existence of Anglo-America are in the hands of its most vulnerable elements. Jane McCrea, potential republican mother, is killed. The unhappy Jemima Boone carried off by the "noble" Indian might never return. Uncertainty, violence, both physical and sexual, and disaster pervade these images.[4]

In John Mix Stanley's *Osage Scalp Dance*, a frontier mother and child, more like a Madonna and child, are the central and riveting figures, surrounded by more than twenty Indians. The drama is the captivity and the potential murder of the pair by an Osage holding a war club; a young mother is alone with her child and in danger of death, with only her own powers of moral suasion and perhaps one of her captors to save her.[5] Light moves across the painting from right to left. It appears that the sun is setting behind the Indians, and the light in the sky draws our attention to a long spear above the white woman held by the "savior" Indian. His spear blocks the club from killing her and her child. Light is used to imbue them both with an almost religious aura. Light emanates from the lower right of the picture as well, striking her and the child fully and illuminating a trio of Indians around them. It strikes the uplifted hand of the young mother, clad in a floor-length, otherwise undecorated and somewhat shroudlike white gown. The babe is cherublike, apparently a boy, with the body and curly hair of a Rubenesque child, clothed only in a white shirt. Light rolls off the outstretched right palm of the mother, down to her elbow, then continues to her face and bodice onto the child and her dress. The child's body is unclothed below the waist, exposing

John Mix Stanley, Osage Scalp Dance *(1845) Oil on canvas.
Courtesy of National Museum of American Art, Smithsonian
Institution, Gift of the Misses Henry, 1908*

a full, rotund, pink and white buttock and fleshy legs. He faces
his mother, his left arm holding her near her right breast.

The mother's face is somber. She is young, and her eyes are
sad. Her gesture is at once hopeless and affecting. It expresses
a desire to effect change but is also not completely hopeless
when backed up as it is by the physical gesture and power of her
Indian protector. The theme is one of Madonna and child, but
in this case, the holy pair are white captives on a field of red. She
is white, her dress is white, the child's underclothes are white.
The colors, clothing, and structure of the painting all reinforce a
sense of danger, of strangeness, of potential savagery over innocence, but mostly of (Indian) male power over (white) female
generativity. On the far left sit musicians with drums and shields
with long eagle feathers. Center left and circling the white captive are warriors, most of whom carry bows, spears, knives,
hatchetlike tomahawks with feathers and a metal protrusion.
The Indians are tawny. Red war paint is worn by several, including the "bad" one. The "good," savior Indian has tattoo marks
on his chest. He wears a pendant around his neck with what
appears to be a white government figure on it.[6] On their right
are Indians with gray-white body paint, wearing wide brace-

lets. Two have red hands painted on their chests. The Indians
in the front line wear necklaces, shells, and beads. One Osage
wears a wildcat head as breechcloth; its face, claws, and teeth
cover the man's private parts. Another has a breechcloth with a
bird covering his buttocks, feathers flying. Feathers, especially
wild, red feathers, surround almost every Indian head, whether
shaved or with a Mohawk-like haircut. Feathers often grow out
of the center of men's scalps.

The "good" Indian saving the woman wears buckskin leggings with red beads and straps hanging from the knee. Men
not wearing fur breechcloths wear red ones, which bring out
the power and sexual force of their supple, firm bodies. These
Indian bodies, naked from the waist up except for paint, necklaces, and feathers, are powerful statements in themselves. Even
the baby is clothed from the waist up. Surrounding a woman
with so much masculinity, so much pagan, strange, exotic, warlike, painted, armed, and dancing masculinity, is itself a highly
gendered physical and sexual threat.

But the Madonna stops the action. She herself in all her weakness, in all her apparent frailty, dominates all this motion and
activity, and white over red, uses it for her own purposes, and
through her Indian savior, calls a halt to it. Her gesture freezes
the flying feathers, the dancing feet, the musicians, the poles
and spears, the moving fur of the wildcat, the jangling earrings
and necklaces and beads, animal teeth, and silver pendants. The
affecting white woman with child, through her gesture, backed
by the shield held by the protective Indian, is powerful enough
to stay not only one Indian's violence but the entirety of their
"savage" world. In an era that touted domesticity and delicate
femininity, it is not by her own physical force or religious fortitude that this Madonna is saved. Rather, the artist allows her
maternity and femininity to be linked with the noble character
of her Indian savior to ensure the safety of the truncated family.
But what could happen after that? How uncertain is the fate of
a wife or a daughter or a child when one must trust to the good
graces of the enemy?[7]

The white female captivity, whether of the Puritan variety or
of the nineteenth century, whether in print or on canvas, etched
or on a pedestal, depicts a woman out of place, surviving in
a world not of her own making (or dying there as in the case

of Jane McCrea). In captivity representations there is often a woman or girl who is separated from her husband or family. Here, white women and children come first. It is presumed that on their courage, stamina, loyalty, and adaptability the various errands in the wilderness stand or fall. Here they are given a role in the epic of Anglo-American nation building.

In his book *Decoding the Past*, Peter Loewenberg suggests that historians study "critical personal traumas" and that "social traumas" can shape the life of a nation much as childhood traumas shape the life of an adult. Groups that live through "a common historical situation" might "possess common features or patterns of response that can be identified decades later." [8] Along America's moving frontier, not just one group but each vanguard of the white American population experienced the traumas of outbreaks of what appeared to be random violence, along with outbreaks that mushroomed into large-scale wars. In both situations the loss of family members was indeed a possibility. The retelling of these stories of loss marked each American generation during the first three centuries of North American life. These tales constituted significant childhood memories, so significant that in their telling we find the education of the next generation of historians who pass the word along. Both childhood memories and family loss are reasons for the longevity of captivity stories.

The theme of family loss, of death in the family, of personal loss and transformation, is present in nearly every narrative of white capture, from the very first lines of Mary Rowlandson's narrative. "Some in our house were fighting for their lives, others wallowing in their blood. . . . Now we might hear Mothers and Children crying out for themselves and one another, Lord, What shall we do? Then I took my Children (and one of my sisters, hers) to go forth and leave the house: but as soon as we came to the dore and appeared, the Indians shot so thick that the bullets rattled against the House." [9] Nor was the theme of a shattered family lost on Cotton Mather when he recited to his congregation the trial of Hannah Dustan, "having lain in about a Week . . . [as] a Body of Terrible *Indians* drew near unto the House . . . to carry on their Bloody Devastations." [10] Family death and estrangement was a theme also of another well-known story of Puritan captivity: that of the Reverend John Williams, in which a final homecoming and family reunion were never effected because of the death of Williams's wife and "loss" of his child Eunice to the Indians. But on the New England frontier, such harrowing stories of women and children also stood as testaments to the strength and durability of the Anglo-American Christian family and its culture, often at the mercy of God and the Indians.

In many of the accounts of young white male captives, it is the loss or return of the white mother or the substitution of the Indian one and her clan that is critical. In the recounting of Jane McCrea stories, her failure to follow her father and brother is emphasized and the role of other women minimized or mocked. But Jane was a potential frontier mother. Her wayward independence was forged in a home in which her own mother was missing as a guide for her life. In Mary Jemison's narrative, we are reminded of Mary's mother, the most potent symbol of her "white" past, and those Christian values which many nineteenth-century editors wanted their readers to assume she was able to carry with her through her trials because of her mother's early instruction. Later we have Jemison's life as a mother and then as a grandmother. In Sarah Wakefield's narrative and in her trial testimony, she appeals to her audience as a mother and claims the necessity of protecting others, who were like brothers, as they protected her and her children. It is as a woman of conscience that she appeals to her community for mercy toward the other. The captive story, then, and especially as its versions evolve in the nineteenth century, features maternity, the mother, the woman alone or alone among the Indians, or a child, like White Chief, or John Tanner, alone until he or she finds a new mother. Captivity materials demonstrate that on the periphery, it is the mother—the woman and her children— who comes first. Their lives must be the focus of our attention because on their survival is based the Anglo-American future in each new "west."

If the captive story increasingly placed women at the center, it was the children who passed on its meaning and who enlisted sympathy in the recreation of the accounts: Hannah Dustan's new baby was killed, Olive Oatman's little sister Mary died, young Olive herself was tattooed. As a young boy John Gyles saw friends tortured and he nearly froze; Matthew Brayton and John Tanner were shipped from one tribe to another. Brayton lost track of his origins altogether. Any number of white children on the Minnesota frontier were orphaned.

Several early historians and compilers wrote about captivity because as children they either experienced or heard stories of life, death, and capture on the frontier. New York historian Charles Neilson told the story of how his stepfather's house was attacked by Indians. Neilson believed the same group who murdered the Allen family and Jane McCrea was responsible. He later wrote an account of the Jane McCrea affair. Asa Fitch, another student of New York history and follower of the trail of Jane McCrea, recounted how as a child after the Revolution, he heard the McCrea and other stories retold. In Minnesota, Marion P. Satterlee explained his interest in tracing the story of the Dakota War for similar reasons: "Coming to Southern Minnesota in 1863, the spring after the outbreak, my boyhood days were filled with its narratives, in which acquaintances were often participants."[11] Childhood war stories and histories heard during childhood were the stuff of which these historians were made. They were not abstractions but the histories of friends and relatives, people they knew. More recently, a neighbor spoke with me about her childhood in Iowa. Her great-uncle wrote a county history of settlement and problems on the Indian border. She had heard of Abbie Sharp, a captive in the Spirit Lake Massacre of 1858. She had been told stories of families murdered and women taken captive from older women in her family. They talked in low voices about women who lived among the Indians and how those women had been "passed under the prairie" (a euphemism for rape). These stories gave her nightmares. In different ways captivity tales imparted to these "frontier" children the dangers of settlement.[12]

Finally, the recountings of captivity are migration stories. The basic assumptions of westward migration from the seventeenth century presumed the righteousness of European relocation. But rather than demonstrating the righteousness of Anglo-American policy, the underside of some narratives such as Jemison's and Wakefield's challenges the reader to rethink the causes behind the seemingly "wild" actions of Indians by giving the reader a sense that the other's side is not merely savage but has political and moral reasons for its behavior. The successive moves west consistently disregarded native peoples with the presumption that the new European order should take over and "civilize" the continent. Placing a woman, a child, or a family at risk functions to depict the darker forces working against "civilization." These representations also functioned to show the "good" Indian, as in Stanley's painting, or Chaska in Sarah Wakefield's story, as stopping the violence and perhaps forcing the viewer to consider how a white woman came to be in such a threatening situation. The woman holding up her hand and, in Sarah Wakefield's narrative, the woman calling a halt, both signal the underside, a more subversive side of the captivity material. Just as the Amazonian woman made clear the danger of the frontier by "unnatural" behavior and the Frail Flower demanded attention by fainting, women and children signaled the distress of migration and, perhaps inadvertently, the questionable side of those policies and propaganda which said all was right with such moves. However the distress was signaled, and obviously some accounts and depictions were used to counsel more force and violence to sustain the move west, these migration stories with women and children at their core expressed the problematic features of the Euro-American enterprise and the consequences of its dealings with other peoples.

The experience and recounting of captivity provided successive Euro-American audiences with stories of close encounters across cultural and gender lines. Along the moving American frontier, captivity focused attention on the most vulnerable members of white society—its own women and children and those men who, at war or with their families, were on that edge of the culture when its future supremacy was in question. On such frontiers, ethnic and gender anxieties were heightened. Men, women, and children were often left undefended, both physically and psychologically. Captivity materials transformed migrants into heroines and heroes or, in some cases, into victims, renegades, or untrustworthy elements. White captives had to survive in any way they could. This meant learning the ways of the other. A captive could go over to the enemy side, marry, or have sexual relations with the enemy or—perhaps more dangerous in some ways in the nineteenth century, when the "enemy" was closer to defeat—might believe in the humanity of the other and call into question the mentality of "we" and "they," so embedded in North American ethnic interactions and ideology.

The ultimate power of captivity materials goes beyond their uses as myth and literature. They represent more than archetypical justifications for the Anglo-American domination of Indians. Although useful ethnographically, such pieces are more than collections of ethnographic data. If anything, they give us ethnographic data about the mentality and claimed experiences of Indian-white interactions, seen through the eyes of Euro-Americans. That mentality was shaped by anxieties based on fear of potential Indian violence and family loss. It was also keenly shaped by fears of personal and social transformation in gender roles and other culturally prescribed behavior and in racial and cultural mixture—all possible as part of the migration process. Of these last, "unnatural" changes might strip a woman from her place as part of a wider family circle and leave her and her children alone and vulnerable, possibly requiring of her Amazonian feats, possibly subjecting her to sexual assault or forcing her to witness the death of her husband and her children, perhaps leaving her unable to cope physically or psychologically. The thought of such remote but known possibilities must have had profound effects on the Euro-American psyche, impressing each generation with the fraught nature of frontier migration.

Placing women and children at the center of so many cultural works expressed these anxieties about frontier migration and interaction with Indians and exposed a basic vulnerability of white women and children, and by extension the entire enterprise of Euro-American settlement. The possible violence against "their" women forced upon migrating men a mammoth responsibility for protection not expected of them in settled rural areas, cities, or towns, except in times of war. The bravado of John Smith, Daniel Boone, and later western heroes was a tactic, in part a facade, to appear strong to oneself, one's family, and one's enemy. The sexual subplot along with women's vulnerability was in part an expression of a variety of anxieties, including the limits of Anglo-American male prowess, both physical and sexual, and the fear that white women might go over to the "enemy" side.

As the frontier receded, white women and children lost their paramount places to resurgent male heroism recast with six-guns and white hats masking real frontier migration and settlement vulnerability behind shoot-outs with attacking Indians in which the white men always won. But earlier generations of white settlers knew the contest was not so easy, the outcome not so clear, and the costs not so light. They mourned and memorialized their "lost" and those who crossed over. In some few cases, they admitted to the losses of those others, and conceived of sharing the bounty of the continent before them.

Appendix
Guide to Captives

Captive (with Indians)	Year Captured	Place/Area of Capture	Publi-cation*
John Smith (Powhatans)	1607	Virginia	(1612)*
Father Isaac Jogues (Mohawks)	1642	New York	1655*
Father Louis Hennepin (Dakotas)	1680	Minnesota	1685*
Mary Rowlandson (Narragansetts accompanied by Wampanoags)	1675/6[1]	Lancaster, Massachusetts	1682*
Quentin Stockwell (Norwooluck, Eastern Abenaki)[2]	1677	Deerfield, Massachusetts	1684
John Gyles (Maliseets)[3]	1689	Pemaquid, Maine	1736*
Sarah Gerish (Penacooks, Western Abenaki)	1689	Dover, New Hampshire	1698
Elizabeth Hull Heard (Penacooks, Western Abenaki)	1689	Dover, New Hampshire	1699
Robert Rogers (Kennebecs, Eastern Abenaki)	1690	Salmon Falls, New Hampshire	1699
Mehetable Goodwin (Kennebecs, Eastern Abenaki)	1690	Salmon Falls, New Hampshire	1699
Thomas Toogood (Kennebecs, Eastern Abenaki)	1690	Salmon Falls, New Hampshire	1699
Hannah Swarton (Abenakis)	1690	Casco Bay, Maine	1697
Hannah Dustin (Dustan, Duston) (Abenakis)	1697	Haverhill, Massachusetts	1697

Captive (with Indians)	Year Captured	Place/Area of Capture	Publication*
Mary Corlis Neff (Abenakis)	1697	Haverhill, Massachusetts	1697
John Williams (Abenakis and Caughnawaga Mohawks)	1703/4[4]	Deerfield, Massachusetts	1707*
Eunice Williams (Abenakis and Caughnawaga Mohawks)	1703/4	Deerfield, Massachusetts	1707
Stephen W. Williams (Abenakis and Caughnawaga Mohawks)	1703/4	Deerfield, Massachusetts	1707
Elizabeth Meader Hanson (Abenakis)	1724	Dover, New Hampshire	1728*
Briton Hammon (black captive)		[?]	1760
Mary Woodwell (Fowler)	1746	Hopkinton, New Hampshire	1846[5]
Isabella M'Coy (Arosaguntacook or St. Francis)	1747	Epsom, New Hampshire	1846
Susannah Willard Johnson[6] (Abenaki)	1754	upper Connecticut Valley, New Hampshire	1796*
Peter Williamson	1754	Delaware Forks, Pennsylvania	1757*
Jemima Howe (Tute) (Abenaki)	1755	Hinsdale, New Hampshire	1788*
Robert Eastburn	1756	Fort Williams, Pennsylvania	1758*
Mary Jemison (Shawnees and Senecas)	1758[7]	Adams County, Pennsylvania	1824
White Chief (original name unknown) (Senecas)	ca. 1750s	Susquehanna River region	1892

Captive (with Indians)	Year Captured	Place/Area of Capture	Publication*	
Colonel James Smith (Caughnawaga, Mohawks)	1755	Bedford, Pennsylvania	1799	... **277** *Appendix*
Mrs. Clendenin (Shawnees)	1763	Green Brier, Virginia	1846	
Daniel Boone (Shawnees)	1769	Kentucky	1784	
Jemima Boone (Shawnees?)	1776	Kentucky	1784	
Frances Slocum (Delawares)	1778	Wilkes Barre, Pennsylvania (Wyoming Valley)	1842	
Experience Bozarth	1779	Dunkard's Creek, Kentucky	1808	
Frances Scott (Delaware)	1785	Washington County, Virginia	1786	
John Marrant (black captive) (Cherokees)	1770	near Charleston, South Carolina	1785*	
Jane McCrea (uncertain, British-allied Indians, usually claimed to be Mohawks)	(1777)	Fort Edward, New York	(1777)	
Charles Johnston (Shawnees)[8]	1790	junction of the Ohio and Scioto rivers	1827*	
Massy Harbison (Herbeson)	1792	Ohio-Pennsylvania frontier	1825	
John R. Jewitt	1803	village on Nootka Sound, west coast of Vancouver Island	1815*	
John Dunn Hunter (Kickapoo, (Osage, Ojibwa)	ca. 1805	not known by Hunter	1823	
Eliza Swan (Osage?)		St. Louis	1815	
John Tanner (Shawnees, Ojibwas, Ottawa)	1789	settlement on Kentucky River	1830	
Caroline Harris (Comanches)	1835	Texas	1838	

Captive (with Indians)	Year Captured	Place/Area of Capture	Publi-cation*
Sarah Ann Horn (Comanches)	1835	Texas	1839
Clarissa Plummer (Comanches)	1835	Texas	1838
Rachel Parker Plummer (Comanches)	1836	Parker's Fort, Texas	1839*
Cynthia Ann Parker (Comanches)	1836	Parker's Fort, Texas	1839
Dolly Webster (Comanches)	1843	Texas	1843
Olive Oatman (Yavapai, Mohave, and Yuma)[9]	1851	Gila Trail, 80 miles east of Yuma, Arizona	1857
Mary Oatman (Yavapai and Mohave)	1851	Gila Trail, 80 miles east of Yuma, Arizona	1857
Abigail Gardiner	1857	Spirit Lake, Iowa	1857
Matthew Brayton (Potawatomis, Winnebagos, Sioux, Snakes, and Copper Heads)	ca. 1830	Ohio	1860
Sarah F. Wakefield (Mdewakanton, Dakotas)	1862	Upper Sioux Agency, Minnesota	1863*
Samuel Brown[10] (Mdewakanton, Dakotas)	1862	Minnesota	1900
Minnie Carrigan (Wilhemina Buce, Minnie Krieger)[11] (Dakotas)	1862	Minnesota	1907*
Urania Frazer (Mrs. N. D. White) (Mdewakanton, Dakotas)	1862	Minnesota	1901*
Benedict Juni (Mdewakanton, Dakotas)	1862	Minnesota	1926*
Nancy McClure (Mdewakanton, Dakotas)	1862	Minnesota	1894

Captive (with Indians)	Year Captured	Place/Area of Capture	Publi-cation*
Mary Schwandt (Mdewakanton, Dakotas)	1862	Minnesota	1864
George Spencer (Mdewakanton, Dakotas)	1862	Minnesota	1863
George G. Allanson (Dakotas)	1862	Minnesota	1899*
Jannette E. De Camp Sweet (Mdewakanton, Dakotas)	1862	Minnesota	1864
Helen Carrothers Mar Tarbel (Mdewakanton, Dakotas)	1862	Minnesota	1862*
Fanny (Wiggins) Kelly (Sioux)	1864	Kansas, west of Fort Laramie	1871*
Edwin Eastman (Apaches and Comanches)	ca. 1870	Southwest	1874
Mrs. Eastman (Apaches and Comanches)	ca. 1870	Southwest	1874
Josephine Meeker (Utes)	1879	Meeker, Colorado	1879*

279
Appendix

Order arranged by approximate date of capture. In many cases, the Indian captors given are highly contested, especially before 1800, when several groups went on war parties together. Publication given is the first edition in which the captivity is published or discussed. I would like to thank Pauline Turner Strong and Tona Hangen for assisting me with the Indian groups involved in these captures.

* Indicates work written by the captive. For exact dates, time in captivity for thirty-one captives, twelve of whom are not mentioned here, and accounts of their captivities, see Samuel G. Drake, *Tragedies of the Wilderness* (Boston: Antiquarian Bookstore and Institute, 1846), Table of Contents.

1. By Julian calendar 1675, by Gregorian calendar 1676. See Pauline Turner Strong, "Captivity in White and Red," in *Crossing Cultures: Essays in the Displacement of Western Civilization*, ed. Daniel Segal (Tucson: University of Arizona Press, 1992).

2. See Richard I. Melvoin, *New England Outpost: War and Society in Colonial Deerfield* (New York: Norton, 1989), 125.

3. Vincent O. Erickson, "Maliseet-Passamaquoddy," in *HNAI/Northeast*, 135.

4. By Julian calendar 1703, by Gregorian calendar 1704.

5. These stories were recorded in local histories earlier but were first anthologized by Drake in this year.

6. Susannah Willard Johnson Hastings (1730–1810) is also called Susanna Johnson. Her narrative along with those of several eighteenth-century captives listed here may be found in *North Country Captives: Selected Narratives of Indian Captivity from Vermont and New Hampshire*, ed. Colin G. Calloway (Hanover: University Press of New England, 1992).

7. The title of the Seaver text says she was captured in 1755, but other evidence indicates 1758. See Chapter 5.

8. Shawnees and Cherokees captured Johnson along the Ohio, and he was then given to a Shawnee, according to *Held Captive by Indians: Selected Narratives, 1643–1836*, ed. Richard VanDerBeets (Knoxville: University of Tennessee Press, 1973), 243. Also see Charles E. Hanson, Jr., "Trade and Terror on the Sandusky in 1790," *Museum of the Fur Trade Quarterly* 25, no. 3 (1989): 1–6. Wyandots is the choice of John R. Swanton, in "Ethnology—Notes on the Mental Assimilation of Races," *Journal of the Washington Academy of Sciences* 16 (Nov. 3, 1926): 493–502, esp. 494.

9. The Stratton narrative claims the Oatman girls were captured by Apaches, but A. L. Kroeber and Clifton B. Kroeber say Yavapai captured them. They were then taken by Mohaves and later Yumas who negotiated for Olive in 1856 and brought her to Fort Yuma and sold her to whites. See R. B. Stratton, *Captivity of the Oatman Girls*, Foreword by Wilcomb E. Washburn (1858; rpt. Lincoln: University of Nebraska Press, 1983); "Olive Oatman's First Account of Her Captivity among the Mohave," *California Historical Society Quarterly* 41, no. 4 (1962): 309–17, esp. 309.

10. For information on editions of Minnesota captives, I would like to thank Alan R. Woolworth, MHS.

11. Buce is her maiden name; Carrigan, the name of her first husband; Krieger, the name of her second husband.

Notes

ABBREVIATIONS

AAS	*Proceedings of the American Antiquarian Society*
ABCFM	American Board of Commissioners for Foreign Missions
AHR	*American Historical Review*
AICRJ	*American Indian Culture Research Journal*
AL	*American Literature*
AMNY	Adirondack Museum, Blue Mountain Lake, New York
AQ	*American Quarterly*
BEHS	Blue Earth Historical Society, Mankato, Minnesota
CA	*Current Anthropology*
EAL	*Early American Literature*
EH	*Ethnohistory*
FEHSNY	Fort Edward Historical Association and Old Fort House Museum, Fort Edward, New York
FS	*Feminist Studies*
Garland Library	*The Garland Library of Narratives of North American Indian Captivities*, 311 titles in 111 vols., selected and arranged by Wilcomb E. Washburn (New York: Garland, 1976–83).
HNAI/IWR	*Handbook of North American Indians*, gen. ed. William C. Sturtevant, Vol. 4, *History of Indian-White Relations*, Wilcomb E. Washburn, vol. ed. (Washington, D.C.: Smithsonian Institution, 1988).
HNAI/ Northeast	*Handbook of North American Indians*, gen. ed. William C. Sturtevant, Vol. 15, *Northeast*, Bruce G. Trigger, vol. ed. (Washington, D.C.: Smithsonian Institution, 1978).
JAEH	*Journal of American Ethnic History*
JAH	*Journal of American History*
JAS	*Journal of American Studies*
JES	*Journal of Ethnic Studies*
LSP	Letchworth State Park, Castile, New York
MHS	Minnesota Historical Society
MHS-DAM	Minnesota Historical Society, Division of Manuscripts

NA	National Archives, Washington, D.C.; Record Groups listed as RG.
NEQ	*New England Quarterly*
NL	Newberry Library, Chicago, Illinois
NMNH/AC	National Museum of Natural History, Anthropological Collection, Smithsonian Institution
NMNH/BAE	National Museum of Natural History, Bureau of American Ethnology, Smithsonian Institution, Washington, D.C.
NSDAR	Library, National Society, Daughters of the American Revolution, Washington, D.C.
NYPL	Special Collections, New York Public Library, New York, New York
Official *Records*	U.S. War Department, *The War of the Rebellion: A Compilation of the Official Records of the Union and Confederate Armies*, 128 vols. (Washington, D.C.: U.S. Government Printing Office, 1880–1901).
PHR	*Pacific Historical Review*
PM	Peabody Museum, Harvard University
RAH	*Reviews in American History*
RG	See NA
WA	Wadsworth Atheneum, Hartford, Connecticut
WHQ	*Western Historical Quarterly*
WMQ	*William and Mary Quarterly*, 3d Series
WPL	William Pryor Letchworth Collections, property of Letchworth State Park and housed at Milne Library, State University of New York at Geneseo, New York

INTRODUCTION

Titles of books and pamphlets issued before 1900 have been shortened. Spelling and punctuation in early titles have been kept as in
the original, but capitalization has been modernized. For full titles
consult the bibliography in June Namias, "White Captives: Gender
and Ethnicity on Successive American Frontiers, 1607–1862" (Ph.D.
dissertation, Brandeis University, 1989).

1. The following are important reference works on scholarly and
popular collections of captivity narratives. The largest reprinted series
taken from the Newberry Library collections is *The Garland Library of
Narratives of North American Indian Captivities*, 311 titles in 111 vols.,
selected and arranged by Wilcomb E. Washburn (New York: Garland,
1976–83). These narratives and modern commentaries are listed in
Alden T. Vaughan, *Narratives of North American Indian Captivity:*

A Selective Bibliography (New York: Garland, 1983), vol. 1. Also see Robert W. G. Vail, "Certain Indian Captives of New England," *Massachusetts Historical Society Proceedings* 68 (1944–47): 113–31. The Garland reprints are taken from the Edward E. Ayer Collection, a complete listing of which may be found in Newberry Library, *Dictionary Catalogue of the Edward E. Ayer Collection of Americana and American Indians in the Newberry Library* (Boston: G. K. Hall, 1961), and *First Supplement* (Boston: G. K. Hall, 1970). For full references of additional narratives see Charles Evans, comp., *American Bibliography: A Chronological Dictionary of All Books, Pamphlets, and Periodical Publications Printed in the United States of America from the Genesis of Printing in 1639 Down to and Including the Year 1820*, 14 vols. (New York: P. Smith, 1941–59). An annotated work most helpful for the various editions of early narratives is R. W. G. Vail, *The Voice of the Old Frontier* (New York: Yoseloff, 1949). For New England captives see Emma Lewis Coleman, *New England Captives Carried to Canada: Between 1677 and 1760*, 2 vols. (Portland, Maine: Southworth Press, 1925). For recent collections of captivity narratives see *Puritans among the Indians: Accounts of Captivity and Redemption, 1676–1724*, ed. Alden T. Vaughan and Edward W. Clark (Cambridge, Mass.: Harvard University Press, 1981); *Held Captive by Indians: Selective Narratives, 1642–1836*, ed. Richard VanDerBeets (Knoxville: University of Tennessee Press, 1973); *The Indians and Their Captives*, ed. James Levernier and Hennig Cohen (Westport, Conn.: Greenwood Press, 1977); *Captured by the Indians: 15 Firsthand Accounts, 1750–1870*, ed. Fredrick Drimmer (New York: Dover, 1985); Howard Henry Peckham, *Captured by Indians: True Tales of Pioneer Survivors* (New Brunswick, N.J.: Rutgers University Press, 1954). For a good collection of essays on the new Indian scholarship see *New Directions in American Indian History*, ed. Colin G. Calloway (Norman: University of Oklahoma Press, 1988).

2. For accounts of Indians captured by Europeans, see James H. Merrell's references to John Smith's capture of Amoroleck, "The Indians' New World: The Catawba Experience," *WMQ* 41 (Oct. 1984): 537, 565, citing Edward Arber and A. G. Bradley, eds., *Travels and Works of Captain John Smith: President of Virginia, and Admiral of New England, 1580–1631*, 2 vols. (Edinburgh: J. Grant, 1910), 2:427; Alden T. Vaughan, *New England Frontier: Puritans and Indians, 1620–1675*, rev. ed. (New York: Norton, 1979), 3–17, and *American Genesis: Captain John Smith and the Founding of Virginia*, ed. Vaughan with Oscar Handlin (Boston: Little, Brown, 1975); John Donald Duncan, "Indian Slavery," in *Race Relations in British North America, 1607–1783*, ed. Bruce A. Glasrud and Alan M. Smith (Chicago: Nelson-Hall, 1983), 85–106, and Carolyn Thomas Foreman, *Indians Abroad, 1493–1938* (Norman: University of Oklahoma Press, 1943).

3. Lewis H. Morgan, *League of the Ho-dé-no-sau-nee or Iroquois*,

ed. Herbert M. Lloyd, 2 vols. (New York: Dodd, Mead, 1904), 331–35; James Axtell, *The European and the Indian: Essays in the Ethnohistory of Colonial North America* (New York: Oxford University Press, 1981), 172–75; David Zeisberger, *History of the Northern American Indians*, ed. Archer Butler Herbert and William N. Schwarze (Columbus: Fred J. Herr, 1910), 40–41. Frank Gouldsmith Speck also saw adoption as a means "to replace population" (*The Iroquois: A Study in Cultural Evolution* [Bloomfield Hills, Mich.: Cranbrook Institution of Science, Bulletin 23, Oct. 1945], 33).

In "The Scholastic Philosophy of the Wilderness," Axtell argued that many captives were adopted and married by Indians in the Northeast during the colonial period and liked their new lives so well that many "refused to return to New England." Axtell's main argument here and in "The White Indians" is a case for what he calls Indian "education." He concludes that Northeast Indians deliberately chose young British Americans and used certain techniques "which would transform their hostile or fearful white captives into affectionate relatives." Axtell claimed "a conservative estimate" of those who did not return would be "from 25–71 percent of English captives" of French and Indians. "A reasonable estimate, based on the proportion of captives in French and Indian hands in 1705 (5 to 3) would be 40 percent, 25 percent (146) becoming French Canadians, 15 percent (90) becoming Indians, and some of them practicing Catholics as well" (Axtell, *European and the Indian*, 131–67, 168–206, esp. 162. Here and in *The Invasion Within: The Conquest of Cultures in Colonial America* (New York: Oxford University Press, 1985) Axtell describes the gauntlet as part of a broader picture of Indian socialization of whites, or "education." These figures have been contested in a quantitative study of 1,085 captives taken by French, Indian, and French-Indian forces between 1675 and 1763 by Alden T. Vaughan and Daniel K. Richter, "Crossing the Cultural Divide: Indians and New Englanders, 1605–1763," *AAS* 90 (Apr. 16, 1980): 23–99. Studies of assimilation include A. Irving Hallowell, "American Indians, White and Black: The Phenomenon of Transculturalization," in *Contributions to Anthropology: Selected Papers of A. Irving Hallowell*, with introductions by Raymond D. Fogelson (Chicago: University of Chicago Press, 1976), 498–529, and J. Norman Heard, *White into Red: A Study of the Assimilation of White Persons Captured by Indians* (Metuchen, N.J.: Scarecrow Press, 1973). For examples of treatment of males see Richard VanDerBeets, "The Indian Captivity Narrative: An American Genre" (Ph.D. dissertation, University of the Pacific, 1973), 78–80. For mention of white capture in areas other than the Northeast, see John R. Swanton, "Ethnology—Notes on the Mental Assimilation of Races," *Journal of the Washington Academy of Sciences* 16 (Nov. 3, 1926): 493–502. On war see Francis Jennings, *The Invasion of America: Indians, Colonialism, and the Cant of Conquest* (New York: Norton, 1975), 15–31, and

Adam J. Hirsch, "The Collision of Military Cultures in Seventeenth-Century New England," *JAH* 74 (Mar. 1988): 1187–1212.

4. Axtell, *European and the Indian*, 172–75. Bruce G. Trigger finds a somewhat different system among the Hurons in the early to mid-seventeenth century. War among the Hurons is based on revenge and steeped in a system of proving male prowess in war. He does not find women-centered demands at the heart of capture, although family replacement does occur. He also finds women and children often killed by war parties and an emphasis on men capturing men for torture. His sources are Reuben Gold Thwaites, ed., *The Jesuit Relations and Allied Documents*, 73 vols. (1896–1901; rpt. New York: Pageant, 1959), which, although the best extant sources, are fraught with problems given the mission of the Jesuits in Indian country. See Trigger, *The Children of Aataentsic: A History of the Huron People to 1660* (Montreal: McGill–Queen's University Press, 1976), 68–75.

5. Daniel K. Richter, "War and Culture: The Iroquois Experience," *WMQ* 40 (1983): 528–59, esp. 537–44. I have emphasized women's role more than his interpretation does. Also see James Lynch, "The Iroquois Confederacy, and the Adoption and Administration of Non-Iroquoian Individuals and Groups prior to 1756," *Man in the Northeast* 30 (Fall 1985): 83–99. For another interpretation of Iroquois adoption as slavery see William A. Starna and Ralph Watkins, "Northern Iroquois Slavery," *EH* 38 (Winter 1991): 3–57. According to some scholars, slavery was a common practice in the Northwest, where it was also a part of the structural hierarchy of the society. See John R. Swanton, "Captives," in *Handbook of American Indians North of Mexico*, ed. Frederick Webb Hodge, 2 vols., *Bureau of American Ethnology Bulletin 30* (1907–10; rpt. New York: Rowman and Littlefield, 1971), 1:203–6, and U. P. [Joyce] Averkieva, "Slavery among the Indians of North America," trans. G. R. Elliott, in *Slavery: A Comparative Perspective*, ed. Robin W. Winks (New York: New York University Press, 1972). For a captivity in the Northwest dealing with captives as slaves see John R. Jewitt's narrative reproduced from its 1851 edition, *The Adventures and Sufferings of John R. Jewitt: Captive of Maquinna*, annotated and illustrated by Hilary Stewart (Seattle: University of Washington Press, 1987). Also see Henry W. Henshaw, "Slavery," in *Handbook of American Indians North of Mexico*, ed. Hodge, 2:597–600.

6. Theda Perdue, *Slavery and the Evolution of Cherokee Society, 1540–1866* (Knoxville: University of Tennessee Press, 1978), chaps. 1 and 2, on aboriginal bondage and the impact of European contact on the Indian slave trade; James H. Merrell, *The Indians' New World: Catawbas and Their Neighbors from European Contact through the Era of Removal* (New York: Norton, 1989), 121–22. Gary Clayton Anderson mentions the Mille Lacs Lake region Dakotas in *Kinsmen of Another Kind: Dakota-White Relations in the Upper Mississippi Valley, 1650–1862* (Lincoln: University of Nebraska Press, 1984), 6, 11.

Richard White finds the taking of captives common in the Great Lakes area among the Algonquians. In the mid-1640s Neutrals attacked an Algonquian village (probably of Fox or Mascoutens) and "killed many on the spot, but they retained eight hundred captives" (*The Middle Ground: Indians, Empires, and Republics in the Great Lakes Region, 1650–1815* [New York: Cambridge University Press, 1991], 2–3, 18, 245).

7. Axtell, *European and the Indian*, 172–73.

8. The origins of capture are somewhat in debate. Bruce G. Trigger traces the practice back to 1642 in eastern Canada between Hurons and Iroquois, relating to the fur trade and European contact. Thomas B. Abler suggests the role of guns, that is, the introduction of a technology that was lightweight, noisy, and powerful greatly influenced ways of war including capture (Abler, "European Technology and the Art of War in Iroquoia," in *Cultures in Conflict: Current Archaeological Perspectives*, ed. Diana Claire Tzaczuk and Brian C. Vivian [Calgary, Alberta: University of Calgary Archaeological Association, 1989], 273–82, citing Trigger, *Children of Aataentsic*, 661). James H. Merrell thinks that among the Indians of the piedmont the indigenous population helped to provide slaves from traditional enemies: "Captives, like scalps, had always been a prize of conflict. . . . Natives simply grafted the traders' demands onto traditional reasons for going off to war" (*Indians' New World*, 37). See also Peter Wood, "Indian Servitude in the Southeast," in *HNAI/IWR*, 407. On white European captives in Latin America see Susan Migden Socolow, "Spanish Captives in Indian Societies: Cultural Contact Along the Argentine Frontier, 1600–1835," *Hispanic American Historical Review* 72 (Feb. 1992): 73–99.

9. Albert H. Schroeder and Omer Stewart, "Indian Servitude in the Southwest," in *HNAI/IWR*, 410–13; Peter Stern, "Captivity Experiences in the Spanish Borderlands," paper presented at the Annual Meeting, American Society for Ethnohistory, Williamsburg, Virginia, 1988. On Spanish capture of Indians and Indian slavery see Socolow, "Spanish Captives," 81–82.

10. Yasuhide Kawashima, "Indian Servitude in the Northeast," in *HNAI/IWR*, 404.

11. Wood, "Indian Servitude," 407–8; Foreman, *Indians Abroad*. On the impact of blacks captured by Indians and blacks who escaped into Indian territory in the South see Hallowell, "American Indians." For the narratives of two black captives see Briton Hammon (captured 1760) and John Marrant (captured 1770, narrative produced 1785) listed in Vaughan, *Narratives*.

12. John Sullivan, *Lettters and Papers of Major-General John Sullivan, Continental Army*, ed. Otis G. Hammond, 3 vols. (Concord, N.H.: New Hampshire Historical Society, ca. 1930–39), 3:127.

13. John D. Unruh, Jr., *The Plains Across: The Overland Emigrants*

and the *Trans-Mississippi West, 1840–1860* (Urbana: University of Illinois Press, 1982), 188; Albert L. Hurtado, *Indian Survival on the California Frontier* (New Haven: Yale University Press, 1988), chap. 8, esp. 180–92.

14. Vaughan and Richter, "Crossing the Cultural Divide," 23–99.

15. *Held Captive by Indians*, ed. VanDerBeets, xi. For more on New England see Colin G. Calloway, "An Uncertain Destiny: Indian Captivities on the Upper Connecticut River," *JAS* 17 (Aug. 1983): 190–210; *North Country Captives: Selected Narratives of Indian Captivity from Vermont and New Hampshire*, ed. Colin G. Calloway (Hanover, N.H.: University Press of New England, 1992); Robinson V. Smith, "New Hampshire Persons Taken as Captives by the Indians," *Historical New Hampshire* 8 (Mar. 1952): 24–36; and Hirsch, "Collision of Military Cultures," 1187–1212. Axtell stresses adoption and white contentment with Indian society in *European and the Indian*, 39–87, 131–67, 168–206, and in *Invasion Within*, 71–90, 287–301, 302–27. On Indian demography and the impact of disease see Alfred Crosby, Jr., *The Columbian Exchange: The Biological and Cultural Consequences of 1492* (Westport, Conn.: Greenwood Press, 1972); S. F. Cook, *The Indian Population of New England in the Seventeenth Century* (Berkeley: University of California Press, 1976); Jennings, *Invasion of America*, 15–31; Russell Thornton, "American Indian Historical Demography: A Review Essay with Suggestions for Further Research," *AICRJ* 3, no. 1 (1979): 69–74; and Melissa L. Meyer and Russell Thornton, "Indians and the Numbers Game: Quantitative Methods in Native American History," in *New Directions in American Indian History*, ed. Calloway, 5–30.

16. Mary Rowlandson, *A True History of the Captivity & Restoration of Mrs. Mary Rowlandson* (1682), *Garland Library*, vol. 1 (New York: Garland, 1977); John Williams, *The Redeemed Captive Returning to Zion* (1707), *Garland Library*, vol. 5 (New York: Garland, 1978), reprinted in *Puritans among the Indians*, ed. Vaughan and Clark, 165–226; John Filson, *The Discovery, Settlement and Present State of Kentucke . . . The Adventures of Col. Daniel Boon* (1784), *Garland Library*, vol. 14 (New York: Garland, 1978).

17. James Fenimore Cooper, *The Last of the Mohicans: A Narrative of 1757*, illustrated by N. C. Wyeth (1826; rpt. New York: Charles Scribner's, 1986); Nathaniel Hawthorne, "The Duston Family," *American Magazine of Useful and Entertaining Knowledge* 2 (May 1836): 395–97, in *Indians and Their Captives*, ed. Levernier and Cohen, 224–30; Herman Melville, *Typee, a Peep at Polynesian Life* (1846; rpt. New York: Viking, 1982); Henry David Thoreau, *A Week on the Concord and Merrimack Rivers* (1849; rpt. New York: Holt, Rinehart and Winston, 1963); Mark Twain, "Huck Finn and Tom Sawyer among the Indians," *Life*, Dec. 23, 1968. For other comments see D. H. Lawrence, *Studies in Classic American Literature* (New York: Viking, 1961),

47–65; David T. Haberly, "Women and Indians: The Last of the Mohicans and the Captivity Tradition," *AQ* 28 (1976): 431–43; Dawn Lander Gherman, "From Parlour to Tepee: The White Squaw on the American Frontier" (Ph.D. dissertation, University of Massachusetts, 1975), 211–13; Henry Nash Smith, *Virgin Land: The American West as Symbol and Myth* (New York: Vintage Books, 1959), 64–76; Richard Slotkin, *Regeneration through Violence: The Mythology of the American Frontier, 1600–1860* (Middletown, Conn.: Wesleyan University Press, 1973).

18. *The Searchers*, 1956, directed by John Ford; Howard Movshovitz, "The Still Point: Women in the Westerns of John Ford," *Frontiers* 7, no. 3 (1984): 68–72; John Boorman, *The Emerald Forest Diary* (New York: Farrar, Straus, and Giroux, 1985). Kevin Costner directed and starred in *Dances with Wolves* (1990) with Mary McDonnell as Stands with a Fist. The picture won seven Oscars, including those for best picture and best director. See Richard W. Stevenson, "7 Oscars for 'Wolves' Lift a Troubled Studio," *New York Times*, Mar. 27, 1991, p. D1, and Chris Chase, "And the Winners Very Possibly, Are . . ." *New York Times*, Mar. 12, 1991, sec. 2, p. 1. See Barbara Anne Mortimer, "From Monument Valley to Vietnam: Revisions of the American Captivity Narrative in Hollywood Film" (Ph.D. dissertation, Emory University, 1991).

19. Rowlandson, *True History*; Williams, *Redeemed Captive*; James Everett Seaver, *A Narrative of the Life of Mrs. Mary Jemison* (1824), *Garland Library*, vol. 41 (New York: Garland, 1977). An available edition is James E. Seaver, *A Narrative of the Life of Mrs. Mary Jemison*, ed. June Namias (Norman: University of Oklahoma Press, 1992). For publishers and details of each edition see James E. Seaver, *A Narrative of the Life of Mary Jemison*, rev. ed. by Charles Delamater Vail (New York: American Scenic and Historic Preservation Society, 1925), 296–97, and discussion in Chapter 5, below. For foreign impact see Ray Allen Billington, *Land of Savagery, Land of Promise: The European Image of the American Frontier in the Nineteenth Century* (New York: Norton, 1981), 25–28; Glenda Riley, *Women and Indians on the Frontier, 1825–1915* (Albuquerque: University of New Mexico Press, 1984), 37–82. According to Socolow, the interest in Latin American captives in Argentina was small. She finds it "perplexing" that there was a "relative lack of dramatic reaction to the continuous loss of settlers to captivity" in the early nineteenth century (especially the 1830s) and suggests this was because those captured were "rural people, illiterate folk with little or no political power" ("Spanish Captives," 99).

20. On differing views of race and culture in early America see Alden Vaughan, "From White Man to Redskin: Changing Anglo-American Perceptions of the American Indian," *AHR* 87 (Oct. 1982): 917–53; Winthrop Jordan, *White over Black: American Attitudes toward the Negro, 1550–1812*, 2d ed. (Baltimore: Penguin, 1969). G. E. Thomas

argues that race was a factor in the scalping and enslavement of Indians by Puritans in "Puritans, Indians, and the Concept of Race," *NEQ* 48 (Mar. 1975): 3–27; *The Great Fear: Race in the Mind of America*, ed. Gary Nash and Richard Weiss (New York: Holt, Rinehart and Winston, 1970); Gary B. Nash, *Red, White, and Black* (Englewood Cliffs, N.J.: Prentice-Hall, 1974), chap. 1. On theories of ethnicity see Harold R. Isaacs, *Idols of the Tribe: Group Identity and Political Change* (New York: Harper & Row, 1975); Werner Sollors, "The Roots of Ethnicity: Etymology and Definitions," in *Harvard Encyclopedia of American Ethnic Groups*, ed. Stephan Thernstrom (Cambridge, Mass.: Harvard University Press), 647–65; Werner Sollors, *Beyond Ethnicity: Consent and Descent in American Culture* (New York: Oxford University Press, 1986); Elizabeth Fox-Genovese, "Between Individualism and Fragmentation: American Culture and the New Literary Studies of Race and Gender," *AQ* 42 (Mar. 1990): 7–34. On the Indian as "other" see Robert F. Berkhofer, Jr., "White Conceptions of Indians," in *HNAI/IWR*, 522–47; and Berkhofer, *The White Man's Indian: Images of the American Indian from Columbus to the Present* (New York: Vintage Books, 1979). Also see Raymond William Stedman, *Shadows of the Indian: Stereotypes in American Culture* (Norman: University of Oklahoma Press, 1982).

21. Joan Wallach Scott, *Gender and the Politics of History* (New York: Columbia University Press, 1988); Natalie Zemon Davis, *Fiction in the Archives: Pardon Tales of Sixteenth-Century France* (Stanford: Stanford University Press, 1987); and Davis, *Society and Culture in Early Modern France: Eight Essays* (Stanford: Stanford University Press, 1975).

22. Jordan, *White over Black*; George M. Fredrickson, *White Supremacy: A Comparative Study of American and South African History* (New York: Oxford University Press, 1981); Tzvetan Todorov, *The Conquest of America: The Question of the Other* (New York: Harper & Row, 1982); Reginald Horsman, *Race and Manifest Destiny: The Origins of American Racial Anglo-Saxonism* (Cambridge, Mass.: Harvard University Press, 1981).

23. The term *frontier* is rejected as ethnocentric in Alfonso Ortiz, "Indian/White Relations: A View from the Other Side of the 'Frontier,'" in *Indians in American History: An Introduction*, ed. Frederick E. Hoxie (Arlington Heights, Ill.: Harlan Davidson, 1988), 1–16, and by Patricia Nelson Limerick as an "all-too-elastic term" and "fuzzy" in "Everything for Your Urban 'Imagining Needs,'" *RAH* 19 (Mar. 1991): 46–47; Robert M. Utley, *The Indian Frontier of the American West, 1846–1890* (Albuquerque: University of New Mexico Press, 1984), xix–xx; William Cronon, "Revisiting the Vanishing Frontier: The Legacy of Frederick Jackson Turner," *WHQ* 18 (Apr. 1987), 157–76, and in conversations at the Seminar on History and the Environment, MIT, Apr. 8, 1991; *The Frontier in History: North America and*

South Africa Compared, ed. Howard Lamar and Leonard Thompson (New Haven: Yale University Press, 1981). For a more expansive multicultural definition of *frontier* see Annette Kolodny, "Letting Go Our Grand Obsessions: Notes toward a New Literary History of the American Frontiers," *AL* 64 (Mar. 1992): 1–18.

24. Paul Hulton, *America 1585: The Complete Drawings of John White* (Chapel Hill: University of North Carolina Press, 1984); Nash, *Red, White, and Black*, 35–43; Hugh Honour, *The New Golden Land: European Images of America from the Discoveries to the Present Time* (New York: Pantheon, 1975); Bernadette Bucher, *Icon and Conquest: A Structural Analysis of the Illustrations of de Bry's Great Voyages*, trans. Basia Miller Gulati (Chicago: University of Chicago Press, 1981).

25. C. Gregory Crampton, "The Archives of the Duke Projects in Indian Oral History," in *Indian-White Relations: A Persistent Paradox*, ed. Jane F. Smith and Robert M. Kvasnicka (Washington, D.C.: Howard University Press, 1981), 119–28.

26. Samuel Eliot Morison, ed., *The Parkman Reader: From the Works of Francis Parkman* (Boston: Little, Brown, 1955), 519–24; George Bancroft, *History of the United States, from the Discovery of the American Continent*, vol. 1 (New York: D. Appleton, 1895).

27. For example, Joseph Pritts, *Incidents of Border Life* (Lancaster, Pa.: n.p., 1841); John Frost, *Indian Wars of the United States from the Earliest Period to the Present Time* (Buffalo: Derby Miller, 1853), Frost, *Daring and Heroic Deeds of American Women* (Philadelphia: G. G. Evans, 1860); Frost, *Thrilling Adventures among the Indians* (Philadelphia: J. W. Bradley, 1851); E[lizabeth] F. Ellet, *Pioneer Women of the West* (New York: Charles Scribner, 1852).

28. J. Lee Humfreville, *Twenty Years among Our Hostile Indians* (New York: Hunter, 1901), 68–73; Carl Coke Rister, *Comanche Bondage . . . with an Annotated Reprint of Sarah Ann Horn's Narrative of Her Captivity among the Comanches* (Glendale, Calif.: Arthur H. Clark, 1955); Frederick Jackson Turner, "The Significance of the Frontier in American History," in *Frontier and Section* (Englewood Cliffs, N.J.: Prentice-Hall, 1961), 37–62. On recent Turner criticism see Richard W. Etulain, "Shifting Interpretations of Western Cultural History," in *Historians and the American West*, ed. Michael P. Malone (Lincoln: University of Nebraska Press, 1983), 414–32, and in the same volume Richard Maxwell Brown, "Historiography of Violence in the American West," 234–69. Also see Martin Ridge, "Frederick Jackson Turner, Ray Allen Billington, and American Frontier History," *WHQ* 19 (Jan. 1988): 5–20; and Donald Worster, "New West, True West: Interpreting the Region's History," *WHQ* 18 (Apr. 1987): 141–56.

29. Richard Drinnon, *White Savage: The Case of John Dunn Hunter* (New York: Schocken, 1972); Drinnon, *Facing West: The Metaphysics of Indian-Hating and Empire Building* (Minneapolis: University of

Minnesota Press, 1980), 443–67; Seaver, *Narrative of the Life of Mrs. Mary Jemison*, ed. Namias. Also see Sidney Lens, *The Forging of American Empire* (New York: Thomas Y. Crowell, 1971), 40–61, 135–49; Jennings, *Invasion of America*; Francis Jennings, "The Indians' Revolution," in *The American Revolution in the History of American Radicalism*, ed. Alfred F. Young (DeKalb: Northern Illinois University Press, 1976), 319–48; Richard Drinnon, ed., *Memoirs of a Captivity among the Indians of North America: John Dunn Hunter* [1824] (New York: Schocken, 1973); *Little Big Man*, 1970, directed by Arthur Penn, based on the novel by Thomas Berger; Richard Slotkin, *The Fatal Environment: The Myth of the Frontier in the Age of Industrialization, 1800–1890* (New York: Atheneum, 1985); Carroll Smith-Rosenberg, *Disorderly Conduct: Visions of Gender in Victorian America* (New York: Knopf, 1986), 90–108.

30. Roy Harvey Pearce, "The Significances of the Captivity Narrative," *AL* 19 (Mar. 1947): 1–20, esp. 3; Pearce, *The Savages of America: A Study of the Indian and the Idea of Civilization*, rev. ed. (Baltimore: Johns Hopkins University Press, 1965), 22; Pearce, *Historicism Once More: Problems and Occasions for the American Scholar* (Princeton: Princeton University Press, 1969); Pearce, "From the History of Ideas to Ethnohistory," *JES* 2 (1974): 86–92. Also see Smith, *Virgin Land*; Slotkin, *Regeneration through Violence* and *Fatal Environment*; Leslie Fiedler, *The Return of the Vanishing American* (New York: Stein and Day, 1968). For a critique of this scholarship see Bruce Kuklick, "Myth and Symbol in American Studies," *AQ* 24 (Oct. 1972): 435–50.

On the captivity genre see VanDerBeets, "Indian Captivity Narrative"; Richard VanDerBeets, *The Indian Captivity Narrative: An American Genre* (Lanham, Md.: University Press of America, 1984); and VanDerBeets, introduction to *Held Captive by Indians*, xi–xxxi. Also see Phillips D. Carleton, "The Indian Captivity," *AL* 15 (Mar. 1943–Jan. 1944): 169–80; James R. Lewis, "Assessing the Impact of Indian Captivity on the Euro-American Mind: Some Critical Issues," *Connecticut Review* 11 (Summer 1989): 14–26; Louise K. Barnett, *The Ignoble Savage: American Literary Racism, 1790–1890* (Westport, Conn.: Greenwood Press, 1975); Dorothy Forbis Behen, "The Captivity Story in American Literature, 1577–1826: An Examination of Written Reports in English, Authentic and Fictitious, of the Experiences of White Men Captured by the Indians North of Mexico" (Ph.D. dissertation, University of Chicago, 1952); Larry Lee Carey, "A Story of the Indian Captivity Narrative as a Popular Literary Genre, ca. 1575–1875" (Ph.D. dissertation, Michigan State University, 1978); James G. Meade, " 'The Westerns of the East': Narratives of Indian Captivity from Jeremiad to Gothic Novel" (Ph.D. dissertation, Northwestern University, 1971); *Indians and Their Captives*, ed. Levernier and Cohen, xiii–xxx; Billington, *Land of Savagery*; Charles E. Hambrick-Stowe, *The Practice of Piety: Puritan Devotional*

Disciplines in Seventeenth-Century New England (Chapel Hill: University of North Carolina Press, 1982), 256–65.

31. A. Irving Hallowell, "The Backwash of the Frontier: The Impact of the Indian on American Culture," in *Annual Report of the Regents of the Smithsonian Institution* (Washington, D.C.: U.S. Government Printing Office, 1959), 447–72, esp. 453–54; Hallowell, "American Indians, White and Black: The Phenomenon of Transculturalization," *CA* 4 (Dec. 1963): 519–31; Swanton, "Captives"; Swanton, "Ethnology," 493–502; and William N. Fenton, *American Indian and White Relations to 1830: Needs and Opportunities for Study* (Chapel Hill: University of North Carolina Press, 1957), 3–27, esp. 18. James Axtell calls ethnohistory a discipline using "a two-culture focus." See Axtell, "The Ethnohistory of Early America: A Review Essay," *WMQ* 35 (1978): 110–44; Axtell, *European and the Indian*, 1–15. For anthropological and cultural approaches to studying the Indian past see Daniel K. Richter, "Up the Cultural Stream: Three Recent Works in Iroquois Studies," *EH* 32 (June 1985): 363–69; Calvin Martin, "The Metaphysics of Writing Indian-White History," *EH* 26 (Spring 1979): 153–59; *The American Indian and the Problem of History*, ed. Calvin Martin (New York: Oxford University Press, 1987); Heard, *White into Red*; Thwaites, ed., *Jesuit Relations*; Cornelius J. Jaenen, *Friend and Foe: Aspects of French-Amerindian Cultural Conflict in the Sixteenth and Seventeenth Centuries* (New York: Columbia University Press, 1976), 128–45. Another critical early source for the French is Joseph-François Lafitau, S.J., *Customs of the American Indians Compared with the Customs of Primitive Times*, trans. and ed. William N. Fenton and Elizabeth L. Moore, 2 vols. (Toronto: Champlain Society, 1974–77). For an analysis of the Jesuit sources see Daniel K. Richter, "Iroquois versus Iroquois: Jesuit Missions and Christianity in Village Politics, 1642–1686," *EH* 32 (June 1985): 1–16. Perdue's research finds that Cherokee practice "spared female captives and young prisoners from the torture inflicted upon young males" (*Slavery and Cherokee Society*, 7–11). Others with a less than sanguine view of capture include Nathaniel Knowles, "The Torture of Captives by the Indians of Eastern North America," *Proceedings of the American Philosophical Society* 82, no. 2 (1940): 151–225; and Erwin H. Acherknecht, " 'White Indians': Psychological Peculiarities of White Children Abducted and Reared by North American Indians," *Bulletin of the History of Medicine* 15 (Jan. 1944): 15–36.

32. For several theoretical and practical applications of the field of American women's history see Gerda Lerner, *The Majority Finds Its Past: Placing Women in History* (New York: Oxford University Press, 1979). For literature on women and the West see Julie Roy Jeffrey, *Frontier Women: The Trans-Mississippi West, 1840–1880* (New York: Hill and Wang, 1979); Lillian Schlissel, *Women's Diaries of the Westward Journey* (New York: Schocken, 1982); Schlissel et al., *Far from*

Home: *Families of the Westward Journey* (New York: Schocken, 1989);
Susan H. Armitage, "Women and Western American History" (Working Paper 134, Wellesley College Center for Research on Women, 1984); Armitage, "Women's Literature and the American Frontier: A New Perspective on the Frontier Myth," in *Women, Women Writers, and the West*, ed. L. L. Lee and Merrill Lewis (Troy, N.Y.: Whitston, 1980); Joan M. Jensen and Darlis Miller, "Gentle Tamers Revisited: New Approaches to the History of Women in the American West," *PHR* 49 (May 1980): 173–213; *Women in the West*, ed. Glenda Riley (Manhattan: University of Kansas Press, 1982); *Frontiers* 7 (1984); Elizabeth Jameson and Darlis Miller, "The Women's West: The Development of a Subfield," paper presented at the Sixth Berkshire Conference on the History of Women, Smith College, June 3, 1984; Susan Armitage and Elizabeth Jameson, *The Women's West* (Norman: University of Oklahoma Press, 1987); John Mack Faragher, *Women and Men on the Overland Trail* (New Haven: Yale University Press, 1979); Allan G. Bogue, "Emigrants West: Male and Female," *RAH* 8 (June 1980): 221–27. For a more conventional view of women's roles see Dee Brown, *The Gentle Tamers: Women of the Old Wild West*, rev. ed. (Lincoln: University of Nebraska Press, 1981).

33. Arthur Roy Buntin was the first to find gender differences in captivity narratives in "The Indians in American Literature, 1680–1760" (Ph.D. dissertation, University of Washington, 1961), 79–159. On women captives see Gherman, "From Parlour to Tepee"; Annette Kolodny, *The Land Before Her: Fantasy and Experience of the American Frontiers, 1630–1860* (Chapel Hill: University of North Carolina Press, 1984), 3–34, 227–41; Kolodny, "Captives in Paradise," paper presented at the Sixth Berkshire Conference, Smith College, June 3, 1984; Laurel Thatcher Ulrich, *Good Wives: Image and Reality in the Lives of Women in Northern New England, 1650–1750* (New York: Knopf, 1982), 202–15. Also see June Namias, "Thrills, Terror, and Suffering: Responses of Captive Women, 1682–1870," paper presented at the Sixth Berkshire Conference, Smith College, June 3, 1984; Leland S. Person, Jr., "The American Eve: Miscegenation and a Feminist Frontier Fiction," *AQ* 37 (Winter 1985): 668–85; Riley, *Women and Indians on the Frontier*, 84–104; June Namias, "Go West, Young Woman," *Women's Review of Books* 3 (Oct. 1985): 18–19; Frances Rowe Kestler, comp., *The Indian Captivity Narrative: A Woman's View* (New York: Garland, 1990).

34. These patterns include the colonial context and the contexts of racial and cultural patterns of domination. For examples see Claudia Koonz, *Mothers in the Fatherland: Women, the Family, and Nazi Politics* (New York: St. Martin's Press, 1987); Helen Callaway, *Gender, Culture, and Empire: European Women in Colonial Nigeria* (Urbana: University of Illinois Press, 1987); Cheryl Johnson-Odim and Margaret Strobel, "Conceptualizing the History of Women in Africa, Asia,

Latin America and the Caribbean, and the Middle East," *Signs* 1 (Spring 1989): 31–62; Elizabeth Fox-Genovese, *Within the Plantation Household: Black and White Women of the Old South* (Chapel Hill: University of North Carolina Press, 1988); and *Unequal Sisters: A Multicultural Reader in U.S. Women's History*, ed. Ellen Carol DuBois and Vicki L. Ruiz (New York: Routledge, 1990).

1: WHITE WOMEN HELD CAPTIVE

1. Mary Rowlandson, *A True History of the Captivity & Restoration of Mrs. Mary Rowlandson* (1682), *Garland Library*, vol. 1 (New York: Garland, 1977), 1.

2. Scott depends on Michel Foucault's use of the word *knowledge*. See Joan Wallach Scott, *Gender and the Politics of History* (New York: Columbia University Press, 1988), 2, 9–10. Also see Scott, "Gender: A Useful Category of Historical Analysis," *AHR* 91 (Dec. 1986): 1053–76; Natalie Zemon Davis, *Society and Culture in Early Modern France: Eight Essays* (Stanford: Stanford University Press, 1975); Davis, *Fiction in the Archives: Pardon Tales of Sixteenth-Century France* (Stanford: Stanford University Press, 1987).

3. Scott, *Gender and the Politics of History*, 6.

4. I am using the word *archetypes* here roughly based on Carl Jung's conception as "an inherited idea or mode of thought . . . that is derived from the experience of the race and is present in the unconscious of the individual," but I would not presume these modes to be present in the unconscious before history and culture placed them there so I am also using the word as "the original pattern or model of which all things of the same type are representations or copies" (*New Collegiate Dictionary* [Springfield, Mass.: Webster, 1975], 59). Roy Harvey Pearce, "The Significances of the Captivity Narrative," *AL* 19 (Mar. 1947): 1–20, esp. 3; Pearce, *The Savages of America: A Study of the Indian and the Idea of Civilization*, rev. ed. (Baltimore: Johns Hopkins Press, 1965), 22. For additional commentary see Leslie A. Fiedler, "The Indian in Literature in English," in *HNAI/IWR*, 573–81; Richard Slotkin, *Regeneration through Violence: The Mythology of the American Frontier, 1600–1860* (Middletown, Conn.: Wesleyan University Press, 1973); Slotkin, *The Fatal Environment: The Myth of the Frontier in the Age of Industrialization, 1800–1890* (New York: Atheneum, 1985). Also see Wilcomb E. Washburn's introduction in Alden T. Vaughan, *Narratives of North American Indian Captivity: A Selective Bibliography* (New York: Garland, 1983), esp. xxxi; and *The Indians and Their Captives*, ed. James Levernier and Hennig Cohen (Westport, Conn.: Greenwood Press, 1977); Scott, *Gender and the Politics of History*, 9.

5. The fifty women are as follows: 1675–1763: Mary White Row-

landson, Sarah Gerish, Elizabeth Hull Heard, Mahetable Goodwin, Mary Woodwell Fowler, Isabella M'Coy, Jemima Howe, Susannah Johnson, Hannah Bradley, Frances Nobel, Eunice Williams, Mrs. Eunice Williams, Elizabeth Hanson, Hannah Dustan (Dustin, Duston), Mary Neff, Mrs. Denis, Hannah Swarton; 1764–1819: Mrs. Clendenin, Frances Slocum, Frances Scott, Jemima Boone, Mary Jemison, Massy Harbison, Experience Bozarth, Mrs. (Samuel) Daviess, Mary Moore, Mrs. Dunham, Jane Gillespie Brown; 1820–70: Caroline Harris, Sarah Ann Horn, Dolly Webster, Fanny Kelly, Olive Oatman, Mary Oatman, Cynthia Ann Parker, Eliza Swan, Hannah Lewis, Mrs. Edwin Eastman, Clarissa Plummer, Sara L. Larimer, Mrs. N. D. White (Urania S. Frazer), Helen Carrothers Mar Tarbel, Mary Schwandt, Nancy McClure, Minnie Carrigan, Sarah F. Wakefield, Susan Fitzpatrick, Alice Fitzpatrick, Josephine Meeker, Arvella Meeker. Except for Mary Jemison, the years of capture determined the date placement. Jemison was captured in the 1750s but remained with Indians into the early nineteenth century, when her narrative first appeared in 1824. Some of these women's captivity accounts are personal narratives; others, like Hannah Dustin's, Eunice Williams's, and Jemima Boone's, appear in the sermons or narratives of others. For Olive Oatman's picture see Lillian Schlissel, *Women's Diaries of the Westward Journey* (New York: Schocken, 1982), 71. I have not included K. White or Mary Barber on this list because I believe theirs are wholly fictive pieces. For more data and a comparison of captives see the Appendix, "Guide to Captives," following the text.

6. For early European and Indian relations in New England see Neal Salisbury, *Manitou and Providence: Indians, Europeans, and the Making of New England, 1500–1643* (New York: Oxford University Press, 1982); Wilcomb E. Washburn, "Seventeenth-Century Indian Wars," in *HNAI/Northeast*, 89–100; William S. Simmons, "Narragansett," in *HNAI/Northeast*, 190–97; Laura E. Conkey et al., "Indians of Southern New England and Long Island: Late Period," in *HNAI/Northeast*, 177–89; Francis Jennings, *The Invasion of America: Indians, Colonialism, and the Cant of Conquest* (New York: Norton, 1975). For accounts of Rowlandson with Metacomet and Weetamoo I refer to Pauline Turner Strong, "Captive Women: Accounts of White Women among North American Indians," paper presented at the Sixth Berkshire Conference on the History of Women, Smith College, June 3, 1984, and Strong, "Captivity in White and Red: Hegemonic and Alternative Representations in Colonial New England," paper presented at the American Society for Ethnohistory, Chicago, Nov. 2, 1989. For a review of recent work in ethnohistory in colonial America see Daniel H. Usner, Jr., "American Indians in Colonial History: A Review Essay," *JAEH* (Winter 1992): 77–85.

7. For a review of the data on captive women I have taken the following statistics from Alden T. Vaughan and Daniel K. Richter,

"Crossing the Cultural Divide: Indians and New Englanders, 1605–1763," *AAS* 90 (Apr. 16, 1980): 55, 58, esp. Figure 2, "Sex of Captives Taken by French, Indian, and French-Indian Forces, 1675–1763" from 1,085 known captives. Of course there were many "survivors" who went to Canada, New England women who stayed, and some who returned. See also Alice Nash, "Choosing Cultures: The Captivity Story of Grizel and Margaret Otis of Dover, New Hampshire," and Barbara Austen, "Captured . . . Never Came Back: Social Networks among New England Female Captives in Canada, 1698–1763," papers presented at the Dublin Seminar for New England Folklife, July 16, 1989; James Axtell, *The Invasion Within: The Contest of Cultures in Colonial America* (New York: Oxford University Press, 1985), 287–301; Richard I. Melvoin, *New England Outpost: War and Society in Colonial Deerfield* (New York: Norton, 1989).

8. James Axtell, *The European and the Indian: Essays in the Ethnohistory of Colonial North America* (New York: Oxford University Press, 1981), 39–87, 131–67, 168–206; Axtell, *Invasion Within*, 71–90, 302–27. On food and ecological survival among New England Indians see Carolyn Merchant, *Ecological Revolutions: Nature, Gender, and Science in New England* (Chapel Hill: University of North Carolina Press, 1989), 63–64, and chaps. 2–3; William Cronon, *Changes in the Land: Indians, Colonists, and the Ecology of New England* (New York: Hill and Wang, 1983).

9. Rowlandson, *A True History*, 3.

10. Ibid., 11.

11. Rowlandson led Puritan New England into what Charles E. Hambrick-Stowe calls "the relocation of the [spiritual] pilgrimage" (*The Practice of Piety: Puritan Devotional Disciplines in Seventeenth-Century New England* [Chapel Hill: University of North Carolina Press, 1982], 256–65). Recent interpretations of Rowlandson see her as challenging rather than going along with traditional Puritan authority, both theologically and in her relations with the Indians. See Mitchell Robert Breitwieser, *American Puritanism and the Defense of Mourning: Religion, Grief, and Ethnology in Mary White Rowlandson's Captivity Narrative* (Madison: University of Wisconsin Press, 1990); Susan Howe, "The Captivity and Restoration of Mrs. Mary Rowlandson," *Temblor*, no. 2 (1985): 113–21; and David Jaffee, "New England Local History: The Myths of Town Formation," paper presented at the Committee for the History of Research on the United States, University of Paris, Feb. 7, 1992. The more conventional view of Rowlandson as part of the establishment and a mythic figure in the creation of an Indian-hating tradition may be found in Slotkin, *Regeneration through Violence*, 95, 101–16, 125–29, and throughout his work. A recent incarnation of this view is in Louis J. Kern, "Savagery, Captivity, and Redemption: Historical Memory and National Myth in Puritan Representations of King Philip's War (1675–78),"

paper presented at the Committee for the History of Research on the United States, University of Paris, Feb. 7, 1992. Amy Schrager Lang incorporates the older view but recognizes some of the new interpretations and adds good biographical references in the introduction to Rowlandson's narrative in *Journeys in New Worlds: Early American Women's Narratives*, ed. William L. Andrews (Madison: University of Wisconsin Press, 1990), 13. On literacy in New England see Margaret Spufford, "First Steps in Literacy: The Reading and Writing Experiences of the Humblest Seventeenth-Century Spiritual Autobiographers," in *Literacy and Social Development in the West: A Reader*, ed. Harvey J. Graff (Cambridge, Eng.: Cambridge University Press, 1981), 149–50; Kenneth A. Lockridge, "Literacy in Early America, 1650–1800," ibid., 183–200, esp. 187; David D. Hall, "The Uses of Literacy in New England," in *Printing and Society in Early America*, ed. William Joyce et al. (Worcester: American Antiquarian Society, 1983), 2:1–47; Hall, "The World of Print and Collective Mentality in Seventeenth-Century New England," in *New Dimensions in American Intellectual History*, ed. John Higham and Paul K. Conklin (Baltimore: Johns Hopkins University Press, 1979), 166–80.

12. Cotton Mather, *Decennium Luctuosum*, in *Narratives of the Indian Wars, 1675–1699*, ed. Charles Lincoln (New York: Charles Scribner's, 1913), 198–99.

13. Samuel G. Drake, *Tragedies of the Wilderness* (Boston: Antiquarian Bookstore and Institute, 1846), 71–72; Harriet Prescott Spofford, *New England Legends* (Boston: James R. Osgood, 1871), 30.

14. Drake, *Tragedies*, 141–45.

15. Ibid., 145.

16. Jemima Howe, *A Genuine and Correct Account of the Captivity, Sufferings & Deliverance of Mrs. Jemima Howe, of Hinsdale, in New-Hampshire* (1792), *Garland Library*, vol. 19 (New York: Garland, 1977), 7–8.

17. Ibid., 11–12.

18. Rowlandson, *True History*, 9, 13; Elizabeth Janeway, *Powers of the Weak* (New York: Knopf, 1980), 3–21.

19. Howe, *Genuine and Correct Account*, 7, 11–12. Henry Nash Smith discusses the rise of the western heroine in *Virgin Land: The American West as Symbol and Myth* (New York: Vintage Books, 1959). In southern Vermont, Howe is called "fair captive." Her life and the legend of her as a romantic figure have been tracked by Kirsten B. Cappy, who finds the real Howe to be a pioneer mother ("The Fair Captive" [paper, Wheaton College, Dec. 1991]).

20. Laurel Thatcher Ulrich, *Good Wives: Image and Reality in the Lives of Women in Northern New England, 1650–1750* (New York: Knopf, 1982), 82–99; John Putnam Demos, *Entertaining Satan: Witchcraft and the Culture of Early New England* (New York: Oxford University Press, 1982), 344. For other biographical data on Dustan

see *Puritans among the Indians: Accounts of Captivity and Redemption, 1676–1724*, ed. Alden T. Vaughan and Edward W. Clark (Cambridge, Mass.: Harvard University Press, 1981), 161; Kathryn Whitford, "Hannah Dustin: The Judgment of History," *Essex Institute Historical Collections* 108 (1972): 304–25; Hon. Albert L. Bartlett, "The Story of Hannah Duston and Mary Neff," *Daughters of the American Revolution Magazine* 105 (1971): 806–9; Robert D. Arner, "The Story of Hannah Duston: Cotton Mather to Thoreau," *American Transcendental Quarterly* 18 (1973): 19–23.

21. Cotton Mather, *Decennium Luctuosum: A History of Remarkable Occurrences in the Long War*, 3 vols. (1699; rpt. New York: Garland, 1978), 3:138–43. On scalping, see Axtell, *European and the Indian*, 207–41. Also see his view of the gauntlet, ibid., 185.

22. Ulrich calls Dustin an "American amazon" in *Good Wives*, 168. Leslie Fiedler calls her "the great WASP mother of Us All" in *The Return of the Vanishing American* (New York: Stein and Day, 1968), 84–119, esp. 95. The Bozarth account is dated April 26, 1779, in Archibald Loudon, *A Selection of Some of the Most Interesting Narratives of Outrages Committed by the Indians in Their Wars with the White People*, 2 vols. (1808), *Garland Library*, vol. 29 (New York: Garland, 1977), 1:80–82. For other Amazon accounts see John Frost, *Thrilling Adventures among the Indians* (Philadelphia: J. W. Bradley, 1851), 28–31; Frost, *Daring and Heroic Deeds of American Women* (Philadelphia: G. G. Evans, 1860); E[lizabeth] F. Ellet, *Pioneer Women of the West* (New York: Charles Scribner, 1852). For additional examples see June Namias, "White Captives: Gender and Ethnicity on Successive American Frontiers, 1607–1862" (Ph.D. dissertation, Brandeis University, 1989), 62–65.

23. *Indian Atrocities! Affecting and Thrilling Anecdotes* (1846), *Garland Library*, vol. 61 (New York: Garland, 1978), 22. Also see a more seductive but equally gory Mrs. Merril in "The Western Mothers," *Family Magazine* 5 (1843): 165, published in Philadelphia, Boston, and New York. A later Amazonian Mrs. Merril is pictured in John A. McClung, *Sketches of Western Adventure* (Louisville, Ky.: Richard H. Collins, 1879), 197. Elise Marienstras commented on these images as being, like Bozarth's, at "the door of the cabin," the entry into civilization, virtue, and womanhood, separated physically by the door, on the other side of which is savagery. She finds that these narratives talk not of white conquest but of "defense" ("The Common Man's Indian: The Image of the Indian as a Promoter of National Identity in the Early Republic, 1783–1835," paper presented at conference "Native Americans and the Early Republic," United States Capitol Historical Society, Washington, D.C., Mar. 5, 1992).

24. *A True and Wonderful Narrative of the Surprising Captivity and Remarkable Deliverance of Mrs. Frances Scott* (1786), *Garland*

Library, vol. 16 (New York: Garland, 1978), 8–9, 13–16; Ellet, *Pioneer Women*, 110–11; *A Narrative of the Sufferings of Massy Harbison* (1825), *Garland Library*, vol. 42 (New York: Garland, 1977), 32–33; [Deposition] "Account of the Sufferings of Massy Herbeson [*sic*] and her Family . . . Given on Oath before John Wilkins, Esq. one of the Justices of the Peace for the Commonwealth of Pennsylvania," dated May 1792, in Loudon, *A Selection of Some of the Most Interesting Narratives*, 85–90.

25. Loudon, *A Selection of Some of the Most Interesting Narratives*, 28; Drake, *Tragedies*, 285–86.

26. Frost, *Daring and Heroic Deeds*, 206–12.

27. Axtell, *European and the Indian*, 174, 206.

28. Mary Rowlandson, *A Narrative of the Captivity, Sufferings and Removes of Mrs. Mary Rowlandson* (Boston: Z. Fowle, 1770). For more on editions see Namias, "White Captives," 65–70.

29. A sermon and preface do not appear in the 1720 edition, but it is unclear if these were lost or excluded. Consult R. W. G. Vail, *The Voice of the Old Frontier* (New York: Yoseloff, 1949), and Charles Evans, comp., *American Bibliography: A Chronological Dictionary of All Books, Pamphlets, and Periodical Publications Printed in the United States of America from the Genesis of Printing in 1639 Down to and Including the Years 1820*, 14 vols. (New York: P. Smith, 1941–59), for editions.

30. See the triptych on the final page of the Coverly 1771 edition. Boyle's woodcut is on the title page, Coverly's woman with musket is a frontispiece; the woodcuts in his 1771 edition are on the second and last pages of the text. A similar observation about the nationalistic use of the Rowlandson narrative and the gun-toting woman in the woodcut is made by Greg Sieminski, "The Puritan Captivity Narrative and the Politics of the American Revolution," *AQ* (Mar. 1990): 35–56, esp. 35–42, 52.

31. Linda K. Kerber, *Women of the Republic: Intellect and Ideology in Revolutionary America* (Chapel Hill: University of North Carolina Press, 1980), 68–113.

32. Vail thinks Fowle's edition was a reprint of Coverly's. Fowle put an advertisement in the September 12, 1771, *Massachusetts Spy*. The woodcut, Vail notes, "passed from printer to printer" (R. W. G. Vail to C. S. Brigham, Oct. 29, 1955, AAS Correspondence File, AAS).

33. *A New Touch of the Times. Well Adapted to the Distressing Situation of Every Seaport Town by a Daughter of Liberty living at Marblehead*, listed in Worthington Chauncy Ford, *Broadsides, Ballads, etc. Printed in Massachusetts* (Boston, 1922), 299, no. 2161, in Kerber, *Women of the Republic*, 107, and in Joan Hoff Wilson, "The Illusion of Change: Women and the American Revolution," in *The American Revolution in the History of American Radicalism*, ed. Alfred F. Young

(DeKalb: Northern Illinois University Press, 1976), 383. There appears to be some disagreement about the date of issue, with Wilson saying 1777 and Kerber, 1779.

34. *A Narrative of Captivity* (Coverly, 1771), 4.

35. Benjamin V. Franklin, ed., *Boston Printers, Publishers, and Book-sellers 1640–1800* (Boston: G. K. Hall, 1980), 56–57, 76–80, 187–91.

36. Ibid. All three Boston printers were known for a variety of other works, including religious tracts, juvenilia, songs, almanacs, poems, and other typical late eighteenth-century American colonial output. Boyle was in the military forces before the Revolution, and his diaries recount the critical events of the war. Also see "John Boyle's Journal of Occurrences in Boston, 1759–1788," *New England Historical and Genealogical Register* (Apr. 1930): 142–43.

37. William Hubbard, *A Narrative of the Indian Wars in New-England, from the First Planting Thereof in the Year 1607, to the Year 1677* (Boston: John Boyle, 1775), v–viii. The title for this edition on Rowlandson reads, "A Particular account of the suffering and captivity of Mrs. *Rowlandson*, written by herself, may be had of the publisher hereof. Price 6s." (ibid., 117).

38. Rowlandson, *True History*, 36. Also see Ann Stanford, "Mary Rowlandson's Journey to Redemption," *Ariel* 7 (July 1976): 27–37; David Downing, "'Streams of Scripture Comfort': Mary Rowlandson's Typological Use of the Bible," *EAL* 15 (1980–81): 252–59. For more historical and geographical information see Douglas Edward Leach, "The 'Whens' of Mary Rowlandson's Captivity," *NEQ* 34 (Sept. 1961): 352–63; Pauline Turner Strong, "Captivated by the Other: English Representations of Identity and Power in Colonial North America, 1682–1736," paper presented at the Western Social Science Association, Denver, Apr. 1988; Annette Kolodny, *The Land Before Her: Fantasy and Experience of the American Frontiers, 1630–1860* (Chapel Hill: University of North Carolina Press, 1984), 17–35; Slotkin, *Regeneration through Violence*, chap. 3; Slotkin, *Fatal Environment*, 63–64; and more recently, Kathryn Zabelle Derounian, "The Publication, Promotion, and Distribution of Mary Rowlandson's Indian Captivity Narrative in the Seventeenth Century," *EAL* 23, no. 3 (1988): 239–61.

39. Frost, *Thrilling Adventures*, 43–44, and engravings 26 and 29. For other views of the transitions in white women's lives as a result of the Revolution see Kerber, *Women of the Republic*; Mary Beth Norton, *Liberty's Daughters: The Revolutionary Experience of American Women, 1750–1800* (Boston: Little, Brown, 1980).

40. *A True Narrative of the Sufferings of Mary Kinnan*, in *Held Captive by Indians: Selective Narratives, 1642–1836*, ed. Richard VanDer-Beets (Knoxville: University of Tennessee Press, 1973), 319–20. My theory here was framed before reading Melvin J. Thorne, who concurs in some respects on Frail Flowers and Amazons in "Fainters

and Fighters: Images of Women in the Indian Captivity Narratives," *Midwest Quarterly* 23 (Summer 1982): 426–36.

41. Pearce, "Significances," 16. Carl C. Rister verifies Horn's narrative and the lives of other Comanche captives in his introductions. Rister is virulently anti–Indian, but his reprint of Horn is more explicit and complete than the Garland reprints (*Comanche Bondage . . . with an Annotated Reprint of Sarah Ann Horn's Narrative of Her Captivity among the Comanches etc.* [Glendale, Calif.: Arthur H. Clark, 1955]).

42. Pearce, "Significances," 16; Richard VanDerBeets, *The Indian Captivity Narrative: An American Genre* (Lanham, Md.: University Press of America, 1984), ix–x, 13–36. Examples of Frail Flower narratives include *Narrative of the Captivity and Extreme Sufferings of Mrs. Clarissa Plummer; History of the Captivity and Providential Release Therefrom of Mrs. Caroline Harris* (1838), *Garland Library*, vol. 54 (New York: Garland, 1977).

43. Eliza Swan (or the writer of her story) does not mention what group of Indians captured her. Only Indian "savages" are discussed. It may be she was with Osage. See Eliza Swan, *An Affecting Account of the Tragical Death of Major Swan, and of the Captivity of Mrs. Swan and Infant Child, by the Savages* (1815), *Garland Library*, vol. 33 (New York: Garland, 1978), 8, 12–14. Glenda Riley indicates that women often became hysterical on the frontier because of feelings of physical weakness, insecurities about their husbands' protection, and propaganda about Indian barbarity fed to them before coming West (*Women and Indians on the Frontier, 1825–1915* [Albuquerque: University of New Mexico Press, 1984], 84–104).

44. *Captivity of Mrs. Caroline Harris*, 27, 38–39; *Sufferings of Mrs. Clarissa Plummer*, 5–6, 12.

45. Sarah Ann Horn, *A Narrative of the Captivity of Mrs. Horn* (1839), *Garland Library*, vol. 54 (New York: Garland, 1977), 4, 21.

46. [Deposition] "Account of the Sufferings of Massy Herbeson," in Loudon, *A Selection of Some of the Most Interesting Narratives*, 1:85–90.

47. On the popularity and publication of these editions see Frank Luther Mott, *Golden Multitudes: The Story of Best Sellers in the United States* (New York: Macmillan, 1947), 305. *Narrative of the Sufferings of Massy Harbison* (1825); *A Narrative of the Suffering of Massy Harbison*, ed. John Winter (Pittsburgh: D. and M. Macleans, [1828]).

48. *Narrative of the Sufferings of Massy Harbison* (1825), iv.

49. Quote from ibid., parts IV and V and letters 13–25; description of the text, 31–33, and St. Clair letters and deposition, 85–90.

50. Rayna D. Green, "The Indian in Popular American Culture," in *HNAI/IWR*, 587–606; Louise K. Barnett traces the rise of the "frontier romance" out of the captivity narrative in *The Ignoble Savage: American Literary Racism, 1790–1890* (Westport, Conn.: Greenwood Press, 1975), 21–43, 48–49; Smith, *Virgin Land*, 64–76; Slotkin, *Re-*

generation through Violence; Pearce, *Savages of America*. On popular literature see Janice A. Radway, *Reading the Romance: Women, Patriarchy, and Popular Literature* (Chapel Hill: University of North Carolina Press, 1984). On images see Vivien Green Fryd, "Two Sculptures for the Capitol: Horatio Greenough's *Rescue* and Luigi Perisco's *Discovery of America*," *American Art Journal* 19, no. 2 (1987): 16–19; Pauline Turner Strong, "Captive Images: Stereotypes that Justified Colonial Expansion on the American Frontier Were a Legacy of a Seventeenth-Century War," *Natural History*, Dec. 1985, pp. 50–56.

51. Rachel Plummer, "Narrative of the Capture and Subsequent Sufferings of Mrs. Rachel Plummer, Written by Herself," in *Held Captive by Indians*, ed. VanDerBeets, 334–42. This edition merges the 1839 and 1844 editions.

52. Carroll Smith-Rosenberg, *Disorderly Conduct: Visions of Gender in Victorian America* (New York: Knopf, 1986), 90–108; Smith-Rosenberg, "Sex as Symbol in Victorian Purity: An Ethnohistorical Analysis of Jacksonian America," in *Turning Points: Historical and Sociological Essays on the Family*, ed. John Demos and Sarane Spence Boocock (Chicago: University of Chicago Press, 1978), 212–47, esp. 217–18, 151–74; John Mack Faragher, *Women and Men on the Overland Trail* (New Haven: Yale University Press, 1979); Barbara Welter, "The Cult of True Womanhood, 1820–1860," *AQ* 18 (Summer 1966): 151–74. Lois W. Banner calls this type of feminine beauty "the steel-engraving lady" and describes it as "sylphlike," "ultra-attenuated," "etherealized," "fragile," "frail," and "slight" (*American Beauty: A Social History through Two Centuries of the American Idea, Ideal, and Image of the Beautiful Woman* [Chicago: University of Chicago Press, 1983], 44–57).

53. Mary Barber, *The True Narrative of the Five Years' Suffering & Perilous Adventures* (Philadelphia: Barclay, 1873), 22.

54. Ibid., 68–70.

55. Ibid. Elizabeth Pleck points out that in this period social purity reformers played on the image of "the Pure Woman and the Brutish Man" to protect the home. This was another plea to protect the Anglo-Saxon home (*Domestic Tyranny: The Making of American Social Policy from Colonial Times to the Present* [New York: Oxford University Press, 1986], 88–107).

56. Pearce, *Savages of America*; Strong, "Captive Images," 50–56; Fryd, "Two Sculptures for the Capitol," 16–19.

57. Mary McDonnell's rendition of Stands with a Fist in Kevin Costner's *Dances with Wolves* (1991) is certainly a survivor type. Gene Quillen notes the connections of her role with an eighteenth-century narrative in her unpublished paper, "*Dances with Wolves* and the Tradition of the Captivity Narrative" (1991), 8–9; Riley, *Women and Indians*.

1. Alden T. Vaughan, *American Genesis: Captain John Smith and the Founding of Virginia* (Boston: Little, Brown, 1975), 37. For Smith's description of the events see John Smith, *A Generall Historie of Virginia, New-England, and the Summer Isles*, The Third Booke, in Edward Arber and A. G. Bradley, eds., *Travels and Works of Captain John Smith: President of Virginia, and Admiral of New England, 1580–1631*, 2 vols. (Edinburgh: J. Grant, 1910), 2:397. Also see Philip L. Barbour, ed., *The Complete Works of Captain John Smith (1580–1631) in Three Volumes* (Chapel Hill: University of North Carolina Press, 1986). For differing views on contact with Indians in Virginia see Nancy Oestreich Lurie, "Indian Cultural Adjustment to European Civilization," in *Interpreting Colonial America: Selected Readings*, ed. James Kirby Martin (New York: Harper & Row, 1973), 36–45; Helen C. Rountree, *Pocahontas's People: The Powhatan Indians of Virginia through Four Centuries* (Norman: University of Oklahoma Press, 1990).

2. Another twenty-one (2.5 percent) of the males probably died as compared to another two (1.2 percent) of the females. Eight male and three female children died or were killed. See Alden T. Vaughan and Daniel K. Richter, "Crossing the Cultural Divide: Indians and New Englanders, 1605–1763," *AAS* 90 (Apr. 16, 1980): 66–67. On assimilation see A. Irving Hallowell, "American Indians, White and Black: The Phenomenon of Transculturalization," in *Contributions to Anthropology: Selected Papers of A. Irving Hallowell*, with introductions by Raymond D. Fogelson (Chicago: University of Chicago Press, 1976), 498–552; J. Norman Heard, *White into Red: A Study of the Assimilation of White Persons Captured by Indians* (Metuchen, N.J.: Scarecrow Press, 1973); Cornelius J. Jaenen, *Friend and Foe: Aspects of French-Amerindian Cultural Conflict in the Sixteenth and Seventeenth Centuries* (New York: Columbia University Press, 1976); William A. Starna and Ralph Watkins, "Northern Iroquois Slavery," *EH* 38 (Winter 1991): 34–57; Richard VanDerBeets, "The Indian Captivity Narrative: An American Genre" (Ph.D. dissertation, University of the Pacific, 1973).

3. Jogues's letter was signed August 5, 1643. The work was first printed in French in 1655 and had a long print history on both sides of the Atlantic, in French and in English. Biographers report that Jogues's head was cut off and placed on a pole in a Mohawk village ("Captivity of Father Isaac Jogues, of the Society of Jesus, among the Mohawks," [1655] taken from John Gilmary Shea, *Perils of the Ocean and Wilderness* [1857] in *Held Captive by Indians: Selective Narratives, 1642–1836*, ed. Richard VanDerBeets [Knoxville: University of Tennessee Press, 1973], 3–40, esp. 4, 9–12, 19). For a comparison of savage behavior, the body of King Philip (Metacom, Metacomet) was quar-

tered and decapitated after the 1675 war in New England. The head was placed on a pole in Plymouth and remained there for twenty-five years (Alvin M. Josephy, Jr., *The Patriot Chiefs* [New York: Viking, 1961], 61–62). One of Philip's hands was sent to Boston for display. His body was not buried but, "having been quartered, was hung upon four trees" (Samuel G. Drake, *Biography and History of the Indians of North America, from Its First Discovery* [Boston: Benjamin B. Muzzey, 1851], 227). For an analysis of the early Indian wars see Wilcomb E. Washburn, "Seventeenth-Century Indian Wars," in *HNAI/Northeast*, 89–100; Washburn, "The Moral and Legal Justifications for Dispossessing the Indians," in *Seventeenth-Century America: Essays in Colonial History*, ed. James M. Smith (Chapel Hill: University of North Carolina Press, 1959), 15–32. For an analysis of the Huron people and Jogues's stay among them see Bruce G. Trigger, *The Children of Aataentsic: A History of the Huron People to 1660* (Montreal: McGill–Queen's University Press, 1976), 522, 541, 645–47, 654–57. Trigger also analyzes the capture and torture sequence among the Hurons. His work indicates that men, women, and children taken by the the Hurons in the early and mid-seventeenth century were often taken alive and tortured. His descriptions relate primarily to Huron captures of Iroquois and other Indian enemies but also include French captives (ibid., 68–75).

4. Daniel K. Richter mentions the fund-raising issues of the Jesuits and "suggests a need for caution" in using the *Relations* as sources ("Iroquois versus Iroquois: Jesuit Missions and Christianity in Village Politics, 1642–1886," *EH* 32 [1985]: 1–16, esp. 1).

5. Vaughan and Richter, "Cultural Divide," 66–67.

6. John Gyles, *Memoirs of Odd Adventures, Strange Deliverances* [1736], in *Puritans among the Indians: Accounts of Captivity and Redemption, 1676–1724*, ed. Alden T. Vaughan and Edward W. Clark (Cambridge, Mass.: Harvard University Press, 1981), 93, 105, 106, 109, 81–83.

7. " 'Quentin Stockwell's Relation of His Captivity and Redemption' Reported by Increase Mather," in *Puritans among the Indians*, ed. Vaughan and Clark, 81–83, 89. On the literature of the pulpit as war propaganda see Richard Slotkin and James K. Folsom, eds., *So Dreadfull a Judgment: Puritan Responses to King Philip's War, 1676–1677* (Middletown, Conn.: Wesleyan University Press, 1978).

8. *Indian Captivities: Life in the Wigwam*, ed. Samuel G. Drake (New York: Miller, Orton, 1857), 109–10, 113.

9. *An Account of the Remarkable Occurrences in the Life and Travels of Colonel James Smith* [1799] in *Indian Captivities*, ed. Drake, 178–252, esp. 182.

10. W. M. Beauchamp says that cases of women (in this case enemies of the Iroquois) being burned and eaten were common in the seventeenth century. He cites Jogues's account among others ("Iro-

quois Women," *Journal of American Folk-Lore* 13 [1900]: 81–91, esp. 84). Frederick W. Waugh, citing sources from the *Jesuit Relations*, says that "ceremonial cannibalism" was "quite a common practice" and body parts were eaten as part of rites of sympathetic magic (*Iroquois Foods and Food Preparation* [Ottawa: Government Printing Bureau, 1916], 134). Buell H. Quain, also using Jesuit sources, stresses the "ritualistic nature" of such practice ("The Iroquois," in *Cooperation and Competition among Primitive Peoples*, ed. Margaret Mead [New York: McGraw-Hill, 1937], 253–54). William N. Fenton documents a number of cases of Indian men and women who committed suicide to escape harm from their Iroquois captors. Most of Fenton's cases are taken from the Jesuit records (*Iroquois Suicide: A Study in Stability of a Culture Pattern* [Washington, D.C.: U.S. Government Printing Office, 1941]).

11. John D. Hunter, *Manners and Customs of Several Indian Tribes Located West of the Mississippi* (1823; rpt. Minneapolis: Ross & Haines, 1957); also *Garland Library*, vol. 39 (New York: Garland, 1977), 27. For an account of the torture of an infant child reported by Rachel Plummer with the Comanches see Rachel Plummer, "Narrative of the Capture and Subsequent Sufferings of Mrs. Rachel Plummer, Written by Herself," in *Held Captive by Indians*, ed. VanDerBeets. On torture see Nathaniel Knowles, "The Torture of Captives by the Indians of Eastern North America" (Ph.D. dissertation, University of Pennsylvania, 1940).

12. "Captivity of Father Isaac Jogues," in *Held Captive by Indians*, ed. VanDerBeets, 9, 7, 38.

13. Rev. Edward V. Neill, *The History of Minnesota from the French Explorations to the Present Time*, 5th ed. (Minneapolis: Minnesota Historical Society, 1883), 128–33; Father Hennepin, *The New Discovery of a Vast Country*, 2 vols., ed. Reuben Gold Thwaites (Chicago: A. C. McClurg, 1903); "Memoir of Duluth on the Sioux Country, 1678–1682," in *Early Narratives of the Northwest, 1634–1699*, ed. Louise Phelps Kellogg (New York: Charles Scribner's Sons, 1917), 331–33, 332, n. 1. The validity of Hennepin's account is discussed in F. Sanford Cutler, "An Evaluation of Documents Useful to the Ethnohistorian: The Writings of Father Hennepin," *Proceedings of the Minnesota Academy of Science* 23 (1955): 23–28.

14. John Williams, "The Redeemed Captive Returning to Zion," in *Puritans among the Indians*, ed. Vaughan and Clark, 167; David Hawke, *The Colonial Experience* (Indianapolis: Bobbs-Merrill, 1966), 329–30. For a museum and shrine to the captives of Deerfield, see the second-floor exhibit in the museum in Historic Deerfield, Massachusetts. For comparisons of British Protestant and French Catholic successes among the Indians, see James Axtell, *The Invasion Within: The Contest of Cultures in Colonial America* (New York: Oxford University Press, 1985), 80, also chaps. 1–6. On the Deerfield experi-

ences of Williams, Stockwell, and others see Richard I. Melvoin, *New England Outpost: War and Society in Colonial Deerfield* (New York: Norton, 1989), esp. chaps. 7–9, and the work of John Demos on Eunice Williams (forthcoming).

15. Williams, "Redeemed Captive," in *Puritans among the Indians*, ed. Vaughan and Clark, 168, 225; Edward W. Clark, *The Redeemed Captive: John Williams* (Amherst: University of Massachusetts Press, 1976), 16.

16. Clark, *Redeemed Captive*, 9; Williams, "Redeemed Captive," in *Puritans among the Indians*, ed. Vaughan and Clark, 173, 178, 180. For the language of Puritan New England's sermons see Sacvan Bercovitch, *The American Jeremiad* (Madison: University of Wisconsin Press, 1978), and Mason I. Lowance, Jr., *The Language of Canaan: Metaphor and Symbol in New England from the Puritans to the Transcendentalists* (Cambridge, Mass.: Harvard University Press, 1980).

17. Williams, "Redeemed Captive," in *Puritans among the Indians*, ed. Vaughan and Clark, 195, 197.

18. Ibid., 204, 209, 212, 215, 218; also 204–20 for correspondence.

19. The small book called itself a "narrative of facts, intended for the instruction and improvement of children and youth taken from an interesting portion of the early history of our country" (A. Phelps, *The Deerfield Captive*, 3d ed. [Greenfield, Mass.: n.p., 1837], 11–12, NL).

20. Vaughan, *American Genesis*, 117. Also see A. L. Rouse, *The Elizabethans and America: The Trevelyan Lectures at Cambridge, 1958* (New York: Harper & Row, 1959).

21. John Smith, "Part of the Travels of Capt. John Smith amongst Turks, Tartars and others," and "A reprint, with variations of the First Part of the *Map of Virginia*," 1612, both in Arber and Bradley, eds., *Travels and Works*, illus. 2:821–24, and illus. 1:342.

22. See Christian F. Feest, "Virginia Algonquians," in *HNAI/Northeast*, 253–70. Richard Drinnon suggests that relationships to the sensual both attracted and frightened Euro-Americans ("The Metaphysics of Dancing Tribes," in *The American Indian and the Problem of History*, ed. Calvin Martin [New York: Oxford University Press, 1987], 106–13). NL photographer Ken Cain pointed out that the woman around the fire looked like a blond.

23. John Smith, *A True Relation*, in *Virginia Reader: A Treasury of Writings from the First Voyages to the Present*, ed. Frances C. Rosenberger (New York: E. P. Dutton, 1948), 77, 78, 81, 84; Barbour, ed., *The Complete Works of Captain John Smith*, 1:43–45.

24. Father Hennepin also found that the mariner's compass dazzled the Dakotas (Neill, *History of Minnesota*, 152). In the film *Dances with Wolves*, actor and director Kevin Costner succeeds in a similar feat, dazzling the Lakotas with a magnifying field glass.

25. See Vaughan, *American Genesis*, 81, 84.

26. Richard Slotkin, *Regeneration through Violence: The Mythology*

of the American Frontier, 1600–1860 (Middletown, Conn.: Wesleyan University Press, 1973), 294–301; Henry Nash Smith, *Virgin Land: The American West as Symbol and Myth* (New York: Vintage Books, 1959), 54–63.

27. John Filson, *The Discovery, Settlement and Present State of Kentucke . . . The Adventures of Col. Daniel Boon* (1784), *Garland Library*, vol. 14 (New York: Garland, 1978); Timothy Flint, *The First White Man of the West* (Cincinnati: H. M. Ruilson, Queen City Publishing House, 1856).

28. Filson, *Discovery*, 51–52, 60, 63–66.

29. Ibid., 52.

30. Ibid., 63.

31. Ibid., 60.

32. Frost gave a chapter to the capture and rescue of the daughters, Elizabeth Ellet gave Mrs. Boone a chapter in *Pioneer Women of the West*, and Timothy Flint devoted a chapter to each episode of capture. See John Frost, *Daring and Heroic Deeds of American Women* (Philadelphia: G. G. Evans, 1860), 26; E[lizabeth] F. Ellet, *Pioneer Women of the West* (New York: Charles Scribner, 1852), 42–57.

33. Flint, *First White Man of the West*, 85–86.

34. Ibid., 86.

35. Ibid., 87–88, 94–95.

36. Edwin Eastman, *Seven and Nine Years among the Camanches and Apaches: An Autobiography* (Jersey City, N.J.: Clark Johnson, M.D., 1873), 210, 216–17.

37. Richard Slotkin emphasizes the role of the other in nineteenth-century narratives and history in the period of industrialization in *The Fatal Environment: The Myth of the Frontier in the Age of Industrialization, 1800–1890* (New York: Atheneum, 1985).

38. Smith, *Virgin Land*, 101 and chap. 9. Smith discusses *Seth Jones* in the first section of the chapter.

39. Edward Sylvester Ellis, *Seth Jones; or The Captives of the Frontier*, 7th ed., Beadles Half Dime Library, vol. 30, no. 60 (New York: Beadle and Adams, ca. 1878).

40. Interview, June 24, 1900, in Albert Johannsen, *The House of Beadle and Adams and Its Dime and Nickel Novels: The Story of a Vanished Literature*, 2 vols. (Norman: University of Oklahoma Press, 1950), 2:32.

41. Ibid. Edward S. Ellis's admiration for Boone is apparent in his biography, *The Life and Times of Col. Daniel Boone: Hunter, Soldier, and Pioneer* (Chicago: Union School Finishing Co., n.d.).

42. Ellis, *Seth Jones*, 3.

43. Ibid., chaps. 3 and 5.

44. Gyles, *Memoirs of Odd Adventures*, in *Puritans among the Indians*, ed. Vaughan and Clark, 93, 101–2, 105–6.

45. Ibid., 107–9, 111, 113–14.

46. Ibid., 95, 116, 103n., 116–20.

47. Gyles spent three of his nine captive years with the French. On Maliseets and Eastern Abenakis see Vincent O. Erickson, "Maliseet-Passamaquoddy," 123–36, and Dean R. Snow, "Eastern Abenaki," in *HNAI/Northeast.*

48. Hunter, *Manners and Customs*, 26–27, 34–35. See Father Jogues on the torture of the Huron chief cited earlier. Also see Richard Drinnon's introduction to his edition of *Memoirs of a Captivity among the Indians of North America: John Dunn Hunter* [1824] (New York: Schocken, 1973).

49. Hunter, *Manners and Customs*, 34–35. My emphasis on mothers and relationship with women differs from Leslie Fiedler's, who stresses the WASP male-Indian male bond (*The Return of the Vanishing American* [New York: Stein and Day, 1968], 24 and chap. 2).

50. Hunter, *Manners and Customs*, 35.

51. Ibid., 43, 62, 64.

52. Ibid., 44.

53. Ibid., 272–73.

54. Ibid., 135.

55. Edwin James, *A Narrative of the Captivity and Adventures of John Tanner* (1830), *Garland Library*, vol. 46 (New York: Garland, 1975), 1–2.

56. John T. Fierst, "Return to 'Civilization': John Tanner's Troubled Years at Sault Ste. Marie," *Minnesota History* 50 (Spring 1986): 23.

57. Edwin James with Noel Loomis, *A Narrative of the Captivity and Adventures of John Tanner* (1830; rpt. Minneapolis: Ross and Haines, 1956), xii, 15, 16, 27.

58. Ibid., 115, 119, 120, 205, 230–32, x–xvi.

59. In 1846 he was accused of murdering James Schoolcraft, brother of Henry Rowe Schoolcraft, Indian agent and compiler of a multi-volume work on North American Indians. On Schoolcraft see Robert E. Bieder, *Science Encounters the Indian, 1820–1880: The Early Years of American Ethnography* (Norman: University of Oklahoma Press, 1986), 146–94; Bieder, "Henry Rowe Schoolcraft," in *HNAI/IWR*, 680–81; P. Richard Metcalf, "John Tanner," in *HNAI/IWR*, 689; Fierst, "Return to 'Civilization,'" 23–36. Fierst says Tanner may have had four wives and ten children (ibid., 27, n. 12).

60. The account is from Henry Sheldon of Vermont, who visited his sister Harriet Caswell at the New York Seneca Mission (Harriet Caswell, *Our Life among the Iroquois Indians* [Boston: Congregational Sunday School and Publishing Society, 1892], 51–62). Other white males who spent their youth among eastern Indians were John Slover among the Shawnees (from age eight to age twenty) in the 1760s and 1770s and John Brickell among the Delawares. John R. Swanton finds that among thirty captives, fifteen male and fifteen female, four males became chiefs and three or four females became the wives of

chiefs. See Swanton, "Ethnology—Notes on the Mental Assimilation of Races," *Journal of the Washington Academy of Sciences* 16 (Nov. 3, 1926): 495–96, 501.

61. James, *Narrative of John Tanner*, 20. White Chief was also taunted for being white.

62. Matthew Brayton with John H. A. Bone, *Indian Captive: A Narrative of the Adventures and Sufferings of Matthew Brayton* (1860), *Garland Library*, vol. 76 (New York: Garland, 1977), 6–10. On the nature of as-told-to traditions among native people of the Americas see Gretchen M. Bataille and Kathleen Mullen Sands, *American Indian Women: Telling Their Lives* (Lincoln: University of Nebraska Press, 1984), 3–26.

63. Natalie Zemon Davis, "Bloodshed and the Woman's Voice: Gender and Pardon Tales in 16th Century France," paper presented at Harvard University, Mar. 6, 1987; Davis, *Fiction in the Archives: Pardon Tales of Sixteenth-Century France* (Stanford: Stanford University Press, 1987).

64. Some scholars attribute a significant part of Rowlandson's narrative to her husband, minister John Rowlandson; others claim Cotton Mather had a hand in it. I would not deny these influences, but I think she was quite capable of doing the writing herself. In any case, John's piece in her original is not as well written as hers.

65. As Leslie Fiedler says, "It is hard to tell history from myth in such accounts, though these earliest attempts to create an image of the Indian for the American imagination usually presented themselves as 'true relations' of fact. Capt. John Smith may seem to have fabricated rather than recorded the story of his encounter with Pocahontas; but his early readers took as literal truth the fanciful tale [of his rescue]" ("The Indian in Literature in English," in *HNAI/IWR*, 573).

66. Charles Johnston, *A Narrative of the Incidents Attending the Capture, Detention, and Ransom of Charles Johnston* [1827] in *Held Captive by Indians*, ed. VanDerBeets, 314.

3: EXPLORING SEXUAL BOUNDARIES

1. "Love-charm Song," Ojibwa (Chippewa) is in *I Am the Fire of Time: The Voices of Native American Women*, ed. Jane B. Katz (New York: E. P. Dutton, 1977), 49. Letter to Sir Thomas Dale from John Rolfe, Apr. 1614, in *The Indian and the White Man*, ed. Wilcomb E. Washburn (Garden City, N.Y.: Anchor Books, 1964), 20–25. See James Axtell, *The Invasion Within: The Conquest of Cultures in Colonial America* (New York: Oxford University Press, 1985), 287–301. There certainly were attempts at early missionary activity and considerable belief in the eighteenth century that the "savage" nature of Indi-

ans could and should be transformed by Christianization. See Roy Harvey Pearce, *Savagism and Civilization: A Study of the Indian and the American Mind*, rev. ed. (Berkeley: University of California Press, 1988), 42–44. On the issue of Catholic versus Protestant churches in the Americas see Carl N. Degler, *Neither Black nor White: Slavery and Race Relations in Brazil and the United States* (New York: Macmillan, 1971), 33–37, as opposed to Frank Tannenbaum's views in *Slave and Citizen: The Negro in the Americas* (New York: Vintage Books, 1946). On Protestant conversion efforts see Richard W. Cogley, "John Eliot in Recent Scholarship," *AICRJ* 14, no. 2 (1990): 77–92.

2. Gary Nash, "Red, White, and Black," in *The Great Fear: Race in the Mind of America*, ed. Gary Nash and Richard Weiss (New York: Holt, Rinehart and Winston, 1970), chap. 1; Rayna Diane Green, "The Only Good Indian: The Image of the Indian in American Vernacular Culture" (Ph.D. dissertation, Indiana University, 1973), 380–87.

3. Winthrop Jordan, *White over Black: American Attitudes toward the Negro, 1550–1812*, 2d ed. (Baltimore: Penguin, 1969); James Axtell, *The European and the Indian: Essays in the Ethnohistory of Colonial North America* (New York: Oxford University Press, 1981), 181–82.

4. Lois Green Carr and Lorena S. Walsh, "The Planter's Wife: The Experience of White Women in Seventeenth-Century Maryland," *WMQ* 3d ser., 34 (1977): 542–71; Edmund S. Morgan, *American Slavery, American Freedom: The Ordeal of Colonial Virginia* (New York: Norton, 1975).

5. Axtell, *European and the Indian*, 156. On the impact of Catholicism see Axtell, *Invasion Within*, esp. chap. 7. For examples of adoption of captives see William N. Fenton, "Northern Iroquois Culture Patterns," in *HNAI/Northeast*, 316; Jack Campisi, "Oneida," citing the *Jesuit Relations*, in *HNAI/Northeast*, 482; Robert F. Berkhofer, Jr., sees more similarities than differences in European settlement policies (*The White Man's Indian: Images of the American Indian from Columbus to the Present* [New York: Vintage Books, 1979], 115–16).

6. Jordan, *White over Black*, 7, 11; Mather on Dustan, in *Decennium Luctuosum*, 138–43, and *Magnalia Christi Americana* in *Puritans among the Indians: Accounts of Captivity and Redemption, 1676–1724*, ed. Alden T. Vaughan and Edward W. Clark (Cambridge, Mass.: Harvard University Press, 1981), 162–64. John Smith, *A Generall Historie of Virginia, New-England, and the Summer Isles*, The Third Booke, in Edward Arber and A. G. Bradley, eds., *Travels and Works of Captain John Smith: President of Virginia, and Admiral of New England, 1580–1631*, 2 vols. (Edinburgh: J. Grant, 1910), 2:400–401. Alden T. Vaughan argues that the use of color words like *red* and *redskin* came in the nineteenth century, in "From White Man to Redskin: Changing Anglo-American Perceptions of the American Indian," *AHR* 87 (Oct. 1982): 917–53. Neal Salisbury disagrees; he argues that color counted,

in "Conquest of the 'Savage': Puritans, Puritan Missionaries, and Indians, 1620–1680" (Ph.D. dissertation, University of California, Los Angeles, 1972), 51. For a comparison of English and Spanish early texts of conquest see Patricia Seed, "Taking Possession and Reading Texts: Establishing the Authority of Overseas Empires," *WMQ* 3d ser., 49 (Apr. 1992): 183–209.

7. John Smith, *A True Relation* and *Generall Historie*, both in Arber and Bradley, eds., *Travel and Works*, 2:709, 74, 79, 94; 1:401. Leslie Fiedler points out how difficult it is "for the child's mind, which loves the story of Pocahontas best of all, to remember, or remembering quite to believe that she married the wrong man" (*The Return of the Vanishing American* [New York: Stein and Day, 1968], 70). See also Smith, *Generall Historie*, 2:529; Mary V. Dearborn, *Pocahontas's Daughters: Gender and Ethnicity in American Culture* (New York: Oxford University Press, 1986), chaps. 5 and 6.

8. Francis Jennings, *The Invasion of America: Indians, Colonialism, and the Cant of Conquest* (New York: Norton, 1975), 223–25; John Underhill, *News from America* (1638; rpt. Amsterdam: Da Capo Press, 1971), 17. Also on the Pequot War see Wilcomb E. Washburn, "Seventeenth-Century Indian Wars," in *HNAI/Northeast*, 89–100; Neal Salisbury, *Manitou and Providence: Indians, Europeans, and the Making of New England, 1500–1643* (New York: Oxford University Press, 1982), 215–25.

9. Benjamin Thompson, *New England's Crisis*, in *So Dreadfull a Judgment: Puritan Responses to King Philip's War, 1676–1677*, ed. Richard Slotkin and James K. Folsom (Middletown, Conn.: Wesleyan University Press, 1978), 215–33 for entire poem, esp. 219.

10. Axtell, *Invasion Within*, 310. Quote from Paul Le Jeune in William A. Starna and Ralph Watkins, "Northern Iroquois Slavery," *EH* 38 (Winter 1991): 50. They do not deal with New England but raise the question of just how benevolent adoption was and conclude that it was a form of slavery. Theda Perdue finds that women were not usually sexually violated among the Cherokees: "This celibacy probably resulted from the widespread practice among the southeastern Indians of abstaining from sexual intercourse for several days before, during, and after their return from war and not from an inactive libido or any particular regard for their female prisoners. James Adair, who accompanied a war-party in the mid-eighteenth century, noted with assurance that after the period of abstinence was over 'some of them forced their captives, notwithstanding their pressing entreaties and tears' " (*Slavery and the Evolution of Cherokee Society, 1540–1866* [Knoxville: University of Tennessee Press, 1978], 6–7).

11. Mary Rowlandson, *A True History of the Captivity & Restoration of Mrs. Mary Rowlandson* (1682), *Garland Library*, vol. 1 (New York: Garland, 1977), 32. "The custom of males and females sleep-

ing indiscriminately together in the same lodge prevails without the thought or association of an idea of impropriety, or a breach of decorum" and "exists without producing any criminal desire" (John D. Hunter, *Manners and Customs of Several Indian Tribes Located West of the Mississippi* [1823; rpt. Minneapolis: Ross & Haines, 1957], 241; also *Garland Library*, vol. 39 [New York: Garland, 1977], 241).

12. Salisbury, "Conquest of the 'Savage,'" 41, 45–46; [Elizabeth Hanson], *God's Mercy Surmounting Man's Cruelty*, in *Puritans among the Indians*, ed. Vaughan and Clark, 26. Privacy was minimal in early colonial New England housing. See John Demos, *A Little Commonwealth: Family Life in Plymouth Colony* (New York: Oxford University Press, 1970), 44, 47; Laurel Thatcher Ulrich, *Good Wives: Image and Reality in the Lives of Women in Northern New England, 1650–1750* (New York: Knopf, 1982), 95.

13. For a different view see Richard Slotkin, *Regeneration through Violence: The Mythology of the American Frontier, 1600–1860* (Middletown, Conn.: Wesleyan University Press, 1973), 128–29.

14. Axtell, *Invasion Within*, 287.

15. John Williams, "The Redeemed Captive Returning to Zion," in *Puritans among the Indians*, ed. Vaughan and Clark, 188–89, 225.

16. Ibid., 188; Emma Lewis Coleman, *New England Captives Carried to Canada: Between 1677 and 1760*, 2 vols. (Portland, Maine: Southworth Press, 1925), 2:54–64; Dawn Lander Gherman called Eunice Williams the first of the "white squaw" legend and one interesting to a public "eager to interpret a woman's history according to its own fantasies" ("From Parlour to Tepee: The White Squaw on the American Frontier" [Ph.D. dissertation, University of Massachusetts, 1975], 71, 79, 86). See also Stephen W. Williams, ed., *The Redeemed Captive Returning to Zion* (Northampton: Hopkins, Bridgman and Co., 1853), 144–61.

17. "Understandably," notes Gherman, "there is that part of any culture which is reluctant to admit that taboos have been violated, but there is as well that part which is intrigued with and publishes those violations" ("From Parlour to Tepee," 84). See John Demos's forthcoming book on Eunice Williams.

18. I refer here to the philosophy of Martin Buber in *I and Thou*, trans. and prologue Walter Kaufman (New York: Scribner, 1970), and to Peter Isaac Rose, *They and We: Racial and Ethnic Relations in the United States* (New York: Random House, 1964).

19. Ulrich, *Good Wives*, 208–14; Axtell, *Invasion Within*, 292–93.

20. I use the term *family books* to refer to the popular nineteenth-century anthologies that emerged in the 1840s and continued through the century. These were anthologies made for family use—equivalent to coffee table books in our own age. They were larger than the typical book (about ten by seven inches) and included full-page illustrations.

21. Jemima Howe, *A Genuine and Correct Account of the Cap-*

tivity, Sufferings & Deliverance of Mrs. Jemima Howe, of Hinsdale, in New-Hampshire (1792), *Garland Library*, vol. 19 (New York: Garland, 1977). See the brief print history in Alden T. Vaughan, *Narratives of North American Indian Captivity: A Selective Bibliography* (New York: Garland, 1983), 1:34.

22. Howe, *Genuine and Correct Account of the Captivity*, 14–15. Howe was later called the "Fair Captive." A historical marker for "Jemima Tute" (1723–1805) memorializes her at Fort Bridgeman in Vernon, Vermont. Kirsten Cappy has tracked this and other elements of her life in "The Fair Captive," paper, Wheaton College, Dec. 1991, esp. 33.

23. "Civilized men who gave in to the temptations of savagism and its simplicities would likewise be destroyed," in Roy Harvey Pearce, *The Savages of America: A Study of the Indian and the Idea of Civilization*, rev. ed. (Baltimore: Johns Hopkins Press, 1965), 49.

24. Roy Harvey Pearce, "The Significances of the Captivity Narrative," *AL* 19 (Mar. 1947): 13. Panther editions are listed in R. W. G. Vail, *The Voice of the Old Frontier* (New York: Yoseloff, 1949). Abraham Panther [pseud.], *A Surprising Account of the Discovery of a Lady Who Was Taken by the Indians* (1785 and 1788), *Garland Library*, vol. 17 (New York: Garland, 1978). This volume also contains *A Very Surprising Narrative of a Young Woman, Discovered in a Rocky-Cave* (1794). Also see *A Surprising Narrative of a Young Woman, Discovered in the Wilderness After Having Been Taken by the Savage Indians* (Leominster, Mass.: Chapman Witcomb by Charles-Prentiss, 1799), and *A Very Surprising Narrative of a Young Woman, Discovered in A Rocky-Cave* (1800; rpt. Fairfield, Wash.: Ye Galleon Press, 1972). The various issues of the Panther narratives may be found at NL. For two different interpretations of Panther, see Slotkin, *Regeneration through Violence*, 257–59; Annette Kolodny, "Turning the Lens on 'The Panther Captivity': A Feminist Exercise in Practical Criticism," *Critical Inquiry* 8 (Winter 1981): 329–45. Gesa Mackenthun notes the "reality of the dispossession of the natives which the text wonderfully inverts" and also agrees as to the Dustan-like quality of the heroine ("Captives and Sleepwalkers: The Ideological Revolutions of Post-revolutionary Discourse," paper presented at the Sixth Biennial Symposium of the Milan Group in Early American History, Milan, Italy, June 22, 1992, pp. 4, 6).

25. All quotes here are from Panther, *Surprising Narrative* (1799), 3–4, 8.

26. Ibid., 3–9.

27. Kolodny notes the first editions, calling the "giant captor" "unidentified." She does not pick up the shift to "Indian." See "Turning the Lens," 338.

28. Panther, *Surprising Narrative* (1799), 10–12.

29. K. White, *A Narrative of the Life, Occurrences, Vicissitudes and*

Present Situation of K. White (1809), *Garland Library*, vol. 27 (New York: Garland, 1978), 34–35.

30. I object to the term *mixed blood* as well as *half-breed* as racist terms as well as inaccurate biology, although the first is commonly used by both Indians and whites. On the mulatto and fictional themes see Mary V. Dearborn, *Pocahontas's Daughters*, chap. 4.

31. Lydia Maria Child, *Hobomok and Other Writings on Indians*, ed. Carolyn L. Karcher (New Brunswick, N.J.: Rutgers University Press, 1986).

32. James Everett Seaver, *A Narrative of the Life of Mary Jemison: The White Woman of the Genesee*, 22d ed., ed. Charles Delamater Vail (New York: American Scenic and Historic Preservation Society, 1925), 44–45.

33. Ibid., 58.

34. The Ebenezer Mix additions remain in each successive edition. See Chapter 5 and James E. Seaver, *A Narrative of the Life of Mrs. Mary Jemison*, ed. June Namias (Norman: University of Oklahoma Press, 1992), 38; Seaver, *Narrative of the Life* (1925), chap. 11, 105–7; originally in James Everett Seaver, *Life of Mary Jemison: Deh-he-wä-mis* (1856), *Garland Library*, vol. 41 (New York: Garland, 1977). See discussion of changes in the Jemison editions in Chapter 5 and in Seaver, *Narrative of the Life*, ed. Namias, Intro.

35. Reginald Horsman, *Race and Manifest Destiny: The Origins of American Racial Anglo-Saxonism* (Cambridge, Mass.: Harvard University Press, 1981), 98–109, 298–303. See *The Indians and Their Captives*, ed. James Levernier and Hennig Cohen (Westport, Conn.: Greenwood Press, 1977), 47–49 and Part III. Also see Robert F. Berkhofer, Jr., "White Conceptions of Indians," in *HNAI/IWR*, 522–47; Berkhofer, *The White Man's Indian: Images of the American Indian from Columbus to the Present* (New York: Vintage Books, 1979), 138; George W. Stocking, *Victorian Anthropology* (New York: Free Press, 1987); Bernard W. Sheehan, *Seeds of Extinction: Jeffersonian Philanthropy and the American Indian* (Chapel Hill: University of North Carolina Press, 1973), 53–54.

36. *A Narrative of the Captivity of Mrs. Horn and Her Two Children with Mrs. Harris* (1839), *Garland Library*, vol. 54 (New York: Garland, 1977), 110–11; *Narrative of the Captivity and Extreme Sufferings of Mrs. Clarissa Plummer; History of the Captivity and Providential Release Therefrom of Mrs. Caroline Harris* (1838), *Garland Library*, vol. 54 (New York: Garland, 1977), 12.

37. *Narrative of Mrs. Clarissa Plummer*, 21; *Narrative of the Captivity of Mrs. Horn with Mrs. Harris*, 11, 12. According to Pearce, "The image of savage ignobility, taken over bodily from the captivity narrative, is in our earliest fiction a means to literary terror" (*Savages of America*, 198); Paul Bibbs, *Moccasin Bill; or Cunning Serpent the*

Ojibwah, a Romance of Big Stone Lake (1873), selection and cover in *Indians and Their Captives*, ed. Levernier and Cohen, 188–99.

38. Joanna L. Stratton, *Pioneer Women: Voices from the Kansas Frontier* (New York: Touchstone–Simon and Schuster, 1981), 121–26.

39. Ibid., 125. The tragic woman whose sexual life causes disgrace and madness was a common nineteenth-century theme (Sandra M. Gilbert and Susan Gubar, *The Madwoman in the Attic: The Woman Writer and the Nineteenth-Century Literary Imagination* [New Haven: Yale University Press, 1979]). Lonnie J. White finds stories of sexual assault common on the southern plains in "White Women Captives of Southern Plains Indians, 1866–1875," *Journal of the West* 8 (July 1969): 327–54. Stanley B. Kimball, however, investigated seven hundred Mormon trail accounts in the West and found "little fear of Indians recorded by men or women pioneers. . . . In fact, Indians were more likely to help women than harm them, if the Mormon record is typical" ("The Captivity Narrative on Mormon Trails, 1846–65," *Dialogue* 18 [Winter 1984]: 82–88, esp. 82–83).

40. Bibbs, *Moccasin Bill*, in *Indians and Their Captives*, ed. Levernier and Cohen, 190.

41. Mary Barber, *The True Narrative of the Five Years' Suffering & Perilous Adventures* (Philadelphia: Barclay, 1873), 38, 85–90, 100–101. Gherman suggests that the Barber narrative was written by a man ("Parlour to Tepee," 156). I have not been able to trace its origins.

42. Edwin James, ed., *A Narrative of the Captivity and Adventures of John Tanner* (1830), *Garland Library*, vol. 46 (New York: Garland, 1975), 100–102.

43. David C. Butterfield, *The Life and Adventures of David C. Butterfield, a Northwestern Pioneer* (1851), *Garland Library*, vol. 63 (New York: Garland, 1978).

44. Ann Sophia Stephens, *Malaeska, the Indian Wife of the White Hunter* (London: Beadle, 187?). According to the *Oxford English Dictionary*, the term *half-breed* was first used in the United States in the late eighteenth century. The term was applied to Indian-white offspring and occasionally to the children of blacks and whites. The racial and animalistic terminology here is in keeping with the growing racial as opposed to cultural fear and hatred of Indian-white unions.

45. Stephens, *Malaeska*, 125.

46. Matthew Brayton, with John H. A. Bone, *Indian Captive: A Narrative of the Adventures and Sufferings of Matthew Brayton* (1860), *Garland Library*, vol. 76 (New York: Garland, 1977), 41, 53–54.

47. Edward Sylvester Ellis, *The Frontier Angel: A Romance of Kentucky Rangers' Life*, Beadles Half Dime Library, no. 123 (New York: M. J. Ivers, 1877), 44, 99, 123–25. A similar problem occurs in Kevin Costner's film *Dances with Wolves* (1991), when the hero falls in love with Indianized white captive Stands with a Fist. Apparently choos-

ing an Indian woman for a mate still creates box office problems. Spike Lee's *Jungle Fever* (1991), a film and media sensation, had as its theme a steamy relationship between an African-American man and an Italian-American woman. The message was that for lasting relationships one should stick to one's own kind.

48. William H. Gerdts finds "the broader captive or slave theme" "attractive" both at home and abroad. He and others see Palmer copying Hiram Powers's *Greek Slave* (1843), the most popular of the bound depictions of women (Gerdts, "The Marble Savage," *Art in America* 62 [July–Aug. 1974]: 64–70, esp. 68). He stresses the popularity of "bondage and attendant chains, manacles, ropes, and such" in American Neo-Classic sculpture including that of Powers and Palmer. See Gerdts, "Marble and Nudity," *Art in America* 59 (May–June 1971): 60–67, esp. 67; Gerdts, *American Neo-Classic Sculpture: The Marble Resurrection* (New York: A Studio Book, Viking Press, 1973). Joy S. Kasson has a provocative analysis. See her work on the Palmer statue, which argues from the responses to it and other captive statues that miscegenation was just what contemporary Americans feared (*Marble Queens and Captives: Women in Nineteenth-Century American Sculpture* [New Haven: Yale University Press, 1990], chap. 4).

49. No one ever told Wimar that one should never stand in a canoe. His gun-toting Indian could wreck the craft. Charles Wimar, *The Abduction of Daniel Boone's Daughter by the Indians* (1853), oil on canvas, Washington University Gallery of Art, St. Louis, and G. W. Fasel, *Daniel Boone & His Friends Rescuing His Daughter Jemima* (1851), lithograph, Library of Congress. For additional comments on Boone and the western paintings see Vivien Green Fryd, "Two Sculptures for the Capitol: Horatio Greenough's *Rescue* and Luigi Persico's *Discovery of America*," *American Art Journal* 19, no. 2 (1987): 16–39, esp. 31–35; Martha Levy Luft, "Charles Wimar's *The Abduction of Daniel Boone's Daughter by the Indians*, 1853 and 1855: Evolving Myths," *Prospects* 7 (1982): 300–314. For more on Wimar see notes in June Namias, "White Captives: Gender and Ethnicity on Successive American Frontiers, 1607–1862" (Ph.D. dissertation, Brandeis University, 1989), 223–24, n. 62.

50. Charles Wimar, *The Abduction of Daniel Boone's Daughter* (ca. 1850), oil on canvas, collection of E. R. Minshall, Jr., of Tulsa. The picture was reproduced on the cover of *American Heritage*, Oct. 1962. Comment on the cover refers to the capture of "Jemima Boone" near Boonesborough, Kentucky on July 7, 1776. I would like to thank Patricia Hills, William H. Truettner, and E. R. Minshall for helping me track down this painting.

51. Gerdts, "Marble Savage," 68, says that "mid-19th-century sculpture often suggests that the Indian male was superior to the white: Indian men are shown as stalwart, strong and almost always nearly naked." I have not looked into the contemporary response to

the paintings under analysis here, but Joy S. Kasson has done this for the sculptures, surveying mid-nineteenth-century magazines, newspapers, and letters and diaries of artists. Her conclusion is similar to mine. See *Marble Queens and Captives*, chap. 4, 91–97. I read her book after I had done most of my research.

52. I wrote this before reading Joy S. Kasson's *Marble Queens and Captives*. She reaches a somewhat similar conclusion after analyzing a variety of ideal sculpture of captives from the pre–Civil War period. She guesses, I think wrongly, that the Ives sculpture may depict Eunice Williams. But her more important conclusions, that Joseph Mozier's *Wept of Wish-ton-Wish* (1869, based on the Cooper novel of New England female captive turned Indian) and the Ives and the Palmer statues all signal viewers, especially female viewers, that if one removes "the chain," then "every captive might be at heart a willing captive." She relates this response to women's confining roles in a changing mid-nineteenth-century America (chap. 4, esp. 93–100).

53. Gerdts finds Indian women more often clothed or, if naked, "always inviolate." My interpretation of the causes here is different from his. See "Marble Savage," esp. 64, 69. But Raymond William Stedman finds the allure of Indian women in popular culture often depicted as sexual from William Byrd, to Alfred Jacob Miller, to Carl Sandburg, Buffy Sainte Marie, and John Barth's *The Sot-Weed Factor*. See Stedman, *Shadows of the Indian: Stereotypes in American Culture* (Norman: University of Oklahoma Press, 1982), esp. 5–6, 17, 31, 38, 93; also Gerdts, "Marble and Nudity," 60–67.

54. William R. Swagerty, "Marriage and Settlement Patterns of Rocky Mountain Trappers and Traders," *WHQ* 11 (Apr. 1980): 159–80; Jennifer Brown, "Company Men and Native Families: Fur Trade Social and Domestic Relations in Canada's Old Northwest" (Ph.D. dissertation, University of Chicago, 1976); Sylvia Van Kirk, *Many Tender Ties: Women in Fur-Trade Society, 1670–1870* (Norman: University of Oklahoma Press, 1980). The word *squaw* has come under recent fire from Indians as derogatory and having been used by whites to mean something akin to *slut*. Many resent its use at all, but according to the *Oxford English Dictionary*, it was taken from the word *squa* meaning woman or wife in Algonquian dialects and picked up by William Wood and other early Puritan settlers. *Squaw-man* has negative, antimiscegenation references dating to the late nineteenth century in popular journals (*The Compact Edition of the Oxford English Dictionary*, 2 vols. [New York: Oxford University Press, 1971], 2:2996).

55. See Calvin C. Hernton, *Sex and Racism in America* (New York: Grove Press, 1965); Robert Staples, *Black Masculinity: The Black Male's Role in American Society* (San Francisco: Black Scholar Press, 1982).

56. David K. Shipler, *Arab and Jew: Wounded Spirits in a Promised Land* (New York: Times Books, 1986), 292–95.

57. Rayna Green, "The Pocahontas Perplex: The Image of the Indian Woman in American Culture," *Massachusetts Review* 16 (1975): 698–714; Dearborn, *Pocahontas's Daughters*, 97–99, 105–8, 116–18, 133–34.

58. John Vanderlyn, *The Death of Jane McCrea* (ca. 1804), oil on canvas, Wadsworth Atheneum.

59. Octavio Paz, *The Labyrinth of Solitude: Life and Thought in Mexico* (New York: Grove Press, 1961), chap. 4.

60. See Leslie Fiedler on sexual appeal across racial lines. He finds the main traditions are white male with Indian male—an "elite" tradition dating to the Leatherstocking Tales. But he finds a "counter-tradition" including Whitman's trapper and Indian maid in "Song of Myself" in Harriet Beecher Stowe's *Old Town Folks* (1869). See "The Indian in Literature in English," in *HNAI/IWR*, 573–86, esp. 578–79. Also see D. H. Lawrence, *Studies in Classic American Literature* (New York: Viking, 1961), 47–64.

61. Jordan, *White over Black*. Because brutality against women was perpetrated mainly on black women by white men in the slave system, the ironic quality of the fetishism of "red" men brutalizing white women should be raised here. The European and American interest in picturing this brutality is discussed and illustrated in Hugh Honour, *The Image of the Black in Western Art: From the American Revolution to World War I: Slaves and Liberators* (Houston: Menil Foundation, 1989; distributed by Harvard University Press), 4:pt. 1, 87–91, with the illustration by William Blake, *Flagellation of a Female Samboe Slave* (1793) from John Gabriel Stedman, *Narrative of a Five Years' Expedition against the Revolted Negroes of Surinam* (1796).

62. *Moccasin Bill, A Dime Novel* (1873) in *Indians and Their Captives*, ed. Levernier and Cohen, 189–99.

63. Albert L. Hurtado, *Indian Survival on the California Frontier* (New Haven: Yale University Press, 1988), 169–92.

64. Daniel Aaron, "The Inky Curse: Race and Sex in the American Imagination," paper presented at Brandeis University, Waltham, Mass., Sept. 3, 1982.

65. According to John D'Emilio and Estelle B. Freedman, middle-class Americans during the nineteenth century frequently saw "the sexuality of minority races" as "a foil against which whites redefined themselves" (*Intimate Matters: A History of Sexuality in America* [New York: Harper & Row, 1988], 108 and chap. 5).

66. Gherman, "Parlour to Teepee"; Alfred Jacob Miller, *The Trapper's Bride* (1845), oil on canvas, Harrison Eiteljorg Collection, Indianapolis; Herman J. Viola with H. B. Crothers and Maureen Hannan, "The American Indian Genre Paintings of Catlin, Stanley, Wimar, Eastman, and Miller," in *American Frontier Life: Early Western Painting and Prints* (New York: Abbeyville Press, 1987, for Amon Carter Museum and Buffalo Bill Historical Center), 160 and detail, 130.

1. Charles Neilson, *An Original, Compiled and Corrected Account of Burgoyne's Campaign* (1844; rpt. Bemis Heights, N.Y.: C. Neilson, 1926), 64, 65; Benson J. Lossing, *The Empire State* (Hartford, Conn.: American Publishing Co., 1892), 268; [Chrisfield Johnson], *History of Washington Co[unty], New York* (1879; rpt. Interlaken, N.Y.: Hearts of the Lake, 1979), 50. Edmund Burke protested Burgoyne's use of Indian troops and the results on the floor of Parliament (William L. Stone, *Washington County, New York: Its History to the Close of the Nineteenth Century* [New York: New York History Co., 1901], 198). Joel Barlow wrote about Jane's tale using the name of Lucinda in his epic poem *The Columbiad, a Poem, with the Last Corrections of the Author* (1807), Book the Sixth in *The Works of Joel Barlow*, intro. William K. Bottorff and Arthur L. Ford (1825; rpt. Gainesville, Fla.: Scholars Facsimiles and Reprints, 1970), 624–37; [Lieut. William Digby], "Some Account of the American War between Great Britain and the Colonies, 1776," in *The British Invasion from the North*, ed. James Phinney Baxter (Albany: Joel Munsell's Sons, 1887), 236, 24–31; David Wilson, *The Life of Jane McCrea, with an Account of Burgoyne's Expedition in 1777* (New York: Baker, Goodwin, 1853), 14.

A short biography, "Jane McCrea," by Martin H. Bush may be found in *Notable American Women, 1607–1950*, 3 vols., ed. Edward T. James et al. (Cambridge, Mass.: Harvard University Press, 1971), 2:456–57. Bush dates her birth in approximately 1754, but her new tombstone near Fort Edward says 1760. Artists who painted the McCrea story include John Vanderlyn, *Death of Jane McCrea* (ca. 1804), oil on canvas, Wadsworth Atheneum, Hartford, Conn.; Asher B. Durand, *The Murder of Miss McCrea* (1839), oil on canvas, Fort Ticonderoga Museum, Ticonderoga, N.Y., and Nathaniel Currier (1846), lithograph, Prints and Photographs Division, Library of Congress. For the collection of McCrea images see Samuel Y. Edgerton, Jr., "*The Murder of Jane McCrea*: The Tragedy of an American Tableau d'Histoire," *Art Bulletin* 58 (Dec. 1965): 481–92. McCrea is also spelled M'Crea, M'Kray, and MacCrea. Other materials on McCrea may be found in FEHSNY. The earliest, longest, and best recounting of her story is James Austin Holden, "Influence of Death of Jane McCrea on Burgoyne Campaign," *Proceedings of the New York Historical Association* 12 (1913): 249–310. The most recent, though short and rather confused account testifying to the continued popularity of the legend is Peter Bauer, "Watersheds: Twenty Decisive Moments That Made Us What We Are," *Adirondack Life* 20 (May–June 1989): 93.

2. The Hartford *Connecticut Courant*, August 3, 1777, said a girl was shot and scalped: "The girl was a sweet heart to an officer in the enemy's service, and a great tory—Hear, O Heavens! and give ear, Oh America!" The Boston *Independent Chronicle*, August 14, 1777, wrote

that "they took a young woman out of a house at Fort Edward . . . and in cool blood, murdered and scalped her." The *Boston-Gazette, and Country Journal*, August 11, 1777, published a letter citing her death on July 28 from Moses Creek, New York. See Kathleen Moss, "The Massacre of Jane McCrea by John Vanderlyn" (paper, WA, Jan. 1948, pp. 15–17); General Horatio Gates to Burgoyne, Sept. 2, 1777, Gates Papers, Box 19b, and General Burgoyne to Gates, Sept. 6, 1777, Gates Papers, Box 7, no. 223, New-York Historical Society, in *The Spirit of 'Seventy-Six: The Story of the American Revolution as Told by Participants*, ed. Henry Steele Commager and Richard B. Morris (New York: Harper & Row, 1967), 560–61; Jay Fliegelman, *Prodigals and Pilgrims: The American Revolution against Patriarchal Authority, 1750–1800* (Cambridge, Eng.: Cambridge University Press, 1982), 138, quoting the *Boston-Gazette*, Aug. 18, 1777, p. 3. For an opposing view arguing that McCrea's death was unimportant in bringing men into battle, see Brian Burns, "Massacre or Muster? Burgoyne's Indians and the Militia at Bennington," *Vermont History* 45 (Summer 1977): 133–44; James Lunt, *John Burgoyne of Saratoga* (New York: Harcourt Brace Jovanovich, 1975), 75. New York officer and captive William Scudder, whose friend Tobias Van Vactor was killed in the assault on Fort Edward and was buried with Jane McCrea, also believed McCrea's death "drove many to arms, who before seemed to appear in suspense" (*The Journal of William Scudder* [1794], *Garland Library*, vol. 22 [New York: Garland, 1977], 13).

3. British and Canadian writers argue that Jane was killed by a stray patriot bullet (Michael Glover, *General Burgoyne in Canada and America* [London: Gordon and Cromonesi, 1976], 154–55; Lunt, *John Burgoyne of Saratoga*, 172–77). A Canadian piece sees Jane as a Canadian patriot (Grace Tomkinson, "Jane McCrea: A Martyr of the Revolutionary War," *Dalhousie Review* 49 [Autumn 1969]: 399–403).

4. The Allens were a loyalist family with three or four children and three slaves, parents, and in-laws, all of whom were supposedly killed by Burgoyne-allied Indians. See Arthur Reid, *Reminiscences of the Revolution* (Utica: Roberts, Book and Job Printer, 1859), 16–17; [Johnson], *History of Washington Co[unty]*, 50, 53; Gates to Burgoyne, in *Spirit*, ed. Commager and Morris, 560–61. For one fairly lucid account see Barbara Graymont, *The Iroquois in the American Revolution* (Syracuse: Syracuse University Press, 1972), 150–52.

5. [Johnson], *History of Washington Co[unty]*, 52.

6. Wilson, *Life of Jane McCrea*, x.

7. Fliegelman, *Prodigals and Pilgrims*, 137–41. Also see Michael Kammen, *A Season of Youth: The American Revolution and the Historical Imagination* (New York: Knopf, 1978).

8. See Linda K. Kerber, *Women of the Republic; Intellect and Ideology in Revolutionary America* (Chapel Hill: University of North Caro-

lina Press, 1980). The debate over women's position in and after the Revolution poses Mary Beth Norton's *Liberty's Daughters: The Revolutionary Experience of American Women, 1750–1800* (Boston: Little, Brown, 1980), which argues that the Revolution transformed women's roles, against Joan Hoff Wilson's "The Illusion of Change: Women and the American Revolution," in *The American Revolution: Explorations on the History of American Radicalism*, ed. Alfred F. Young (DeKalb: Northern Illinois University Press, 1976), 383–446. For other works on women in the Revolution see Walter Hart Blumenthal, *Women Camp Followers of the American Revolution* (New York: Arno Press, 1974); Joy Day Buel and Richard Buel, Jr., *The Way of Duty: A Woman and Her Family in Revolutionary America* (New York: Norton, 1984); Elizabeth Evans, *Weathering the Storm: Women of the American Revolution* (New York: Scribners, 1975). For additional clarification on the role of women after the Revolution see Jan Lewis, "The Republican Wife: Virtue and Seduction in the Early Republic," *WMQ* 3d ser., 44 (Oct. 1987): 689–721; Ruth H. Bloch, "American Feminine Ideals in Transition: The Rise of the Moral Mother, 1785–1815," *FS* 4 (June 1978): 101–26; and Bloch, "The Gendered Meanings of Virtue in Revolutionary America," *Signs* 13 (Autumn 1987): 37–58; Rosemarie Zagarri, "Morals, Manners, and the Republican Mother," *AQ* 44 (June 1992): 192–215; Mary Kelley, "Reading the Revolution: Women, Literacy, and Learning," paper presented at the Sixth Biennial Symposium of the Milan Group in Early American History, Milan, Italy, June 19, 1992.

9. John Demos, *Past, Present, and Personal: The Family and the Life Course in American History* (New York: Oxford University Press, 1986), 92–113, esp. 99–104, and on the premodern and modern periods, xi; Robert V. Wells, "Family Size and Fertility Control in Eighteenth-Century America: A Study of Quaker Families," *Population Studies* 25 (Mar. 1971): 173–82; Daniel Scott Smith, "Parental Power and Marriage Patterns: An Analysis of Historical Trends in Hingham, Massachusetts," in *The American Family in Social Historical Perspective*, ed. Michael Gordon, 2d ed. (New York: St. Martin's Press, 1978), 87–100; David Hackett Fischer, *Growing Old in America* (New York: Oxford University Press, 1977); Joseph Kett, *Rites of Passage: Adolescence in America, 1790–the Present* (New York: Basic Books, 1977); Daniel A. Cohen, "Arthur Mervyn and His Elders: The Ambivalence of Youth in the Early Republic," *WMQ* 3d ser., 53 (July 1986): 362–80; Jack Larkin, *The Reshaping of Everyday Life, 1790–1840* (New York: Harper & Row, 1988). Joan Gunderson finds that a "reluctance of state and federal governments to recognize married women as independent citizens is paradoxically related to the Revolutionary era's emphasis on independence and freedom." Though the choice of mates has increased, she sees a mixed picture of dependence and independence

in "courtship patterns, divorce records, and marriage settlements" ("Independence, Citizenship, and the American Revolution," *Signs* 13 [Winter 1987]: 59–77, esp. 71–72).

10. Leary's introduction cites Joseph Sabin in *Bibliotheca Americana* for the book's publication history. Michel René Hilliard-d'Auberteuil, *Miss McCrea: A Novel of the American Revolution*, trans. Eric LaGuardia, intro. by Lewis Leary (1784; rpt. Gainesville, Fla.: Scholars' Facsimiles and Reprints, 1958), intro., 5–10. In 1781, Hilliard-d'Auberteuil (1751–89) published a political history supporting the emerging English states in America, following it with a second volume in 1782. Also see Michel René Hilliard-d'Auberteuil, *Miss Mac Rea* (1784), *Garland Library*, vol. 16 (New York: Garland, 1978).

11. Hilliard-d'Auberteuil writes, "We deemed it wise to change the name of the English officer; to embellish his subject, the author has added everything that could be allowed." He is true to his word (Hilliard-d'Auberteuil, *Miss McCrea*, 20). The book's first North American edition was published in Philadelphia.

12. Ibid., 26. Leary gives a detailed account of the connections between this novel and other English, French, and American sentimental novels of the period (ibid., 15–16). Terence Martin cites a "Richardsonian formula" for early American fiction—"virtue in distress, but virtue inevitably rewarded, or conversely, the punishment of villainy or a lapse from the normal moral code. The characters, and especially the young women, who go astray in these novels pay a mighty price" ("Social Institutions in the Early American Novel," *AQ* 9 [Spring 1957]: 72–84, esp. 74). For a discussion of the "codes" of early American fiction and the possible responses of readers see Cathy N. Davidson, *Revolution and the Word: The Rise of the Novel in America* (New York: Oxford University Press, 1986), esp. chaps. 1 and 2.

13. Hilliard-d'Auberteuil, *Miss McCrea*, 26–29, 33.

14. Ibid., 40–42.

15. Ibid., 57, 55, 48.

16. Henry William Herbert, "Jane McCrea," in Wilson, *Life of Jane McCrea*, 149.

17. "The Murder of Miss M'Kray" in *Indian Atrocities! Affecting and Thrilling Anecdotes* (1846), *Garland Library*, vol. 61 (New York: Garland, 1978), 18–19.

18. Wilson, *Life of Jane McCrea*, 6–9, 29–35.

19. Ibid., 82, 71, 44. Wilson says he interviewed the son of Daniel Jones, who verified such correspondence (Sept. 1853, Brockville, Canada). David Jones lived out his life as a bachelor in his home in Canada. Alexander Freel is said to have delivered the critical letter. Holden, who did well in cutting through the contradictory McCrea information, succumbs to reproducing this fabricated letter in "Influence of the Death of Jane McCrea," 274–75. The letter is cited as

late as Bush, "Jane McCrea," in *Notable American Women*, ed. James et al., 2:456.

20. Wilson, *Life of Jane McCrea*, 65–66.

21. Ibid., 65, 82, 84, 89, 90. On women and sentimental novels see Nina Baym, *Novels, Readers, and Reviewers: Responses to Fiction in Antebellum America* (Ithaca: Cornell University Press, 1984); Baym, *Woman's Fiction: A Guide to Novels by and about Women in America, 1820–1870* (Ithaca: Cornell University Press, 1978). Also see Janice A. Radway, *Reading the Romance: Women, Patriarchy, and Popular Literature* (Chapel Hill: University of North Carolina Press, 1984).

22. Wilson, *Life of Jane McCrea*, 117. See Lawrence Cortesi, "The Tragic Romance of Jane McCrea," *American History Illustrated* 20 (Apr. 1985): 10–15. Kenneth Silverman also notes the irony of loyalist lover turned patriot heroine as a nineteenth-century transformation of Jane into a "folk heroine" in *A Cultural History of the American Revolution: Painting, Music, Literature, and Theater in the Colonies and the United States from the Treaty of Paris to the Inauguration of George Washington, 1763–1789* (New York: Thomas Y. Crowell, 1976), 330.

23. Philip Henry Carroll, *Jane McCrea: A Tragedy in Five Acts* (Albany: Fort Orange Press, 1927). A copy may be found at AMNY.

24. Ibid., 24.

25. Ibid., 47–49, 75–76, 81–83.

26. Ibid., 4, 20, 46, 121–24. Robert W. Venables discussed the visual indictments of Wyandott Panther in "The Iconography of Empire: Images of the American Indian in the Early Republic, 1783–1835," paper presented at "Native Americans and the Early Republic," a conference sponsored by the United States Capitol Historical Society, Mar. 5, 1992.

27. James McCrea's ministry began in 1739 in a Presbyterian church in Lamberton, New Jersey. Jane's brother John, his oldest son, moved to Albany in 1760. Jane came to live with John in New York after her father's death in 1769. John studied and practiced law, married a member of the Beekman family, and had two sons. He later moved to the west side of the Hudson, five miles south of Fort Edward, opposite the mouth of Moses Kill. John is mentioned in the records of Washington County (formerly Charlotte County) as "a leading attorney and counsellor." In 1775 he and Philip Schuyler organized a Committee of Safety for Saratoga district. He later became a colonel in the Saratoga regiment. Stephen McCrea, another of Jane's brothers, became a doctor and was a surgeon in a New York regiment during the Revolution. See Asa Fitch, "History of the McCrea Family, and the Murder of Jane by Indians," in *Revolutionary Memorials, Embracing Poems by Rev. Wheeler Case*, ed. Stephen Dodd (New York: M. W. Dodd, 1852), Appendix 2, 56–61; Bush, "Jane McCrea," in *Notable American Women*, ed. James et al., 456.

28. Mrs. Campbell was first Miss Fraser from Scotland, cousin to

General Fraser, who was in the campaign with Burgoyne during the Hudson invasion. Her first husband, by the surname Campbell, is said to have been lost at sea, as was her second husband, McNeil (Fitch, "History of the McCrea Family," in *Revolutionary Memorials*, ed. Dodd; Robert O. Bascom, *The Fort Edward Book Containing Some Historical Sketches with Illustrations and Family Records* [Fort Edward, N.Y.: James D. Keating, 1908], 49; Bush, "Jane McCrea," in *Notable American Women*, ed. James et al., 456).

29. Wilson, *Life of Jane McCrea*, Appendix and concluding pages; Asa Fitch, "Notes for a History of Washington County, New York," 7 vols., 1:selection 104, manuscript, New York Genealogical and Biographical Society; Fitch, "Notes," Mary Gillespie Bain, 1:selection 124 [77–78]. The manuscript pages have a numbering system which includes page brackets along with section numbers. Both sets of numbers are used in the manuscript. Fitch, "History of the McCrea Family," Appendix 2, 56–61, esp. 60.

30. In the Mozart opera, Pamina falls into the clutches of a bad black man. She asks young and handsome Tamino to rescue her. In the process, Tamino is told by the male rulers that the Queen of the Night is also to be avoided (Wolfgang Amadeus Mozart, *The Magic Flute* [1791]); Wilson, *Life of Jane McCrea*, 35. Mrs. Campbell's name is also spelled M'Neil and McNeill. Stone's *Washington County* claims that Americans could have killed Jane. See also Edgerton, "*Murder of Jane McCrea*," *Art Bulletin*, 492.

31. Wilson, *Life of Jane McCrea*, 18; Benson J. Lossing, *The Pictorial Field-Book of the Revolution*, 2 vols. (New York: Harper and Brothers, 1869), 1:98.

32. Fitch, "Notes," Mary Gillespie Bain, 1:selection 88 [45]; Timothy Eddy, 2:selection 259; Blake interview, Oct. 1847, 1:selection 51.

33. Ibid., Bain, 1:selections 87 and 88 [45]. Mary Gillespie Bain [b. 1770], later Mrs. Casparus Bain. No exact date is given for this interview, but after it, in October 1847, Fitch asked Robert Blake to comment on Bain's remarks. Blake said it was all false except for Campbell's being lifted through the trap door (ibid., 1:selection 51 [46]).

34. Lossing, *Pictorial Field-Book*, 98; Fitch, "Notes," T. Eddy, 3:selection 583; [Johnson], *History of Washington Co[unty]*, 51; Stone, *Washington County*, 188; Fitch, "Notes," Blake, 1:selection 51 [6].

35. [Johnson,] *History of Washington Co[unty]*, 55; Wilson, *Life of Jane McCrea*, 104, 110. On her state of dress Blake says, "Nor was any of her clothes stripped off & taken from her that I ever heard of" (Fitch, "Notes," 1:selection 51 [6]). Fraser's name is also spelled Frazer and Frazier. See Neilson, *Burgoyne's Campaign*, 74–75.

36. Wilson, *Life of Jane McCrea*, 110. According to Lossing, General Fraser gave her his coat, but Mrs. McNeil was not stripped (*Pictorial Field-Book*, 99).

37. Hilliard-d'Auberteuil, *Miss McCrea*, 44–45, 57–58.

38. Ibid., 47.

39. Kerber, *Women of the Republic*.

40. Rev. Wheeler Case, "The Tragical Death of Miss Jane M'Crea," in *Revolutionary Memorials*, ed. Dodd, 37; Barlow, *Columbiad*, Book the Sixth, 634–36; Philip Freneau, "America Independent and Her Everlasting Deliverance from British Tyranny and Oppression" (1809), in *Poems of Philip Freneau: Poet of the American Revolution* (New York: Russell and Russell, 1963), 279. In 1913, Holden, usually an even-handed historian, follows the only alleged eyewitness account of Jane's death in which it is claimed Jane was first shot and then scalped and adds that the "body was then mutilated by the knives of the party and the scalp taken. It is of course very probable she was tomahawked." Her body was then rolled into a ditch and covered with leaves, and her shoes were hung on a branch. The document from which this information comes was a petition of Samuel Standish to his local congressman of the Washington-Saratoga district. Holden does not tell us how many years or perhaps decades passed between Jane's death and this petition ("Influence of the Death of Jane McCrea," 279). A still more violent account is Lauran Paine, *Gentleman Johnny: The Life of General John Burgoyne* (London: Robert Hale, 1973), 112–13.

41. Freneau, "America Independent," 279; Barlow, *Columbiad*, Book the Sixth, 628, 633, 636. Also see Patrick M. Malone, *The Skulking Way of War: Technology and Tactics among the New England Indians* (Lanham, Md.: Madison Books, 1991).

42. Graymont, *Iroquois in the American Revolution*, 150. One reason for this conflict is that there were British troops coming from the West and from Canada and each had Indian allies, but it is also symptomatic of wanting to blame any Indian one can find and not knowing one from another. The recent conglomeration is in Bauer, "Watersheds," 93.

43. The theme of Indians and savagery is most fully documented by Roy Harvey Pearce, *Savagism and Civilization: A Study of the Indian and the American Mind*, rev. ed. (Berkeley: University of California Press, 1988), 58, 110–12, 198–99, and intro. Edgerton has reproductions of twelve works on the murder of McCrea in "*Murder of Jane McCrea*," *Art Bulletin*.

44. Samuel Y. Edgerton, Jr., says the Vanderlyn painting was "exhibited in Paris in 1804" and "was the first instance of a purely American historical subject being accepted by the prestigious French *salon* ("*The Murder of Jane McCrea* and Vattemare's System of International Exchange," *Bulletin of the Fort Ticonderoga Museum* 11 [1965]: 336–42).

45. Barlow, *Columbiad*, Book the Sixth, 624–37; Edgerton, "*Murder of Jane McCrea*," *Art Bulletin*, 481–92. The sketches are at Fordham

University; see ibid., 483–84, n. 13. Vanderlyn was born in Kingston, New York, in 1775, worked with Gilbert Stuart (1795–96), and was supported in his training in Philadelphia by Aaron Burr. He then studied in Paris with a member of the French Academy, Andre Vincent B. Cathles. For a discussion of Vanderlyn's work see Kenneth C. Lindsay, "The Works of John Vanderlyn: From Tammany to Capitol," University Gallery, State University of New York at Binghamton, A Loan Exhibition, Oct. 11 to Nov. 9, 1970. "John Vanderlyn," notes, WA correspondence between Barlow and Vanderlyn is cited by Kathleen H. Pritchard, in "John Vanderlyn and the Massacre of Jane McCrea," *Art Quarterly*, Autumn 1949, pp. 361–66, esp. 361–62.

46. William Townsend Oedel, "John Vanderlyn: French Neoclassicism and the Search for an American Art" (Ph.D. dissertation, University of Delaware, 1981), 1–2, 9, 203–29. The painting is variously called *The Murder of Jane McCrea*, *Death of Jane McCrea*, and *The Death of Jane McCrea*.

47. See Ellwood Parry's comments in "The Last of the Mohicans," in *The Image of the Indian and the Black Man in American Art, 1590–1900* (New York: G. Braziller, 1974), 59–63.

48. Richard Drinnon, *Facing West: The Metaphysics of Indian-Hating and Empire Building* (Minneapolis: University of Minnesota Press, 1980), 101. Also see Pauline Turner Strong, "Captive Images: Stereotypes That Justified Colonial Expansion on the American Frontier Were a Legacy of a Seventeenth-Century War," *Natural History*, Dec. 1985, pp. 51–56, and for a countermyth see Leland S. Person, Jr., "The American Eve: Miscegenation and a Feminist Frontier Fiction," *AQ* 37 (Winter 1985): 668–85.

49. Edgerton, "*Murder of Jane McCrea*," *Bulletin of the Fort Ticonderoga Museum*, 336–42.

50. Edgerton, "*Murder of Jane McCrea*," *Art Bulletin*, 487. I have no references that tell how the work was received by contemporary critics or the public.

51. Traditional paintings of the Virgin Mary dress her in red, white, and blue, with the baby Jesus wearing similar colors (telephone conversation with Carol Zemel, Mar. 6, 1988).

52. J. L. Ferris and F. C. Yohn, "Capture of Jane McCrea," The Glens Falls Collection: A Series of Eleven Paintings (Glens Falls, N.Y.: Glens Falls Insurance Co., n.d., ca. 1931), AMNY. A copy of the 1912 version is in Holden, "Influence of the Death of Jane McCrea," opposite 249.

53. Her present gravestone in Fort Edward, New York, dates her birth to 1760, making her seventeen; George Bancroft says she was twenty in *History of the United States of America*, 6 vols. (New York: D. Appleton, 1886), 5:164. Digby's journal (written while he was with Burgoyne) claims she was eighteen (*British Invasion from the North*, ed. Baxter, 236). Neilson puts her age at twenty-three (*Burgoyne's*

Campaign, 70). General Horatio Gates to Burgoyne, Sept. 2, 1777, in Gates Papers, Box 19b, New-York Historical Society, cited in *Spirit*, ed. Commager and Morris, 560. Holden claims she was in her early twenties, "not her 'teens' " ("Influence of the Death of Jane McCrea," 285). Contemporary biographer Bush estimates her birth around 1752 making her twenty-four or twenty-five ("Jane McCrea," in *Notable American Women*, ed. James et al., 2:456–57).

54. Poem by Herbert in Wilson, *Life of Jane McCrea*, 151; Stone, *Washington County*, 186; Ferris and Yohn, "Capture of Jane McCrea"; Interview with Bell by Asa Fitch, Nov. 19, 1847, in Bascom, *Fort Edward Book*, 70; Alfred B. Street from "Burgoyne," a narrative poem, 278–319, in Allen C. Beach, *The Centennial Celebrations of the State of New York* (Albany: Weed, Parsons and Co., 1879), 293. Asa Fitch also says her hair was black, in Fitch, "Notes," 1:selection 129. Holden writes on the confusion of colors but guesses that "she was of the light complexioned type" ("Influence of the Death of Jane McCrea," 260).

55. These descriptions are "golden brown and silken hair," Stone, *Washington County*, 186; "glorious tresses" and "glossy-locks," Street in Beach, *Centennial Celebrations*, 293–94; Lossing talks of "the long glossy hair of Jenny" in *Pictorial Field-Book*, 99, and of her "glossy tresses" in *Empire State*, 268. Wilson, citing Mrs. Neilson, describes the hair as "uncommonly beautiful," *Life of Jane McCrea*, 16, see also 102–3; [Johnson], *History of Washington Co[unty]*, 51, uses "luxuriant" and "ample"; Reid, *Reminiscences of the Revolution*, 25. A recent biographer says her hair "reportedly reached the floor when tied in a braid" (Bush, "Jane McCrea," in *Notable American Women*, ed. James et al., 456).

56. "The Murder of Miss M'Kray," in *Indian Atrocities!*, 19.

57. Street from "Burgoyne," in Beach, *Centennial Celebrations*, 278–319, esp. 293–94.

58. Stone, *Washington County*, 186; Wilson, *Life of Jane McCrea*, 112, 41; Lossing, *Empire State*, 268; Neilson, *Burgoyne's Expedition*, 74; [Johnson], *History of Washington Co[unty]*, 51. Earlier, Joel Barlow in *The Columbiad* called Jane's "gory scalp, their horrid prize of blood" and admonished the British for the "British gold" paid for them: "Are these thy trophies, Carleton!" (635–36); Sydney Jackson, ed., *With Burgoyne from Quebec: An Account of the Life at Quebec and of the Famous Battle at Saratoga* (Toronto: Macmillan of Canada, 1963), 210, n. 76.

59. Reid, *Reminiscences of the Revolution*, 19.

60. Lossing, *Empire State*, 269.

61. Carroll, *Jane McCrea*, 99.

62. Germaine Greer, *The Female Eunuch* (New York: McGraw-Hill, 1971); "The Massacre at Fort Edward," Fort Edward High School Historical Club, *Yorker*, Nov.–Dec. 1952, pp. 26–27, FEHSNY. On the issue of scalping see James Axtell, *The European and the Indian:*

Essays in the Ethnohistory of Colonial North America (New York: Oxford University Press, 1981), 16–38; Bernard W. Sheehan, "Indians in the American Revolution"; and Mary Beth Norton, "Indians and the American Revolution: Approaches to Teaching," in Newberry Library, *The Impact of Indian History on the Teaching of United States History*, No. 4, Occasional Papers in Curriculum Series, Washington Conference, 1985 (Washington, D.C.: Newberry Library, 1986), 171–204, 205–12, esp. 205. Here Norton echoes Francis Jennings's earlier essay "The Indians' Revolution," in *American Revolution*, ed. Young, 319–49.

63. Isabel Thompson Kelsay comes close when she says, "Jane was killed, by somebody or other in some way or other, on July 26" (*Joseph Brant, 1743–1807: Man of Two Worlds* [Syracuse: Syracuse University Press, 1984], 204). Also see Gerald Howson, *Burgoyne of Saratoga* (New York: New York Times Books–Quadrangle, 1979), 176–80, 320, n. 9.

64. Robert Blake came to New York from Scotland at age ten and was interviewed at age eighty-five by Asa Fitch in October and November of 1847 for Fitch's history of Washington County. Blake claimed to remember hearing Mrs. Campbell and others tell the story of the capture and murder. He says, "I never understood that Miss McCrea was scalped . . . I always supposed she was left by the Indians where she was shot" (Blake in Fitch, "Notes," 1:selection 51 [4] and biographical information, 1:selection 42 [10]).

65. Kerber, *Women of the Republic*, chap. 3, esp. 73. Kerber quotes Ann Gwinnett to John Hancock and the "other Members of the Grand Continental Congress" [Aug. 1777?], Papers Continental Congress, M-247, Roll 87, Item 73:135, NA, 79 and 85–104, also in broadsides, 104–5. Mary Beth Norton shows that by organizing boycotts, women did find these political means (*Liberty's Daughters*, chaps. 6 and 7). The heroic view of McCrea was voiced by New York officer William Scudder. Scudder, captured by Indians at Fort Stanwix and friend of Tobias Van Vactor (who was also killed at the time of the Fort Edward attack as Jane was and originally buried in the same grave), claimed that Jane's death "spread a general alarm, particularly through the New England states, and I believe drove many to arms" (*Journal of William Scudder*, 13).

66. Wilson, "Illusion of Change," 383–445; Norton, *Liberty's Daughters* (see note 8 above); also Gordon S. Wood, *The Radicalism of the American Revolution* (New York: Knopf, 1992), 183–84, 356–57.

67. Deborah Sampson's memory is being revived. She dressed as a man and joined the Fourth Massachusetts Regiment of Foot and fought for a year and a half in the New York campaign before her injury led to the discovery that she was a woman. "Private Robert Shurtleff Well-Camouflaged Fighter" was inserted as part of a full-

page piece, "Should Women Be Sent Into Combat?," *New York Times*, July 21, 1991, p. E3.

68. A thick book of such articles, many undated and without names and places of origin, can be found in "Scrap Book. All the Known Accounts of the Massacre of Jane McCrea" (n.p., n.d.), FEHSNY. They range from papers in Dubuque, Iowa, to ones in Ohio and Pennsylvania, to the *New York Times*, the *Boston Herald*, and local papers such as *Glens Falls Republican*. See "Influence of the Death of Jane McCrea," 257, 304–7.

69. Carroll, *Jane McCrea*; Bauer, "Watersheds," 93. The early reburial rites are documented in the local papers beginning with "Jane McCrea Disinterment," *Washington County Post*, Apr. 25, 1822; a later discussion is "Jane McCrea and Her Remains," *Salem Press*, Mar. 14, 1887, copied from *Albany Journal* (no date given); "Fence Around Grave of Jane McCrea," *Fort Edward Advertiser*, Sept. 18, 1894. The sentimental ritualizing of death in the Victorian era is discussed in Karen Halttunen, *Confidence Men and Painted Women: A Study of Middle-Class Culture in America, 1830–1870* (New Haven: Yale University Press, 1982), 124–52.

70. Requests range from the Museum of Modern Art exhibit "Romantic Painting in America," Nov. 15–Feb. 6, 1944, to the *Weekly Reader*, Mar. 23, 1977. For a more complete listing see June Namias, "White Captives: Gender and Ethnicity on Successive American Frontiers, 1607–1862" (Ph.D. dissertation, Brandeis University, 1989), 295, n. 78.

71. The traditional rendering of the nineteenth-century narrative often sets up the home as a romantic idyll before captivity destroys it. I first recognized this in a captivity narrative sent to me by the Keller family of western Pennsylvania. The narrative was of a family captured on the Pennsylvania frontier in the 1750s but retold in the nineteenth century. It was sent to me through a request I had placed in the magazine of the Daughters of the American Revolution. Joy S. Kasson notes that this kind of narrative can be read in the captive statues as well (*Marble Queens and Captives: Women in Nineteenth-Century American Sculpture* [New Haven: Yale University Press, 1990], 97–98).

72. Clifford Geertz, *The Interpretation of Cultures: Selected Essays* (New York: Basic Books, 1973), 412–53, esp. 452–53.

73. Lynn Hunt, *Politics, Culture, and Class in the French Revolution* (Berkeley: University of California Press, 1984), 88. Hunt's recent work explores the connections between revolution and the family in France (Lecture to the History and Literature Colloquium, MIT, May 6, 1991). Also see Ruth H. Block, "The Gendered Meanings of Virtue in Revolutionary America," *Signs* 13 (Winter 1987): 37–58.

74. Abigail Adams to John Adams, Mar. 31, 1776, in L. H. Butterfield, Marc Friedlaender, and Mary-Jo Kline, eds., *The Book of Abigail*

and John: Selected Letters of the Adams Family, 1762–1784 (Cambridge, Mass.: Harvard University Press, 1975), 121.

. . .

5: MARY JEMISON: THE EVOLUTION
OF ONE CAPTIVE'S STORY

1. Most references to the Seaver narrative are from James Everett Seaver, *A Narrative of the Life of Mrs. Mary Jemison* (1824), *Garland Library*, vol. 41 (New York: Garland, 1977); James Everett Seaver, *A Narrative of the Life of Mary Jemison: The White Woman of the Genesee*, ed. Charles Delamater Vail, 22d ed. (New York: New York Scenic and Historic Preservation Society, 1918); and James Everett Seaver, *A Narrative of the Life of Mary Jemison: The White Woman of the Genesee*, rev. ed., Charles Delamater Vail, ed. (New York: New York Scenic and Historic Preservation Society, 1925). After the first citation, editions will be referred to by shortened title with the year of publication. For an available edition of the 1824 text and Seaver's introduction see James E. Seaver, *A Narrative of the Life of Mrs. Mary Jemison*, ed. June Namias (Norman: University of Oklahoma Press, 1992), 49–58. According to Seaver, Daniel W. Banister, Esq., "at the insistence of several gentlemen," wanted him to get together with Jemison "to publish to the world, an accurate account of her life." He met Jemison in the house of Jannet Whaley, in Castile, New York, "in the company of the publisher." Jemison arrived with Thomas Clute (*Narrative of the Life* [1925], ix–x).

2. Lois Lenski, *Indian Captive: The Story of Mary Jemison*, 15th printing (Philadelphia: J. B. Lippincott, 1941). Tom Cook, part-Mohawk teacher, writer, and historian, spoke on August 12, 1986, at Letchworth State Park, Castile, New York.

3. In Seaver's account, Mary says her capture was in 1755, but a newspaper account in the *Philadelphia Gazette*, Apr. 13 and 20, 1758, verifies the date as April 5, 1758. C. D. Vail cites these articles and indicates that all of Jemison's dating is three years off (*Narrative of the Life* [1918], 310). It appears rather that some of her dating before the Revolution is off. See Chronology in *Narrative of the Life* (1992), xii. Also see Eleanor Robinette Dobson, "Mary Jemison," *Dictionary of American Biography*, 10:39–40.

4. Seaver, *Narrative of the Life* (1824), 25, and *Narrative of the Life* (1992), 66–70. The two brothers eventually wound up in Virginia at the home of her maternal grandparents, the Erwins (Allen W. Trelease, "Mary Jemison," in *Notable American Women, 1607–1950*, 3 vols., ed. Edward T. James et al. [Cambridge, Mass.: Harvard University Press, 1971], 2:271–74).

5. Tom Cook, "White Woman of Genesee Legend Endures," *Outdoors* [central New York] 1984, pp. 2–4, WPL.

6. These works include James Axtell, ed., *The Indian Peoples of Eastern America: A Documentary History of the Sexes* (New York: Oxford University Press, 1981), 138–39; and Anthony F. C. Wallace, *The Death and Rebirth of the Seneca* (New York: Vintage Books, 1972), 33, 135, 200–201, 300, 317.

7. Roy Harvey Pearce, *The Savages of America: A Study of the Indian and the Idea of Civilization*, rev. ed. (Baltimore: Johns Hopkins University Press, 1965.)

8. J. Niles Hubbard, *An Account of Sa-Go-Ye-Wat-Ha or Red Jacket and His People, 1750–1830* (1848; rpt. Albany: Joel Munsell's Sons, 1886), 185–86. On English and American ideology of the Indian see Robert F. Berkhofer, Jr., *The White Man's Indian: Images of the American Indian from Columbus to the Present* (New York: Vintage Books, 1979); Reginald Horsman, *Race and Manifest Destiny: The Origins of American Racial Anglo-Saxonism* (Cambridge, Mass.: Harvard University Press, 1981), chap. 6 and 105–6, 189–209, 298–303.

9. Gretchen M. Bataille and Kathleen Mullen Sands, *American Indian Women: Telling Their Lives* (Lincoln: University of Nebraska Press, 1984), 3–46, esp. 3–4, 10–17; Mary V. Dearborn, *Pocahontas's Daughters: Gender and Ethnicity in American Culture* (New York: Oxford University Press, 1986), 9, 18, 23, 31–47. See Susan Walsh, " 'With Them Was My Home': Native American Autobiography and *A Narrative of the Life of Mrs. Mary Jemison*," *American Literature* 64 (March 1992): 1–18. Her work was unavailable while I was writing.

10. Jesse Seaver, "The Seaver Genealogy: A Genealogy, History and Directory," typescript (Philadelphia, 1924), 2, 5, 41–43, 45, 49, in NSDAR; William Blake Trask, *A Genealogy of Robert Seaver: The Seaver Family, A Genealogy* (Boston: David Clapp and Son, 1872), NSDAR; "Family Skeletons and Ghosts," "Hunt," and "Everett" Families, copied by David Seaver from genealogies printed at Boston, Mass., Seaver Family Collection, NSDAR. Edward Everett ran on the Constitutional Union ticket in the 1860 election with John Bell.

11. F. W. Beers, ed., *Gazetteer and Biographical Record of Genesee County, N.Y., 1788–1890* (Syracuse: J. W. Vose, 1890), 403; Safford E. North, ed., *Our County and Its People* ([Boston]: Boston History Co., 1899), 387–88.

12. Fredrick Strecker gives a complete listing to 1929 in *My First Years as a Jemisonian* (Rochester, N.Y.: Fred'k Strecker, 1931); or see C. D. Vail, "Tabulation of Editions of 'The Life of Mary Jemison,' " in Seaver, *Narrative of the Life* (1925), 296–97. For a listing of major editions see *Narrative of the Life* (1992), 197–98.

13. Frank Luther Mott, *Golden Multitudes: The Story of Best Sellers in the United States* (New York: Macmillan, 1947), 20; Seaver, *Narrative of the Life* (1918), k–l. A 16 mo is a particularly small book.

14. Seaver, *Narrative of the Life* (1824), viii; *Narrative of the Life* (1992), 54.

15. Seaver, *Narrative of the Life* (1824), 18, 23, 27–28.

16. Barbara Welter, "The Cult of True Womanhood, 1820–1860," *AQ* 18 (Summer 1966): 151–74.

17. Seaver, *Narrative of the Life* (1824), xii–xiv. According to Arthur C. Parker, Hiokatoo's real name was Hogedowa, meaning Great Spear. Others called him Big Lance. See Arthur C. Parker, "Mary Jemison, Historic Character Made Deep Imprint upon Region," Address at 100th anniversary ceremonial of the death of Mary Jemison, Letchworth State Park, Sept. 19, 1933, unnamed newspaper, LSP.

18. Seaver, *Narrative of the Life* (1824), 105; *Narrative of the Life* (1992), 129–30.

19. Wallace, *Death and Rebirth*, 30–48.

20. Seaver, *Narrative of the Life* (1824), xiv. Even contemporary scholars take the torture scenes of George Jemison as the words of Mary and use them as firsthand evidence of Indian brutality (Barbara Graymont, *Iroquois in the American Revolution* [Syracuse: Syracuse University Press, 1972], 232).

21. Beers, ed., *Gazetteer of Genesee County*, 195.

22. James E. Seaver, *Deh-he-wä-mis: or A Narrative of the Life of Mary Jemison*, 2d ed. (Batavia, N.Y.: William Seaver and Son, 1842). For more detail on the print history see June Namias, "White Captives: Gender and Ethnicity on Successive American Frontiers, 1607–1862" (Ph.D. dissertation, Brandeis University, 1989), 355–56, nn. 27, 30.

23. The "original" chapters were 5, 18, 19. James E. Seaver, *Deh-he-wä-mis* (1842), published by William Seaver and Son; same title, 3d ed. (Batavia, N.Y.: William Seaver and Son, 1844), vii–viii.

24. Dr. E. H. Hall to C. D. Vail, in Seaver, *Narrative of the Life* (1918), 229–300, also see Vail's notes in the foreword, 1.

25. Mix in *Deh-he-wä-mis* (1842), chap. 5, p. 60. The additions appear in chap. 5, pp. 58–70, chap. 18, pp. 165–68, chap. 19, pp. 169–73, and chap. 20, pp. 174–78, and include the Sullivan expedition selection in the Appendix, 182–91, for a total of 32 new pages (Strecker, "Tabulation," in *My First Years*).

26. Seaver, *Deh-he-wä-mis* (1847), viii.

27. Seaver, *Deh-he-wä-mis* (1844), 166–67.

28. See Michael Kammen, "'The Promised Sunshine or the Future': Reflections on Economic Growth and Social Change in Post-Revolutionary New York," in *New Opportunities in a New Nation: The Development of New York after the Revolution*, ed. Manfred Jones and Robert V. Wells (Schenectady, N.Y.: Union College Press, 1982), 109–43; William H. Siles, "Pioneering in the Genesee Country: Entrepreneurial Strategy and the Concept of a Central Place," ibid., 35–68.

29. Seaver, *Deh-he-wä-mis* (1844), 173–74, 177–78. The original paragraph may be found in Seaver, *Narrative of the Life* (1824), 90.

30. Seaver, *Narrative of the Life* (1824), 73–74. On the Sullivan campaign see Graymont, *Iroquois in the American Revolution*. Also see Introduction by Namias in *Narrative of the Life* (1992). For another Seneca view of the Revolution see Thomas S. Abler, ed., *Chainbreaker: The Revolutionary War Memoirs of Governor Blacksnake as told to Benjamin Williams* (Lincoln: University of Nebraska Press, 1989). For another captive's view see *The Story of Jasper Parrish: Captive, Interpreter and United States Sub-Agent to the Six Nations Indians* (1903), *Garland Library*, vol. 105 (New York: Garland, 1976). I have expanded these themes on the Senecas' Revolution in "The Life of Mary Jemison: Toward a Fuller Vision of Frontier America, 1758–1812," paper presented at the Annual Meeting of the Organization of American Historians, Washington, D.C., Apr. 1990; "Remembering, Omitting, and Reconstructing: Mary Jemison's Story and Indian-White Relations on the Early American Frontier," paper presented at conference, "Private Memory, Collective Memory in Pre-Industrial America," at the Institut d'Anglais, Université Paris 7, Paris, France, Feb. 5, 1992; and "Mary Jemison's Story and Indian-White Relations on the Early American Frontier," paper presented at the Workshop for History and Literature, Feb. 20, 1992, and forthcoming from the Literary and Cultural Studies Program at MIT. Also see Kenneth M. Morrison, "Native Americans and the American Revolution: Historic Stories and Shifting Frontier Conflict," in *Indians in American History: An Introduction*, ed. Frederick E. Hoxie (Arlington Heights, Ill.: Harlan Davidson, 1988), 95–115.

31. Seaver, *Deh-he-wä-mis* (1884), 188–91.

32. Mott, *Golden Multitudes*, 305–6.

33. Michael Kammen, *A Season of Youth: The American Revolution and the Historical Imagination* (New York: Knopf, 1978).

34. Biographical information is from the *Buffalo Evening News*, Dec. 2, 1910. The firm was also known as Malleable Iron Works.

35. James A. Tuck, "Northern Iroquoian Prehistory," in *HNAI/Northeast*, 322–33; Tuck, "Regional Cultural Development, 3000–300 B.C.," in *HNAI/Northeast*, 28–43. On religion see Arthur C. Parker, "An Analytical History of the Seneca Indians," *Researches and Transactions of the New York State Archaeological Association* 6 (1926); Edward Hagaman Hall in *New York Evening Post*, Dec. 10, 1910.

36. *Buffalo Evening News*, Dec. 2, 1910.

37. *New York Evening Post*, Dec. 10, 1910; "Friend of Indian Is Dead," *Washington Post*, Dec. 3, 1910; "Friend of Indian Dies in New York," *Washington Times*, Dec. 3, 1910.

38. Lewis H. Morgan, annotated by Herbert M. Lloyd, *League of the Ho-dé-no-sau-nee or Iroquois*, 2 vols. in 1 (New York: Dodd, Mead, 1904); Seaver, *Narrative of the Life* (1918), 292–93, for details. The 1877 edition, which was reprinted for several years, had seventeen

illustrations, twelve more than the 1860 edition. James Everett Seaver, *Life of Mary Jemison: Deh-he-wä-mis* (Buffalo: William P. Letchworth, 1880). By 1913 there were twenty-two illustrations.

39. Letter "To the American Scenic and Historic Preservation Society," Sept. 10, 1910, in Seaver, *Narrative of the Life* (1918), 238. Laura Wright's words first appeared in the Letchworth edition of 1877 and are reprinted on pages 208–12 in the 1918 edition. On Asher and Laura Wright among the Senecas see Wallace, *Death and Rebirth*, 94, 323.

40. The Wrights spent the better part of their lives as Christian missionaries to the Senecas. William N. Fenton suggests Reverend Asher Wright needed to "justify the failure of his mission." Laura Wright too seems less than a neutral witness as to the state of Jemison's soul. See W. N. Fenton, ed., "Documents: Seneca Indians by Asher Wright (1859)" (from American Board of Commissioners for Foreign Missions), *EH* 4 (Summer 1957): 302–20, esp. 303; Bernhard J. Stern, "The Letters of Asher Wright to Lewis Henry Morgan," *American Anthropologist* 35 (Jan.–Mar. 1933): 138–45; "Copy of Manuscript prepared by Mrs. Asher Wright relating Indian Mission burial ground and to 'The White Woman,'" in the hand of Letchworth, n.d., WPL. Mary Ormsbee Whitton also doubts the conversion (*These Were the Women: U.S.A., 1776–1860* [New York: Hastings House, 1954], 24–25).

41. For a listing of contemporary displays see the Inventory of American Sculpture at the National Museum of American Art, Smithsonian Institution, and Glenn B. Opitz, *Dictionary of American Sculptors: "18th Century to the Present"* (Poughkeepsie, N.Y.: Apollo, 1984), 55.

42. Letters from H. K. Bush-Brown, Nov. 30, 1906, July 4, 17, Oct. 6, 1907, Mar. 2, 1908, photographs of Jemison statue in plaster, undated, WPL.

43. Letters from Bush-Brown, Nov. 30, 1907, Jan. 2, 1908, WPL.

44. Vail says that the belt, leggings, and "baby board" were all modeled from the Morgan collection. See Seaver, *Narrative of the Life* (1918), 240–41; Richard Rose, "The Morgan Collection at the Rochester Museum and Science Center," *American Indian Art* 12 (Summer 1987): 32–37. A step-by-step accounting of Jemison's journey of over six hundred miles from southern Ohio may be found in which Vail suggests that it took six months from about July 1, 1762, to January 1, 1763, going from Wiishto, Ohio, to Genishau, New York (Seaver, *Narrative of the Life* [1925], 373–79).

45. In a letter of January 14, 1908, Bush-Brown says he designed the statue of Jemison walking; "however I will make another design representing her standing, as suggested in yours the 13th., and then submit the two designs to you" (WPL). "Copy of Manuscript prepared by Mrs. Asher Wright relating Indian Mission burial ground and to 'The White Woman,'" in the hand of Letchworth, n.d., WPL, reprinted in Seaver, *Narrative of the Life* (1918), 209, 212. Mrs. Wright

said Mary "did not look much larger than a child of ten years old" and "Mary Jemison must have been small in stature."

46. Letter "To the American Scenic and Historic Society," Sept. 19, 1910, in Seaver, *Narrative of the Life* (1918), 238–39; *New York Evening Post*, Dec. 10, 1910.

47. See section of this chapter, "Indian Woman," for further discussion of Morgan. Charles Delamater Vail was a bibliographer who took over Letchworth's editions and in 1918, under the aegis of the American Scenic and Historical Preservation Society and G. P. Putnam's Sons, issued a 475-page twentieth edition with forty-one illustrations, gold page edgings, and a gold embossed replica of the Bush-Brown Jemison statue on the cover.

48. Parker, "Mary Jemison, Historic Character."

49. Parker never received a Ph.D. degree; rather, he used his influence among the Iroquois to gain information which then earned him professional acceptance (William N. Fenton, ed., *Parker on the Iroquois: Iroquois Uses of Maize and Other Food Plants; The Code of Handsome Lake, the Seneca Prophet; The Constitution of the Five Nations* [1910, 1913, 1916; rpt. Syracuse: Syracuse University Press, 1968], 2, 6, 10; Parker, "Mary Jemison, Historic Character").

50. Clare D. Kinsman, *Contemporary Authors: A Bio-Bibliographical Guide to Current Authors*, 44 vols. (Detroit: Gale Research, 1975), 1:372–73; Taimi M. Ranta, "Lois Lenski," in *American Writers for Children, 1900–1960: Dictionary of Literary Biography*, ed. John Cech, 115 vols. (Detroit: Gale Research, 1985), 22:241–52, citing May Hill Arbuthnot on *Tom Sawyer*, 251. For another children's version of the Jemison story see Will W. Whalen, *The Golden Squaw* (Philadelphia: Dorrance, 1926).

51. Lenski, *Indian Captive*, xvii–xviii; Ranta, "Lois Lenski," 246. For the foreign print history see Namias, "White Captives," 362, n. 66.

52. Arthur C. Parker, intro. in Lenski, *Indian Captive*, ix–x. Stepsisters lend a Cinderella quality to this section. See 67–69.

53. Seaver's comments, *Narrative of the Life* (1824), xi. Laura Wright's statement is reproduced in Seaver, *Narrative of the Life* (1918), 212. Despite my contention that Jemison's hair was not blond, in my own edition of her narrative I chose to have a descendant and Seneca artist, G. Peter Jemison, draw the cover. He depicts her hair as blond. When I called to his attention that she was not a blond, he said he knew, but the contrast on the cover simply would not be as strong with a brunette. Art and legend win again over "the facts." See Cover, *Narrative of the Life* (1992). Helena Michie says that the focusing on and "fetishizing" of particular body parts, including hair, was common in nineteenth-century fiction (*The Flesh Made Word: Female Figures and Women's Bodies* [New York: Oxford University Press, 1987], esp. 98–102). Also see a discussion of this in sculpture, especially for the Palmer statue *White Captive*, in Joy S. Kasson, *Marble Queens*

and Captives: Women in Nineteenth-Century American Sculpture (New Haven: Yale University Press, 1990), 83–85, and William H. Gerdts, "Marble and Nudity," *Art in America* 59 (May–June 1971): 60–67.

54. *An Account of the Remarkable Occurrences in the Life and Travels of Colonel James Smith* (1799) in *Indian Captivities: Life in the Wigwam*, ed. Samuel G. Drake (New York: Miller, Orton, 1857), esp. 185.

55. Lenski, *Indian Captive*, 38–39.

56. Ibid., 53–54.

57. Ibid., 77.

58. Ibid., 269–70.

59. Dawn Lander Gherman, "From Parlour to Tepee: The White Squaw on the American Frontier" (Ph.D. dissertation, University of Massachusetts, 1975), 211–13.

60. I refer here to Joyce Antler's use of the idea of a woman's life as lived as a measure of her feminism and development. See *Lucy Sprague Mitchell: The Making of a Modern Woman* (New Haven: Yale University Press, 1987). Also see John Demos, *Past, Present, and Personal: The Family and the Life Course in American History* (New York: Oxford University Press, 1986), x–xi.

61. See *The Reader in the Text: Essays on Audience and Interpretation*, ed. Susan R. Suleiman and Inge Crosman (Princeton: Princeton University Press, 1980), esp. Susan R. Suleiman, "Introduction: Varieties of Audience-Oriented Criticism," 3–45; Jonathan Culler, "Prolegomena to a Theory of Reading," 46–68; Tzvetan Todorov, "Reading as Construction," 67–83; Wolfgang Iser, "Interaction between Text and Reader," 106–19.

62. Feminist critics have been influenced by a number of poststructuralist French writers. See Roland Barthes, *Writing Degree Zero*, trans. Annette Lavers and Colin Smith, Preface by Susan Sontag (New York: Hill and Wang, 1968), xii–xiii. Also see Elaine Showalter, "The Feminist Critical Revolution" and "Toward a Feminist Poetics," in *Feminist Criticism: Essays on Women, Literature, and Theory*, ed. Elaine Showalter (New York: Pantheon, 1985), 3–18, 125–43. In the same collection see Annette Kolodny, "A Map for Rereading: Gender and the Interpretation of Literary Texts," 46–61. On heroines see Nancy K. Miller, *The Heroine's Text: Readings in the French and English Novel, 1722–1782* (New York: Columbia University Press, 1980).

63. Seaver, *Narrative of the Life* (1824), 20, 22, 24–25.

64. Ibid., 26–27.

65. Ibid., 27–28.

66. Ibid., 28–29, and *Narrative of the Life* (1992), 70.

67. Ibid., 36–37.

68. See discussion in the Introduction. Also see Daniel K. Richter, "Ordeals of the Longhouse: The Five Nations in Early American History," in *Beyond the Covenant Chain: The Iroquois and Their Neigh-*

bors in Indian North America, 1600–1800, ed. Daniel K. Richter and
James H. Merrell (Syracuse: Syracuse University Press, 1987), 16–
17; Daniel K. Richter, "War and Culture: The Iroquois Experience,"
WMQ 3d ser., 40 (1983): 537–44. The mourning-war behavior of cap-
ture and adoption was first mentioned by Marian W. Smith, "The War
Complex of the Plains Indians," in *The American Indian: Past and
Present*, ed. Roger L. Nichols and George R. Adams (Waltham, Mass.:
Xerox College Publishers, 1971), 146–56, and in *Proceedings of the
American Philosophical Society* 78, no. 3 (1937): 425–61. The role of
women in this ceremony is highlighted in James Lynch, "The Iroquois
Confederacy, and the Adoption and Administration of Non-Iroquoian
Individuals and Groups prior to 1756," *Man in the Northeast* 30 (Fall
1985): 83–99. See a discussion on capture in the Introduction. For a
bleaker view of Iroquoian captive practices see William A. Starna and
Ralph Watkins, "Northern Iroquoian Slavery," *EH* 38 (Winter 1991):
34–57.

69. Seaver, *Narrative of the Life* (1824), 36

70. Ibid., 36–40, 56–57. Seaver says this name was Dickewamis,
meaning "a pretty girl, a handsome girl or a pleasant, good thing."
Arthur C. Parker claims that no such construction exists in Seneca;
rather, her name was Dehgewanus, meaning the sound of falling
voices, and he claims that the Iroquoian languages have no sounds like
the other name. The folklore and the various editions, however, hold
to Dickewamis, and the childlike and romantic meaning of her name.
In the Lewis Henry Morgan edition NMNH/BAE, J. N. B. Hewitt, an
important Iroquois ethnographer at the Smithsonian Institution, has
penned in a correction to Morgan's subtitle, *Life of Mary Jemison:
Deh-he-wä-mis* (New York and Auburn: Miller, Orton and Mulligan,
and Rochester: D. M. Dewey, 1856). He wrote, "De-gi-wa-'ne^{un}'s—
'Two women's voices falling.' "

71. *Life of Mary Jemison: Deh-he-wä-mis* (1856), 39–43, and second
rejection of returning, 60–62. For another example of Indian women's
role in initiating daughters and younger women see Jay Miller, ed.,
Mourning Dove: A Salishan Autobiography (Lincoln: University of
Nebraska Press, 1990), chap. 2.

72. *Life of Mary Jemison: Deh-he-wä-mis* (1856), 45, and "Kin of
Mary Jemison Hold Onondaga Reunion," *Branford Expositor*, June
1956, LSP. C. D. Vail claims the trek was more like 682 miles: 236
miles by canoe, 75 miles by foot, 270 miles with horses, and another
101 miles on foot. See Seaver, *Narrative of the Life* (1918), 269, 372–75;
also Namias, "White Captives," 365, n. 95.

73. Seaver, *Narrative of the Life* (1824), xii–xiv; Janice A. Radway,
Reading the Romance: Women, Patriarchy, and Popular Literature
(Chapel Hill: University of North Carolina Press, 1984).

74. Seaver, *Narrative of the Life* (1925), 98–99, 102, 120–21.

75. Nina Baym first discusses women as readers in *Novels, Readers,*

and Reviewers: Responses to Fiction in Antebellum America (Ithaca: Cornell University Press, 1984), 39, 50–54, and in *Woman's Fiction: A Guide to Novels by and about Women in America, 1820–1870* (Ithaca: Cornell University Press, 1978). See forthcoming work by Peter C. Mancall, "The Bewitching Tyranny of Custom: The Social Costs of Indian Drinking in Colonial America," paper presented at the Boston Area Seminar in Early American History, Feb. 20, 1992.

76. Seaver, *Narrative of the Life* (1824), 98–99.

77. Allen Trelease also comments on Seaver's use of Jemison's language in his introduction to James E. Seaver, *A Narrative of the Life of Mrs. Mary Jemison* (New York: Peter Smith, 1961), vii. Statistics are from Carl N. Degler, *At Odds: Women and the Family in America from the Revolution to the Present* (New York: Oxford University Press, 1980), 181.

78. Seaver, *Narrative of the Life* (1824), 102.

79. Her first child died two days after her birth. Ibid., 143.

80. Seaver has her say directly following, "My mother and her family gave me all the consolation in their power, and in a few months my grief wore off and I became contented" (ibid., 58).

81. Ibid., 125–26, 139. The will was published in the *Rochester Post-Express*, Dec. 15, 1894, and is printed in Vail's editions and discussed there by William Holland Samson. By Samson's account, the will was admitted to probate April 7, 1835 (Seaver, *Narrative of the Life* [1925], 243–50).

82. John Tebbel, *A History of Book Publishing in the United States*, Vol. 1, *The Creation of an Industry, 1630–1865* (New York: R. R. Bowker–Xerox, 1972), 203–62, esp. 221; Martha Vicinus, "Heroines for 19th-Century Girls: Popular Biographies in Florence Nightingale," paper presented at the Seventh Berkshire Conference, Wellesley College, June 20, 1987. On the importance of fiction in the education of women see Cathy N. Davidson, *Revolution and the Word: The Rise of the Novel in America* (New York: Oxford University Press, 1986), 8.

83. Seaver, *Narrative of the Life* (1824), 142, and *Narrative of the Life* (1992), 159.

84. Based on the first, second, and third translations of J. N. B. Hewitt, *Iroquoian Cosmology* (First Part), extract from the *21st Annual Report of the Bureau of American Ethnology* (Washington, D.C.: U.S. Government Printing Office, 1904), 221–28. This translation was done looking at Hewitt's direct and literal translation from the Seneca. I have deliberately chosen Hewitt and the Seneca version over Hewitt's other versions (Mohawk, Oneida, and others) and over other versions by other authors because Hewitt was a Tuscarora and well versed in the Seneca language. With all due respect to his linguistic skills, his poetic sense was sacrificed to his linguistic training. I have taken artistic and linguistic liberties here in an attempt to create both fluidity

and clarity. I have no knowledge of the Seneca language but hope this translation is a fair one.

85. For other cosmologies see Namias, "White Captives," 416–17, n. 2.

86. G. Peter Jemison, a descendant of Mary's, says that Seneca children are still told these explanations of the world (telephone conversation, July, 12, 1987). Other Native Americans have had similar experiences (N. Scott Momaday [Kiowa], "Personal Reflections," and Henrietta Whiteman [Cheyenne], "White Buffalo Woman," in *The American Indian and the Problem of History*, ed. Calvin Martin [New York: Oxford University Press, 1987], 156–61, 162–70). Jesse Cornplanter refers to his sisters' versions as well as those of his father in Jesse J. Cornplanter of the Senecas, Told to Sah-Nee-Weh, the White Sister, *Legends of the Longhouse* (Philadelphia: J. B. Lippincott, 1938), 19–33.

87. Seaver, *Narrative of the Life* (1824), 46. It seems that Thomas's birth and the move took place in 1762. This was the first year of a two-year epidemic in Jemison's area of the Ohio. In that year a disease, possibly smallpox, moved through the Mingo, Delaware, and Shawnee (Helen Hornbeck Tanner, ed., *Atlas of Great Lakes Indian History* [Norman: University of Oklahoma Press, 1987], 173). Annette Kolodny finds the work itself "swerved radically from conventional formulae" after chapter 3, when Jemison identifies with her Indian surroundings (*The Land Before Her: Fantasy and Experience of the American Frontiers, 1630–1860* [Chapel Hill: University of North Carolina Press, 1984], 74–75).

88. Seaver, *Narrative of the Life* (1824), 40, 46–47.

89. Ibid., 47, and *Narrative of the Life* (1992), 84; Arthur C. Parker (Gawaso Wanneh), *The Indian How Book* (1927; rpt. New York: Dover, 1975), 193–202.

90. Seaver, *Narrative of the Life* (1824), 47–48.

91. Ibid., 44.

92. Ibid., 45.

93. The river is said to mean "Between Beautiful Fields or Brooks." The Seneca town Jemison went to was Genishau. Gardow (or Gardeau Flats) is the area in which Jemison lived from about 1780 to 1824. It was called Ga-Da-O ("Map of Ho-De-No-Saw-Nee-Ga or the People of the Long House," compiled about 1851 by Lewis H. Morgan and Ely S. Parker, NYPL).

94. Seaver, *Narrative of the Life* (1824), 51. On Iroquois dominance of the Delaware see Ives Goddard, "Delaware," in *HNAI/Northeast*, 213–39, esp. 220–23; Francis Jennings, "The Delaware Indians in the Covenant Chain," in *A Delaware Indian Symposium*, ed. Herbert C. Kraft (Harrisburg: Pennsylvania Historical and Museum Commission, 1974), 89–102. For a sense of the multicultural Indian society

along the Ohio in the 1760s, see Tanner, ed., *Atlas*, 43–47, 58–59, 62–63.

95. Seaver, *Narrative of the Life* (1824), 68. For more on Butler and Brant and their roles during the Revolution see Graymont, *Iroquois in the American Revolution*, 64, 86, 115–57, 208–9.

96. Seaver, *Narrative of the Life* (1824), 48, 64.

97. Ibid., 58, 93. Jemison says this was soon after the Revolution. If this was the mid-1780s, her son Thomas would have been in his early twenties. Her first daughter to live was Nancy, born about 1773 (using Vail's stipulation of her three-year time error). Her next daughter, Betsey, was born between then and 1778–79, when the third, Polly, was born. Jane was born in 1782 and son Jesse in 1784. See Chronology in *Narrative of the Life* (1992), xiii.

98. Wallace, *Death and Rebirth*, 179–83 and chap. 7, and Anthony F. C. Wallace, "Origins of the Longhouse Religion," in *HNAI/Northeast*, 443–44. After the Revolution, Indians were not party to the Treaty of Paris (1783). The second treaty of Fort Stanwix (1784) stripped both land and sovereignty from the Iroquois people. Some, including Jemison's brother, chose to move to Canada, where they set up the Grand River Reserve in Ontario. Seneca lands were also disputed between New York and Massachusetts. In an agreement made in Hartford (1786) New York was given legal rights to most of these lands, and Massachusetts sold its rights in a series of deals that led to land developers—first Oliver Phelps and Nathaniel Gorham, then Robert Morris, then the Dutch banking house the Holland Land Company—taking over (Thomas S. Abler and Elisabeth Tooker, "Seneca," in *HNAI/Northeast*, 508–9). See the shape of these reservations after individual land sales in Elisabeth Tooker, "Iroquois since 1820," in *HNAI/Northeast*, 450.

99. Jemison says Red Jacket also opposed her receiving money she was due and was compelled to pay it by Indian agent Jasper Parrish and interpreter Captain Horatio Jones, both of whom had been Iroquois captives (Seaver, *Narrative of the Life* [1925], 92–95, Vail's notes, 407, and on naturalization, 136, and Vail's notes, 438).

100. Reservations such as the Allegany and Tonawanda still exist and are scenes of a revived Seneca consciousness. There is a museum on the Allegany Reservation, and teaching of the Seneca language is in process.

101. Seaver, *Narrative of the Life* (1824), 122–26, Seaver note, 123. Karen Oakes argues that Jemison's is a "transethnic journey" in which Jemison's use of "the sacredness of language" may be traced to her becoming a Seneca ("A Tale of Two Cultures: The Story of Mary Jemison," paper presented at the New England American Studies Association Conference, Boston, Apr. 26, 1992).

102. Seaver, *Narrative of the Life* (1824), 137–38; Treaty on the Buffalo Creek Reservation, Aug. 31, 1826, and letter to Letchworth from

W. H. Lawson, Jan. 22, 1898, WPL; Francis Jennings, *The Invasion of America: Indians, Colonialism, and the Cant of Conquest* (New York: Norton, 1975), 128–45.

103. Annette Kolodny agrees in *Land Before Her*, 71–72, and see *Women in the Field: Anthropological Experiences*, ed. Peggy Golde, 2d ed. (Berkeley: University of California Press, 1986), 1–15.

104. See Robin Ridington, "Fox and Chickadee," in *American Indian and the Problem of History*, ed. Martin, 128–35; Introduction by Robert Coles in June Namias, *First Generation: In the Words of Twentieth-Century American Immigrants* (Boston: Beacon Press, 1978), xvii–xviii, and rev. ed. (Urbana: University of Illinois Press, 1992).

105. Seaver was not alone in this regard. Theda Perdue says that James Adair married and lived among the Cherokee most of his life and never asked about or recognized the essentially matriarchal nature of clan and kin networks ("Amerindian Women: Old World Perceptions, New World Realities," paper presented at Harvard University, Mar. 8, 1988).

106. Tom Cook, historian and park attendant at Letchworth State Park, took me down to Gardeau Flats in August 1986.

107. Seaver, *Narrative of the Life* (1824), ix–x.

108. Ibid., 28; James Axtell, *The European and the Indian: Essays in the Ethnohistory of Colonial North America* (New York: Oxford University Press, 1981), 180.

109. Conversation with R. H. Ives Goddard, National Museum of Natural History, Smithsonian Institution, May 1, 1987; Joseph Doddridge, *Notes on the Settlement and Indian Wars of the Western Parts of Virginia and Pennsylvania from 1763–1783* (Pittsburgh: John S. Ritenour and Wm. T. Lindsay, 1912).

110. Jemison claims that in looking out for her health, she "never once attended an Indian frolic." Nevertheless, this would not exclude seasonal rituals. Seaver uses *frolic* to mean something close to a wild party with liquor (*Narrative of the Life* [1824], 141).

111. Ibid., Appendix, 157–79. For my analysis see Namias, "White Captives," 383–85, and Intro. to Seaver, *Narrative of the Life* (1992), 3–45.

112. The Rochester collection's copy of the 1856 edition is signed by Morgan. The Lewis Henry Morgan Papers (1839–85) are at Special Collections at Rush Rhees Library, University of Rochester. The 1856 edition is attributed to Morgan by Letchworth, J. N. B. Hewitt, and Wilcomb E. Washburn. For further discussion on Morgan and citations see Namias, "White Captives," 388–90, 422, n. 39.

113. Seaver, *Deh-he-wä-mis* (1856), 7–9. See references to women's work in ibid., 70–71, not to be found in the first edition. Morgan, or whoever else edited the 1856 edition, cut and pasted chapters together differently than in the first edition and added material to the text. The

statement, "the reverse of the order of nature," concurs with Morgan's evolutionary theory of culture.

114. Trelease in Seaver, *Narrative of the Life* (1961), viii.

115. For more on early Seneca and Iroquois history and culture see *Beyond the Covenant Chain*, ed. Richter and Merrell; J. N. B. Hewitt, "Seneca," in *Handbook of American Indians North of Mexico*, ed. Frederick Webb Hodge, 2 vols., *Bureau of American Ethnology Bulletin 30* (1907–10; rpt. New York: Rowman and Littlefield, 1971), 2:502–8; John R. Swanton, "Iroquois," in *The Indian Tribes of North America* (Washington, D.C.: U.S. Government Printing Office, 1952), 33–40.

116. On postwar settlement see Francis Paul Prucha, *The Great Father: The United States Government and the American Indians*, abridged ed. (Lincoln: University of Nebraska Press, 1986), 17–19; Arrell Morgan Gibson, *The American Indian: Prehistory to the Present* (Norman: University of Oklahoma Press, 1980), 257–69. "Genesee fever" is described in *Description of the Settlement of the Genesee Country* (New York: T & J. Swords, 1799); *A View of the Present Situation of the Western Parts of the State of New-York, Called the Genesee Country* (Frederick-Town, N.Y.: Author, 1804); Paul E. Johnson, *A Shopkeeper's Millennium: Society and Revivals in Rochester, New York, 1815–1837* (New York: Hill and Wang, 1978); Mary P. Ryan, *Cradle of the Middle Class: The Family in Oneida County, New York, 1790–1865* (Cambridge, Eng.: Cambridge University Press, 1981).

117. Elizabeth Tooker places the historical documentation of the league from the 1600s, but the traditions of the Iroquois on the league go back as far as the 1400s ("The League of the Iroquois: Its History, Politics, and Ritual," in *HNAI/Northeast*, 418–20). Why the league expanded is contested by historians. Some claim European intervention and the quest for furs for the European market and their exchange for weapons was central; others include an internal dynamic relating to more spiritually driven imperatives; still others center the conflict around inter-Indian rivalries. See Eric R. Wolf, *Europe and the People without History* (Berkeley: University of California Press, 1982), 158–94; Francis Jennings, *The Ambiguous Iroquois Empire: The Covenant Chain Confederation of Indian Tribes with English Colonists from Its Beginnings to the Lancaster Treaty of 1744* (New York: Norton, 1984); Calvin Martin, "The Covenant Chain of Friendship, Inc.: America's First Great Real Estate Agency," *RAH* (Mar. 1985): 14–22; James W. Bradley, *Evolution of the Onondaga Iroquois: Accommodating Change, 1500–1655* (Syracuse: Syracuse University Press, 1987), 106–11; Morgan, *League*; Paul A. W. Wallace, *The White Roots of Peace* (1946; rpt. Saranac Lake, N.Y.: Chauncy Press, 1986); Wallace, *Death and Rebirth*, 42, 44, 97–98. For Seneca names see "Map of Ho-De-No-Saw-Nee-Ga," comp. Morgan. For Jemison's world, see map in this chapter and in *Narrative of the Life* (1992) and Tanner, *Atlas*, 98–99. On diplomacy see *The History and Culture of Iroquois Diplomacy: An*

Interdisciplinary Guide to the Treaties of the Six Nations and Their League, ed. Francis Jennings, William N. Fenton, et al. (Syracuse: Syracuse University Press, 1985).

118. Telephone conversation with Joseph Bruchac, Jan. 9, 1988. Also see William N. Fenton, "Northern Iroquois Culture Patterns," in *HNAI/Northeast*, 296–306, esp. 300–302.

119. Wallace, *Death and Rebirth*, 28–30; Judith K. Brown, "Iroquois Women: An Ethnohistoric Note," in *Toward an Anthropology of Women*, ed. Rayna R. Reiter (New York: Monthly Review Press, 1975), 235–51, esp. 238–43; George S. Snyderman, *Behind the Tree of Peace: A Sociological Analysis of Iroquois Warfare* (1948; rpt. New York: AMS Press, 1979); Fenton, ed., *Parker on the Iroquois*.

120. Morgan, *League*, 317; Wallace, *Death and Rebirth*, 28–30.

121. Parker, *The Indian How Book*, 29–35; Fenton, "Northern Iroquois Culture Patterns," 303; and George R. Hamell, "From Longhouse to Log House: At Home among the Seneca Iroquois, 1783–1828," paper presented at "Native Americans and the Early Republic," a conference sponsored by the United States Capitol Historical Society, Mar. 5, 1992.

122. This was not a static system and there were changes over time.

123. Frank Gouldsmith Speck cites Hewitt on the nine clans of the Senecas: "wolf, bear, turtle, hawk, sandpiper (snipe), plover (killdeer), deer, heron" (*The Iroquois: A Study in Cultural Evolution* [Bloomfield Hills, Mich.: Cranbrook Institute of Science Bulletin 23, Oct. 1945], 28–29). See also Fenton, "Northern Iroquois Culture Patterns," 309–14.

124. Jennings, Fenton, et al., *Iroquois Diplomacy*; Cadwallader Colden, *The History of the Five Indian Nations: Depending on the Province of New-York in America* (1727 and 1747; rpt. Ithaca: Cornell University Press, 1986); Seaver, *Narrative of the Life* (1925), 41.

125. Seaver, *Narrative of the Life* (1824), 46–47, and Seaver, *Narrative of the Life* (1925), 46–47. These editions have similar but not identical pagination. They have the identical text, but the 1824 (Garland) is an exact reprint.

126. The different editions cut and paste the original narrative, but I could not find this piece in the first edition. My conclusion is that Morgan wrote it himself based on his knowledge of planting methods among Iroquois women and tacked it on to the original chapter 4 of *Narrative of the Life* (1824), 46–47.

127. Speck, *Iroquois*, 38–39.

128. For a discussion of corn, its recipes, preparation, and storage see Frederick W. Waugh, *Iroquois Foods and Food Preparation* (Ottawa: Government Printing Bureau, 1916), 77, 71–75, 9–43.

129. According to Neal Salisbury, Hochelaga was a village in which an Iroquoian language was spoken, but it was not a member of the league (note on MS 1989). Quoting French colonial sources, Parker

calls this figure an overestimation (Parker, "Iroquois Uses of Maize," in Fenton, ed., *Parker on the Iroquois*, 15, 18).

130. Ibid., 18–20; Graymont, *Iroquois in the American Revolution*, 192–222. The forty towns destroyed are detailed in "Indian Towns Destroyed in Sullivan's Campaign, 1779," in "Sullivan's Campaign 1779: Journals, Notes and Biography," *Cayuga County Historical Society Collections* 1 (1879): 83–87, and intro. to Seaver, *Narrative of the Life* (1992), 3–45. For another view see Pierluigi D'Oro, "Savage and Civil: Indian Violence and Non in the Revolutionary Context," in *Quaderno 3 People and Power: Rights, Citizenship and Violence*, ed. Loretta Valtz Mannucci [1990], 15–26.

131. On his trip out of Pennsylvania he also met George Slocum, trying to track down his daughter Frances Slocum, "Lost Daughter of the Wyoming," a captive in Indian country for the past five years (*Narrative of the Journey of Col. Thomas Proctor to the Indians of the North-West* [1791; rpt. *Pennsylvania Archives* 4 (1876): 594]).

132. Ibid., 555. The land was in Northumberland and along Big Fishing Creek on the west side of the Susquehannah (ibid., 560, 577, 580, 554).

133. Horatio Jones is mentioned first as helping out on April 1, 1791, and later while Proctor was in negotiations (ibid., 562, 602, 579, and earlier pages for the whole journey).

134. Ibid., 590.

135. Ibid., 600.

136. Ibid., 601.

137. The Senecas sent a delegation across Lake Erie to accompany Proctor to Fort Niagara, to the Miamis, and then to the Ohio River to Fort Washington (ibid., 601–2, 605).

138. Ibid., 565.

139. Frank G. Speck says he found at least sixteen "sound-pounding instruments" in his fieldwork among the Canadian Cayuga (*Iroquois*, 77–81). See also Gertrude Prokosch Kurath, "Dance and Song Rituals of the Six Nations Reserve, Ontario," *National Museum of Canada Bulletin* 220, Folklore Series 4 (1968): 201–2. Elisabeth Tooker, "The Iroquois White Dog Sacrifice in the Latter Part of the Eighteenth Century," *EH* 11 (Spring 1965): 129–40.

140. Kurath, "Dance and Song Rituals," 91–93. For Seneca drawings of women in the rituals, see Parker, "Iroquois Uses of Maize," in Fenton, ed., *Parker on the Iroquois*, from a drawing by Jesse Cornplanter (Gannundaiyeoh), a Seneca boy, ibid., Fig. 2, p. 27. Proctor saw women dance in a circle (*Journey of Thomas Proctor*, 578–79).

141. Robert F. Berkhofer, Jr., "Faith and Factionalism among the Senecas: Theory and Ethnohistory," *EH* 12 (Spring 1965): 99–112; Wallace, *Death and Rebirth*.

142. Rev. James H. Hotchkin, *A History of the Purchase and Settlement of Western New York and the Rise, Progress, and Present State*

of the Presbyterian Church in That Section (New York: M. W. Dodd, Brick Church Chapel, 1848), 126–29. See Johnson, *Shopkeeper's Millennium*, and Ryan, *Cradle of the Middle Class*. My thinking here was shaped in part by a series of programs, "Traditional Dance and Song of the Seneca," organized by Rayna Green in April 1987 and the programs of Iroquois and Algonquian music and dance including members of the longhouse from the Allegany Reservation at Salamanca, New York, presented as "The American Sampler: Musical Life in America, 1780–1800," April 16, 18, and 23, 1987, and the Iroquois "social dance" at National Museum of American History, directed by men from the Allegany Reservation.

143. Morgan, *League*, 192. "Our Supporters" are the Three Sisters, Corn, Beans, and Squash, also called, "Our Life" (ibid., 153). See Fenton, "Northern Iroquois Culture Patterns," 300.

144. J. N. B. Hewitt, "A Constitutional League of Peace in the Stone Age of America: The League of the Iroquois and Its Constitution," *Annual Report of the Smithsonian Institution for 1918*, 527–45, in *An Iroquois Source Book: Political and Social Organization*, 3 vols., ed. Elisabeth Tooker (New York: Garland, 1985), 1:543. Hewitt has an excellent essay titled "Women," expressing this conception. See *Handbook of American Indians North of Mexico*, ed. Hodge, 2:968–72. "The Tuscarora were the sixth nation of the Six Nations Iroquois. They lived among the Iroquois and were adopted formally in the early 1720s" (David Landy, "Tuscarora among the Iroquois," in *HNAI/Northeast*, 518–22).

145. Recent studies have brought about a reexamination of the stereotypes and conventional wisdom about Amerindian women. See Namias, Intro. to Seaver, *Narrative of the Life* (1992). Hewitt addressed this debate in 1910, stating that the view of the Indian woman as "abject slave and drudge of the men of her tribe" was "one of the most erroneous beliefs relating to the status and condition of the American Indian woman" (J. N. B. Hewitt, "Women," in *Handbook of American Indians North of Mexico*, ed. Hodge, 2:968–73). See Rayna Green, "The Pocahontas Perplex: The Image of the Indian Woman in American Culture," *Massachusetts Review* 16 (1975): 698–714; Green, "The Only Good Indian," 374–79; Green, *Native American Women: A Contextual Bibliography* (Bloomington: Indiana University Press, 1983); Bataille and Sands, *American Indian Women*; Patricia Albers, "Introduction: Perspectives on Plains Indian Women," in Patricia Albers and Beatrice Medicine, *The Hidden Half: Studies of Plains Indian Women* (Washington, D.C.: University Press of America, 1983), 1–29. On the impact of white male interpretation on explicating Indian women's roles see Eleanor Burke Leacock, *Myths of Male Dominance: Collected Articles on Women Cross-Culturally* (New York: Monthly Review Press, 1981); Sally Slocum, "Woman the Gatherer: Male Bias in Anthropology," and Paula Webster, "Matriarchy: A

Vision of Power," in *Toward an Anthropology of Women*, ed. Reiter, 36–50, 141–56. The ethnographic debate goes back to the eighteenth century and then to the mid-nineteenth century and Lewis Henry Morgan's work on the Iroquois. From then to the present, controversy over the precise role of Iroquois women has been sharp. Morgan saw the Iroquois as a highly male-dominated society (*League*, 315). Harriet Maxwell Converse lived close to the Iroquois. Her work sometimes praises their views of women, other times says the opposite (Harriet Maxwell Converse, "Miscellaneous Papers by Harriet Maxwell Converse, Iroquois Indians of the State of New York: The Ho-dee-no-sau-nee or People of the Long House" and "Women's Rights among the Iroquois," in *Myths and Legends of the New York State Iroquois*, Museum Bulletin 125, Education Department Bulletin 437 [1908; rpt. Albany: University of the State of New York, 1974]). Elisabeth Tooker and Judith K. Brown represent the contemporary version of this debate, with Tooker following the Morgan position, Brown the feminist one (Elisabeth Tooker, "Women in Iroquois Society," in *Extending the Rafters: Interdisciplinary Approaches to Iroquoian Studies*, ed. Michael K. Foster et al. [Albany: State University of New York Press, 1984], 109–23; Brown, "Iroquois Women"). Also see Father Joseph François Lafitau, *Customs of the American Indians Compared with the Customs of Primitive Tribes*, 2 vols., ed. and trans. William N. Fenton and Elisabeth L. Moore (1724; rpt. Toronto: Champlain Society, 1977), 2:54–55; Deborah Welch, "American Indian Women: Reaching beyond the Myth," in *New Directions in American Indian History*, ed. Colin G. Calloway (Norman: University of Oklahoma Press, 1988), 31–48. Also see Katherine Sheila Livingston, "Contemporary Iroquois Women and Work: A Study of Consciousness of Inequality" (Ph.D. dissertation, Cornell University, 1974). On the persistence of different views of women in regard to white contact see Carol A. Devens, "Separate Confrontations: Indian Women and Christian Missions, 1630–1900" (Ph.D. dissertation, Rutgers University, 1986).

146. Early 1800s Iroquois moccasins of black deerskin trimmed with porcupine quills with two types of beading, collected by George Catlin, quills of orange and buff, high on the ankle, circular designs, no. 50795, PM; child's moccasins probably Iroquois, undated, apparently for tourist trade, mid- to late nineteenth century, leaf and floral designs with white beading, no. 85445, PM. On the making of moccasins see Parker, *The Indian How Book*, 170–76.

147. Knife holder, no date, no. T7373, NMNH/AC. Unfortunately, many museum items are vaguely dated or undated. Quill work was abandoned sometime in the nineteenth century, replaced by European-style glass beads. Finding porcupines, taking the quills, and making them into colored beads was no easy task. Iroquois and other Indian women knew a good thing when they saw the glass bead. For

another, more religious interpretation of glass beads and the trade in them, see Chris L. Miller and George R. Hamell, "A New Perspective on Indian-White Contact: Cultural Symbols and Colonial Trade," *JAH* 73 (Sept. 1986): 311–28. Iroquois small tobacco pouch of deerskin, with quill beading, no date, no. 53071, Iroquois belt with porcupine quills and "tin jinglers," ca. 1800, no. 53062, Iroquois quilted belt with wide orange stripes, no. 53063, quilted black skin pouch Iroquois, no date, no. 53061, PM; Arthur C. Parker, *History of the Seneca Indians*, Empire State Historical Publication 43 (1926; rpt. New York: Dover, 1975), 111. Carrie A. Lyford says the New York Iroquois "were the leaders of silver jewelry, with a silversmith in almost every Iroquois village" and that silver trading remained profitable until about 1865 (*Iroquois Crafts* [Stevens Point, Wisc.: R. Schneider, 1982], 67–69, including designs). The Iroquois copied the work of Montreal and other silversmiths involved in Indian trade. A picture of brooches may be found in Speck, *Iroquois*, 49.

148. Iroquois dolls, NMNH/AC. It would be incorrect to argue that objects made in the recent past or even in the late nineteenth century were identical to those in Jemison's time, but continuity in crafts does exist. See Marjorie Lismer, *Seneca Splint Basketry*, ed. Willard W. Beatty, Education Division, U.S. Office of Indian Affairs [Washington, D.C., n.d.].

6: SARAH WAKEFIELD AND THE DAKOTA WAR

1. Sarah F. Wakefield, *Six Weeks in the Sioux Tepees: A Narrative of Indian Captivity* (1864), *Garland Library*, vol. 79 (New York: Garland, 1977), 3. The only known copy of the first edition, with the same title (Minneapolis: Atlas, 1863), is in the Western Americana Collection of the Beinecke Library, Yale University.

2. In 1849 the administration of Indian affairs was moved from the War Department to the Department of the Interior. Commissioners of Indian affairs were responsible for reservation and land allotment policy. After 1851 there were three regional divisions east of the Rockies and north of Texas. With statehood in 1856 Minnesota became part of the Northern Superintendency. In 1861 Clark W. Thompson became the new Republican superintendent of Indian affairs for the Northern Superintendency, Thomas J. Galbraith, the Minnesota agent. See Francis Paul Prucha, *The Great Father: The United States Government and the American Indians*, abridged ed. (Lincoln: University of Nebraska Press, 1984), 109–14; Gary Clayton Anderson, *Kinsmen of Another Kind: Dakota-White Relations in the Upper Mississippi Valley, 1650–1862* (Lincoln: University of Nebraska

Press, 1984), chap. 11, esp. 246; David A. Nichols, *Lincoln and the Indians: Civil War Policy and Politics* (Columbia: University of Missouri Press, 1978), 5–24. The change in agents is mentioned by Big Eagle (Wamdetonka), a Mdewakanton chief, in "Chief Big Eagle's Story of the Sioux Outbreak of 1862," *Minnesota Historical Society Collections* 6 (1894): 382–401, esp. 387. For some of the Indian sides of the story see *Through Dakota Eyes: Narrative Accounts of the Minnesota Indian War of 1862*, ed. Gary Clayton Anderson and Alan R. Woolworth (St. Paul: Minnesota Historical Society, 1988). For the official discussions by the Indian Affairs establishment, including Galbraith's on the background and causes of the Dakota War see *Report of the Commissioner of Indian Affairs for the Year 1861* (Washington, D.C.: U.S. Government Printing Office, 1862); *Report of the Commissioner of Indian Affairs for the Year 1862* (Washington, D.C.: U.S. Government Printing Office, 1863), 11–23, 49–69. For other work on the Sioux and the war see Jack W. Marken and Herbert T. Hoover, *Bibliography of the Sioux* (Metuchen, N.J.: Scarecrow Press, 1980).

3. Deposition of J. L. Wakefield, Mar. 31, 1863, Ramsey County, Minnesota, in Sioux Claim of John L. Wakefield (hereafter J. L. Wakefield Sioux Claim), Sioux Uprising Collection, Box 3, John L. Wakefield, MHS. Lucy E. Wakefield's nickname was Nellie, the name used by Marion Satterlee in his listing of the captives in *A Detailed Account of the Massacre by Dakota Indians of Minnesota in 1862* (Minneapolis: Marion P. Satterlee, 1923), no. 101, p. 93. See also *Obituary Record of Graduates of Yale College*, no. 33, 1847 (New Haven, 1880), 154; Obituary, n.p., ca. 1901, in Sioux Uprising Collection, Box 3, John L. Wakefield, MHS. Wakefield had been a physician in Shakopee since at least 1857 (U.S. Census Schedule, Shakopee, Scott County, Minnesota, Sept. 21, 1857, p. 117). Other data on family ages and places of birth from U.S. Census Schedule, Shakopee, Scott County, Minnesota, July 27, 1860, p. 146, and Aug. 5, 1870, p. 9; and Sioux Uprising Collection, Box 3, John L. Wakefield, MHS. Lucy E. Wakefield was born in January 1860. See U.S. Census Schedule, Ramsey County, Minnesota, 1900. Her married name was Lucy E. Bourke.

4. Wakefield family history and political activity may be found in Payne Kenyon Kilbourne, *A Biographical History of the County of Litchfield, Connecticut* (New York, Austin, 1851), 372–73, 375, 404, 410; *Obituary Record of Graduates of Yale College*, 154. Other biographical information was taken from *Collections of the Minnesota Historical Society: Minnesota Biographies, 1655–1912*, comp. Warren Upham and Rose Barteau Dunlap, vol. 14 (June 1912), 816–17; "J. B. Wakefield Is Dead; One Time in Congress," *Mankato Daily Free Press*, Aug. 26, 1910, p. 1; Trinity College file, Trinity College, Hartford Conn.; John Luman Wakefield of Winsted, candidate for the degree of Doctor of Medicine, "Dissertation on Cynanche Trachealis," Dis-

sertation 22, 1847, Yale Medical School Library, Historical Library.

5. *Journal of P. C. Tiffany Detailing His Trip Across the Plains from Mt. Pleasant, Iowa, to the Gold Diggings of California in 1849*, No. 475, Diary, typescript, 123–24, 161, 163, and manuscript, 3:3–4 (unnumbered pages), Western Americana Collection, Beinecke Library, Yale University; *Mankato Daily Free Press*, Aug. 26, 1910, p. 1; J. A. Kiester, *The History of Faribault County, Minnesota* (Minneapolis: Harrison & Smith, Printers, 1896), 579; Homer Wakefield, comp., *Wakefield Memorial Comprising an Historical, Genealogical and Biographical Register of the Name and Family of Wakefield* (Bloomington, Ill: Printed privately, 1897), 67. On Wakefield's role see "The Battle between the Sioux and Chippiwas at Shakopee," *Shakopee Weekly Pioneer and Democrat*, June 3, 1858.

6. Julius A. Collier II, *The Shakopee Story* (Shakopee, Minn.: Lakewood Press, 1960), 15–17, 42–43. After $30,000 for the land was turned over, some of the Mdewakanton returned. Three bands lived in the county: Shakopee's (the elder), Big Eagle's, and the Sand Creek. See Rev. Edward D. Neill, *History of the Minnesota Valley Including the Explorers and Pioneers of Minnesota* (Minneapolis: North Star Publishing, 1882), 292–94; Samuel W. Pond, *The Dakota or Sioux in Minnesota as They Were in 1834*, Intro. Gary Clayton Anderson (1908; rpt. St. Paul: Minnesota Historical Society Press, 1986), 12–13; *St. Paul Minnesota Pioneer*, Dec. 29, 1853; *Shakopee Daily Minnesotian*, Apr. 14, 1856; *Shakopee Weekly Pioneer and Democrat*, Apr. 30, 1857; *Shakopee Daily Minnesotian*, Apr. 30, 1856; *Shakopee Daily Minnesotian*, Sept. 4, 1856. These articles exist in typescript copies in the Writers' Project Annals for Scott County, Minnesota, 1852–69, MHS-DAM. The year 1857 was one of financial panic (Kiester, *History of Faribault County*, 78).

7. *Shakopee Weekly Pioneer and Democrat*, Nov. 26, 1857; *St. Paul Minneapolis Pioneer*, Aug. 24, 1854; *Shakopee Weekly Pioneer and Democrat*, Jan. 29, 1857; Collier, *Shakopee Story*, 42–43; *Shakopee Daily Minnesotian*, Dec. 30, 1856, Dec. 21, 1857, July 1, 1858, typescript articles in Writers' Project Annals files, MHS-DAM.

8. Sarah F. Brown was born to Sarah and William Brown of North Kingston, Rhode Island, Sept. 29, 1829 (Alden G. Beaman, *Washington County, Rhode Island: Births, 1770–1850* [Princeton, Mass.: Published by the Compiler, 1977], 25). The 1857 census shows John but not Sarah in Shakopee. Both are listed in Shakopee on the 1860 census (U.S. Census Schedule, Shakopee, Scott County, Minnesota, July 27, 1860, p. 146, and Aug. 5, 1870, p. 9. Obituary, n.p., ca. 1901, Sioux Uprising Collection, Box 3, MHS). Her maiden name is listed as Butts in the recording of the marriage in the Scott County records of marriages, 1856. Minnesota was still a territory, and marriage certificates were not kept. Her grandson and other relatives with whom I spoke

said the name was Brown and it was so listed in the family Bible (telephone conversations with daughter of Lucy Wakefield Bourke, Oct. 1987, and James Orin Wakefield II, Oct. 1987).

9. This is a partial listing of clothing from J. L. Wakefield, Sioux Claim.

10. Wakefield, *Six Weeks* (1864), 3. Such appreciation of the prairie was typical of women moving west, according to Annette Kolodny's analysis of Anglo-American women going west (*The Land Before Her: Fantasy and Experience of the American Frontiers, 1630–1860* [Chapel Hill: University of North Carolina Press, 1984]).

11. Wakefield, *Six Weeks* (1864), 3–4. On early Mississippian, Adena, and Hopwell cultures and mound building see James E. Fitting, "Regional Cultural Development, 300 B.C. to A.D. 1000," in *HNAI/Northeast*, 44–57; Melvin L. Fowler and Robert L. Hall, "Late Prehistory of the Illinois Area," in *HNAI/Northeast*, 560–68; David S. Brose, "Late Prehistory of the Upper Great Lakes Areas," in *HNAI/Northeast*, 569–82. See Map 5, "Distribution of Late Prehistoric Cultures, c. 1400 to 1600," in Helen Hornbeck Tanner, ed., *Atlas of Great Lakes Indian History* (Norman: University of Oklahoma Press, 1987), 26. For maps of Dakota villages and hunting grounds see Tanner, map 28, "Indian Villages c. 1830 Minnesota region," and before 1851 and in the reservation period 1851–62, Gary Clayton Anderson, *Little Crow: Spokesman for the Sioux* (St. Paul: Minnesota Historical Society Press, 1986), 12, 120.

12. Wakefield, *Six Weeks* (1864), 4, 6.

13. Ibid., 7. See Charles Alexander Eastman's (Ohiyesa) Dakota family exile and his grandfather's "demographic" sense of white population growth in Minnesota (*Indian Boyhood* [1902; rpt. Williamstown: Corner House Publishers, 1975], 279–83). According to Jonas Pettijohn, who had settled in Minnesota to teach and whose family escaped capture during the outbreak, Indians were to be given "teams, wagons and plows," but were given left-handed cast-iron plows "as no Minnesota farmer would have on his farm" (*Autobiography, Family History and Various Reminiscences of the Life of Jonas Pettijohn* [Clay Center, Kan.: Dispatch Printing House, 1890], 84).

14. Wakefield, *Six Weeks* (1864), 7. Big Eagle's analysis is very close to Wakefield's ("Big Eagle's Story," esp. 384–85; *Through Dakota Eyes*, ed. Anderson and Woolworth, 21, 35–36).

15. Wakefield, *Six Weeks* (1864), 6–7.

16. Ibid., 5.

17. Ibid., 5–6. They smoked bark from the red willow tree that was shaved. The tobacco is called knicknic (conversation with Theresa Morrison, Sioux Community Center, Prior Lake, Minnesota, Oct. 19, 1987).

18. Pond includes the Yankons as a fifth (*The Dakota or Sioux*, 4–13). The figure cited is from ibid., 5. Alan Woolworth mentions

nineteen hundred, based on a census of 1861 (telephone conversation, July 26, 1991). Ruth Landes finds this figure too large and says the villages of these Santee bands in the Mdewakanton villages ranged from under fifty to four hundred (*The Mystic Lake Sioux: Sociology of the Mdewakonan Santee* [Madison: University of Wisconsin Press, 1968], 13–14). On "Sioun" languages and the choice of the word *Dakota* to refer to these people, see Anderson, *Little Crow*, 6. Dakota, Nakota, and Lakota are linguistic designations, with Dakota being made up of Mdewakanton, Sisseton, Wakpekute, and Wahpeton. There are 181 eastern and western Siouan language groups. See Ruth Underhill, *Red Man's America: A History of Indians in the United States*, rev. ed. (Chicago: University of Chicago Press, 1971); John R. Swanton, *The Indian Tribes of North America* (Washington, D.C.: U.S. Government Printing Office, 1952), 280–85, 827–29. The name *Sioux* was first used by their enemies, Winnebago and Ojibwa (Chippewas), as recorded by Jean Nicolet and first used in the *Jesuit Relations* in 1640. " '*Naduesiu*' was a variation on the Algonquian '*Nadouess-iw*', a diminutive for snakes, adders, and by extension, enemies," which the French shortened to Sioux (Roy W. Meyer, *History of the Santee Sioux: United States Indian Policy on Trial* [Lincoln: University of Nebraska Press, 1967], 5). Although some scholars still prefer *Sioux*, I have generally used the name *Dakota* because of the original negative connotation of *Sioux* and because it is the preferred name of Dakota people today (conversations with Herbert T. Hoover, St. Paul, Oct. 16, 1987, and with Chris Cavender, St. Paul, Oct. 18, 1987).

19. Pond, *The Dakota or Sioux*, 4–13; Wakefield, *Six Weeks* (1864), 7. Also see Stephen E. Feraca and James H. Howard, "The Identity and Demography of the Dakota or Sioux Tribe," *Plains Anthropologist* 8 (May 1963): 80–84.

20. Wakefield, *Six Weeks* (1864), 4–5; Kenneth Carley, *The Sioux Uprising of 1862* (St. Paul: Minnesota Historical Society, 1976), 17. Also see the reconstruction of the Upper Agency, destroyed in the uprising, drawn by Chester Kozlak, ibid., 20. The exact number of buildings and layout of the Upper Agency is drawn as eight buildings. "Location of Buildings at the Upper Agency, 1862" by George E. Olds, has a total of six buildings and map, "Vicinity of the Upper Sioux Agency, 1862," in William Watts Folwell, *History of Minnesota*, 4 vols., rev. ed. (St. Paul: Minnesota Historical Society, 1978), 2:116–17. See maps of Lower Agency (Redwood) and discussion of Upper Agency in *Through Dakota Eyes*, ed. Anderson and Woolworth, 9–12.

21. J. L. Wakefield Sioux Claim, "*Family room*," "Dining room," and "Help's room." Reconstructing the Wakefields' quarters and possessions was accomplished by using the Sioux Claim document, a deposition signed by J. L. and Sarah F. Wakefield, both of whom claimed losses and stipulated each item's worth. Whether the Wakefields padded this claim by adding items, exaggerating the worth of

their possessions, or both we can only guess. I have tried to compensate for padding by not using items that seem repeated too often or are unusually expensive. For comparison see Records of the Depredation Division, "Records Relating to Claims for Depredations by Sioux Indians in Minnesota in 1862," E-702, six boxes, RG 75, NA. There are 326 claims in the Record Book but only about 12 claims for over $1,000 in damages. The Wakefields claimed $4,316.05. Most are for under $100. See "Records Relating to Claims for Depredations by Sioux Indians in Minnesota in 1862," entry 704, "Claims for Sioux Damages Sustained by the Sioux Outbreak in Minnesota in 1862," and "Record Book," RG 75, NA. Close to 3,000 claims were filed for lost property valued at $2,500,000 (Edward D. Neill, *History of Ramsey County and the City of St. Paul* [Minneapolis: North Star Publishing, 1881]).

22. J. L. Wakefield Sioux Claim, "Kitchen," "Groceries," and "Closet," and "Store room," and "Outhouse."

23. The Wakefield claim contains six legal-sized pages listing clothing items. Excluding thirty-seven items that seem to be John's, Sarah itemized more than seventy pieces of her own clothing. The children were listed as having forty items, including two red cashmere dresses, fur-lined shoes, overcoats, and the like. For more detail see June Namias, "White Captives: Gender and Ethnicity on Successive American Frontiers, 1607–1862" (Ph.D. dissertation, Brandeis University, 1989), 442–47.

24. See chart, Minnesota Population, 1850–70, in Namias, "White Captives," Appendix, 584–87. For the growth of the Minnesota Valley counties see *Schedules of the Minnesota Census of 1857*, National Archives Microfilm Publications T1175, Minnesota State Population Census Schedules, MHS (microcopy), for Brown and Blue Earth counties. See Minnesota State Population Census Schedules, 1865–1905.

25. *St. Paul Pioneer and Democrat*, Jan.–Aug. 1862; *Mankato Semi-Weekly Record*, July 12, 1861–Dec. 1862; *Winona Republican*, Feb.–Nov. 1862; *Mankato Semi-Weekly Independent*, Aug. 15, 1862–Jan. 2, 1863. Almost all of the nineteenth-century Minnesota newspapers used are found on microfilm at MHS.

26. In May 1858, Minnesota entered the Union. Minnesota voted for Lincoln, who received 22,069 votes as against 11,920 for Douglas; less than a thousand combined votes went for Breckinridge and Bell (Neill, *History of Ramsey County*, 131; Folwell, *History of Minnesota*, 2:84–108).

27. President A. Lincoln to Gov. Ramsey, July 3, 1862, Alexander Ramsey Papers, 1815–1903 (microfilm), MHS.

28. U.S. Census, 1860.

29. Folwell, *History of Minnesota*, 2:228. On the controversy over the role of the population drop in Minnesota as a cause of the war

see *Minnesota History* 45 (Summer 1976), esp. Priscilla Ann Russo, "The Time to Speak Is Over: The Onset of the Sioux Uprising," 97–106. Anderson's research indicates that Myrick's statement was not made the day before the war but probably between August 5 and 8 (*Kinsmen*, 250–53). For fuller summaries of the causes and the start of the war see ibid., 226–60; "Big Eagle's Story"; *Through Dakota Eyes*, ed. Anderson and Woolworth; and the standard histories mentioned above. A study that sees the causes of the war as Indian as well as white is Duane Schultz, *Over the Earth I Come: The Great Sioux Uprising of 1862* (New York: St. Martin's Press, 1992).

30. Folwell, *History of Minnesota*, 2:109–10; Carley; *Sioux Uprising*; Anderson, *Kinsmen*. The early attacks of the war give good reason for calling it an uprising in the sense used by some in the late 1960s, as in the Newark uprising or riots. When Newark and other American cities reacted to the death of Martin Luther King, stores and store owners were the first to be attacked. Similarly, in the spring of 1992, after the Rodney King verdict, Korean stores were attacked in Los Angeles. There is a relationship here to recent research on food riots and revolution both in Europe and in colonial America.

31. Wakefield, *Six Weeks* (1864), 11–12. Samuel Brown, his mother, and twenty-two others were captured by members of Cut Nose's and Shakopee's bands on August 19 and brought to Little Crow's camp (Samuel J. Brown, "In Captivity: The Experience, Privations, and Dangers of Samuel J. Brown and Others While Prisoners of the Hostile Sioux during the Massacre and War of 1862," in *Senate Document 23*, 56th Cong., 2d sess., Dec. 5, 1900, 1–36, esp. 2–3; "Big Eagle's Story"; Anderson, *Kinsmen*, chap. 12; Carley, *Sioux Uprising*, 1–15; William E. Lass, *Minnesota: A Bicentennial History* [New York: Norton, 1977], 166; Anderson, *Little Crow*, esp. 130–34).

32. Wakefield, *Six Weeks* (1864), 11–13; Mary Butler Renville, *A Thrilling Narrative of Indian Captivity* (Minneapolis: Atlas Company's Books and Job Office, 1863), 9.

33. Wakefield, *Six Weeks* (1864), 13.

34. Ibid., 13–14. Sarah Wakefield did know some Dakota so she may have understood this conversation, if indeed it took place. Samuel W. Pond, the missionary who lived near (northern) Shakopee village, says that Shakopee (also called Shapaydan and Shakpay), meaning Little Six, was of the Tintatonwan band. Pond says Shakopee's brother Hocholaduta was a powerful force and that the first August murders were by men of the brother's "party." Whether he means the Acton murders or Gleason's is unclear; probably Gleason's (Pond, *The Dakota or Sioux*, 12–13).

35. Alex. Ramsey to E. M. Stanton, Aug. 21, 1862, *Official Records*, 13:590.

36. Jas. Craig to E. M. Stanton, Aug. 23, 1862, *Official Records*, 13:592.

37. H. W. Halleck to Brigadier-General Schofield, Aug. 22, 1862, and and H. W. Halleck to Alex. Ramsey, Aug. 24, 1862, *Official Records*, 13:591, 595; Alex. Ramsey to H. W. Halleck, Aug. 22, 1862, H. W. Halleck to Ramsey, Aug. 21, 1862, Alex. Ramsey to E. M. Stanton, Aug. 25, 1862, Alex. Ramsey to President Lincoln, Aug. 26, 1862, M. S. Wilkinson, W. P. Dole, and Jno. G. Nicolay to President of the United States, Aug. 27, 1862, Lincoln to Alex. Ramsey, Aug. 27, 1862, all in Ramsey Papers, MHS, the latter also in *Official Records*, 13:599. In this and other cases when I have used letters or wires in the Ramsey Papers rather than the *Official Records*, it is because emphasis or punctuation has been changed in the *Official Records* and using the originals gives a more authentic sense of the moment.

38. Jno. G. Nicolay to E. M. Stanton, Aug. 27, 1862, *Official Records*, 13:599–600; Folwell, *History of Minnesota*, 2:186.

39. Jas. Craig to General James G. Blunt, Aug. 30, 1862, Samuel J. Kirkwood to E. M. Stanton, Sept. 8, 1862, *Official Records*, 13:607, 620.

40. Alex. Ramsey to President Lincoln, Sept. 6, 1862, E. M. Stanton to Maj. Gen. John Pope, Sept. 6, 1962, *Official Records*, 13:617. Alvin M. Josephy has reached a similar conclusion about the import of these wars in the west in *The Civil War in the American West* (New York: Random House, 1991).

41. Nick Coleman, "The Last, Futile Struggle of the Dakota," *St. Paul Pioneer Press Dispatch*, Oct. 11, 1987, sec. G, p. 4. Actual white death tolls, civilian and military, came to just under five hundred (Satterlee, *Detailed Account*).

42. H. H. Sibley's letters, Aug.–Oct. 1862, in Henry Hasting Sibley Papers, 1815–1930 (microfilm), MHS; "Big Eagle's Story"; Benedict Juni, *Held in Captivity: Benedict Juni, of New Ulm, Minn. Relates His Experience as an Indian Captive during the Indian Outbreak in 1862* (1926; rpt. New Ulm, Minn.: Lowell F. Juni, 1977). The original date of the writing of the narrative is unclear. Juni died in 1922. Samuel Brown reported that 738 Indians were killed at Wood Lake and that sticks were counted as warriors went out and came back. After his release, Brown became a scout with Major Thomas J. Galbraith and acted as an interpreter. This testimony was given on December 5, 1900, some thirty-eight years after the event (Brown, "In Captivity," 22). Sibley's forces saw the human side of war. Thomas Scantlebury from New Auburn wrote in his diary of August 19 of meeting "families and teams" "leaving that part of the country for their lives," and he "saw several whose families had been murdered or taken captive." On September 21 he wrote, "The Sabbath—but again no rest." On September 26 he wrote how they passed two children, age nine and eleven, "their parents and most of their family had been killed; a little baby belonging to the family was left in a cradle by the Indians to starve to death" ([Diary of Thomas Scantlebury] in *Wanderings in*

Minnesota during the Indian Troubles of 1862 [Chicago: F. C. S. Calhoun, 1867], NL). For a history of those Dakotas who finally settled in Canada see "One Century Later: Western Canadian Reserve Indians since Treaty 7," in George F. G. Stanley et al., *Displaced Red Men: The Sioux in Canada* (Vancouver: University of British Columbia Press, 1978), 55–81.

43. Samuel Brown described the scene. Brown enumerated 2,188 at Camp Release (excluding the soldiers): Indians 1,918, captive white men 4, captive white women and children 104, captives who were part Indian 162 (Brown, "In Captivity," 21–23).

44. Wakefield, *Six Weeks* (1864), 52–53.

45. Ibid.

46. 37th Congress, Records of the Military Commission that tried Sioux-Dakota Indians for barbarities committed in Minnesota, 1862, SEN 37A-F2, RG 46, NA (hereafter cited as Dakota Trials). Indians who aided whites were called "friendlies," those opposed, "hostiles." I have used this language to point out the mentality of the period.

47. Dakota Trials, Case No. 3, p. 1; Folwell, *History of Minnesota*, 2:192, n. 3, mentions the full names of these officers and the substitution of Major George Bradley of the Seventh for Marshall. The handwriting and names on the record show a variety of recorders. See Isaac V. D. Heard, *History of the Sioux War and Massacres of 1862 and 1863* (1864; rpt. Millwood, N.Y.: Krause Reprint, 1975), 251–71.

48. See Folwell's reaction in *The Court Proceedings in the Trial of Dakota Indians Following the Massacre in Minnesota in August 1862* (Minneapolis: Satterlee Printing, 1927), 9–11, MHS; Meyer, *History of the Santee Sioux*, chap. 6; Karen Thiem, "The Minnesota Sioux War Trials" (M.A. thesis, Mankato State University, 1979).

49. Stephen R. Riggs, *Tah-Koo Wah-Kan; or, The Gospel among the Dakotas* (Boston: Congregational Sabbath-School and Publishing Society, 1869), 333–34; Stephen R. Riggs, *Mary and I: Forty Years with the Sioux* (Chicago: W. G. Holmes, 1889), 180. Heard claims that the charges made against the men were "based upon information furnished by the Rev. S. R. Riggs," from the testimony of "half-breeds" and others, and that Riggs "was, in effect, the grand Jury of the court." Heard called him "eminently qualified" for the job (*History of the Sioux War*, 261, 268, 270).

50. Conversations with Chris Cavender, St. Paul, Oct. 18, 1987, and with Theresa Morrison, Sioux Community Center, Prior Lake, Minnesota, Oct. 19, 1987. There is also the issue of actual kin and those who are thought of as kin. There seems to be a cultural misunderstanding here (Anderson, *Kinsmen*, and his comments on reading an earlier version of this chapter, Feb. 10, 1990).

51. Dakota Trials, Case No. 3, pp. 1–2.

52. Agnes Robertson was probably the Indian wife of a "mixed blood" by the name of Robertson mentioned as a neighbor by Bene-

dict Juni, *Held in Captivity*, 11. Nancy McClure mentions the Robertson boys and that Agnes was part Indian in "The Story of Nancy McClure," *Minnesota Historical Society Collections* 6 (1894): 439–60, esp. 457. Agnes Robertson's testimony was more ambiguous as to Chaska's role. Her status as an Indian or half-Indian woman would make anything she said in his favor even more insignificant to the court than Wakefield's words. See Dakota Trials, Case No. 3.

53. Dakota Trials, Case No. 3, pp. 2–3. The transcript continually moves between spelling Indian with both upper- and lower-case letters. The punctuation here is as in the original. See [Little Crow], "Taoyateduta Is Not a Coward," *Minnesota History* 38 (Sept. 1962): 115, and in *Through Dakota Eyes*, ed. Anderson and Woolworth, 40–42.

54. Gary Clayton Anderson says that the real issue is the different meaning of kinship terms in Dakota and in English (letter and notes on manuscript, Feb. 10, 1990).

55. Dakota Trials, Case No. 3, pp. 3–5.

56. Riggs, *Mary and I*, 179–80; Wakefield, *Six Weeks* (1864), 55. On rape cases, see Dakota Trials, Case No. 2 against Te-he-hdo-ne-cha, and Case No. 4 against Ta-zoo or Ptandoota. Both men were hanged at Mankato. As usual, the rape issue was highly contested. See comments by George Spencer, a white clerk who was captured and one of the few white men in the camp of Little Crow and the Dakotas in rebellion. He claimed that although he was treated well, "the female captives were, with very few exceptions, subjected to the most horrible treatment. In some cases a woman would be taken into the woods and her person violated by 6, 7, and as many as 10 or 12 of these fiends at one time" (The Sioux Commission, 1863, entry 663, George H. Spencer, Jr., "The Sioux War" [1862], p. 15, RG 48, NA). See Folwell, *Trial of Dakota Indians*, 9–11. Another man who saw those released said the captives "had suffered agonies indescribable and indignities revolting and unspeakable" (Oscar Garrett Wall, *Recollections of the Sioux Massacre: An Authentic History of the Yellow Medicine Incident* [Lake City, Minn.: N.p., 1909], 137). Colonel H. H. Sibley wrote to his wife of "one young lady, very respectable and of fine personal appearance, a Miss Williams, who has been very much abused; indeed I think all the young ones have been" (Sept. 27, 1862, in R. I. Holcomb's hand, Sibley Papers). For other references see Namias, "White Captives," chap. 7, and 545, n. 103.

57. H. H. Sibley to Sarah Sibley, Aug. 28, 1862, Sibley Papers.

58. Chronological bibliography at the beginning of the microfilm; H. H. Sibley to Sarah Sibley, Aug. 22, 31, Sept. 4, 27, 1862, ibid.

59. H. H. Sibley to Sarah Sibley, Oct. 10, 11, 1862, ibid.

60. Nichols, *Lincoln and the Indians*, 94–118; H. H. Sibley to Sarah Sibley, Oct. 17, 20, 1862, Sibley Papers.

61. H. H. Sibley to Sarah Sibley, Sept. 28, 1862, Sibley Papers. "By

17 October Sibley had close to 400 prisoners, only 68 of whom were deemed to have been 'friendly' throughout the entire war. Their dependents totaled another 1,400 people. Perhaps 200 hostile Mdewakanton warriors were still at large on the plains" (Anderson, *Kinsmen*, 276).

62. Wakefield, *Six Weeks* (1864), 54–56. From this point on I have chosen the final spelling used in the sentencing, Dakota Trials, Case No. 3.

63. Wakefield, *Six Weeks* (1864), 54–56.

64. Ibid.; H. H. Sibley to Sarah Sibley, Oct. 22, 1862, Sibley Papers.

65. H. H. Sibley to Sarah Sibley, Oct. 15, 22, 31, Nov. 3, 1862, Sibley Papers; S. R. Riggs to S. B. Treat, Nov. 24, 1862, ABCFM.

66. Folwell, *History of Minnesota*, 2:200. There were twenty women according to Williamson (Williamson to S. B. Treat, Dec. 1, 1862, Williamson Papers). Papers from Thomas S. Williamson and Stephen Return Riggs are used by permission of the American Board of Commissioners for Foreign Missions (ABCFM) and the Houghton Library, Harvard University, Cambridge, Massachusetts, and the United Church Board for World Ministries. See Michael C. Coleman, *Presbyterian Missionary Attitudes toward American Indians, 1837–1893* (Jackson: University Press of Mississippi, 1985), chap. 2. Folwell, citing the December 2, 1862, census, says there were 1,601 at Snelling (*History of Minnesota*, 2:252).

67. H. H. Sibley to Sarah Sibley, from Camp Lincoln, one and one-half miles from Mankato, Nov. 12, 1862, Sibley Papers. According to Folwell, the people of New Ulm were reburying their dead on the day the group came through the town (*History of Minnesota*, 2:200–201). "New Ulm had been selling whiskey to the Indians for several years, wholesale and retail," according to Jonas Pettijohn, *Autobiography*, 82.

68. There were 303 accused. Father Ravoux claimed there were 360 men in the Mankato prison when he arrived on December 19, 1862 (Father Ravoux to Rt. Rev. Bishop Grace, Dec. 29, 1862, reprinted in English in A. Ravoux, *Reminiscences, Memoirs and Lectures of Monsignor A. Ravoux* [St. Paul: Brown, Treacy, 1890], 72–86). See also Rev. T. S. Williamson to S. B. Treat, Dec. 1, 1862, Williamson Papers, ABCFM; Rev. S. R. Riggs, *A Memorial Discourse on Rev. Thomas S. Williamson, M.D., Mission to the Dakota Indians* (New York: American Tract Society, n.d.), 15–17; Henry Benjamin Whipple, *Lights and Shadows of a Long Episcopate* (New York: Macmillan, 1899), 133, and quotes in Jon Willand, *Lac Qui Parle and the Dakota Mission* (Madison, Minn.: N.p. 1964); Meyer, *History of the Santee Sioux*, 137–39. On Whipple's role with the Chippewas see Martin N. Zanger, " 'Straight Tongue's Heathen Wards': Bishop Whipple and the Episcopal Mission to the Chippewas," in *Churchmen and the Western Indians*, ed. Clyde A. Milner II and Floyd A. O'Neil (Norman: University of Oklahoma Press, 1985), 177–245.

69. S. R. Riggs to S. B. Treat, Nov. 24, 1862, Riggs Papers, ABCFM; Williamson to S. B. Treat, Dec. 1, 1862, Williamson Papers, ABCFM. In this letter, Williamson asked Treat to go to influential members of Congress and call on Lincoln for "a new trial by unprejudiced men." See also S. R. Riggs to S. B. Treat, Nov. 26, 1862, Riggs Papers, ABCFM.

70. President Lincoln to H. H. Sibley, Dec. 6, 1862, Sibley Papers; Heard, *History of the Sioux War*, 287.

71. *New York Times*, Aug. 24, 1862, pp. 1, 6, Aug. 25, 1862, p. 4, Aug. 29, 1862, pp. 4, 8; *Harper's Weekly*, Sept. 13, 1862, p. 592.

72. M. S. Wilkinson, Cyrus Aldrich, and William Windom, letter to President Lincoln, in "Message of the President of the United States in Answer to the resolution of the Senate of the 5th instant in relation to the Indian barbarities in Minnesota." The letter and the list of accused along with those charged were published Dec. 11, 1862, in "Records of the Trial of Sioux-Dakota Indians in Minnesota," *Senate Executive Document* 7, 1862, 37th Cong., 3d sess., pt. C. The letter was also run in several major Minnesota newspapers. On the sensationalizing of rape and captivity in mid-nineteenth-century exotic literature see Sarah Carter, "A Fate Worse Than Death," *Beaver* 68, no. 2 (1988): 2–28.

73. Senator Wilkinson protest to Lincoln, "Indian News from Washington," *Faribault Central Republican*, Dec. 3, 1863.

74. Message of the President, Dec. 11, 1862, in "Records," *Senate Executive Document* 7, p. 1, pt. D, pp. 6–7. There is some reason to suspect that more than two women were abused sexually. See Mrs. N. D. [Urania S. Frazer] White, "Captivity among the Sioux, August 18 to September 26, 1862," *Minnesota Historical Society Collections* 9 (Apr. 1901): 395–426. See Case No. 22, Do-Wan-Sa, SEN 37A-F2 44D.

75. *Harper's Weekly*, Dec. 20, 1862, p. 39.

76. Message of the President, Dec. 11, 1862, list of "Indians and half-breeds sentenced to be hanged by the military commission," Dec. 6, 1862, and pt. E, list of "those who were convicted of rape and murder," Dec. 5, 1862, pt. D, pp. 5–6, all in "Records," *Senate Executive Document* 7.

77. Scattered through the Sibley Papers from August through December 1862 are letters he exchanged with Miller, who asked Sibley to write in his favor for a commission. Miller became governor of Minnesota soon thereafter. Stephen Miller to Sibley, Nov. 31, 1879 [1862], Sibley Papers, War Department.

78. Rev. T. S. Williamson to S. B. Treat, Apr. 10, 1863, Williamson Papers, ABCFM. This letter is not in Williamson's hand. Also see Riggs, *Mary and I*, and Riggs Papers, Dec. 1862–Jan. 1863, ABCFM; Folwell, *History of Minnesota*, 2:250–51; Riggs, *Memorial Discourse*, 15–17.

79. Ravoux to Rt. Rev. Bishop Grace, Dec. 29, 1862, in Ravoux, *Reminiscences*, 73–74.

80. Ravoux, *Reminiscences*, 76–79.

81. Williamson to Treat, Jan. 20, 1863, ABCFM. Rda-in-yan-ka, was Case No. 9 and was accused of urging men into battle at New Ulm and Wood Lake. David Faribault alleges that he offered wampum for scalps. A Christian Indian testified that he opposed the return of captives (Heard, *History of the Sioux War*, 281, 284). It is unclear whether this letter was given to Williamson or to one of the other chaplains.

82. Williamson to Treat, Apr. 12, 1863, Williamson Papers, ABCFM; Riggs, *Mary and I*, 184; Heard, *History of the Sioux War*, 274–75, citing the *St. Paul Press*; Riggs to Treat, Jan. 21, 1863, Riggs Papers, ABCFM.

83. Riggs, *Mary and I*, 184; Heard, *History of the Sioux War*, 289–90; Ravoux, *Reminiscences*, 80–81. Oscar Garrett Wall claims that keepsakes were given by Indian prisoners to friends and family who visited them before the execution (*Recollections of the Sioux Massacre*, 165–66).

84. Some accounts spell Daly's name as Duley (Meyer, *History of the Santee Sioux*, 129). On the Lake Shetek captives see the Duke Oral History Collections at the University of South Dakota. I would like to thank Herbert T. Hoover for bringing these papers to my attention.

85. Ravoux, *Reminiscences*, 78; A. P. Connolly, *A Thrilling Narrative of Minnesota Massacre and the Sioux War of 1862–63* (Chicago: A. P. Connolly, 1896), 172–73. I have found no corroborating evidence on this story of the attempt at touching among the dying Dakotas. This account is in a history of 1896. The author writes as if he had been there, but this might have been part of the lore passed around later (Heard, *History of the Sioux War*, citing a St. Paul news report, 291, 296). One might well question how men could reach out to grasp hands if their hands were tied behind them, but it is possible.

86. Riggs wrote to Treat that it pained him to read the names, but he did it nevertheless (Riggs Papers, ABCFM). See also Folwell, *History of Minnesota*, 2:198–99, n. 16; references to *St. Paul Press*, Nov. 29, 1862, and Riggs's response to a review of Isaac V. D. Heard's book, which claimed Riggs as "a kind of grand jury" at the commission. Riggs's books and writings attest to his role as translator for the trial. His letters say he supervised the records before they went to Washington (Riggs Papers, ABCFM).

87. Message of the President, Dec. 11, 1862, in "Records," *Senate Executive Document 7*, pt. E, pp. 8–9. Chaska-don is also spelled "Chaskay-etay." See President Lincoln to H. H. Sibley, Dec. 6, 1862, Sibley Papers.

88. Wakefield, *Six Weeks* (1863), 52–53. Bishop Henry Whipple also publicized this error, saying, "The marshall of the prison told Rev.

Dr. Knickerbacker and myself that a man was hanged by mistake. 'The day after the execution,' said the marshal, 'I went to the prison to release a man who had been acquitted for saving a woman's life, but when I asked for him, the answer was, 'You hung him yesterday.' I could not bring back the redskin'" (Whipple, *Lights and Shadows*, 131–32).

89. Wakefield, *Six Weeks* (1864), 59.

90. This is yet another spelling of the name (ibid., 59).

91. Wakefield, *Six Weeks* (1864), 51; Ravoux, *Reminiscences*, 73.

92. Wakefield, *Six Weeks* (1864), 59, 42, 48.

93. Wakefield, *Six Weeks* (1863), Preface. The Dakota War produced other instant publications besides histories and captivities. There were instant dime novels of the most lurid type such as Ann Coleson, *Miss Coleson's Narrative of Her Captivity among the Sioux Indians!* (Philadelphia: Barclay, 1864); Edward S. Ellis, *Indian Jim: A Tale of the Minnesota Massacre* (London: Beadle, [1864]); and Ellis, *Nathan Todd; or The Fate of the Sioux Captive*, vol. 4 (London: George Routledge and Sons, 1861).

94. Wakefield, *Six Weeks* (1863), and Wakefield, *Six Weeks* (1864).

95. Wakefield, *Six Weeks* (1864), 3–8, and Preface to this and the 1863 edition.

96. Wakefield, *Six Weeks* (1863), 3.

97. Ibid., 3.

98. Wakefield, *Six Weeks* (1864), 14.

99. "The wounded are under the care of Drs. WAKEFIELD and WIESER of Shakopee." In the one-hour battle with 176 Ojibwa, 3 Dakota were killed and 14 wounded. It was reported that 4 of these might survive ("The Battle between the Sioux and Chippewas at Shakopee," *Shakopee Pioneer Democrat*, June 3, 1858, Shakopee, Scott County, Writers' Project Annals files, MHS-DAM).

100. Wakefield, *Six Weeks* (1864), 14.

101. Wakefield, *Six Weeks* (1863), 14–15.

102. Wakefield, *Six Weeks* (1864), 22, and in the first edition as well.

103. Ibid., 18.

104. There is the possibility that it is Mrs. Adams to whom Sibley refers in letters to his wife. Schwandt continued, "Mrs. Adams was a handsome young woman, talented and educated, but she told me she saw her husband murdered, and that the Indian she was then living with had dashed out her baby's brains before her eyes. And yet she seemed perfectly happy and contented with him!" ("The Story of Mary Schwandt. Her Captivity during the Sioux 'Outbreak,'—1862," July 26, 1894, *Minnesota Historical Society Collections* 6 [1896]: 461–74, esp. 472–73; "Narrative of Mary Schwandt" in Charles S. Bryant and Able B. Murch, *A History of the Great Massacre by the Sioux Indians, in Minnesota* [Cincinnati: Rickey & Carroll, 1864], 335–42).

On multiple editions see Namias, "White Captives," 548, n. 125, for listings in the Brown County Historical Society.

105. Wakefield, *Six Weeks* (1864), 11, 16. Wakefield never talks about the trunk full of clothes, which were probably distributed around the camp. But Mary Butler Renville does in *A Thrilling Narrative of Indian Captivity*. Mrs. J. E. De Camp Sweet describes warriors decked out in "ladies bonnets," "furs," "brooches and chains," "silks . . . made into skirts," "shawls . . . used for saddle cloths" on the march from Little Crow's camp near the Lower Agency to the Upper Agency ("Mrs. J. E. De Camp Sweet's Narrative of Her Captivity in the Sioux Outbreak of 1862," *Minnesota Historical Society Collections* 6 [1899]: 368). Also see White, "Captivity among the Sioux," 405.

106. Wakefield, *Six Weeks* (1864), 18, 29.

107. Ibid., 19, 55.

108. Williamson was a Carolina missionary who was part of the American Board of Commissioners for Foreign Missions' effort to convert the Dakotas. He set up his first mission in Lac qui Parle and later near the Upper Agency. Williamson learned Dakota and began to translate the Bible into Dakota between 1837 and 1842 (Riggs, *Memorial Discourse*, 4–16).

109. Wakefield, *Six Weeks* (1864), 40–41.

110. Ibid., 3–7, 61–63.

111. Ibid., 60. Wakefield may mean Minnie Buce Carrigan, who shared a tent with her at Camp Release. Carrigan wrote of sharing a tent with other captives: "We were nearly starved, as we had eaten almost nothing all that day" (*Captured by the Indians* [1907 and 1912], *Garland Library*, vol. 106 [New York: Garland, 1977]). But Benedict Juni of New Ulm (aged ten, almost eleven at the time) said that meat, cattle, sheep, and hogs were in "abundance" as Dakotas took them "and held them in common" (*Held in Captivity*, 11, 19).

112. Wakefield, *Six Weeks* (1864), 60.

113. Ibid., 62. The Riggs and Williamson papers discuss these issues. Also see William E. Lass, "The Removal from Minnesota of the Sioux and Winnebago Indians," *Minnesota History* 38, no. 8 (1963): 353–64.

114. Wakefield, *Six Weeks* (1864), 62–63.

115. Ibid., 63.

116. Ibid.

117. Sophie Bost to in-laws, Nov. 21, 1862, in Ralph H. Bowen, ed. and trans., *A Frontier Family in Minnesota: Letters of Theodore and Sophie Bost, 1815–1920* (Minneapolis: University of Minnesota Press, 1981), 220–21.

118. Parker I. Peirce, *Antelope Bill* (n.d.; rpt. Minneapolis: Ross and Haines, 1962), 18, 34–37; "Statement of Parker Pierce" [*sic*], *Mankato Independent*, Aug. 29, 1862, p. 2.

119. "The Indian War . . . Statement of Parker Pierce," *Mankato*

Independent, Aug. 29, 1862, p. 2. Lucy Wakefield Bourke's daughter Leah (b. 1887) married Dr. Jacob Prinzing, who studied at the Mayo Clinic. After he and Leah moved to Oregon, her mother, Lucy Bourke, followed (conversation with Dorothy Prinzing of Beaverton, Oregon, granddaughter of Lucy Wakefield Bourke, Oct. 1987). The papers of James Beach Wakefield are in the John Wakefield Papers, BEHS, the J. B. Wakefield House Museum, Faribault County Historical Society, Blue Earth City, Minnesota, and James B. Wakefield Papers, MHS-DAM. Sister Elizabeth's letter is in the John Wakefield Papers at BEHS.

120. 1870 U.S. Census Schedule, Shakopee, Scott County, Minnesota, 9.

121. *Mankato Daily Free Press*, Aug. 26, 1910, p. 1.

122. *St. Paul Daily Pioneer*, Feb. 19, 1874, p. 4.

123. *Shakopee Argus*, Feb. 19, 1874, p. 4.

124. Unsigned Will, Wakefield Papers, BEHS.

125. 1870 U.S. Census Schedule, Shakopee, Scott County, Minnesota, 9.

126. *Shakopee Argus*, Feb. 19, 1874, p. 4; Certificate of Death, No. 128, Feb. 17, 1874, John L. Wakefield, notarized Oct. 16, 1987, cemetery listing, J. L. Wakefield Papers, MHS-DAM.

127. Affidavit and Claims Report of Commissioners, Mar. 22, 1875, Probate Records of John Luman Wakefield, Scott County Court House, Shakopee, Scott County, Minnesota.

128. Ibid.

129. Petition for Appointment of Guardian for son James O. Wakefield, Mar. 2, 1874, ibid.

130. Report of Administratrix, signed Sarah F. Wakefield, Dec. 1, 1875, Petition of Widow for Allowance of Support for Family, Mar. 10, 1875, ibid.

131. Ibid.; telephone conversation with James Orin Wakefield II, Oct. 1987.

132. *Campbell's St. Paul City Directory*, 1876 (microfilm), MHS, collection of city directories, 1872–76, p. 306; *St. Paul City Directory, 1883–84* (St. Paul: R. L. Polk and A. C. Danser, [1884]), 306; *St. Paul City Directory* (St. Paul, 1884), 795 (microfilm), MHS; *R. L. Polk & Co.'s St. Paul City Directory, 1898* (St. Paul: R. L. Polk, 1898), 1364; telephone conversation with James Orin Wakefield II, Oct. 1987; St. Paul, Ramsey County, Minnesota, Census, 1900, Roll 186.

133. "Submit or Stay," *St. Paul Pioneer Press*, May 27, 1899, p. 1; "The Saints Give the Game Away," *St. Paul Pioneer Press*, May 27, 1899, p. 3; "National League Whitewash Day," *St. Paul Pioneer Press*, May 27, 1899, p. 3; "Ellen Osborn's Fashion Letter," *St. Paul Pioneer Press*, May 28, 1899, p. 16; "Death of Mrs. Wakefield, In Minnesota since 1854. She Was a Prisoner of the Sioux for Six Weeks during Their Outbreak," *St. Paul Pioneer Press*, May 29, 1899, p. 8.

134. On the 125th anniversary of the Dakota War, the *St. Paul Pioneer Press Dispatch* ran a series of articles by Nick Coleman and John Camp called "The Great Dakota Conflict." Wakefield's life and narrative were discussed in a full-page article, "Woman Endured Captivity, Taunts of 'Indian Lover,'" Oct. 11, 1987, p. 5G. The picture reproduced here was in the article.

135. *St. Peter Tribune*, Oct. 9, 1861, p. 3, and Oct. 30, 1861, p. 2.

136. George Spencer's protection by Wa-Kin-yan-tu-wa (His Thunder, also Chaska) is found in The Sioux Commission, entry 663, 1863, George Spencer, Jr., pp. 1–3, 8½–11, 14, RG 48, NA. For a modified version of this story see "The Sioux War," "Captivity and Release of George Spencer, as Told by Himself," in modified form in Harriet E. Bishop McConkey, *Dakota War Whoop; or Indian Massacres and War in Minnesota*, ed. Dale L. Morgan (1863; rpt. Chicago: R. R. Donnelley & Sons, 1965); "Taopi's Statement," in *Through Dakota Eyes*, ed. Anderson and Woolworth, 255–56. Also see *Sketches Historical and Descriptive of the Monuments and Tablets Erected by the Minnesota Valley Historical Society in Renville and Redwood Counties, Minnesota* (Morton, Minn.: Minnesota Valley Historical Society, 1902), on Snahnah, 49, 62, on Mahkahta-Heiya-Win, 61–64, and the narratives of Mary Schwandt and Mrs. N. D. White. Many Dakotas made efforts to save white men and women, often at the risk of their own lives. In the white recounting, such efforts often have something of a "faithful Indian companion Tonto" quality about them (ibid., 75). See the accounts of the Dakota in Whipple, *Lights and Shadows*.

137. Riggs, *Tah-Koo Wah-Kan*, 313–24.

138. Wakefield, *Six Weeks* (1864), 54.

139. From the Audio-Visual and Photograph Collections, MHS. I showed copies of these pictures to several Mdewakanton women at the Prior Lake Reservation, and they agreed that the two men were one and the same (Theresa Morrison, Oct. 1987). For a dissection of the name, Chris Cavender and Theresa Morrison helped, as did Stephen Return Riggs, *A Dakota-English Dictionary* (Washington, D.C.: U.S. Government Printing Office, 1890), and John P. Williamson, comp., *An English-Dakota Dictionary* (New York: American Tract Society, 1902).

140. Robert Utley, *The Last Days of the Sioux Nation* (New Haven: Yale University Press, 1963).

141. Riggs to Treat, Jan. 21, 1863, ABCFM.

142. Riggs, *Memorial Discourse*, 18–19; Rev. T. S. Williamson to S. B. Treat, Apr. 10, 1863, Williamson Papers, ABCFM.

143. J. F. Meagher, Mankato, Minnesota, Dec. 26, 1887, to J. F. Fletcher Williams, St. Paul, Secretary of the Minnesota Historical Society (typescript), George Gleason folder, Box 1, P 1369, Sioux Indian War Manuscripts, MHS-DAM.

144. Meagher letter, all spelling and punctuation, or lack thereof,

are as in the letter. Other doctors took bones from the grave (C. M. Oehler, *The Great Sioux Uprising* [New York: Oxford University Press, 1959], 223). According to Dr. William Worrall, Mayo's biographer, "medical men, including Dr. Mayo," came to the hanging "in the hope of getting a body for dissection." They went to the grave at night, opened it, and "removed and distributed the bodies." Dr. Mayo got the body of Cut Nose (Helen Clapesattle, *The Doctors Mayo* [Minneapolis: University of Minnesota Press, 1941], 77–78).

145. Meagher letter. The Minnesota Historical Society now says it "has returned skeletal remains formerly in its collections to appropriate tribal people," including the remains of Little Crow, which were on exhibit in the State Capitol until removed in 1915 after protest from his descendants and were returned for burial to the family in 1971 (*Minnesota History News* 28 [Nov.–Dec. 1987]: 2).

146. The eagle as a U.S. symbol was taken from the Indians. The Sioux especially used the eagle and eagle feathers as symbols of sacred power. See Charles A. Eastman (Ohiyesa), "The American Eagle, an Indian Symbol," *American Indian Magazine* 7 (Summer 1919): 1–2; Mrs. [Henderson] Mary Eastman, *Dahcotah: or, Life and Legends of the Sioux around Fort Snelling* (New York: Wiley, 1849), ii, xxviii; Interview of Amos Owen from Nick Coleman and John Camp, "The Spirit of a People" in the series "The Great Dakota Conflict," *St. Paul Pioneer Press Dispatch*, July 19, 1987, pp. 7–8G. The Coleman and Camp story calls the return of the eagles "well documented. They have become symbolic of the ceremonies at Mankato, a powwow which is annually growing in prestige."

147. Wakefield, *Six Weeks* (1864), 60.

148. Ibid., 56.

149. Richard Slotkin, *Regeneration through Violence: The Mythology of the American Frontier, 1600–1860* (Middletown, Conn.: Wesleyan University Press, 1973). Harry J. Ross traces captivity themes in history and literature, indicating a dual paradigm of freedom and escape within the genre ("Trapped by Society, Imprisoned in the Wilderness: Captivity in American Literature, 1680–1860" [Ph.D. dissertation, Northwestern University, 1989]).

150. Wakefield, *Six Weeks* (1863).

151. The other contemporary captive narrative written by a woman is Renville, *Thrilling Narrative*. References to the many versions of Minnesota women's narratives: Mrs. Helen Carrothers [Helen Mar Paddock Carrothers, later Tarbel], Mattie Williams, Mary Schwandt, Minnie Buce Carrigan, Mrs. N. D. [Urania S. Frazer] White; "Mrs. J. E. De Camp Sweet's Narrative" [Janette E. Sykes also Mrs. J. E. De Camp]; Nancy McClure [Mrs. Nancy McClure Faribault Huggan] (Namias, "White Captives," 555–57, n. 169). There are also heroic stories of women such as Mrs. Alomina Hurd, Justina Kreiger, and Mrs. Eastlick (somewhat in the Amazonian tradition) who got

away, and George C. Allanson's account, which focuses on his mother, Suzanne Frenier Brown. For George Spencer's manuscript and other male accounts of those who had been children or adolescents at the time of their capture see Juni, *Held in Captivity*, Samuel J. Brown, "In Captivity," and Parker I. Peirce, *Antelope Bill*. Alan Woolworth and Darla Schnurrer helped me find these accounts.

152. The most popular of these histories are Bryant and Murch, *History of the Great Massacre*; Connolly, *Thrilling Narrative of the Minnesota Massacre*; McConkey, *Dakota War Whoop*; Fred M. Hans, *The Great Sioux Nation: A Complete History of Indian Life and Warfare in America* (n.d.; rpt. Minneapolis: Ross and Haines, 1964); Heard, *History of the Sioux War*.

153. Anderson, *Kinsmen*.

154. Jane P. Tompkins, *Sensational Designs: The Cultural Work of American Fiction, 1790–1860* (New York: Oxford University Press, 1985), 122–46.

155. Wakefield, *Six Weeks* (1864), closing paragraph, 63.

CONCLUSION

1. *A Narrative of the Captivity of Mrs. Johnson. Containing an Account of Her Sufferings, during Four Years with the Indians and French* (1796), *Garland Library*, vol. 23 (New York: Garland, 1976), 4.

2. As D. H. Lawrence noticed, it is only late in the Leatherstocking Tales that "we get actual women," but as a way of showing off male prowess (*Studies in Classic American Literature* [New York: Viking, 1961], 58). Also see Philip Fisher, *Hard Facts: Setting and Form in the American Novel* (New York: Oxford University Press, 1987). Lillian Schlissel mentions that women's diaries "taught me that a family on an American frontier—wherever that frontier might be—was a family separated from some part of itself. Frontier settlers were fragments of families, maintaining outposts on uncharted land" (*Far from Home: Families of the Westward Journey*, ed. Lillian Schlissel et al. [New York: Schocken, 1989], xv). For a similar observation which points to the importance of the break between the first English immigrants and their families see Kai T. Erikson, *Wayward Puritans: A Study in the Sociology of Deviance* (New York: Wiley, 1966).

3. Natalie Zemon Davis, "Women on Top" and "The Rites of Violence," in *Society and Culture in Early Modern France: Eight Essays* (Stanford: Stanford University Press, 1975), 124–51, 152–88. For the concept of center and periphery I have taken a geopolitical analogy and applied it in a gendered and ethnic context. See Immanuel Wallerstein, *The Modern World-System I: Capitalist Agriculture and the Origins of the European World-Economy in the Sixteenth Century* (New York: Academic Press, 1974).

4. *The Captive* by Irving Couse (oil on canvas, 1892) was the focus of a review on a controversial exhibit at the National Museum of American Art (Michael Kimmelman, "Old West, New Twist at the Smithsonian," in *New York Times*, May 26, 1991, sec. 2, pp. 1, 27). The painting and comments on it are found in Alex Nemerov, "Doing the 'Old America': The Image of the American West, 1880–1920," in *The West as America: Reinterpreting Images of the Frontier, 1820–1920*, ed. William H. Truettner (Washington, D.C.: National Museum of American Art by the Smithsonian Institution, 1991), 306–9.

5. John Mix Stanley, *Osage Scalp Dance* (1845), oil on canvas, National Museum of American Art, Smithsonian Institution. For additional comments see William Kloss, *Treasures from the National Museum of American Art* (Washington, D.C.: Smithsonian Institution, 1985), 38; Julie Schimmel, "John Mix Stanley and Imagery of the West in Nineteenth-Century American Art" (Ph.D. dissertation, New York University, 1983), esp. 168–79, 228–29, 272–73, 296; *John Mix Stanley: A Traveller in the West* (Ann Arbor [University of Michigan Museum of Art], exhibit 1969–70); W. Vernon Kinietz, *John Mix Stanley and His Indian Paintings* (Ann Arbor: University of Michigan Press, 1942).

6. This suggestion was made to me by Julie Schimmel, telephone conversation, May 6, 1987, and is mentioned by her in "Inventing 'the Indian,'" in *The West as America*, ed. Truettner, 149–90, esp. 163–65.

7. *Portraits of North American Indians, with Sketches of Scenery, Etc.*, painted by J. M. Stanley (Washington, D.C.: Smithsonian Institution, 1852).

8. Peter Loewenberg, *Decoding the Past: The Psychohistorical Approach* (Berkeley: University of California Press, 1985), 27–28.

9. *A True History of the Captivity & Restoration of Mrs. Mary Rowlandson*, in *Narratives of the Indian Wars, 1675–1699*, ed. Charles H. Lincoln (New York: Charles Scribner's, 1913), 118–20.

10. Cotton Mather, *Decennium Luctuosum: A History of Remarkable Occurrences in the Long War* (1699), *Garland Library*, vol. 3 (New York: Garland, 1978), 138.

11. Charles Neilson, *An Original, Compiled and Corrected Account of Burgoyne's Campaign* (1844; rpt. Bemis Heights, N.Y.: C. Neilson, 1926), 82–85; Marion P. Satterlee, "Explanatory Remarks," in *A Detailed Account of the Massacre by Dakota Indians of Minnesota in 1862* (Minneapolis: Marion P. Satterlee, 1923). R. W. G. Vail also recounts such childhood stories as being important in his life work as a New York frontier historian and bibliographer ("A 'Halloo' from the Hilltop," *New-York Historical Society Quarterly* 28 [Oct. 1944]: 167).

12. Conversations with Camille Smith, Dec.–Jan. 1983–84, R. A. Smith, *A History of Dickenson County, Iowa Together with an Account of the Spirit Lake Massacre, and the Indian Troubles on the Northern Frontier* (Des Moines: Kenyon Printing, 1902).

Index